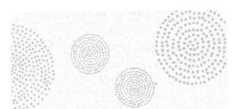

A selection from
the 2010 J.P. Morgan
Holiday Reading List

With best wishes for

Tom Brooks, Sr.

J.P.Morgan

A
GLOBAL
LIFE

A GLOBAL LIFE

My Journey among Rich and Poor,
from Sydney to Wall Street to the
World Bank

JAMES D. WOLFENSOHN

PublicAffairs • New York

For Elaine, Sara, Naomi, and Adam—
With Love and Gratitude

CONTENTS

PROLOGUE

THE IDEA OF WRITING an account of my life originally grew out of a desire to leave to my children a record of the events that shaped me, something that I wish my own parents had done. Hyman and Dora Wolfensohn settled in Australia in the late 1920s, leaving their home in London, where my father was born and where my mother was brought shortly after her birth in Belgium. I have long been frustrated by my lack of knowledge of their families and their early lives and resolved to leave a record of my own experiences, beginning in Sydney and moving to study abroad and eventually settling in the United States.

I have been blessed by opportunities to build a career in business and in public service and by living during a time of fascinating transformation on our planet. I profited from the enormous changes of the last fifty years in economics, technology, and global development. I benefited from the arrival of the jet aircraft, advances in all forms of communication, and the revolution in information made possible by the computer and Internet. The second half of the twentieth century must have been one of the most exciting and challenging periods ever in human development. As a young and proud Australian, I was able to build a life that has been global, to travel to more than one hundred countries, and to both witness and participate in the changing economics and demographic balance of our planet. I had opportunities that my father never had, and I doubt that my journey would have been possible even a decade or two earlier.

During the more than half century of my professional career, the whole world of international finance changed. The global markets developed with centers operating twenty-four hours a day in New York, London, the Middle East, Hong Kong, Japan, Australia, and other locations. It was as though the world became smaller, but for me and others like me from many countries, it presented the chance to become a global player, to feel more a citizen of the world than a member of one nation.

And I learned that there were really two worlds—the developed world of one billion people, which in the year 2000 had 80 percent of the global income, and the developing world of more than five billion people, with 20 percent of the benefits. This stark contrast and the resulting poverty became, early in my life, a challenge and a passion. Equity and social justice became part of my vocabulary and a growing focus of my activities and interests. In 1980, I was considered, briefly, for the position of president of the World Bank, and I became an American citizen to give myself the opportunity to be nominated. But the time was not right. In 1995, I was nominated by President Clinton and served in the job for a decade. The World Bank presidency was, for me, and for my wife, Elaine, the opportunity of a lifetime. It somehow put the rest of my career into perspective.

I have been fortunate. I have talented, creative, supportive, and loyal friends, who can be found around the world. My interests beyond my career have been fulfilling and rich, in music, education, sports, and public service. It has been a great life.

More than anything else, I have been blessed by the support of Elaine, an enormously gifted and balanced person, who has been a wonderful companion of more than fifty years, and by my three children, Sara, Naomi, and Adam, whose families enrich me every day.

My hope is that this book may be of interest as an account of a period of more than half a century of extraordinarily fast and profound change in the global economy. I also hope that it may encourage some younger readers to embrace life at many levels—professional, social, and international. It is a moment unique in history, when anyone might build "a global life" in the service of humankind and create that life to one's personal satisfaction and joy as a citizen of an ever-shrinking planet.

A
GLOBAL
LIFE

1

A LONG WAY
FROM NEW YORK

As the white paint dripped off my hair and onto my best suit of clothes, I remember thinking, *I deserved that.* A farmhand had just picked me up by the ankles and put my head into a bucket of diluted lime wash. He'd had enough of my anxiety about getting my shoes dirty. There I was, a plump, precocious eight-year-old, out for a day in the country with my father. We were perfectly dressed, perfectly English, and perfectly out of place on a farm in the outer suburbs of Sydney. That dunking broke the ice for me. The farmhand told me I was "a little prick," and when I got over the indignity, I knew he was right.

I was a miniature version of my father, Hyman, known as Bill Wolfensohn, who had never adjusted to Australian life. With his English upbringing, it had not occurred to him that one could visit a farm without a jacket and tie. As young as I was, the farmhand's lesson made me realize I somehow needed to be more of an Australian. But when I looked at my father I wanted to be like him, too. He spoke beautifully and was polite and polished. Although others found him formal, I knew another side of him. His eyes twinkling, he would tell me wonderful stories and keep me engaged for hours. That was when he was at peace with himself—and I craved those moments. Mostly, however, he seemed preoccupied and worried.

Every afternoon, toward 5:00 PM, I would sit at the front of our apartment block waiting for my father to return from work. A tram would appear at the bottom of the little hill, and a few minutes later his familiar figure, in a dark suit and Homburg, would come into view. Although I would jump off the wall and run to meet him, my enthusiasm was always touched with caution. His moods were a mystery. If I sensed lightness, I would take his hand and we would go inside. Some other days, though, his worry was palpable. Then I would climb back onto the low wall above the mailboxes and in the shade of a frangipani tree and wait for my mother, Dora, who would walk the same path toward home a short time later. Her face always broke into a smile when she saw me.

We had lived in that redbrick block of apartments since I was three. Although it stood in Edgecliff, one of Sydney's affluent eastern suburbs, it was modest. There were two very small bedrooms, a living room with a sofa and two armchairs in which my parents sat every night, and a miniscule dining room that had previously served as a bedroom for my sister, Betty, ten years my senior. It was a close environment where I was the focus of my parents' attention, particularly after my sister married when I was ten years old. Our family was not like other families I had observed. We had no relatives or grandparents or real connection with Australia. All we had was my mother's elderly uncle, Harry Feinmesser, who was at our table most Friday nights. Our grandparents and cousins were in England or America, and although they wrote on birthdays and we responded with grateful postcards, we grew up without any real feeling for them. My parents had friends, and there was the Jewish community, but when we switched off the lights at night, once Betty had left, it was just the three of us—and music.

I would lie in bed with strains of my mother's music floating down the hall into my room. Often, I would drift into sleep hearing German or Spanish songs in the air, knowing she was at the piano. My mother was from another age. She had come out of Europe with all the accomplishments that a fine life in Belgium could provide. Fluent in several languages and gifted with literary sensibility, she also had a deep knowledge of music and could sketch and paint. Although we were thousands of miles from the old centers of Western culture, its influences stretched into our home.

But even though we had the values and the cultural influences of that world, materially we had little to sustain it. My father pretended to a grander lifestyle than he could possibly manage, and within the limits of my young life, I copied him. My mother had a much firmer grip on reality and had the advantage of a background that made her comfortable in any company. I heard later that when people met her socially, they assumed she came from untroubled wealth. The truth was that when she and my father clashed, it was always about money. Life in that little apartment was mostly quiet, but sometimes my parents' concern about finances was so intense they would shout. The money question made me terribly upset. I grew up knowing we didn't have much of it and hating the fact that it was such a dominating problem.

* * *

My father arrived in Australia in 1928 with great optimism. Amazing advances in aviation that year brought hope that this antipodean continent was at last being opened to the world and new opportunities. About a year later, my mother and Betty, then five years old, left Antwerp for Australia. My mother had been biding her time teaching at a school while my father scouted the new land. He missed them so much that when their ship, the SS *Largs Bay* docked in Sydney, he couldn't wait for the gangway to be put in place. Spotting a Jacob's ladder hanging from the side of the boat, he leaped across, climbed up, and scrambled onto the deck to embrace them. As my parents looked around this new land, with its eucalyptus trees, raucous bird calls, wide-open spaces, and surf beaches, they must have felt a long way from everything familiar. But they had each other, they were young—my father thirty, my mother twenty-eight—and they were hopeful of a fresh start.

As it happened, the Great Depression was already upon the country and there couldn't have been a less opportune time for them to be striking out. By the following year, the economy was sliding so rapidly that the government brought out two advisers from the Bank of England to try to apply the brakes. It took until 1934 for the country to recover, and in the intervening years, my father lost much of the small stake he had brought with him. Although he consistently worked hard, for all his talent and effort he could never attain financial security in Australia. He worked first in advertising and later in business consulting, an endeavor in which he brought more success to others than to himself.

As a boy, I knew something was not right in his life. Some Saturdays, he and I would walk from our house to a cinema in Double Bay for the 5:00 PM show. He always tried to catch the late-afternoon show because there was no intermission between the double feature and little risk of bumping into anyone if we left between movies. Just as the main film ended and the credits were rolling, we'd slip out early to avoid notice. Out in the open again, my father's usual imposing presence and self-possession would melt away. He seemed wounded, and I became like a watchdog, always looking at people and trying to guess if they knew him and if they were friendly. It was instinctive. I knew the rules, but I didn't understand them. Without any discussion, I'd realized while very young that there were a few people he never wanted to see, and without knowing who they were, I was constantly on the lookout for them. For the first ten years of my life, I sensed that as a family we weren't quite within the community.

From the stories my father told, I knew he had not always been like this. Before coming to Australia, he'd moved with ease through the upper echelons of English society. He'd even been made a freeman of the City of London in 1919 for helping to organize the Victory Parade after World War I. He was proud of this recognition, which was given to important citizens of that city for their contributions to community life. We all knew that he had been on a brilliant career trajectory that had lifted him out of the crowded East End and had shown him and my mother the finest that England had to offer. I understood that back in those days, my father was playful and full of mischief. Betty remembers his impishness and how he would put her up to tricks she didn't understand. A classic family example of this revolved around that fact that my parents were married on September 6, 1922, and Betty arrived a year later, on September 5. But whenever anyone asked Betty about her birthday, my father had schooled her to joke: "I was born a day before Mummy and Daddy were married."

In those early days in Australia, as a gentlemen's hobby, my father and some friends bought a brewery in Lithgow, a suburb in the Blue Mountains about an hour's drive from Sydney. On the weekends, while my mother was busy with music, he and Betty would take the train to a rented cottage in the mountains. It had a garden where she played and he grew large white asparagus. But this rural idyll was short-lived; the brewmaster was lured to a better job and the business began to slide. Toward the end of the following year, when I was born, there were signs that the Great Depression was easing, although my parents were still having problems establishing themselves in a new land. Their struggle was to continue throughout my childhood. Whereas other families had cars and holidays, for many years we did not even have a telephone, although we always appeared to be doing well.

In 1933, the family was living in the Sydney suburb of Elizabeth Bay. Betty recalls being thrilled when Father came back from the hospital and announced she had a baby brother. She vividly remembers jumping up and down on the bed, saying, "You promised, you promised I could name him!" She promptly chose the name "David." My father replied that "David" was too widely used and asked if she'd accept "James David." Between bounces, she agreed. My father was naming me after James Armand de Rothschild, a man who had been pivotal in his life and coincidentally shared my birthday of December 1.

Although I never met or saw a Rothschild until I was close to thirty, the name had almost magical qualities in our home. My father had worked for James de Rothschild, first in the army and then in private life. For nearly a decade he traveled with him extensively. When Dad reminisced about his life in London with James and his wife, Dorothy, his voice sounded soft and unstrained. This was another world, where there was no stress and where—dare I say it?—my father had been genuinely happy. Without realizing it, I carried this legend inside me. Years later, as a grown man, I was doing a tour of merchant banks in London and found myself at NM Rothschild and Sons. I remember going into the head office in New Court, seeing the tapestry in the front hall and almost evaporating with emotion at being in the Rothschild Bank. Swirling around my head was the fairytale of my father's relationship with the Rothschilds and the mystery of why it had come to an end. I took some pink paper and a couple of pencils from the waiting room and put them in my pocket. I carried a piece of that pink paper in my wallet for years.

For all his Rothschild stories, my father never said why he left their employ. His recollections always ended abruptly. He kept diaries, though, and when he passed away I read them, hoping to understand what had happened, but I never found out exactly why he decided to set out on his own for a career in Australia. Most of the diary pages had been torn out, except for some innocuous recollections about good parts of his life. It seemed he wanted no one to know the whole story. While he was alive, I never could discuss this period with him, and it would be decades before I even came close to a hint of an understanding of the events. I did learn later that Rothschild introduced my father to horse racing and to gambling in a minor way. My father never dropped his interest in these pursuits, which continued throughout his life.

*   *   *

My father's decision to go to Sydney might have been influenced by the fact that James de Rothschild himself had once sought a kind of refuge in Australia. As a young man, Rothschild sailed for Australia under an assumed name. He left without informing any of his family or friends, because, as he later explained, he wanted "to find out what it was like not to be called a Rothschild." He took no money or checkbook and earned his living first as a bookmaker's runner on a Melbourne racecourse and later as a cattle drover, herding cattle from the far north of the country down to the sale yards in the south. After eight months, his family traced him and he returned to London.

My father had grown up in London, in a large house on Whitechapel Road, just short of the Aldgate Pump, which marks the entrance to the City of London from the east side. The family's tobacco factory took up most of the ground floor, together with a shop that was leased out to various tenants. For a man who had come to London from a tiny shtetl in eastern Europe, my grandfather, Nathan Wolfensohn, had done well. Using the name of an official of the Turkish occupation of Odessa, he called his business the Gadji Bey Tobacco Company and gained a reputation for producing high-quality tobacco and handmade cigarettes. These he supplied to the best London retailers and to the House of Commons.

It was a boisterous household, enlivened by my father's older sister, Millie, who played the piano, and his mother, Mary, only five feet one inch, teetering on her very high heels. An exuberant character, she would break into Russian dancing when the mood took her. Hyman was the youngest of the three, and while Millie studied music and his brother, Morris, was being trained as a tobacco blender downstairs, he took his own path. My father won a place at the prestigious City of London School, and at just fourteen, he graduated. After some years working with his father, he began studying medicine at St. Thomas's Hospital. He was a young man with a future. He kept at his studies, but eventually the overwhelming presence of World War I broke through. His brother had already signed up, and before my father could complete his degree, he felt compelled to sign up, too. Relentless petitioning had caused the British War Office to agree to form new Jewish combat units, and fudging his age, my father left medical school to join a new battalion of the Royal Fusiliers. This decision removed the possibility of his having a professional life as a physician, but it took him to Palestine, where he met James de Rothschild, who was then a major.

My father and Rothschild were both in the Jewish Brigade of the Royal Fusiliers, which—a first for the British army—had Hebrew as a regimental language. Because of his fluency, my father was assigned the task of issuing the British army's first Hebrew orders. He handwrote them, and when a few days later he received a typewriter with Hebrew characters, he typed them up. I have a copy of both historic documents, signed by him as adjutant to the regiment. The unit was actively recruiting and drew in men, including David Ben-Gurion and Itzhak Ben-Zvi, who would go on to become esteemed figures in modern Israel. Although my father was commissioned as a subaltern and later became a captain, the most significant position he was given was as aide to Major de Rothschild. They developed a close and effective working relationship, and upon their return to England after the war, my father remained with Rothschild as his private secretary.

For a boy from the East End, the Rothschild lifestyle was intoxicating. There he was at twenty, wearing fine tailored suits and spats, sailing on magnificent yachts, and later working in London and at Waddesdon Manor, the family mansion in Buckinghamshire, styled after a sixteenth-century French chateau. As they traveled the world, he kept Rothschild's diary and wrote the occasional speech. Despite the twenty-year age gap, the relationship between them deepened and over the next eight years grew into a close friendship.

But my father still hankered for professional qualifications and while in Rothschild's employ enrolled at Gray's Inn to qualify as a barrister-at-law. He did well academically, but before completing the final examinations to be called to the bar, he met my mother. He left Gray's Inn, and the two of them had a traditional London wedding. People remember a glamorous couple, with Hyman being somewhat pompous and dashingly good-looking. Dora, my mother, with her sturdy build, was handsome rather than pretty but very warm and accomplished. The Rothschilds must have had a hand in arranging the lavish honeymoon in Germany, because it saw my parents chauffeured around Berlin in the kaiser's Rolls Royce.

Dora, while accustomed to wealth, was also familiar with its absence. Her father, Emanuel Weinbaum, had made and lost fortunes. I never knew my grandfather Emanuel, but according to family legend he was a diamond merchant, an adventurer, and a pilot. At the turn of the century, he was in Haiti making one of his fortunes, this time in the shipping business. While provisioning ships, he apparently managed to acquire the rights for railroads and many acres of prime land that today is part of Port-au-Prince. The legend, which is no doubt highly exaggerated, holds that some time after the civil war of 1902, he performed the functions of an acting British consul. Over the next few years, Haiti continued to be plagued by political unrest, and at one point the government offered him the position of finance minister. He took the job—but two days later, in an outburst of violence, he was ousted. Fortunate enough to be rescued by a British gunboat, he lost his Haitian fortune.

Emanuel was a gambler and a speculator, and for a time, he and my grandmother, Yetta, and their six children lived splendidly, alternating between London and Antwerp. He had been born in Odessa and Yetta in Warsaw, but they fell in love with everything English. Yetta was a woman of considerable social pretension, acutely aware of class and quite certain of her place in the world. While she took care maintaining the family's position, Emanuel immersed himself in the diamond business. He was a member of the Antwerp Diamond Exchange and was said to be the first person to have a private airplane so he could fly diamonds in and out of Belgium. But he was diabetic, his sight was failing, and eventually he was trading diamonds blind, assisted by my grandmother, who would describe the gems to him. The challenge was too great. He lost his fortune and resettled the family in London, where he bravely tried to resume his trade at Hatton Gardens. By the time I met my grandmother, she was close to eighty, though she still retained traces of old grandeur. Yetta, whose surname, Feinmesser, was later changed by different members of the family to Fine or French, wouldn't tolerate company she imagined to be below her standing. Forgetting her origins, she instructed her children, including my mother, that breeding was everything.

My mother believed she had married well and had expectations of a comfortable life. In their first years, she wasn't disappointed. My parents took an apartment in the affluent suburb of Maida Vale on the northwest

side of London and indeed lived well. Working for James de Rothschild
was always exciting and stimulating, and it gave my parents opportunities
for travel and an active social life. However, this lifestyle changed dramatically when they moved to Australia, for them a new and unknown country in which they were to build a quite different life. My father set out
working hard and trying to build up new relationships and opportunities.

There was nothing snobbish about my mother, and in Australia, her
versatility and education served her well. She could turn her hand to anything and would roll up her sleeves and serve soup to the homeless,
scrub the floors, and then give a French lesson before going to sing on
the government-sponsored national Australian broadcasting radio, where
she performed under the name of Dora Marquita. Later, her work at the
Council of Jewish Women meant she would address gatherings in outlying
Jewish communities. Jana Gottshall, whose husband was the rabbi of the
community in Newcastle, north of Sydney, remembers Dora's visits clearly:

> Her personality was something outstanding. She would put everyone
> at ease and as soon as she stood to speak, she impressed you. You knew
> this was *someone,* so warm, so elegant, so groomed. We were so poor.
> My rabbi didn't speak any English and we had two small children. But
> Dora, she was like a queen. I thought the Wolfensohns, they must be
> very well off.

I treasured the moments my mother and I spent alone. She gave me a
taste of the upbringing she had enjoyed and would share her passion for
music, encourage me to try new things on the piano, and show me how to
draw on large blocks of creamy paper.

My childhood friend and neighbor Jan Hunter remembers:

> The Wolfensohns were different. They had a piano and were always
> playing classical music. To me, Mrs. Wolfensohn was lovely. She was
> pretty, with a big, soft face and hair that she would roll back in the
> style of those days. She seemed soft and cuddly and really interested in

what I had to say. Mr. Wolfensohn was a bit frightening. He wore very dark suits and a dark Homburg and had a deep voice. Although he was kind, he was otherworldly and I never engaged much with him.

To supplement my mother's casual instruction, it was arranged that one of the nuns at my first school would give me real piano lessons. But she was an old-fashioned disciplinarian, so whenever I hit a wrong note, she hit my hands with a ruler. When my parents noticed my hands sweating in anticipation of the lessons, they found another teacher. Miss Coburn, who lived a couple of blocks from us, prepared me for a competition at the Conservatorium. I must have been about seven, and although the judge declared I was a "bright little fellow" and a "musical" one, he remarked that I was not well trained. I rarely practiced, but young as I was, I delighted in music.

In the living room we had an old radio with a separate record player atop it that was attached to the speakers in the radio. We listened to many of the latest recordings, which we received as gifts from an adopted uncle, Walter Simpson, the sales director of EMI, the recording company. Some years later, Uncle Wal gave me a windup record player and the first record I ever owned—the pianist William Kapell playing Rachmaninoff's Third Concerto. I discovered that if I put the record player in the little cupboard in my bedroom, it sounded almost stereophonic. If I climbed into the cupboard, too, I felt like I was in the concert hall with Kapell.

After a few months, those piano lessons were over. I was never told why, but I sensed it was because we could not afford them and there was probably an outstanding bill. That started my embarrassment about not paying people. I remember the same feeling with doctors and dentists. My mother would take me to appointments, and then suddenly treatment would end. I still have a protruding tooth that reminds me of that period. My parents wanted me to have this corrected, but it would have required several expensive visits to the dentist. When it became clear we could not afford this, the dentist told me I could fix it myself if I just pushed my finger against it at night for ten minutes at a time. I never did.

When my mother wasn't at work or doting on me, she attended to all my father's needs. Life revolved around his armchair, where he would sit reading, listening to music or the radio. Everything would be brought to him, and although he was usually at peace within the walls of the apartment, he could not completely escape the stress of his financial situation. He was struggling with himself and the world. He was indeed the warm center of our lives and was tremendously demonstrative, but he was also volatile. He could spend hours listening to what I had to say, but then a wall would come up around him and it would be impossible to get close. It shut me out, but somehow I knew it had little to do with me and I learned to manage on my own until he was with us again.

The lack of money drove my mother to work without break. At one point, she was a teacher at a nearby kindergarten, which was convenient because I was the right age for the class and could become part of it. Before that, it was Betty who so often looked after me, if my babysitter, Rose, could not be there. Although I cannot remember those early years well, when I look at photographs of Betty and me together, I can see the love and the care she gave me. It must surely have been a burden on her own private life.

With the income from my mother's jobs, I started going to Monte Oliveto, a small Catholic school around the corner from our apartment block. In class with me was my friend Jan Hunter. I was a law-abiding five-year-old, but she was a year younger and an absolute free spirit. I loved her company and we played together almost every afternoon after school. As she was Church of England and I was Jewish, neither of us went to school prayers. Our parents had requested that we not receive religious instruction, but we were given the important task of carrying the crucifix to the front of the class every day before prayers. Then we'd go and sit on the veranda and listen intently to what we were missing inside. After we had been at Monte Oliveto for a couple of years, one of the nuns remarked to Mrs. Hunter that Jan and I were becoming better Catholics than the other children because we could recite all our Hail Marys perfectly. The Hunters began making plans to move Jan to another school.

Where we lived on Ocean Street, there were three blocks of apartments in a row, connected by a quiet, almost communal garden at the back. My family lived at one end and the Hunters at the other. In the middle of the garden, there was a stately camphor laurel tree. Some afternoons I'd hang out of my first-floor window and chat to Jan, who was sitting among its branches. We were almost inseparable and had memorable games of "doctor," sometimes joined by David Allsop, who also lived in the apartment complex. That garden was our paradise, and in summer my mother's music would waft out of the open windows and through the trees. Jan and I would jump down the terraces, swing under the railings, and scale the wobbly trellis that hid the washing lines. Mrs. Hunter was unusually tolerant, so we'd drag her lounge cushions and sheets onto the veranda to build what we thought was an elaborate structure, under which we would play "house." Jan remembers that on many occasions, just as our house was complete, my mother would lean out of the window and call, "Yooo-hooo, Jimmy, piano lessons!" This, she says was most annoying.

> Jimmy would immediately jump up and say: "Terribly sorry, got to go now. Good-bye!" And he would scamper off, up the terraces, like a little hare in short pants. I would stand there and shout: "You come back here Jimmy Wolfensohn, you horrible boy, you come back here and help me tidy up." My mother said it was a scream because I would always shout and he would always leave me with all the things to clean up and never ever come back and help.

I was a coddled child, but my parents couldn't protect me from the reality of our financial situation. One night I was playing in my pajamas when the peacefulness of the flat was broken by loud, urgent knocking. At the door was a man wearing a cap with a large crown ornament on it. He was unlike any policeman I'd ever seen before. I remember this crown vividly because, as he entered, my father picked me up and held me at a height where I could get a close look at the man's cap. My father grew pale and took me into another room before speaking to the man in hushed tones. Although nothing was ever said about this incident, in the drama of the moment I registered that something awful was happening. In retrospect, I think the man was a court officer serving papers on my father for outstanding debts.

When I think of it now, it's amazing that I was never sent or permitted to go out to earn money like children in other poor families. At one point I tried to deliver newspapers, but that didn't last. Working would have meant total defeat because my parents didn't want to admit to me that they had very few resources. There was a deception going on. They were clearly under financial pressure, but the pressure stopped at me. The one thing they were investing in was me.

Since Betty had her own dreams and was a very good student, it must have been difficult for her to see so much of my parents' attention focused on me. Betty left home when she married at twenty, moving overseas soon thereafter. At the time when I could have developed a relationship with her, our lives diverged. I have very few memories of her from those early years, but I remember well, and with great affection, my visits to her apartment after she married and our long talks together about her life and her hopes. I am very saddened that I couldn't spend more continuous time with her in my teenage years.

The year I started high school, Betty eloped with one of my father's close friends. Vijaya Raghavan was the Indian consul general in Sydney and was always at our house, chatting, playing cards, and staying on for dinner. It was great for me because whenever a Royal Indian Navy boat, corvette, or destroyer came in, I met some of the officers and crew. Once I met the entire Indian cricket team and got a seat at the test match. But when Vij and Betty married, it caused great surprise in the Jewish community and enraged my father. He found it too difficult to accept the marriage. My mother paused, considered the options, embraced Vij as part of the family, and moved on with life.

Although my father was initially unhappy about the marriage, he soon invited Betty and Vij regularly to our apartment before their departure to diplomatic ports overseas. Some years later their son, Derek, was born, and it was soon clear that he was gifted. My father loved being a grandfather. Derek's journey has since been extraordinary. He is now professor and division chairman of the Cleveland Clinic's Taussig Cancer Center. Over time, my father and Derek became great friends.

*   *   *

Financial strain was another cause of frequent stress in our household. In later years my father's business improved, and it eventually gave me great happiness to be able to ease my parents' burden myself. But as a child, the impact of witnessing their financial worries was enormous from the age of seven or so. I was always doing contingency planning in my head. My needs were small, but I remember thinking that if I could have just £10, my life would be safe. As I grew older, I would do calculations on scraps of paper and work out how long I could live on £100 if I only ate cheese and bread. If I had a box of raisins, what would that do to the calculation? Not surprisingly, such obsessing carried over into my adult years. When my wife, Elaine, and I got married, my big aim was to have $100,000 because I knew with that amount of money, I could look after the family, at least for a few years, and we would be safe no matter what happened. Monetary insecurity was a fact of life from childhood, and I was always looking for a cushion to protect myself from it.

Whenever the financial pressures at home became acute, I could see in my father a heartbreaking mixture of pride and embarrassment. As he wouldn't say what was wrong, my mother, who was finely tuned in to the situation, would somehow have to make money appear. She would get extra work or save from the work that she was already doing and manage quietly to feed her earnings into the family finances without humiliating her husband. If we wanted something and couldn't afford it, Dad's reaction was anger. Even then I sensed it was anger against himself.

In all this, I only felt let down by him once. For my bar mitzvah, my granduncle Harry had given me a collection of gold sovereigns carefully arranged between layers of paper in an old cigar box. He continued to add to the collection over the years until it reached thirty-two sovereigns. This precious box was kept in a drawer in my father's closet and I used to visit it, feel the weight of the coins in my hands, and hold them up to the light. One day the cigar box was gone. I searched the apartment. There was no sign of it. When I inquired, I got into trouble with my parents for asking. Confused and bitterly disappointed, I tried to surmise what had happened. Clearly, my father had sold them.

Although it makes perfect sense now, then I couldn't understand how my coins were related to my father's financial problems. I have no memory of my mother explaining things or trying to comfort me. She kept silent when financial strain broke through the surface and always defended my father. I never questioned her loyalty to him, but with Betty gone, I was left to try to sort the matter out in my head.

What made the coin episode even more painful was Uncle Harry's reaction. I loved Uncle Harry very much. Once he learned about the coins, he stopped coming to our table on Friday nights, which was a huge loss to me, as I already felt claustrophobic in our family of three. My mother and I continued to visit Uncle Harry in the single room where he lived and worked. In beautiful gold script, the window of his ground-floor room announced he was "Harry Feinmesser, Watchmaker." He seemed worn out and disheartened, and my mother took to cooking chicken soup that I would ferry across a couple of times a week. During these regular visits, as I became familiar with the tools, eyeglasses, and paraphernalia of his life, he grew visibly weaker.

Eventually, taking food to him became part of my daily routine. One day, I let myself into the apartment and found Uncle Harry in bed, barely conscious. He was coughing, and in his distant eyes I saw the recognition that I had arrived. I sensed he had been waiting for me, and I climbed onto his single bed. But for the sound of his slow breathing, the room was quiet and airless. Nothing else moved. Then, the breathing stopped. I tried to hold him tightly as I cried silently. Instinctively, I started to recite the Shema: "Hear, O Israel, the Lord our God, the Lord is one . . ." I recited the full prayer over and over again, seven times. I was fourteen, and it was my first experience with death. I was strangely calm. I remember laying him down and covering his head with the sheet before sprinting home to get my mother. I knew with Uncle Harry gone, at close to eighty years of age, our family would be entirely alone in Australia. He was a relic from another world and my only point of reference in the older generation.

I never forgot the incident of that cigar box. Fifty years later, I commissioned a dealer in Australia to collect sets of thirty-two gold sovereigns for each of my three children. It took time and diligence, but after some months the sets were completed. I also had the dealer build a complete set, in mint and uncirculated condition, of every sovereign ever minted in Australia, which took him several years. When the collection arrived at my office in New York, I held the heavy box for a long time. Seeing it intact and in my possession gave me a sense of deep satisfaction. Five years later, the dealer called to say the collection had increased substantively in value. Of course I was pleased, but I had done it for Uncle Harry—and for myself—not as an investment.

*   *   *

Luckily, during my youth we had our angels. One of them was my mother's sister Hannah, who would send us envelopes bearing a New York postmark and filled with dollar bills. In 1939, she sponsored my mother's trip to Europe and the States for a year to visit her family and have a holiday. One day, I heard my father shouting down the phone, "For God's sake, Dora, get on a boat." The Germans had invaded Poland in September, causing Britain and France to declare war, with Australia joining in soon thereafter, and there was growing anxiety about the safety of ocean travel and shipping. My father wanted my mother home quickly and safely.

At home, there were few signs of the war. The most tangible was an air raid shelter in the garden, and occasionally we climbed under the dining room table when a bomb warning was issued. I remember my father and his friends talking intensely about two-man Japanese mini-submarines in Sydney Harbour, but the main thing that affected me was my mother's absence.

On her return, in addition to her other activities my mother found time for voluntary work at the ANZAC Buffet, run by the lord mayor's Patriotic War Fund. She also took a job with the navy and applied to become a translator for the defense services. Before being added to the official censorship list of translators, security officials checked her out. They approached and questioned three women she worked with at the buffet. I found their confidential character references in a file on my mother held by what is now the Australian Security Intelligence Organisation (ASIO), which took over from the Commonwealth Investigations Branch (CIB).

While one branch of investigators was approving my mother, another branch had my father under surveillance as a suspected German spy. The documentation reveals that they had little insight into what was happening in the Australian Jewish community in the years immediately before World War II. At the time, Australia, like much of the rest of the world, was disinclined to allow widespread immigration by Jewish refugees from Europe. However, in 1938, after Hitler's Anschluss with Austria, the Australian government relented and began to grant up to 100 permits a week to Jewish refugees. The government did this partly on humane grounds, but also because they were suitable "white" immigrants. Many of these refugees had been prominent professionals and businessmen in Europe and began using the existing Jewish networks in Sydney and Melbourne to rebuild their lives. Although there were points of conflict between the established Jewish community and the immigrants, my father remained sympathetic and willing to help wherever he could. Then, at the beginning of World War II, all immigration stopped and those who had come from Germany and Austria were classified as "enemy aliens." Many were interned.

According to documents in my father's ASIO file, in November 1939, an informant gave a long and detailed interview at police headquarters explaining how he had heard that a chap called Wolfensohn, who was a German Jew, was in the pay of the German Secret Service. Acting on the allegations, in January 1940, the police interviewed my father and found nothing incriminating, concluding: "It would appear that he is a man of good character." His ASIO files fell silent for a year until February 1941, when a letter arrived from another informant who was certain there were "suspicious circumstances surrounding the business of H Wolfensohn." The informer had repeatedly noticed German men and women entering this office. For the next two months, two officers kept my father under surveillance and finally submitted a report that found no evidence of untoward activity. A month later the case was closed. In those days, any foreigner was a "German." Despite the fact that my father was a former British army officer and had been born in London, to some Australians he must have been German.

From the interviews and the climate of paranoia, my father would have known there was a question mark over him and this would have added to his stresses. Despite this, he never stopped helping others. A constant stream of poor foreigners, refugees, and soldiers passed through our apartment, and I often found people sitting with him in the living room, having long discussions. My parents never let these visitors go away hungry, sharing our meal or whatever small luxuries we had in the house. On more than one occasion, I saw my father get up from his chair, go to his bedroom, return with a shirt or article of clothing and give it to a guest who had less than he. I saw the pleasure this gave to our visitors, but more so, I saw the pleasure it gave my father.

My father was fascinated by international politics and instilled in me the idea that regardless of where people came from, they were essentially the same. His views went beyond British liberalism, and rather than simply tolerating racial differences, he seemed not to notice them. When he was feeling secure in himself, he was a wonderful presence and a charming host.

My problem, however, was that he had too much invested in me. After Monte Oliveto, my father enrolled me at the Woollahra Public School. Although I was young even for third grade, he insisted I go directly into fourth grade. He and my mother were convinced that I was the cleverest child on earth and that my abilities were endless. They pushed and pushed. But from the moment I entered that school, I was a couple of years ahead of myself. The biggest problem was the disadvantage I had in sports. Always small and fat compared to the other boys, I could never keep up. I was always the last boy selected for a team. On top of everything else, running made me wheeze. I couldn't keep up socially, either, though I remember grasping the necessity of befriending a certain boy, Pat Stanley, who was the most powerful student in our class. He was strong, he lifted weights, and he had photographs of nude girls. I gave him chocolate.

I wasn't always able to develop survival skills on my own. My parents were so intent on seeing me succeed that they tried to do everything for me. My father viewed my homework as his homework. He would try to explain things to me, but the reality was that he was robbing me of the ability to learn. Because of his help and my natural intelligence, my early years appeared to go smoothly and I was promoted to the "opportunity" class for fifth and sixth grades. All the kids in the district competed for this special class because it was a gateway to the elite government high school in the region.

My father swiftly befriended the teacher, George Unwin, giving him cigarettes or peaches, which were hard to get in those days. In turn, Mr. Unwin would visit my father's office. I felt a vague discomfort about their friendship and worried that my father was sort of buying him off. Mr. Unwin didn't always look the other way, and I remember the uneasiness I felt when on one of my projects, he remarked that the language and presentation seemed beyond the ability of someone of my age. "It's a shame he didn't do it himself," he wrote. Still, with the help of my good teacher and classmates, and with my natural ability in examinations, my results were decent enough to gain admission to Sydney Boys High School, the selective government school that was on a par with the private schools of the city. It was, however, a big strain on me, and I still wish I could have started high school and university two years later, in my proper peer group.

I was always eager to look outside our little apartment and see what was happening in other people's lives. By the beginning of high school, I had made friends with a couple of boys my own age. Among these was Robert Naumann, who later served for decades as a professor of chemistry at Princeton University. Together, we often visited a large house on Edge-cliff Road, where our friend Tiger Johnson lived. As we explored in the catacombs below the house or played in the grand living rooms, I became aware of the differences between Tiger's family and mine. I hardly ever saw his father, and it seemed there was much more air in the Johnson family relationships than in the Wolfensohn household.

Tiger would tell me wonderful stories about their country house and how the whole family would gather there during the holidays. I was fasci-nated by his accounts and privately wished for an invitation. I never got one. But so strong was that wish that fifty years later I would buy a farm in Australia, just for the comfort of having it.

On other afternoons I would take the tram down to Rose Bay to meet Earl Owen. Earl, who would later become a distinguished professor and surgeon, ended up spending a lot of time with us because his parents went off to the war. He loved the fact that my father was home so much and took such an interest in his schoolwork. Earl and I were extremely com-petitive and would turn everything into a contest. We would each practice marbles so we could beat the other. In the evenings, while we waited for my mother to cook dinner, we'd throw a ball down the hallway. With that—as with everything else we did—we figured out a way to keep score.

On several occasions, my father's lawyer, Lionel Dare, invited me to stay at his small farm on the outskirts of Sydney. There was space, the air was fresh, and I related easily with his family and his daughter, Robin. There was an ordinariness about the Dares' lives that I craved. I loved their healthy engagement with the wider world and the expansiveness of their discussions, and that they had breakfast together in the kitchen—a meal we never had together in my home. There was an openness, a straightforwardness I'd never experienced before. No subject was off-limits, and Lionel himself was extremely irreverent and brilliant.

*   *   *

There was one meal I always looked forward to. On Friday night we gathered around the Sabbath table, laid with a white cloth. Candles were lit, and there was wine, sweet plaited loaves of challah, and a special feeling in the air. We were a traditional Jewish family and kept a kosher home. This was the big event of the week, and if there had been tensions in the days before, everybody would make up on Friday night. It was the night when peace returned—and I would wait for it. Sometimes, though, we went through the meal without clearing the air. My parents rarely argued openly, but I could sense a lot from the cold looks. These dinners would proceed in silence. There was no singing and no easy chatter. This meant things were very bad, and I would run off and cry into my pillow.

Most of our Friday dinners were cozy, however, and more often than not, refugees or servicemen joined our table. My parents saved the best for the Sabbath, and whatever food my mother had managed to get together, we shared. Somehow we always had the freshest peaches, strawberries, and John Dory fish. It didn't matter whether our guests spoke French, German, Spanish, Italian, or even Flemish. My mother could talk to them all. If they spoke Hebrew or Yiddish, my father took over. We had memorable festivals, always with interesting guests. Intellectually, life in our apartment was rich.

Every Saturday morning, Dad and I would go to the Great Synagogue in Sydney, which stands on the edge of Hyde Park. This magnificent sandstone building, with its mixture of Byzantine and Gothic styles, was like no other place I'd ever seen. Wherever I looked, there was something extraordinary to see, from the gold-leaf stars on the ceiling to the richly inlaid mosaic floor. And whatever was uttered in that space was made profound by the surroundings. I knew this was a serious place for the serious business of prayer. Despite constant conversation among congregants, there was an air of formality and a strong sense of decorum. People behaved with modesty and courtesy. The leading families had sat in certain pews for generations, and the president was a very important man, revered by the whole community.

Dad and I would walk to synagogue unless the weather was bad and he happened to have money that week, in which case we'd get a taxi. He had a favorite driver, Joe Symes, who would arrive to collect us in taxi number 121 and then drop us at the back of the synagogue. Everyone else went through the ornate front entrance on Elizabeth Street. We always entered through a small rear door on Castlereagh Street and slipped into the main sanctuary early. There were two or three people Dad would greet, but he never mixed the way other men did before and after the service. To me, he seemed lonely. But to others during this period, I expect he appeared distant and cold. His seat was in the center of the front row, and eventually I had a seat there, too. I would remain next to him for the whole morning because I wasn't allowed to go to the children's service. My father wanted me to sit there and absorb the service, but he also wanted me close. I sensed it gave him a feeling of security. This experience built in me a kind of defense mechanism. It was part of my learning whether someone approaching us was antagonistic or friendly. It taught me how to read a room.

My father had developed an unexplained antipathy for Rabbi Porush and I was prohibited from attending the synagogue's Hebrew school. He didn't want that rabbi instructing me in anything and arranged for me to be privately tutored both for my bar mitzvah and in conversational Hebrew. A woman named Gerda Zundheimer began by coming to our apartment for lessons in the afternoons. Soon the arrangement changed and I had to walk to her apartment after school. Then the lessons stopped altogether, for what, I am sure, were financial reasons.

My father stepped in and continued teaching me himself. Then, just before my bar mitzvah, he did something quite novel for the time. He took me to a commercial studio to record the portion of the law that I would sing in Hebrew. It was recorded onto a number of 78 vinyl records that were then sent overseas, to family members who couldn't attend the ceremony. I doubt that many family members listened to the whole recording, but it gave my parents a sense that our distant family was participating.

After synagogue, my father and I would stroll through the city together. When we passed the photo store, I would put my nose up against the window and look for a camera. There was always a Leica in the window and although I had never touched one, I was an expert in their qualities because I used to read *Popular Mechanics* magazine, which contained advertisements for cameras. One day, my father let me go into the shop and I actually held one of the mythical Leicas. In later life, I could never bring myself to buy one because in my mind they remained unattainable objects. Then, about twenty-five years ago, I was asked to join the board of Leica when friends bought the Leitz company. I declined but told them about my childhood love affair with the camera. A short while later, a box arrived. Finally, I had my own Leica with every lens and every possible accessory. Although I don't know how to use it very well—I leave that to my children—I draw pleasure just knowing I have it.

Sometimes, on our walk after synagogue, we would look in at Dad's office at 14 Spring Street. We'd climb the stairs to the first floor and come to a door announcing "H Wolfensohn." It was one big office with a large desk, two chairs for clients, a table with chairs, and a couple of filing cabinets. To me, the room seemed rather sparse, with nothing on the walls and lots of books, mainly Australian regulations in green bindings. It was peaceful and smelled of cigars, like my father. Dad would open the windows outward, and while he looked at papers, I would sit quietly and draw. Occasionally, during school holidays I'd take a bus to his office and we would go out for lunch. If clients were visiting, he'd let me listen to the discussion, and if I was lucky, he would take me on his rounds. I never knew what he was doing with clients, but he seemed to know a lot of people and to help many new immigrants. At those times, I felt happy in his orbit.

2

SETTING OUT

MY FIRST REAL JOURNEY FAR FROM HOME WAS A YOUNG AUSTRALIA League trip to the Great Barrier Reef in far northern Queensland, almost 1,500 miles from Sydney. We took a long slow train up the east coast of Australia, toward Cairns. Up north, it was so hot and the train crept so slowly, we would jump down and walk alongside. But the conditions didn't matter because everything was interesting. At Cairns, we all piled into a bus that took us to a sugar mill and then out into the fields to see the workers burning the cane stubble. The highlight of the trip was when we sailed off the coast to a tiny coral cay. We learned that Captain Cook had called it Green Island after the astronomer aboard his ship, the *Endeavour,* but that the Aborigines called it Wunyami, or "place of the haunted spirits." The Gungandji people once used the island for initiation rites, leaving young men there for weeks at a time to demonstrate their survival skills. This was my first exposure to Aboriginal culture, and I soaked it in. During that trip to northern Queensland, I was not homesick for a second. I loved the feeling of exploration, which I have never lost, and I was filled with excitement at seeing something new and different. Home was the base from which I could explore the world, and even going to school could be seen as an adventure.

When I returned to Sydney, I started at my new school. My parents loved the fact that I was at Sydney Boys High School, affectionately known as High. The first day, they could hardly take their eyes off their protégé, dressed as they believed in one of the most prestigious school blazers a Sydney boy could wear. High was not only the leading high school, but it was free and entry was determined competitively, based on performance in the primary school system.

High's alumni held positions in politics, the judiciary, the foreign service, and the arts, and my parents naturally assumed that I, too, would shine. Although the teachers were not as accessible as they had been in my previous schools, my parents still found ways to push me forward. My mother took care of my French and encouraged me to read Lamb's *Tales from Shakespeare*, in place of the original. I am not sure that this was constructive advice. My father was my private math, history, and Latin tutor. But for all their effort, and indeed partly because of it, I didn't hold my own. After the entrance examinations, I had started at High ranked eleventh out of the 132 boys in the year. When I completed fifth form (roughly eleventh grade), I ranked 123rd. This prompted the headmaster to note in my final report card that I was "a nice young man but totally lacking in ambition." My parents continued to make excuses for me, but I simply didn't know it was possible to depend on myself. I didn't know how to think or learn—I just vaguely knew how to make it look like I had.

Then it got worse. I failed the final school exam and could not matriculate for entrance to the university. After a dismal Christmas break, I had to drag on my school uniform and return to class. Although the boys were now closer to me in age, I felt like the epitome of failure. My parents immediately urged me to apply to have my examinations reassessed and to sit for one exam again. This I did, reluctantly, and the resulting upgrade to a passing grade in that one subject was enough to get me over the line and into university with my original classmates, though still far ahead of my age group.

All the same, there was one realm at High that I felt was my own: music. Each term we performed a Gilbert and Sullivan operetta. The wit, the melody, and the easy harmony caught my imagination, and I discovered I had a voice. This excited my mother, who coached me and made the costumes—and that required some skill, because I was always cast in a female role. My first triumph was playing Ruth in *The Pirates of Penzance*. Then came Little Buttercup in *H.M.S. Pinafore,* followed by the Duchess of Plaza-Toro in *The Gondoliers*. My success was, however, tinged with the personal shame that my "soprano" voice meant I would never be given a male role. But after three years, my voice broke and my singing career was over anyway.

Although sport was not my forte, in my early years of high school I also discovered I could play a reasonable game of tennis. Every Sunday morning I would walk down to White City tennis courts, where I had been given a junior membership and a tennis racquet as a gift from Betty and Vij. It was the home of the New South Wales Lawn Tennis Association and the training ground for the state's best players. The association was sponsoring young kids, so we would get lots of games, many with adults. Occasionally, I'd even play with legendary figures such as Adrian Quist and John Bromwich, who were Australian heroes. These two men would go on to win the doubles at Wimbledon, but they had already set a record for the remarkable way they had won the Davis Cup. Their non-playing captain, Harry Hopman, was *my* coach, too.

I was in the perfect spot at the perfect time. Harry had a towering reputation, and by chance, I was in his squad. With me were two slightly younger boys, Ken Rosewall and Lew Hoad, who would rocket to tennis fame as the "tennis twins." They were already way beyond me in skill, but under Hopman's tuition I became last string in the Under Thirteen State Squad. Harry believed in me and wanted me to leave school to devote myself to tennis. My father, of course, wouldn't hear of it, as he insisted that nothing would prevent me from gaining professional qualifications. As much as I wanted to drop out of school and train with Hopman, I could not challenge my father. I dropped out of the squad. Rebellion was not an option.

As mentioned, the Sabbath normally meant peace and freedom from worry about the stresses of the week. But there was one unpredictable and not very consistent element of the Sabbath that I feared—the gathering for the Saturday afternoon horse races, usually at the Einfeld's place in Bellevue Hill, which we attended nearly every weekend. Dad's mood for the coming week would be determined by whether he won or lost. Sometimes, he would wager £1 or more on a horse. This was such a stress on the family that I grew to hate the horses. So much depended on racing that I just couldn't bear it. Betting exacerbated our already tenuous financial situation, as we never had a steady income. If Dad lost badly on Saturday afternoon, it usually meant no 5:00 PM movie. We'd go home in silence.

In order to give me some experience of life in the country, my resourceful parents made a discovery. They found a dairy farm at Rooty Hill, on the outskirts of Sydney, that had a few horses and took guests on the weekends. For no charge, the farmer agreed to let me stay for a week during my vacation—a privilege I was to accept many times. In return, I had to clean out the stables and milk the two cows. My mother came with me to settle me in the first couple of times, but after that I went alone. I loved this arrangement, partly because for the first time in my life, I had become interested in a girl. Rae looked after the horses, and although she was a few years older than I, she was the first woman I thought I would love. I was given a little room at the back in a bunkhouse near the stables and I would lie on my bed and think of Rae. She was probably oblivious to my affection, but that didn't dampen my interest. Among the horses was a chestnut mare, Nelly, who was very fast and difficult to ride. I managed her very well, and Nelly and I became great friends. This gave me a point of contact with Rae that was not available to my competitors. My crush never developed into anything, but I cherished the time I spent in Rooty Hill, for it was a glimpse at the world beyond my family.

When I had entered high school at eleven years old, my parents allowed me to join a group called the Great Synagogue Youth, or GSY. The organization had been established to foster a closer relationship between Jewish youth and engender a love for Orthodox Judaism. My parents were unlocking a door and allowing me to walk into a peer group that was perfect for my stage of life. For the first time, I didn't have to worry about trying to keep up with the boys in my class who were physically more mature and had interests beyond me. These were girls and boys my own age who accepted me without question, and I slipped into the group with ease. GSY offered activities like drama classes and stamp collecting, but it also encouraged us to attend meetings and have some fun with regularly scheduled parties. Most of the kids lived around the area, and I developed a network of places to visit. We'd go to someone's house and sit around chatting, or we might play tennis or hang out at the One Two Three milk bar in Double Bay. The little store was always so full that we would spill out onto the pavement, where we'd drink our milkshakes out of large metal containers. Someone would buy a bag of broken cookies for a penny or two, which we'd pass around. Leaving my GSY pals to start at the University of Sydney at the age of sixteen was daunting. I knew I'd miss them and wondered whether I'd ever replace our camaraderie.

*   *   *

At the university, with its Gothic revival architecture, quadrangle, cloisters, and beautifully kept lawns, I didn't know where I was at first. I'd gaze up at the great tower and all around, seeing gargoyles staring back at me. I hadn't decided to go to this place, I just found myself there. In fact, in those days I didn't decide much. I didn't choose my subjects, or even my clothes, and I didn't have much money.

Practically everybody my family knew had a scholarship to the university, but I had such a mediocre record that I didn't qualify. The fees were something like £30 (about $75) a semester, and I never had enough. That first year, I went up to the registrar's office with £5 or £10 at a time, feeling tremendously embarrassed. I must have absorbed my father's habits because I couldn't deal with it directly. I could not say: "Terribly sorry, the family is having a difficult time and I can't pay the fees in full right now, but please understand I'll pay the rest in three weeks' time." I simply felt embarrassed and could not state directly what would have been understood as a problem but no great crisis.

As a first-year student, I had no self-possession and no idea how things worked. I did, however, recognize that I was getting older and that life was changing when I was offered a Sydney University Union credit card, which I readily accepted. Our family had never had any credit cards before, and we initially used to run up bills on my card. Then I would grow embarrassed all over again because I couldn't pay them on time. Thereafter, I took control of the card and used it sparingly. Financial insecurity was my constant companion. I never suffered in the sense of not having enough to eat, and in a world context, I lived in middle-class security. But at that time I was living out a tremendous personal drama, trying to keep up with other students who seemed to have no such financial problems in Australia's most sophisticated university. I wasn't worldly; in fact, I was behind my peers in age and experience.

One of my father's wealthier acquaintances, Arthur Flanders, had a son named Eric who was also in first year, though two years older than I was. Every morning, Eric would give me a ride to the university. He collected me in his blue-green Austin A90, a top-of-the-line sports car in those days. It was an impressive piece of machinery. I marveled that at the touch of a button, he could roll the roof open or closed. Without fail, every time I climbed into that car, I felt a sting. Eric was a pretty hot ticket at the university because of that A90—the girls liked him, he was the right age, and he had a tutor for all his subjects. I compared badly. I hadn't even begun shaving yet, and it would be more than two years before I could get a driver's license. Although I tried to keep up my end of the conversation while we drove along, as soon as we arrived at the campus, he'd dump me and go off to meet the girls.

I would head straight for the students' union, where the chess club was housed. If I had a few coins, I'd go down to The Buttery and have coffee or sit around in the armchairs, reading the newspaper and magazines. I felt comfortable there: It was bigger than the apartment I still lived in with my parents, I was allowed to be there, and although I didn't talk to many people, just being there made me feel part of the community. I went to the chess club every day and I was a decent player, but like everything I did at that time, I did not excel. I followed the books of the chess masters' games, but instead of spending hours playing out the games and learning the theories thoroughly, I would pick up just enough to get by. I played an enormous amount of chess in my first year, and all too often missed class to do so.

When Eric and other boys chatted about girls, I had little to contribute. Once Eric produced a packet of condoms his father had given him. I had no idea what they were. I pretended to know, of course, and had to quickly find out. But sex was something that you never talked about explicitly in those days, and like many boys, I had a set of strange but firmly held views that remained uncorrected for years. I knew that if you got close to a girl, you'd have a baby, and that would ruin your life. The things I didn't know would make a sex-ed teacher cringe. I knew that I liked girls and had the normal fantasies, expectations, and hopes, but I had incredible inhibitions and fears. It barely mattered; all the girls were beyond me, and I sank deeper into my armchair.

I hardly went to lectures but would come home every night, give the impression that all was well, and show my parents bits and pieces from university life, like pens stamped with the Sydney University crest. I don't know how suspicious they were, or whether I was deluding them as much as I was deluding myself. One of the mainstays of my delusion was Eric's tutor. Eric's father had hired Dr. Plant to make sure his son's work was handed in correctly and that he obtained a respectable passing grade. Using a typewriter, Dr. Plant compiled notes and summaries of lectures and gave them to Eric. Often, Eric would share them with me, which meant we were both working off his tutor, except that I never saw him. Eric reported that all we needed to do was read the summaries and memorize ten key points. We never picked up a textbook. This was absolutely the

worst conceivable thing for our education, and an extension of my re-
liance on others. I went on to fail three out of my four subjects.

I experienced the full force of failure, and it transformed me. Failing
that first year woke me from my boyhood somnolence and completely
changed the way I saw the world. There was no escape from the reality of
failure, nor any explanation that would shield me. Throughout the year
I could sense that academically I was drifting toward disaster, but I
thought that with the aid of Dr. Plant's notes it would somehow work
out. It was as if I were floating downstream in a dreamlike state, knowing
that there was a precipitous waterfall ahead but believing that someone
would eventually intervene and save me. This time, no one did. Crashing
over the edge finally marked the beginning of my taking charge of my
life. I recognized not only that I had to rescue myself but that it was
quite possible to do so. Understanding this was an enormously empower-
ing process and one that, once I had begun, I wanted to do more and
more. I wanted to think for myself, plan for myself, and execute my own
plans. For the first time, I felt in command. Within a couple of years, I
had dumped the crutch of my upbringing and was making my own way
in the world.

The fact that my parents couldn't save me became my salvation.
Things between us changed. As they had always praised me regardless of
my performance, I no longer trusted their judgment. Of course, I was always thrilled to do good things to make them happy, but only when I
knew they were good. I stopped using their yardstick of success and used
my own. I would tell them what I'd done, but I was now the judge of
whether or not it was successful. I took charge of the calibrations of success. Even so, I was still left with a need for approval. I had jettisoned my
parents' praise, but I still craved external recognition and absolutely required that someone else tell me I was doing well. In the subsequent decades, whatever I did, I would have to call someone and ask, "Did I do
well?" Even now, in my seventies, I catch myself doing it. No matter what
I've accomplished, part of me can't break the addiction.

Although failure became my catalyst for change, initially it sent me into a mixture of panic and despair. I wanted to run away. I turned for advice to Lionel Dare, my father's lawyer, whom I trusted and admired, and who had owned the farm near Sydney where my head had been dunked in a bucket of lime wash. At first he said I should study accounting, make a living, and stop being a spoiled brat. Then he modified his position, saying to hell with that: "Go and toughen yourself up, work someplace like a timber yard, make some money, and when you've made a man of yourself, then you can think of studying." It was excellent advice—I *was* soft and coddled—but I did not follow it, although I did take part-time work in a timber yard. In retrospect, this was a turning point. I could very well have quit and become an accountant.

Instead, I sought further advice, this time from Julius Stone, another of my father's friends, a renowned jurist and professor of jurisprudence and international law at Sydney University. "No, no, no!" he said emphatically. "You stay and get on with it. You cannot quit."

Quite literally, Julius saved me. He took me in hand and gave me remedial instruction. I spent weekends at his home trying to return the enormous favor by doing work around the house on his many construction projects. While we laid cement paths and built a compost heap, we'd talk. He was astonished at my complete lack of methodology. We'd go indoors and he'd sit me down, give me some material to read, and show me how to make flash cards to remember my key points. From his wife, Reca, I learned to write out summaries of what was important in my reading, each week showing her the notes I took in my university lectures. Until then the only structural advice I'd ever absorbed was from an English teacher at school who taught me that an essay has an introduction, a body, and a conclusion. I'd been totally impoverished academically because of my inability to take advantage of my high school education due to my age and immaturity, so Julius's instruction was enlightening and life-changing. He and Reca taught me the lessons I should have learned in high school, if not primary school.

Julius was a symbol of the real integrity of scholarship and during his forty-year career was both feared and revered. He was arguably one of the greatest international lawyers of his time. He profoundly influenced generations of students who went on to make major contributions to the life and culture of Australia, to the bench, in politics, and in the professions. Like my father, Julius was intellectually formidable, but because I was accustomed to my father, I wasn't intimidated by him. The son of Lithuanian Jewish refugees, he had been educated at Oxford and Harvard, and the powerful combination of the British and American traditions marked his work. He went on to teach at both universities. I am enormously lucky that he chose to come to Australia and that he took an interest in me. Without his intervention, I might have settled for a midlevel career. I eventually had the privilege of working on footnotes during the editing of his epochal book on jurisprudence, *The Province and Function of Law.*

In the late 1940s, as I was emerging from the cocoon of my parents' protection, my father was coming out of the worst period of his life. His consultancy started to gather momentum. Many Jewish immigrants had arrived, and he advised them about beginning businesses and the relevant regulations, and helped them acquire approvals from the different layers of government. He also began publishing an innovative monthly newsletter about commercial and economic affairs in Australia, which he wrote and distributed himself. His mood had lightened, and consequently our domestic life had improved. For the first time, we even had a few pounds to give away to charities.

We were finally able to have a telephone in the house and, amazingly, a car. My mother had taken a job at a business college and managed to save enough to buy a 1937 Morris 8/40. Although this red-and-black coupe with its little jump seat in the back was probably tenth-hand, it was a thrilling purchase and, on the weekends, we'd go for drives in the country. My parents were both overweight and would squeeze into the front seats while I climbed into the jump seat. I loved those trips. Often I would drive, and because of the small engine, I would have to find routes that avoided steep hills. It didn't look like much to my friends, but I felt wonderfully free in that little car.

My father, relieved of financial stress, was beginning to come out of the shadows and socialize freely. He began making his entrance through the front door of the synagogue and greeted people openly. By 1949, so much of his confidence had returned that he accepted a communal leadership position as head of the public relations committee of the Jewish Board of Deputies. Australia was feeling the effects of the Holocaust, growing anti-Semitism, and the establishment of the state of Israel. During his five-year appointment, my father found himself at the heart of controversies about immigration, Zionism, and fascism. It's true that Australia was not an overtly anti-Semitic country. The first native-born governor general, Sir Isaac Isaacs, had been Jewish and so had a great general of World War I, Sir John Monash. But there were occasional flash points, and my father, by then, was not afraid to make his voice heard.

When he spoke out, however, the security police were listening, particularly on the subject of German immigration. Immigration, in general, was a contentious issue. The White Australia Policy, which was put into effect in 1901 and held sway for well over half a century, aimed to restrict non-European migration to Australia by requiring all immigrants to pass a dictation test in a European language. Although a belief in the biological inferiority of some races no doubt underpinned this policy, revisionist historians now take a benign view and say the policy was also an attempt by some politicians to preserve social harmony and a strategy by the fledgling trade-union movement to keep cheap labor out of the country. By the early 1950s, intellectuals were drawing attention to the offense this policy caused in Asia and were beginning to question why an immigrant trading nation based in the Asian region would ban Asian immigrants because of their race.

In my later years at university, my friend Laksiri Jayasuriya, who was the university medalist in psychology, was refused permission to stay in Australia. He had come from Ceylon by grace of the Colombo Plan, which gave Asian students scholarships in Australia. However, the plan did not allow graduates to remain in the country. This was of some benefit to these students' home countries, but it nevertheless revealed the spirit of antagonism toward Asians that prevailed in Australia at that time. Laksiri's situation infuriated me and many other students, and we wrote letters and demonstrated, though with little immediate effect. But students continued to make noise, and ultimately the legislation was revoked several years later. I felt that my efforts had gone full circle when I was at the World Bank and was able to establish the Virtual Colombo Plan, which relied on videoconferencing between Australian and Asian educational institutions to supplement and expand Australia's role in Asia. The Australian government put up $50 million in the first year to establish distance-learning facilities and enrich educational life in the region, and continued the program for several more years. Jayasuriya went on to become a distinguished university professor in Western Australia, where he and his wife still live.

A crude line had initially been drawn between white and nonwhite in Australia, but finer distinctions were under discussion about which particular European immigrants were most suitable. It was against this background that the debate about German immigration took place. By the late 1940s, Australia was having difficulty finding what it regarded as suitable migrants from Europe, meaning British or western Europeans as opposed to migrants from southern and eastern Europe, who were seeking Australian residency permits in much greater numbers. To boost western European migration, a proposal was put forward saying that Volksdeutsche, or ethnic Germans, who were excluded at the time because of World War II memories, should be encouraged to come to Australia. This was rejected by the Labour government, but in 1950, the new Liberal government supported the scheme and proposed sponsoring 100,000 Germans over four years. The administration argued that in the past, Germans had been good and industrious settlers who were easily absorbed into the country. It argued further that ex-members of the Nazi Party should not necessarily be excluded because membership in the party had been compulsory.

The Jewish community protested fiercely, and my father, as head of the public relations committee, found himself directing part of its campaign. As usual, and completely unknown to him or our family, his activities were being reported to the Australian Security Intelligence Organisation (ASIO) and recorded in a dossier. The Jewish community pointed out that the Volksdeutsche in displaced persons (DP) camps who were eligible for migration had cooperated with the German army in concentration camps and auxiliary units and were now too afraid to return home. The Jewish opponents also added that young Germans whom the government considered suitable migrants had been educated under the Nazi regime and would be indoctrinated with racist and authoritarian beliefs that were incompatible with the type of democracy enjoyed by Australians.

The Liberal government rejected these arguments, declaring them based on emotion. But the controversy continued, and in 1953, officers from the Commonwealth Investigations Branch (CIB) reported that my father and the well-known Sydney personality Sydney Einfeld (then vice president of the Jewish Board of Deputies and later a member of State Parliament) had removed a confidential file from the Department of Immigration. According to the CIB report, "This file showed conclusively that Jewish migration to Australia has been curtailed and that German migration is to be encouraged." I never found out whether the allegation was true or how the file was used. But it showed me an aspect of the work my father and Einfeld were doing.

We would later learn that between 1947 and 1951, Australia accepted 200,000 people from DP camps, of whom only 17,000 were Jews. There were many stories told by Jewish survivors about coming to Australia by boat and recognizing among the passengers certain people who had collaborated with the Nazis, had been camp guards, or had persecuted them. Many of the collaborators were from the Baltic countries or Eastern Europe. On arrival, the survivors would sometimes make a report to the Jewish Council. These reports were compiled in dossiers and sent to the government.

There was much dissent in the Jewish community about how to handle these sensitive issues, and when my father took his position, he reversed some of the previous decisions that had inflamed the Jewish community and was able to diffuse the tensions. He also introduced a program of promotions and goodwill within the wider community to try to combat anti-Semitism and promote the protection of the rights of Jews. Many people have told me that my father was a man ahead of his times. He trained speakers to go out and represent the Jewish community at schools and other public venues. But his most forward-looking venture was to establish a legal subcommittee to work on antidefamation legislation. He wanted to sponsor legislation for group libel but was thirty years too early; the proposed legislation was never introduced into Parliament. In the late 1980s, racial vilification legislation finally came into being in Australia.

*   *   *

During spring break of my second year, I was watching the university's tennis team practice when the captain of the fencing team, Rupert Bligh, whom I knew slightly, came over to speak to me. The fencing team trained in the tennis pavilion. He asked if I wanted to come to Melbourne the next day, to the national university championships, and fence for Sydney University. "You've got to be mad," I answered. "I've never fenced in my life." He said he knew that, but someone had just fallen ill, there was an empty place, and it needed to be filled, urgently, so the team would have enough members to meet the requirements to compete. I quickly accepted the offer and went home thinking that this must be a totally unique way to get a university blazer—a major status symbol—without my ever having played the sport.

The problem, apart from my complete lack of knowledge of the sport, was that I now needed money to cover train fare and a few days' expenses in Melbourne. My parents were able to come up with the necessary funds, and the next day I was heading south. As the train rattled forward, I stood, sword in hand, swaying with the movement of the train, trying to follow the commands of my teammates and lunge against an imaginary target. It was not an easy way to learn the basics of fencing and must have been a unique sight for other passengers.

The plan was to equip me, show me how to hold the épée, and make it look like I knew what I was doing. In order to make my performance less than ludicrous, we developed a series of signs that would launch me into a couple of very simple moves. I was told to put out my arm, aim it at the opponent, and run toward him. If I could hit him, I would get a point. When we got to the championships, I carried this out well enough, but the opposing teams quickly recognized that I had absolutely no strategy after I started running. So they would induce my action, knock aside the épée, and then hit me. I found it a lot of fun and tried to invent new ways to score points on the opponent. Of course I lost every bout and never scored a single point, but our team beat the University of Melbourne without my contribution. I could not remember having such a good time ever before. I'd fallen into a group of sportsmen in a terrific sport, and I decided right then that I would become a fencer. As I slimmed down, I became increasingly hungry for victory. That old fear of failure that used to hobble me on the tennis court was gone. For the next five years, I pushed myself, ending up many times as national universities champion.

Fencing taught me a new form of discipline. I had to stay fit. I had to train for the national championships four or five nights a week in order to represent the state of New South Wales. This forced me to plan how I spent the rest of my time, because I now had an obligation to my teammates to show up on time for training most evenings. I built close relationships, particularly with Hil Van Dijk, a Dutchman some ten or more years older than I was. He became my teacher, protector, and close friend. In 1953, he included me in a small group he was preparing with the aim of getting into the 1956 Olympic Games. With Van Dijk driving us, we worked hard, and for me there was no escape from reality because the scoreboard was always there. I soon learned that only one person was responsible for my success.

I had followed Julius Stone's advice and kept at my studies, but I did not entirely disregard Lionel Dare's suggestion and I continued my part-time job in a lumberyard behind the university. It was hard work but it did me good, and for several months, as I lugged timber, I also made money to contribute to my tuition. Then I took the more lucrative and comfortable position of salesclerk in the shoe section of the David Jones department store in the city. That wasn't making me wealthy, so I persuaded a friend from law school, George Masterman, who later went on to a distinguished legal career, to start a little business with me. We would visit houses where a birth had been registered and offer to have our professional employers photograph the mother and new baby together. The system worked on commission, so we had to learn to be good salesmen. Our enterprise only lasted a few months. George recalls barely making enough to cover the cost of having to buy the street directory.

After a couple of years at the university, I finally found a girlfriend and was deeply smitten. Two years younger than me, athletic, and from a private school, this girl was more beautiful to me than any other woman who ever existed. We'd arrange furtive rendezvous, meet at the library, drive off and hold hands and kiss in a local park in her car. Then she'd drop me off at the bottom of my street. But I wasn't deemed a proper suitor by her family. Jewish, penniless, and with no career prospects, I didn't make the grade. So we went underground, and at stipulated times I would call her from the local telephone booth, for two pennies. I could never understand why my parents swallowed the fiction that I needed a nightly walk, but they did not object. The relationship ended when I completed my law degree and set off for study abroad.

By my third year at Sydney University, the Korean War was underway. As the Liberal government urged us to prepare for war, antiwar activists on campus were becoming increasingly vocal. Memories of World War II were still fresh, and the peace movement staged rallies featuring passionate speeches about the waste of war. I knew they had a convincing case but felt conflicted. My father's military background had instilled in me a deep respect for the defense force. As a child, I was mesmerized by the gallantry and adventure of the air force that I saw in films. Vivid newsreel scenes of the Berlin Airlift were still in my mind when I had the chance to apply for a place in the newly formed Sydney University Squadron of the Royal Australian Air Force (RAAF). It was modeled on the squadrons at Oxford and Cambridge that had supplied pilots for the Battle of Britain. Getting through the rigorous selection process and being recruited was a real honor. From hundreds of applicants, only thirty students from Sydney University would make it as cadets that year.

In 1952, my friend Tony Robb and I were recruited together and joined the same squadron. Apart from the real possibility of serving our country, it conferred a kind of rank that gave us access to the world of officers without our actually being officers. The commitment was for two years, after which we would graduate, receive a commission, and be put on reserve for five years. Apart from being issued an impressive blue uniform, complete with a white band to go around our officer's cap, we were paid for participating in parades and for our attendance at periods of training on air force bases. They only paid us a few shillings per day, but for many students, including me, it was welcome beer money. Occasionally we'd have to wear our uniforms to the university. This drew a mixed response; some students were respectful, but others directed their antiwar sentiments against us. We thought this was a small price to pay for the honor and education the squadron provided. We heard lectures from men we would never otherwise have encountered, including a pilot from the Dambusters of World War II and the navigator of the queen's flight. I loved the tradition and was very proud to wear my country's uniform.

On campus, I was looking for ways to have more responsibility. I had discovered ambition and had acquired some confidence to try initiatives on my own. Together with another student, I came up with the idea of expanding orientation week, which was then no more than an academic introductory week for new students. Why not use this valuable time, when the students were fresh and enthusiastic, to give them a feel for campus life and show them the range of clubs and activities the university had to offer? I remembered well my own insecurity at the start of my university career and wished that someone had shown me around and introduced me to the rich texture of university life. We did our planning in the student newspaper offices, which were housed in two trailers, but there we found the phones, the typewriters, and the infrastructure we needed. By the beginning of my third year, we had the social aspect of orientation week up and running. I was the director that inaugural year and the next, when we improved on it.

At the university where I had started out so badly, I was increasingly comfortable and confident. With the distance my new life afforded, I came to view life at home more critically. I was beginning to understand the unhealthy aspects of the dynamic between me and my parents and was consciously pulling away. I still tried to include them by giving them detailed descriptions of everything I did. The joy on their faces made it worthwhile, but I knew I had to separate myself and make my own decisions.

Each year just at the end of December, when the Australian summer is in full sway, I would close myself in my bedroom with a pad of paper and plot out the options for all my areas of activity—family, finance, sport, romance, academics, and career. Then I would set goals in each, completely without limit. I let my mind run free. What would I have to do to become prime minister, a leading banker, a judge of the Supreme Court, an Olympian, a Rhodes scholar? I wrote down my name and attached all sorts of labels of achievement to it. What would it look like to be Mr. Justice Wolfensohn, or Governor-General Wolfensohn, or Sir James Wolfensohn, or Lord Wolfensohn? What would it be like to have £100,000 or £1 million, or a bachelor's apartment, or a car? Did I want a permanent girlfriend? Initially I had planned to study medicine, but when I worked out how many years it would take and how much it would cost, I crossed it off the list. This was both a thrilling and a soul-searching exercise, a heady mixture of fantasy and real possibility. Lending power to these ideas meant going against the conventional wisdom by starting at the top and working down. It was a bold exercise that opened real possibilities to me. I conceived of the future and then worked out how to make it a reality. I wrote down "Olympic fencer." What would it take? There would be practice four nights a week, I would have to turn myself into a better athlete, I would have to keep at my studies and contribute at home. I made long lists and planned a month at a time for the coming year. Sitting at the small table in my room that night, with the warm summer air coming through the window, I believed I could do anything—it was just a matter of planning and organizing it.

To this day I keep up the practice at the start of the new year. I reflect, dream, and plan, although at this late stage of my life my options are certainly more limited. I do not know why or how I started this annual practice, but I look forward to the several days I take to complete the exercise—and I have no doubt that my career and life have been enriched by this practice.

3

∞∞∞

STEPPING UP

THE OFFICE OF ALLEN ALLEN & HEMSLEY WAS LOCATED ON MARTIN Place in an elegant, imposing building that was the headquarters of an insurance company. Allens was *the* iconic, establishment law firm in Sydney. I was nervous and eager as I entered Norman Lethbridge Cowper's large office. In some ways, I had no business being there. I did not have the top grades to seek with confidence a clerkship at Sydney's top firm of attorneys. But I did have Julius Stone. He had encouraged me to study law, and Cowper, the firm's senior partner, was his close friend. Like other firms, Allens maintained the tradition of passing legal knowledge, experience, and practice from generation to generation, through master solicitors to articled clerks who had to serve three years to gain a professional license. I had three years of university left, having completed my Bachelor of Arts degree and one year of legal studies. I was anxious to work at the center of the legal community—and Allens, which had clients like the Bank of New South Wales and the Church of England, was a dream.

Julius put his formidable legal reputation behind me and guaranteed Cowper that if I were only given the chance, I would excel. I managed not to mess up the interview with Cowper and the subsequent ones with several other partners, and the firm decided to take a chance on me. I accepted their offer immediately, believing I could manage to keep up with my university obligations and still work through my clerkship with the firm, as was mandated by law for solicitor's accreditation.

A couple of weeks into my clerkship, Cowper invited me to a group luncheon in the partners' dining room. This was unknown territory for me. Feeling a little apprehensive, I walked in to find a formal but clubby atmosphere where everyone knew each other. I was shown my seat at the table next to Cowper, and after meeting the assembled group, I never said a word until the main course arrived. I looked down at my food—and stared at it nervously for a minute: It was ham. Everyone else began eating. I thought: *Either I do it now or I don't do it at all.* Summoning all my courage, I said: "Mr. Cowper, I'm Jewish, I don't eat pork, ham, or shellfish, and I would like to have the Jewish holidays off." In my anxiety, all this tumbled out. My neighbors stopped eating and stared at me. Cowper looked at me, too. "No problem," he replied. "Order something else, and yes, you can have the holy days off."

I doubt anyone else remembers that exchange. I will never forget it. I was young, insecure, and the first Jew in Sydney's leading establishment law firm. I could have said, "I love ham," but something in me decided not to hide. The traditions of the Jewish faith were important to me—and would continue to be—but the bigger choice that day was to represent myself honestly. I never felt that I would meld into the landscape. There was an innate insecurity in being Jewish because I was different. I could often spot the Jews when I walked into a room. And I could spot the people pretending they weren't Jews. But that insecurity developed into an advantage. I developed the practice of always assessing any room as I entered to see where people fit and to observe their characteristics, strengths, and weaknesses.

Cowper, who had reformed Allens, didn't seem to care much about convention. There was an air of glamour and mystery about him, and even suggestions that he had once been on the fringes in the world of Australian espionage. He had founded the United Australia Party in 1931 and had twice stood unsuccessfully as a candidate for Parliament. The grandson of a former premier of New South Wales and great-grandson of one of its governors, he had an impeccable pedigree, and yet he was entirely without social pretension. I felt extremely lucky to have him as a mentor.

Allens demanded a whole new mentality. I got up at 7:00 AM every day, attending law school lectures early in the morning before going to the office and doing my professional work until late in the evening, and most days squeezed in two or more hours of fencing practice before returning home. I was on my own, and the challenge was to meet absolute standards. I couldn't fudge my results, and I couldn't rely on anyone else to do my work. This challenge changed the way I did everything, from the way I worked for exams to the way I fenced. I had entered the real world, and I felt enormous pressure to perform. But I was ripe for it. The partners around me established the highest standards and stood ready to help. I put in a tremendous number of hours and tried always to be one step ahead. If my master solicitor, Robert William Dill Stevenson, told me to get a list of cases or organize the evidence in a certain way, I'd always prepare more than was needed. First, I'd take his instructions and mull them over. I'd learn as much as I could about the reason for his request, the client, and the transaction or litigation involved. Then I would try to anticipate ways in which the information could be used. I'd learn all I could about the client, pick up news on the street, and never close the doors to more. I looked for linkages, trying to imagine what the representatives on the other side would think and to anticipate what they would do. I'd try to play their game.

When one of Allens' most feared trial lawyers, Gabriel Selmar Reichenbach, requested that I leave Bob Stevenson to become his clerk, I was proud but fearful. Working in his office with him was the best thing that could have happened to me. Reichy, as he was known to all of us, represented the finest quality, methodology, and attention to detail. He was very demanding and tough, but he was a great teacher with a great heart. I was tremendously stimulated. Nothing was good enough for Reichy.

Often, he would question me on my research. He would sit at his desk, look at me intently, and ask about some issue before us:

"Have you looked up the law reports?"

"Yes, sir."

"Have you looked up the monthlies?"

"Yes, sir."

"Have you looked up the dailies?"

"Well, no, sir."

"Well, on Wednesday last week a case was decided in the Supreme Court which offset everything you have told me. Go back and do the research again."

I would feel mortified. Reichy breathed fire down my neck to get the best out of me. I had to master every brief completely in order to feel secure and serve our client well. This was how I learned to overprepare, driven by a mixture of fear of failure and a desire to excel at my job. I learned to hold a totally new set of standards for myself. I began to drop my student mentality and adopt the professionalism required in real life.

Reichy had for many years advised one of the firm's largest clients, Consolidated Press, and most important, its chairman, Sir Douglas Frank Hewson Packer. Because I worked for Reichy, I found myself working for Frank Packer, too. And I worked my heart out to please them both. I worked such long hours that Packer made me an offer to join his company. The money was tempting, but after a few days of agonizing, I decided I wasn't ready to tie myself to one company—there was so much more I wanted to explore in the law. Years later, he would again ask me to join Consolidated Press, but even then I still felt there was much more to do. Anyway, by that time I had come to know his sons and to count them as friends, and I did not want to compete with them.

Sir Frank was a big and demanding man in every sense. A former boxing champion, he was rough, but he was a tremendous leader and had great instincts in the publishing business and was among the first to recognize the potential of commercial television and establish a channel. He later mounted the first Australian Challenge for the America's Cup with a boat called *Gretl*, which was named after his wife. I developed enormous respect for him, and though I saw nothing of him socially, he was extraordinarily kind to me in a personal way. When I went to study overseas, he gave me two letters of introduction to the Australian high commissioner in London and to the ambassador in the United States. I don't think I ever used them, but I was proud to have them.

Sir Frank was very close to barrister Anthony Larkins, QC, whom we regularly asked for advice on legal matters and who represented us in court when there was litigation. Larkins and I connected the moment we met. As the representative of a firm of solicitors, it was necessary to brief (or engage) a barrister to plead in court when there was litigation. He was a brilliant lawyer, from whom I learned a great deal. But we also became lifelong friends. Visiting his stylish apartment, decorated with paintings by the young Robert Hughes, who later became a distinguished art critic and author living in New York, I felt that I'd entered a different world. Impeccably dressed, wearing a monocle, and tremendously polite, he taught me to make martinis. Tony's lifestyle and his personal warmth made a big impression on me, and he helped me learn how to be a member of the broader social community while building my values.

One day in the office I overheard Cowper say: "Give me a clerk with Wolfensohn's willingness and Masterman's brains and I will have a good one." My heart sank. George Masterman was my impressive Oxford friend in the firm, and I wanted to match his talents. It was Larkins who convinced me that it was not only my diligence but also my skills of observing, understanding people, and tuning in to the environment that added value. Once again I found it valuable that I had developed that self-protective mechanism on outings with my father and on the playground when I was two years younger than the other guys and needed to identify the bullies and my allies. This instinct never left me, and Larkins taught me that it could be turned into a legal skill.

As articled clerks we were paid a pittance, a ridiculous £2 ($5) a week, which would buy lunch but not much more. With a couple of other clerks, I headed a group of young activists at the law school to try to campaign

for a living wage. We went to the major firms and the Law Society, arguing that although £2 had been pretty good in the 1800s, it was virtually
nothing in the 1950s. They expected slave labor because in the British tradition you went to a law firm for training, and it was a privilege. In fact,
clerks once paid for tutelage, and when the £2 was introduced, it was regarded as generous. To me, that was just a wall ready to be knocked over.
As a result of our first piece of collective bargaining, we increased the rate
to something like £12 a week, moving up in our third year as articled
clerks to £25. This meant I could contribute at home, pay for gas for the
car, and help with bills. We were always paid in crisp new notes provided
by the bank. The partners at Allens did not mind the increase and were
rather amused that someone had not asked for it before.

I was still living with my parents, and at that time Reginald Gourgey,
a British naval commander, entered our life. He rapidly established independent friendships with my mother, my father, and me. He'd go to fencing with me, to synagogue with my father, occasionally to the horse races
with my mother. He loved to accompany us all to symphony concerts at
the Town Hall. Later, he turned up to watch me at the Olympic Games
and even visited me at Harvard. He and my father would chat for hours, and
years later, Reggie told me my dad used to say: "If I had had more money,
Jimmy would have devoted his life to music." Although our circumstances had improved, Reggie sensed money was an issue. He remembers
my father talking about all the refugees he had helped: "Just look at
Joseph living in splendor in Bellevue Hill! I helped him get started and
now he barely acknowledges me."

When Reggie asked why he didn't just send the person in question an
invoice, my father's reply was: "If they don't recognize what I've done, I
wouldn't dream of pointing it out to them."

Reggie made sense of this, saying that although my father was a business consultant, he had not made it clear that his advice was his business.
Using a rather old-fashioned model of English behavior rather than making it clear in advance what he would charge his clients, he waited to settle
the matter until later and all too often he received nothing.

But my father had taken on more responsibility in communal life, and as a result his circle enlarged and he made several new friends. He grew particularly close to Dr. Joachim Schneeweiss, who became my parent's doctor and gave them great care. This was a huge relief for me. Joachim was a good listener, and the friendship flourished. My father talked endlessly about commercial affairs and about his favorite subject— me. He talked so much that Joachim formed the view that I was more his creation than his son. My father placed all of his unrealized hopes on me, and I certainly felt the responsibility. Still, I had moved out of his immediate orbit and was beyond his daily reach.

I happily watched others gravitate toward him. Friends began to ask him to act as godfather, and he went on to have a number of godsons. Whereas I found my family situation claustrophobic, my university friends found it appealing. Toby Hammerman, my father's first godson, remembers my father taking his mentoring responsibilities seriously, instructing him in Judaism and always being present at the major events in his life. Dad spread his fatherly care generously. There was a time when my friend Michael Diamond felt like a son, too. It was not unusual for Michael, who was Greek Orthodox and a bit irreverent, to spar with my father over religion. Michael was fond of the whole family. He liked my mother and had an eye for Betty, whom he found striking. He'd been told that when she walked into a room, everyone would stop and look at her. When he actually met her, he found this to be entirely true.

While I was working at Allens, I continued to train with the fencing squad, and Michael and I were fencing buddies. Once when he forgot to put on his protective gear, which was worn under the white jacket and was not visible, my épée snapped and entered his body through his armpit. I was petrified as I took him to the hospital with my sword firmly stuck in him and fearful it would reach his heart. Although he did not hold it against me, his injuries meant he had to drop out of our squad of Olympic hopefuls.

It almost felt like punishment when, several weeks later, I was also struck down. I developed appendicitis and was rushed to the hospital just as the selection trials for the 1956 Olympics were beginning. After the operation, I lay in the ward, wracked with disappointment. Luckily, Hil Van Dijk, the team captain, kept one position back in the épée team. I'd been training for the past two years, and the team decided I should have the spot, with the understanding that I could not be nominated without an open competition. Accordingly, they prepared a full-day competition for about fifty people, to be held when I recovered.

I entered that competition determined to win. With my physical build, people thought I'd be best suited to the saber. But I preferred the épée. Épéeists tend to be tall and lean and have a long reach. I made up for my physical disadvantage with quick reflexes, and I was really well trained. Fencing is a little like chess; you must project a few moves ahead and outthink your opponent. I loved this aspect of fencing, and after a tough and exhausting one-day competition, I emerged as the clear winner and secured my position on the team. This was a huge break for me, and my teammates were extremely supportive. It was a great confidence boost. Although being on Australia's fencing team was not like being on its Olympic athletics team or swimming squad, both of which were favored to win gold medals, we worked hard and developed a discipline that I could call on for the rest of my life.

*   *   *

As the Games approached, we began working with the coach of the swimming and pentathlon team, Forbes Carlisle, who had once represented Australia in the Olympics. Forbes was a university lecturer and an early sports psychologist who promoted the use of self-hypnosis during competition. We would often train with Forbes at the Drummoyne swimming baths, where he was coaching the swimming squad. I remember his explaining that swimmers were more susceptible to hypnosis than fencers. He would grab a swimmer by the wrist and the swimmer would somehow go into a trance. Forbes would say, "On the last lap you are going to be chased by a shark," and then release the wrist. The swimmer would not consciously remember what had been said but, predictably, on the last lap would swim at a tremendous pace. When the swimmer got to the end of the pool, he would jump out with the remark, "The bloody thing nearly got me." The fencers were not quite as malleable, but we did teach ourselves to relax. I remember months of training myself to imagine the pendulum of a clock swinging with my eyes closed. That would calm me down. Our whole team would sit, like zombies, beside the fencing strip with our eyes back in our heads, mentally rehearsing our moves.

On November 22, 1956, I walked into the Olympic Stadium in Melbourne, wearing the Australian blazer in front of 120,000 cheering people. I would never forget it. These were the first Games to be held in the southern hemisphere, and they were opened by Prince Philip, Duke of Edinburgh. They attracted competitors from seventy-two countries, and Australia performed outstandingly, winning thirteen gold medals in swimming, track and field, and cycling. These were the golden days of Dawn Fraser in the pool and Betty Cuthbert on the track. I loved being in the Olympic Village, in the company of the world's greatest athletes.

Prior to Opening Day, when I was issued my tracksuit, I went out onto the cinder track—the first of its kind in Australia—and ran around. Running had never been part of my training routine because of my bronchial problems, but I had to try out the track. Then a Russian ran by. When he waved to me on the track, I felt a rush of adrenaline. Here I was, running with famous athletes from around the world. Not surprisingly, the Russians were passing me. But then I realized that I was running as hard as I could—and they were speed walking. The next morning I was so stiff I couldn't get up for the team photo.

Often, kids at the gate to the Olympic Village would ask for my signature, because we all wore the same green-and-gold tracksuits with "Australia" in large letters on the back. They would say, "What sport do you do?" I'd tell them I fenced, and they'd yell out to another kid: "Oh, don't worry about him, he's only a fencer." It certainly brought me down to earth, but it didn't matter. It was thrilling to be part of the spirit and international camaraderie of the Village.

The 1956 Games were probably the last that were relatively apolitical and, in a sense, amateur. Like me, about one-third of the fencers had full-time jobs or were students. Some of the Russians and Eastern Europeans and even Americans were in the army, which meant they could devote 100 percent of their time to training. I was proud of my Olympic achievements, but I was not quite at the top Olympic level, as our team lacked the experience of constant international competition. Our first Olympic round was against the Italian team, and I had to fence a match against each of the four Italians. They were the gold medalist team, and I was so revved up that I won my first two bouts, surprising everyone, including myself. I was in the lead again in my third match, but then the Italian team members came to the side of the *piste* and started chanting to my opponent: *"Viva il campione del mondo!"* Realizing I was up against the world champion, I promptly lost focus and he then hit me four times in succession to win. Next up was competition against the British team, and in my first bout I fenced against a man named Alan Jay. He was a Jewish solicitor who had been in the Olympics before and who would subsequently become world champion. Alan was a left-hander, and I was leading him 3–0 in a match to five points. I was in the zone. Then Alan said his weapon was not working and stopped the bout so the armorer could repair it. While we waited, he told me about a party planned that night for the athletes. I hadn't heard about it, so he described a wonderful Israeli swimmer who would be there and suggested we go together and meet her. He completely broke my concentration. When the bout resumed, he quickly won, 5–3.

"You know, you're a twit," Alan said afterward. "You really had me down, I've got a lot of lessons to teach you! Never talk to anybody and don't let people distract you." It was good advice. I was disappointed, but that feeling was later overwhelmed by my awe at simply having participated in the Olympics.

At the time, many athletes from Eastern Europe wanted to defect to Australia. On one occasion, a Romanian competitor from the modern pentathlon with whom we'd been training in fencing came up to us in the dining room. He wanted to defect, and after talking to him for a while, we decided to help him. The next day while having lunch, I got up and walked into the men's room wearing two Australian tracksuits in order to give him one. He followed me in, quickly changed, and ran out with us. That tracksuit allowed him to get out of the Olympic Village and seek asylum. At the end of the Games, forty-five members of the Hungarian team also sought asylum in Australia.

*   *   *

That Olympic year was also my final year of law school, and I had five subjects to pass before I could graduate. I had not attended many lectures during the year because I'd been working at Allens, putting in long hours training for fencing, and participating in student union affairs. After the Games, however, I shut out the excitement and buried myself in my books. I moved into the home of my friend Rodney Rosenblum, as I'd been doing during exam period for the last three years, and we studied together. He was the better student, and I suspect had attended more classes, so at night, after he turned out his lights, I stayed up studying for several more hours, trying to close the gap. When we got sick of working, we went downstairs and played mammoth games of table tennis. Rodney had reached the university's doubles championships in table tennis, so by the end of the six weeks, I had gotten pretty good, too.

With Rodney, I learned that when you want to get a job done, you just work until it is done. This is a mentality I've had ever since. On one trip during my last years at the World Bank, I had to give a speech about federalism to the European Parliament. At the hotel the night before, I looked through the notes I'd received and they were terrible. It was 11:00 PM and I was exhausted. But I took out my laptop and started researching federalism on Google. At 4:30 AM, I logged off. As I was sitting there, I thought about when I'd developed the ability to drive myself through that first round of exhaustion. It was at the Rosenblum house.

Rodney and I were at different law firms and rarely saw each other professionally. Rodney worked with his uncle, but we worked together once on the legal settlement of a transaction. Our styles were very different. He remembered a discharging mortgagee showing up without the certificate of title to the property he owned. "I would never have settled," Rodney said. His uncle had advised him to hold out unless he got everything to which he was entitled. But the fellow said to Rodney and me, "Look, I'm terribly sorry; I left the certificate on my desk. Can I bring it up to you later on?" Rodney recalled the rest of the particulars this way:

> Jim's [Wolfensohn's] response was, "Yes. That'll be fine." And he was just an articled clerk at Allens at the time. Now, because I wouldn't have settled, the fellow would have been at least slightly annoyed at me for having put the settlement off and embarrassing him in that way. Jim, on the other hand, did settle. The fellow went straight back, got the certificate of title, brought it back up again. He saved face, and he was, I'm sure, grateful to Jim. And I'm sure there were lots of circumstances where Jim thought that the gratitude of somebody to him was something very valuable.

But I was never as strategic as Rodney or as disciplined as some of my other friends thought. Although my choices may have looked wonderfully planned—organizing orientation week to make myself known, selecting fencing because it was a little-patronized sport, joining the University Squadron—there was a large arbitrary element in operation. I went into each of these activities with all the energy and commitment I could muster, but really with no sense of the architecture of my decisions. I was not trying to prepare a good-looking resume. Rather, I jumped at opportunities as they arose. I was hungry for new experiences in life and had a desire to explore the possibilities that came my way.

*   *   *

When I graduated from law school and was admitted as a solicitor to practice law in early 1957, my wages shot up sixfold and I realized that earning real money was possible. I was growing more secure and finally felt in control of my life. But I had a strong urge to move beyond Australia. Most of the Australians who intrigued me engaged in activities with some sort of global dimension. It probably started with my father. I wanted to reach out to the rest of the world, too.

It seemed to me that Australia would inevitably have a much bigger relationship with Asia, so I wrote to the School of Commonwealth Studies at Hokkaido University in Japan. It only had one scholarship, and I couldn't get it. Then I decided to go for a Rhodes scholarship. It was completely unrealistic. I had a chance of fulfilling the sport and leadership criteria, but my academic record was certain to put me out of the race. Even so, I hoped that by some magic, my academic setbacks would be lost among my other achievements. I had slipped under the radar and into Allens, so why couldn't I slip into Oxford? Somehow I made it into the final round. In my interview, Sir John Northcott, the governor of New South Wales, asked if I had studied Latin in school. I replied that it had been my worst subject; in fact, I had failed it outright.

"You what?" was Northcott's astonished reply.

"I failed it."

"Well, you can't go to Oxford if you don't know Latin."

"Why? Is it a requirement?" I asked politely.

"For me it is. I'm not sure whether it is for anybody else, but I'm a classicist."

And that was the end of the interview. I shouldn't have gotten my hopes up, but I still felt crushed as I walked out of the gate at Government House.

I began practicing as a fully qualified solicitor at Allens in 1957, backed by my three years' experience there as an articled clerk. In my first year of practice, I worked nonstop on a $300-million treble damages suit known as the RCA-Zenith antitrust action. It was an American monopoly case, in which treble damages were sought from Radio Corporation of America (RCA) for incursions on the rights of the plaintiff, Zenith Corporation. American lawyers had come to Australia to gather extraterritorial evidence for use in the case in Chicago. RCA was represented by Robert Zeller from the American firm Cahill Gordon Reindel & Ohl. To help gain the Australian evidence, RCA retained my boss, Reichenbach, at Allens to work with Zeller. Our special adviser was the Melbourne advocate and distinguished law professor Zelman Cowen, who later became the governor-general of Australia.

The proceedings took place before an appointed judge whose duty it was to get the evidence on record for the U.S. court. We had been preparing the case for a year, but the night before we were due to start, Reichenbach had a heart attack (from which he would only recover months later). It was too late to bring in anyone else as senior Australian legal adviser, and as I had put the thousands of pages of evidence together and knew my way around them, Bob Zeller suggested I should work on the case with him. There were other U.S. lawyers working with us, including Ken Clarke, a lawyer from RCA, as well as John MacDonald, a Scot from Harvard Business School who was assisting on the commercial aspects of the case, and who later became an international partner of McKinsey & Company and a great friend. On the first day of the proceedings in Sydney, I was nervous, though I knew I was very well prepared. Whenever I was asked by Zeller for evidence to support his examination or his argument, I found it readily. At the end of the day, my head swelled to a degree that could scarcely be believed. I was the Australian expert and the master of all the facts and files.

A few days afterward, we moved to Canberra. During the proceedings, Bob turned to me and asked, "What is the current ratio of AWA [Amalgamated Wireless of Australia, one of the leading companies with activities similar to RCA]?" I had no idea. I pulled out the AWA annual report and frantically flipped through it, looking for the words "current ratio." I couldn't find them and kept fumbling. Bob asked again, and I looked at him blankly. As he grabbed the report from me, he snapped, "Why the hell don't you go to Harvard Business School?" I was deflated instantly.

That night, from my room at the Hotel Rex in Canberra, I wrote to Harvard Business School in Cambridge, Massachusetts, requesting an application form. When it arrived some days later, I quickly realized I didn't have the three essential things necessary to pursue an MBA. I did not have the personal history that showed my interest in a business career, or the money to pay for the course work, or any means of getting to the United States. But after my crisis that morning, I had plenty of enthusiasm and determination, so these obstacles did not seem insurmountable.

I decided that getting into Harvard would be easier than winning a Rhodes scholarship to Oxford. At Harvard, they appreciated a broad educational and extracurricular base. Perhaps the fact that I had a couple of degrees, experience in a law firm, an officership in the air force, experience in the Olympics, and a student leadership position would hold more weight than my pure academic record. Once again, in his unconventional way, Julius Stone stepped in to help. Although I had only asked him to oversee my application, I later found out that he had written a letter strongly urging my acceptance on the basis that I had "some indefinable attributes" that were likely to make me "very successful in business." In the end I scored high on the entrance exam, but I have no doubt that this recommendation helped the admissions committee accept me.

I began looking around for financial assistance, but I had left it until too late. The deadline for applying for a Fulbright scholarship had passed, and there were no other travel grants. I decided to use the little background

I had in the Royal Australian Air Force Reserve to get to the United States. This was the brilliant idea of my dear friend Tony Larkins. At his prompting, I telephoned the federal minister for air, Fred Osborne, at his offices in Sydney. I had never spoken to a federal minister before, but I boldly asked for an appointment. When his secretary asked why I wanted to see him, I said it was about air force training and my hopes of doing postgraduate work in the United States.

The secretary was somewhat skeptical, but a subsequent phone call from Larkins got me the meeting. I was nervous but determined when I walked into the ministerial offices in Sydney. Osborne, a lawyer himself, fired the first question:

"Why have you come?"

"Sir, I've come because I would very much like to see if there is a way of getting a free ride to the United States on an air force plane, if anyone happens to be flying over there."

He looked at me as though I were crazy.

"Are you in the air force?"

"Well, I'm in the Air Force Reserve, the University Air Squadron, and I've recently been made a pilot officer in the reserve. I spent two years there, part-time, of course."

"Well, what are you going to do in the United States?"

"As you know, I'm a lawyer, and I'm going to study business administration in the United States. I thought it might be a great help to have someone in the reserve who could do all the clever things that they teach you at Harvard, if there is a war."

"That's fine. But are you going to join the air force permanently when you return?"

"Good heavens, no," I blurted out without thinking.

"You're a very arrogant young man."

"Well, sir, I don't have any money and I have to get there and I need your help."

Without hesitation, Osborne picked up the phone to the air vice-marshal in charge of transportation services and asked if there were any planes flying to England or America in September. Looking at me, he explained into the phone: "I've got a brash young fellow here who is a pilot officer in the reserve and who wants to get an indulgence passage to the United States." For whatever reason, he seemed to like my nerve, or had already been persuaded by his friend Larkins.

*   *   *

In early August 1957, the air vice-marshal informed me that a prop-driven Hastings aircraft used by the chief of air staff of the New Zealand Air Force would soon be flying to London. They could put me on in the back. It would take six days to get from South Australia to London, with stops in Darwin, Singapore, Ceylon, and Iraq, among other places. It would fly six or seven hours a day, at the rate of about 250 knots per hour. The New Zealanders agreed to grant me the indulgence passage, and all I had to do was get myself to the air force base in South Australia. The trip would cost me $30, for food and lodging. At the time the process seemed amazingly effortless, but decades later, when I read my own Australian Security Intelligence Organisation files, I learned that the air force had done a thorough assessment before granting me permission. They checked my credentials in the reserve and my father's record. An ASIO file document stamped "Secret" read: "The assessment attached hereto considers the subject is clear and that there is no case against his father. Clearance is recommended." I was free to go.

When I arrived at the base in South Australia, a staff sergeant ordered me to report immediately to the quartermaster's store to pick up my new emblem of rank. I hadn't expected this, and when I went over, an officer said:

"Well, lad, you've been promoted."

"What do you mean I've been promoted?"

"Someone has promoted you from a pilot officer to a flying officer. There's a message here that if you are going to be with an air marshal from New Zealand, you can't be outranked by everyone."

I was speechless.

"In any event, you've shown such a sense of leadership, they thought you should go to the next rank."

They promoted me on the spot. I never knew if the promotion came from Osborne or the air vice-marshal, but it got me to England feeling extremely proud—and very lucky.

To fill the idle flying time, I bought a typewriter in Singapore and spent the rest of the trip in the noisy back of the aircraft learning to touch type. I had never been out of Australia, and after several days I was in Baghdad. It was August 1956, and the Iraqis were trying to get rid of the British base. As soon as we landed at the air force base, we decided to go into town to look around without changing out of our uniforms. We got out of our car and found ourselves surrounded by a mob eager to get its hands on us. We were all terrified. Somehow we found our taxi and made a getaway. But every time we were stopped, by a goat or sheep or something else in the road, the luggage compartment of the taxi would pop up before we could get going again. I kept asking the driver about this, and eventually he explained: "That's my second gear, he's my brother." Only then did I realize there was a man in the back, jumping out every time we stopped and pushing until we picked up sufficient speed to enter third gear, when he would jump into the trunk again.

Waiting for me at the Royal Air Force air station in Northolt, London, were my cousin Eric Wolfensohn and my mother's brother, Ellis Weinbaum. I didn't know what they looked like or what to expect, because apart from Uncle Harry, I'd never met any of our extended family. We had a motley collection of photographs at home, but I had no sense of the larger family, no grasp of our history, and no understanding of where anyone fitted. Eric told me that I'd climbed off the plane in my RAAF uniform, looking around and looking a bit mystified. He also said there was a distinctive Wolfensohn look about me.

It was comforting to be in the company of family, and Uncle Ellis and Eric did their best to refresh and equip me. I had only a few days in London before leaving for Harvard, so I didn't have much time to appreciate what London had to offer. Uncle Ellis took me to the department store sales racks and bought me a serviceable brown checked sports jacket and a few odds and ends. I made sure to visit the City of London, remembering that my father had been awarded the ancient accolade of Freedom of the City of London. Being a freeman meant you and your children could go to the City of London School, you could walk through the city carrying a drawn sword, and if you were sentenced to death, you could be hanged by a silken cord. It also meant you could be a member of the guilds and become lord mayor of London. These were very old traditions, and of course I didn't expect to take advantage of any of these benefits. But being a freeman meant a great deal to my father, and it was one of the few things that he could pass on to me by patrimony. So I went to the clerk's office in the city, where it was confirmed that my father was a freeman, and I applied for my freedom. They gave me my Freedom of the City of London on parchment paper and a little red book, entitled *Rules for the Conduct of Life*.

In London, I got my first real sense of British aristocracy. I'd met a young Englishman named Eric Drummond in Australia when I took the qualification exam to get into Harvard. He introduced himself as Lord Strathallan. We didn't have much time to chat, but he said if we both got into Harvard and I came through London, I should call him and we would have lunch before heading to the United States. I had never met a viscount before, nor indeed anyone with an English title, and I was intrigued. I called Eric and was duly invited for lunch at Hyde Park Gardens, the home of Eric's parents—David, the Earl of Perth, and his American wife, Nancy. Like most Australians, I had little knowledge of what an earl was except that it was high in the hierarchy.

I was torn between the Australian habit of mocking aristocracy and following my father's lead and giving title great respect. I gravitated toward the latter course and felt proud to be in the Perths' home. As I entered the beautiful drawing room in Hyde Park Gardens and was handed a sherry, I had butterflies in my stomach. Eric's parents were gracious, and we proceeded into the dining room, where David had decanted a bottle of red wine. He talked about the process of decanting and how to let a wine breathe. This was all new to me. David, who was later to become a senior colleague of mine as a director at Schroders, was particularly kind. He had recently been a minister in the Macmillan cabinet and, following the tradition of his family, gave much of himself to public service. Our lives would remain intertwined, with Eric later spending time with me in Lausanne and his parents also becoming my close friends as a result of our Schroders association.

I mentioned to Eric that I needed some shoes and a hat. He told me that the only places to get these were on St. James Street at Lobb's and Lock's—two different establishments, one for shoes and one for hats—and that I must be properly measured for these items if I was to get appropriate-quality clothing. I did not have the money for this top-of-the-line shopping, so I returned to the department store sales. But Eric's words echoed in my head. For years afterward, I would walk by Lobb's and Lock's wondering when I could afford to go in. They seemed entirely out of reach. To this day, Lobb's, shoemaker to kings, is one of the shops I do not have the courage to enter. Once, however, I did enter Lock's and bought a ready-made hat. I also found a tailor in my later years in Savile Row. I support the notion that many Australians *never* get over their feelings of insecurity with respect to the English.

* * *

When it was time for me to sail for America, Uncle Ellis and Aunt Florie generously paid the £75 ($200) for my third-class passage on the *Queen Elizabeth*. This was a fortune and meant that I could arrive in the United States with my own $300 intact. On accepting the position at Harvard, I had been told without any ambiguity that unless I had $3,000, I shouldn't bother to come. But everything else had fallen into place, and I figured this would, too. So I delayed the worry. I had an almost delusional belief that when the time came, I could handle anything.

My feeling of omnipotence was tempered onboard the *Queen Elizabeth,* though, when I met an Irishman named Jim Doolan. He put the fear of God in me about the competition I was about to face at Harvard. After studying to be a priest for several years, Jim had studied accounting and became, as he told me, the top graduate in his field in Ireland. He recounted many of his triumphs in the accounting profession, and by the time he'd finished with me, I thought I was done. I couldn't even read a balance sheet. As it turned out, he had an undistinguished academic career at Harvard. However, Jim would eventually become my partner in a laundry service on the campus and one of the groomsmen at my wedding. He went on to become a senator in the Irish government, having worked for a time at the World Bank and as professor of business administration in Ireland. But at that moment, he terrified me.

My most memorable experience on the boat, however, had nothing to do with academics. It involved a girl from Texas whose name I can no longer remember. The incident, however, became etched in my mind. I had befriended a steward who arranged for me to go to the first-class area of the ship for a party. I stood back, watching what the first-class passengers were doing. Eventually, they started a game in which a couple had to hold an apple under their chins while dancing together. The couple that kept dancing the longest without dropping the apple would win a bottle of champagne. Somehow I found myself dancing with a beautiful Texan girl, and we won the champagne.

I had no idea what to do next. So I decided I would sit down and have the champagne with her and when the champagne was finished, I'd invite her for a walk on the deck. As we strolled along the deck, I thought I should hold her hand. Hand in hand, we walked toward the lifeboats, where it was slightly dark, and I put my hand on her shoulder, hoping that she would be overcome by the moment and fall into my arms. She turned to me:

"It's been a wonderful evening, Jim, but you know, I'm pinned."

I had never heard of the American custom of pinning—which meant getting a pin from a boyfriend, the pin of his fraternity. "I'm terribly sorry, can I help you un-pin it?" I said, thinking that this was the moment for further excitement.

She looked at me like I was crazy. Then she carefully explained to me the importance of pinning; it was just short of an engagement to marry, and she was already taken by another man in Texas. I went back to tourist class and never saw her again. I did, however, write to my father about this incident, asking him to send me a dozen Sydney University pins. I thought they might come in handy with the girls at Harvard.

After six days on the ocean, we docked in New York City. When I disembarked, a customs officer said something to me that I couldn't understand because of his thick Brooklyn accent. He was apparently asking if I had anything to declare. I stared at him blankly. Annoyed at my stupidity, he pointed to my two bags and slowly said:

"O-p-e-n t-h-e-m."

I looked at him.

"Don't you speak English?" he asked, growing more irritated.

"I do, I do."

This made him even angrier, and he leaned over and pulled open the first bag. He saw my Australian air force uniform. He looked up at me. "Are you an Aussie?"

"Yes."

"Oh, now I understand. I flew with you bastards during the war. Close it up!"

He picked up my bags and carried them through to the arrivals area, telling me as we walked along how much he liked the Australians. There my mother's sister, Hannah, and her husband, Joey Sonnenberg, were waiting. I recognized them immediately. Hannah was younger than my mother but there was an unmistakable likeness. I knew she and Joey had been wonderfully generous to my parents and I liked them immediately. My aunt and uncle took me in, in the most welcoming and accepting way possible, making me feel comfortable in their Forest Hills apartment in Queens. Seeing how little I possessed, they immediately spent nearly

$100 buying me the basic necessities for college life, including a plastic clock radio I would keep for years. Hannah had the genteel poise of the Weinbaum women, and she and Joey ran a very successful wholesale diamond business on Fifth Avenue in Manhattan. Their son Maurice was close to my age, and he went out of his way to be there for me during my early years in New York.

At the Sonnenbergs' apartment, I was greeted by a message from Bob Zeller, the lawyer with whom I had worked in Australia and who had suggested the Harvard adventure. He knew I had been dreaming of seeing *West Side Story*. With his message were two tickets. I adored Leonard Bernstein's music—the second record I ever owned was his *Jeremiah Symphony*—and I could not believe someone who could write that piece could also write *West Side Story*. I would eventually see *West Side Story* thirteen times, because over the next few years, many friends and foreigners would come through New York and I would take them to see the musical. But that first time was the best. I felt happy and carefree sitting in that theater in New York, hearing the music performed live and watching the story unfold. I could not believe that within less than twelve months, my life had changed so much. The entire trip from Australia had a dreamlike quality, but I sensed that reality was about to descend on me when I entered Harvard.

4

HARVARD

In September 1957, accommodation and tuition at Harvard Business School cost about $3,000 a year. I had received a grant-in-aid of $3,000 for two years, which meant I would be given a loan of $1,500 a year. It also meant I immediately had to supply the other half myself. Once I walked into Harvard, I could no longer avoid this problem. Given that I had a grand sum of $300 in my pocket, I needed a miracle.

My room was located on the top floor of Gallatin Hall. I found my roommate, Bob Shanks, lying on the couch surrounded by beer cans. He didn't get up. He just lay there laconically. We tried to figure out why we were selected to live together in a triple room. We soon learned that a triple was the cheapest—and why we had been matched. It turned out that Bob had been an American field hockey player in the Melbourne Olympics. Happy at least to have this point of contact, we started talking. A couple of hours later, we heard someone coming up the stairs. We would hear a few heavy steps, then the sound of metal hitting the ground, then a few more steps and more metal scraping. Eventually a small, extremely fit man walked into the room, dragging weights behind him. David Penning was a weightlifter from Yale, and he announced that he had requested a room with other athletes. He was clearly annoyed that all he got was a beer-drinking hockey player and an unknown fencer, neither greatly interested in training.

On that first day, I went down to the cafeteria at Kresge Hall, collected my tray for dinner, and sat down next to an American classmate named Mark Wray and his sister.

"Where are you from?" the girl asked.

"Australia."

"When did you get to the States?"

"A week ago."

"My, my!" She sounded surprised. "You've learned the language quickly."

A few days later, in class, Mark posted pictures on the board of Aborigines from Central Australia, holding their spears. So this was the view Americans had of my country. It was of course done in good humor, but it was a reminder of our differences in culture. Little reminders like this popped up everywhere. Although my American classmates were welcoming and kind, for a long time I felt like one of the foreigners who made up 10 percent of our class.

The second day, knowing that bankruptcy was upon me, I went to the financial aid department and met a cheerful, rotund woman named Florence Glynn. She was an ageless woman, probably only in her forties. I told her how I had managed to travel to the United States and how grateful I was for the advance in aid. She congratulated me and remarked that I was one of the first Australians to attend the Business School.

"But, I have to tell you that I've not been quite honest. I have arrived with only $300."

"You are a very naughty boy," she said sternly.

"Yes, I suppose I am, but I have very little money to contribute to the fees in the first year and certainly have no money to go home."

"Well, let's see. Maybe we could use some of your grant to cover the first term. In fact, let's just draw down your first-term fees and we'll see how you do, and then let's see if we can conspire to get things going."

Florence became my regular confidante and supporter, and I did well enough for our conspiracy to continue. Our plan was to draw down in the first year a good part of the total amount that was available for me for the full two years and then worry about the second year when I got to it. For the moment, I was saved. I never forgot her kindness and support and eventually, with my Canadian classmate John McArthur, we financed a scholarship at the Business School in her name.

On the first day of classes, a tremendous amount of work was thrown at us, and the pattern never let up. Our curriculum was founded on the case method. We were given detailed accounts of real business situations and asked to address problems from the perspective of a general manager. We were assigned an average of three sets of case materials a night, which we studied on our own before preparing our strategies in group discussions. The next day, the professor would introduce the case and then cold call the students, so we always had to be ready to present our analysis and recommendations. The pressure was enormous and exhilarating. It was an extraordinary learning experience because it taught me how to deal with far more work than I thought possible, to assimilate a great deal of material in one night and dig for the essential issues.

This academic experience opened my eyes to global business; the cases were built not only around U.S. corporations but focused on multinational and international companies as well. How lucky I was to be at Harvard. The educational methodology was first-rate and the campus welcoming and beautiful. Had I gone to Oxford, my further education would have been an extension of many elements of Australian society. In England and in Australia, there were social and educational frameworks that everyone understood. Education stressed the importance of the Crown, the queen, and the Commonwealth. As part of the British Commonwealth of nations, Australia had an uninterrupted sense of colonial history and had not yet fully benefited from European and Asian migration.

America was something quite different. Harvard was outside the colonial norm. It was a global institution, big, challenging, and wonderful, and the academic and intellectual standards were as good as or better than anything in the world. Because Harvard attracted students worldwide, the competition there was several notches above anything I'd experienced previously. I learned immeasurably from my professors and classmates—lessons that have lasted a lifetime.

In our first year, we met daily with the same class of sixty people. A few of us formed a hub of friendship that would last the course of our lives. Everyone at Harvard seemed to have a different point of view. At the onset of the year, I had no idea how to calibrate and account for the diverse backgrounds, but as the year progressed I began to discern the richness of the group. It made me even more aware of difference—and of sameness.

Harvard gave my classmates and me the chance to grow up, both in and outside the classroom. Through role-play within the case studies, I could enter the world of steel, airlines, or banking, express my views and spend billions of dollars on investments or make decisions about marketing programs. This gave all of us the chance to experience business in a compressed way, to test our skills, analytical capacities, negotiating capabilities, and persuasive powers. We had the opportunity to live a life—albeit an imaginary life—that covered a wider range of experiences than a person would encounter in decades of business. At the beginning, I was weak in finance and accounting, but I soon realized I had both an aptitude and a voracious appetite for these subjects.

*   *   *

A week after arriving at Harvard, I marked the Day of Atonement by attending prayers for Jewish students and staff at Hillel House. During the day of prayer, there is a memorial service, Yizkor, that is attended mostly by those who have lost one or both parents. Those with living parents usually wait outside. It was a beautiful fall day, and I found myself talking to a quiet, dark-eyed young woman who had just returned from a year in Europe.

"Where are you from?" she asked.

"Australia."

She was surprised. "Oh, when I was cycling in Scotland this summer, I met my first-ever Australian at a youth hostel. Now you're the second. Where do you study?"

"I have just begun at Harvard Business School," I said proudly.

She looked disappointed.

Elaine Botwinick was just twenty and in her final year at Wellesley. I later learned that her father was a hardworking, successful, socially responsible accountant and businessman. Although Elaine had originally studied math and physics with great success, she had changed majors to French literature and spent her junior year in Paris studying at three institutes—La Sorbonne, L'École du Louvre, and L'Institut des Sciences Politiques, where she took a course called "Condorcet et l'idée du progrès." Initially, what seemed to interest her about me was the fact that I was Australian, which she regarded as exotic. Unfortunately for me, the fact that I was at the business school only *lessened* my appeal.

Elaine later wrote about our meeting in terms I quote to her whenever I am in trouble:

Standing outside during Yizkor, somehow I met this charming Australian with the darkest most twinkling eyes you could ever see, dark hair and to an American, a rather beautiful English accent. He was not only very good looking, but he seemed confident and worldly. I'd never seen anyone like him, some charm exuded from him that was like a magnet, at least for me. To me—feeling very alienated in America and missing Europe—here was someone who seemed to be the most worldly person you could ever meet. He was the only person I knew who, when we started comparing Australia and America, said it doesn't matter where you live because we're all world citizens.

Although we spent perhaps ten minutes together, we made enough of a connection to pick up the conversation the next time we met, which was at the Boston Symphony rehearsal where we both had student season tickets. I now had a double incentive to use my tickets, as we began meeting regularly at intermissions. In order to improve my chances with Elaine, I stretched the truth a little and told her I'd majored in music. I had studied one year of music theory at Sydney University and figured my passion and knowledge of the arts would carry me past her apparent distaste for students of business.

Our brief meetings at the Boston Symphony went on for several months and never developed much until we came across each other in different circumstances. One night, my friend Mike Nightingale and I dropped in at the Wurst House, a restaurant on Harvard Square, and spotted Elaine and a friend having dinner. They'd just come from a Boston Opera performance and her friend happened to know Mike, so we went over and joined them. I could see that Elaine had a terrific mind and a comfortable social manner, and from that time forward we began to spend a good deal of time together and grew even closer.

Elaine came from a well-to-do family in Westchester, New York, and had one older brother, Edward, in whom the family's aspirations were invested. He was to become a highly successful engineer and entrepreneur. Edward was smart, and although she was, too, there was less interest in her achievements. But she grew into an academically confident young woman who identified with her talented and ambitious father, Ben. His parents were extremely poor Russian immigrants, and as a bricklayer, his father barely made a living. This meant that through elementary school, high school, and college, Ben worked to help feed the family. He qualified as an accountant and threw himself into the business of giving financial advice, eventually building a successful medium-size accounting and tax practice with many clients, including the association representing all the taxicab owners in New York City.

Elaine's mother came from the Kaplan family in Georgia. They regarded themselves as a better class of immigrant, originating from Bialystock, Poland, which was a thriving Jewish center of learning, commerce, industry, and fashion. The day Elaine took me home for the first time, I

could feel her mother's disappointment. She was convinced I was an interloper, and anyway, she didn't believe there could possibly be Jews in Australia. But Elaine's father warmed to me. I think he saw in me qualities
that he recognized in himself—ambition and a drive to rise out of financial hardship. He didn't see many of these qualities among the privileged
Westchester boys and he made me feel very welcome.

Elaine had loved living in Europe, and upon returning had difficulty
readjusting to American college life. Her mother had remarked that she
would probably fall in love with the first foreigner she met. I hadn't realized I was this foreigner, and with nothing to my name, I was certainly
not thinking of marriage. Elaine told me later that my complete lack of
wealth appealed to her. She had met few poor people before she went to
France, which was still in its postwar state. Those were the days of good
socialism, when it was admirable to be poor, and now that she was back in
America, she was thrilled to meet someone without money. In me, she
could probably hear echoes of her father, who had started with nothing.

Elaine was a contemplative young woman, a serious reader. She
seemed always engrossed in a book. Some weekends she'd come to Harvard
and sit quietly in my room, reading for hours, as I wrote the case analysis
that was due at 6:00 PM every Saturday. Then we'd go out together. Some
Saturday afternoons I would play cricket with other Commonwealth students. Elaine would gather my case notes, write them up while I was playing, and together we would speed through my assignment. We would
then run across the lawn, often barefoot, to get my paper in on time. We
usually spent Saturday evenings together, having dinner and meeting
friends. Elaine always seemed to have her work done and generously
helped me get organized. In return, I tried to show her some fun, and our
relationship deepened.

*   *   *

In the spring of 1958, Sandy White, the fellow living across the hall, invited me to come to the country with him for a long weekend. I said I

would be delighted. He told me to get myself to Oyster Bay in New York. I hadn't seen much beyond Cambridge that year and was looking forward to some time in the country. I imagined that the place in "the country" would probably be a charming but unassuming farm.

I did not have much clothing or luggage. My most useful bag was a little green plastic overnight bag from the Olympics, with a map of Australia on one side and the Olympic rings on the other. It was not handsome, but into it I packed T-shirts, a pair of khaki shorts, some sneakers, and a sweater. Then I dressed in my finest piece of weekend wear—a pair of gray trousers issued for the Olympics in Australia—and the brown checked sports jacket my uncle had bought for me in London. I put on my green Olympic tie and set off for Oyster Bay. On the way, I stayed overnight with my relatives, the Sonnenbergs, in Forest Hills and was very grateful when Uncle Joey slipped me $100 and my cousin Maurice squired me to the drugstore to pick up a few more things I needed.

At the Oyster Bay railroad station, Sandy picked me up in an estate car, and as we drove past one manicured mansion after another, I quickly recognized that this was not "the country" as I knew it in Australia. Sandy was Alexander M. White Jr., the son of Alexander White, a leading New York investment banker at White, Weld & Company and an important figure on the Harvard Board of Overseers, and I was getting the picture that his family was quite grand. We finally turned into a driveway where each blade of grass seemed to have been polished. We arrived at a large house with a circular driveway, where huge double doors, a maid, a butler, and Sandy's mother were waiting to greet me.

Suddenly I felt completely ridiculous in my brown jacket and gray trousers. I had totally misunderstood the nature of the invitation. In Australia, an invitation to the country meant dressing in just about anything, riding horses, and mucking about. This was a form of aristocracy with which I was completely unfamiliar.

Mrs. White asked the butler to take my bag inside and unpack it for me. Thinking about the contents, I turned to the butler and begged him not to bother. The butler took it anyway, and we went into the spacious living room, where there was a fire burning. Sandy introduced me to his father and their next-door neighbor, Thomas Lamont. Mr. White was very gracious. He told me how pleased he was to have an Australian guest, that he had heard a lot about me from Sandy, and that they had planned a great weekend for me. Their boat, *Blue Water,* was available if we wanted to go sailing. They always played croquet in the afternoons at the Lamonts' next door, and that evening, Mr. White told me, they had arranged a black-tie dinner so that I could meet some of their friends. He hoped I'd have a relaxing weekend.

I grabbed a strong drink from the white-gloved butler and looked Mr. White straight in the eye.

"Sir, I am thrilled at the invitation to come here and to meet you, but I have to tell you that I misunderstood what Sandy was inviting me to. I only have the clothes I am standing in and certainly have no black-tie attire."

He listened, and I went on. "My only time spent in New York has been at my aunt's house in Forest Hills, and this is a very different world for me. I'd love to have lunch and spend the afternoon here, but I really think I should go back to stay the night with my aunt."

Without blinking an eye, Mr. White said, "Don't be ridiculous." He turned to Mr. Lamont and added, "And the dinner tonight, why don't we have it in sports clothes?" That night we sat at a table graced with silver candelabra and surrounded by butlers, and everyone wore sports jackets so I wouldn't feel out of it. It was a moment I would never forget. After that weekend I became devoted to the White family and often visited them at their New York apartment and in Maine. Years later, I would invite Sandy to be a partner at my boutique investment bank when White Weld was bought out by Merrill Lynch and he wanted a new affiliation.

There was an extraordinary openness and generosity about the White family that seemed distinctly American to me. I explained to them in detail what it meant to be Jewish. I described Forest Hills and people with surnames like Sonnenberg, and they seemed interested. In their house, I saw that it was possible to build links between cultures and classes. They made me feel more, not less secure. They took me for what I was. I probably romanticized the Whites a bit at the time, but my experience that weekend made me think that I might be able to build my life without feeling any difficulties arising from my background and faith. The White family was for me the gold standard.

*   *   *

My grades at Harvard were generally solid and unremarkable, but there was one course that I excelled in without effort. It was called "Administrative Practices" and was essentially instruction in how to read a room. We learned how to judge a situation in a negotiation, to observe the relationships among people, to note who is sitting where, to identify the dynamics of the discussion. The experience of tiptoeing around Sydney with my father had made me acutely sensitive to the dynamics between people. That instinctive vigilance I developed as a boy would serve me well for years to come, although to be sure, once or twice it let me down spectacularly.

For my first summer, I landed a job in New York City. Years earlier in Australia, my father and our family had been friendly with Angus Lightfoot Walker, who had since become chairman of the Rheem Manufacturing Company in the United States. He offered me a position. Over the three months, drawing on my legal background and year at Harvard, my task was to contribute to a comprehensive tax study for the company's international division. I was very grateful for the work and learned an enormous amount about the workings of the global tax system. At this time, American business leaders were starting to expand more aggressively abroad, and Rheem was at the forefront. I was fortunate to have colleagues of great experience and generosity.

For the summer, I shared an apartment on East Fifty-fifth Street with fellow Australian Rod Carnegie. He was the top man in my class at Harvard and already had a reputation for high achievement. After graduating from Melbourne University, he had gone to Oxford, where he served as captain of boats and had been written up in *Time* magazine for introducing a new method of rowing, which helped Oxford beat Cambridge. To me, he was a sort of Australian hero.

Our apartment was very gaudy, with gold-and-green walls and too many couches crammed into the living room. But it was a reasonably inexpensive two-bedroom summer lease and usually quiet. Occasionally, we would be disturbed late at night by knocking on the door. The owner of the apartment lived upstairs, so we'd refer callers to her. I was so naïve that a couple of weeks passed before I figured out that our landlady was a "woman of the night." She obviously had several apartments for her girls, and as there wasn't much business during the summer, she rented them out. Some of her customers had clearly forgotten about the new arrangement. We got along well with the landlady, but unfortunately she never offered us anything very much in the way of services, except for dinner one night.

Rod and I had a terrific time spending our salaries, and at the end of the three months, neither of us had saved as much as we should have. Although I was constantly aware that I had to face Florence Glynn at Harvard when the new semester began, saving was almost impossible. We were young, alone in New York for the first time, and couldn't help but live it up. Still, Rod was in a better position to do this than I, because he received off-campus accommodation from Harvard in return for some services working with college students. Rod was doing very well, and he impressed me. I thought he was brighter and much more organized than I, and that his background would also help him excel. My assessment was correct, and he went on to McKinsey and Company and later became chairman of the giant mining company Conzic Riotinto of Australia—which on his watch went from number fourteen in the world to number four. During business school and later, the two of us maintained a healthy rivalry, and he still tells people that even on fishing trips in the remotest parts of Alaska, I'll look for competition and someone to cast a line against. At the time, though, with our New York summer coming to an end, I was worried about how to pay for my second year, had no idea what I was going to do, and was floating through school—and life—just absorbing everything and trying to grow up. Rod remains a lifelong and much-treasured friend.

*   *   *

That same summer, Elaine was living in New York, getting ready to do graduate work in French literature at Columbia University, and she would regularly come around and help me cook. Our relationship was becoming more serious. I was taken with her marvelous sense of structure, culture, and values, which had been well established from her upbringing. She had clear beliefs about everything and a deep knowledge of the arts that I lacked. Elaine began to teach me about the connections between painting, music, and literature, consistently impressing me with her encyclopedic knowledge. Although she read everything and seemed to me to know everything, what I admired about her most was her honesty and direct-ness. She had almost no diplomatic skills and just said it the way it was. At times I found this wonderful, and at other times I hated it. But she was pure gold in terms of values, and that was what I needed. I was searching for a way to live my life, feeling drawn in a million different directions. Elaine centered me and made me feel needed and loved.

When the summer break was over, Rheem agreed to let me continue working from Harvard part-time. This gave me a trickle of income and also kept me connected to the company. Back in Cambridge, I discussed my financial situation with my savior, Florence. We did some calculations and agreed I would have to find more income-generating work. So Jim Doolan, my friend from the *Queen Elizabeth,* and I became the proud co-proprietors of Teddy's Laundry Service on the Harvard Business School campus. Our only means of transport was a secondhand bicycle purchased for $25, which we shared, but somehow, with the help of an increased loan from Harvard, we made enough money during the year for me to pay the remainder of my fees.

Elaine had begun her graduate studies in New York, and we remained in close touch. We exchanged affectionate letters, and sometimes I'd travel to New York for the night and stay in a cheap hotel or at my uncle and aunt's apartment. Elaine would stand in endless queues to get tickets to some of the best concerts in New York. There was a thaw in Russian-American relations at the time, and she once stood in line for six hours to get seats for Sviatoslav Richter's piano recital and almost as long again to get tickets for the Bolshoi Ballet. Elaine loved the ballet, and it was the height of George Balanchine's days as choreographer and ballet master of the New York City Ballet. The company was probably the most creative force in America at the time. We drank it all in.

Harvard was one of the happiest times in my life. There were always financial issues, but I worked them out, and in the end, money didn't really matter. For just $2.50 I could buy a roast beef sandwich at Elsie's Diner that was so huge I could save half for the next night. Rehearsal concerts of the Boston Symphony cost 25 cents, including the subway fare. Once I'd managed tuition with Florence's help, money was just not a consideration. With the odd handout from Uncle Joey and my laundry income, my life ran smoothly. I adored the independence and realized that under the right circumstances, which surely are not always present, you can really make it on very little money. In New York in the summer, Elaine and I didn't have to go to the New York Philharmonic because there were free concerts at the Frick Museum on Sunday afternoons and concerts at Lewisohn Stadium. When we spent time together in New York, we lived on spaghetti and cheap wine, with the occasional treat from a liquor store her father bought as an investment. One New Year's Eve, we went in and signed a bottle of Lafitte Rothschild to his account. Then we drank it out of paper cups, in her car, overlooking the East River.

I hadn't seen my parents for a year, but detailed letters, written in my father's beautiful hand, came every day. These letters were suffused with affection. In one, he wrote:

> It is the source of the greatest pride and pleasure to me to think of you, as I do during all my waking moments, and the experiences I have enjoyed through, and with you, have constituted one of the sweetest episodes in my life. I should not be writing so many pages to you, so consistently, unless I had the highest regard and deepest affection for

you, and I pray that I may be spared to continue this delightful exercise. When, P.G. [Please God], in due course, we can meet once again in person, then, indeed, will my cup of joy be running over . . .

In their content and tenderness, these letters never failed to move me. In their formality and endless reminders of my role in his life, they were in some ways a burden. But I also saw them as a way for my father to release his thoughts and tensions—and to stay close to me. To be sure, writing every day with the limited life that he had, it was often hard for him to come up with exciting news. I wrote back infrequently, maybe once a week. I would call, however, and whenever I had it, I would put money in an envelope and send it home. For decades, I would have nightmares about whether I gave enough to my mother and my father and would wake up in a sweat, thinking how I promised my mother £25 and never sent it.

*   *   *

As my time at Harvard drew to an end in the spring of 1959, I began to dread the prospect of returning directly to Sydney. Part of me wanted to please my parents by returning to Australia, but I was too full of fire to go back right away. I wanted to see more of the world. I wanted, particularly, to live in Europe. I applied for a research and teaching position at the Institut pour l'Étude des Méthodes de Direction de l'Entreprise in Switzerland. IMEDE was run by Harvard and financed by Nestlé. Each year, Harvard University sent half a dozen of its brightest graduate students to spend a year as research assistants in Lausanne before commencing their doctorates.

The interviews for IMEDE were being conducted by Hugo Uyterhoeven, a brilliant man who was then a research assistant on his way to becoming a distinguished senior professor at Harvard. Competition was predictably tough, but I went to see him on the off chance that I could sneak in.

"Do you want to get into academic life?" he asked as I sat in his Harvard office.

"I'm afraid not."

"What about trying to bring to the Europeans a sense of American management?"

"That sounds like a good idea," was all I could think of saying.

"Well, would you spend a tremendous amount of time doing research work at IMEDE?"

"I am sure I will work hard, but to be quite honest with you, Mr. Uyterhoeven, I am an Australian and haven't seen much of the world. I would really love to spend a year in Europe."

"Do you understand that you are in competition with Baker scholars and people who are very focused on work?"

"Yes, I do, but I thought I'd come by and see you anyway, and I can assure you that if you choose me, I will do the work very well."

Uyterhoeven looked at me for a moment, then stood up, walked around his desk, and put out his hand: "You're a man after my own heart," he said, and immediately assigned me to one of the positions. Everyone, including me, was surprised.

The Royal Australian Air Force Reserve had made special arrangements for me while I was in the United States, and on arrival in 1957, I had been instructed to report to Group Captain Parker, then the Australian air attaché in Washington. I thereupon visited the embassy in Washington and told him I was fulfilling my orders in reporting to him. I described my free trip with the New Zealand Air Force and said if there was ever anything I could do in return, I'd be most willing. He thought my trip had been a great joke and said if I was eager to continue, he would help me.

"How?" I asked.

"If you want to see the United States, they have an outfit called the Military Air Transport Service, or MATS. Why don't I assign you to the Pentagon to do a report on the American Air Force Reserve?"

"That sounds terrific."

"You'll be given a secret clearance and then you can go around bases and if you want, for example, to go to Alabama, you call up the colonel [with whom he had made the arrangements for my reporting expeditions] and report to an air force base near Boston. You wear your uniform, jump a plane, ask some questions about the U.S. Reserve, and everyone will give you a good time."

As it happened, I didn't have much spare time, but I did manage to fit in two of these trips. Recognizing my Australian uniform, American officers would collar me, buy me meals and drinks, and tell me about their experiences in Australia during World War II. I got to see parts of the States in the South and the Midwest that I would otherwise never have seen. I was overwhelmed by the warmth of the military's welcome.

At the end of my two years at Harvard, the report to the Australian Air Force was due. I had taken very few notes and frankly had not given this assignment much priority. Luckily for me, the U.S. Air Force Reserve had just celebrated a major anniversary that was commemorated in a magazine circulated to 30,000 reservists. It contained a comprehensive history and description of the current activities of the U.S. Air Force Reserve. I remember my last weekend at Harvard vividly. I spent it with Hugo Uyterhoeven's wife-to-be, Sandy, who had graciously agreed to help me type my magnum opus. We took my notes and the formidable history and together crafted a report.

The magazine proved invaluable, and I used it to fill large gaps in my knowledge. We marked the report "Confidential" and addressed it to the "Minister for Air" in Australia. She charged a very modest fee for the thirty typed pages, which I put in the mail as I was leaving Harvard. The minister loved it. As I flew across the Atlantic, I felt at ease. I had completed my Harvard course, fulfilled my responsibilities to the air force, and was now about to begin my next adventure. I began daydreaming about what was in store for me in Europe.

*   *   *

In Switzerland, no longer a student, and with no exams to face, I found myself untrammeled and working in completely new ways. The year starting in September 1959 was one of intellectual curiosity and exploration. I was finally independent, living in my own apartment, and well paid. In many ways, IMEDE provided the perfect transition out of university and into business. Although my main responsibility was to assist the professors who taught at the business school, I was also doing my own research, which took me inside major European companies to write cases.

IMEDE was one of the latest initiatives taken by European business to emulate the activities of American business schools. Nestlé picked up the tab for the institute and had renovated a charming old estate in the suburbs of Ouchy, on the lake in Lausanne, and constructed modern classrooms and a library to complement the historic surroundings. The faculty was drawn from around the world, and an experienced American educator named Clarke E. Myers was dean. Myers had begun teaching at the age of sixteen in a one-room schoolhouse in Kansas, and later, after years of university lecturing in the United States, became the founding director of IMEDE. With his keen intellect and astonishing memory, he created a unique environment that was bursting with innovation.

It was a thrilling intersection of academia and business. I remember my eyes widening at my first opening session when one of the joint managing directors of Nestlé, Jean Corthésy, rose to his feet. "I am the western hemisphere," he said, then pointing to his partner, Enrico Bignami, "and he the eastern hemisphere." I looked from man to man, and the description was completely accurate. They seemed masters of the universe. But more important, they were deeply interested in the educational process and understood that through serving both their own executives and those of other countries and other industries, IMEDE would serve everyone to the best advantage.

For me, landing in Lausanne was like winning a prize. My small modern apartment was on the hill but looked out over Lac Léman, and I spent hours walking along the water's edge and absorbing the sheer beauty of the lake and the Alps. New friends took me to cafés and the theater, and there was even a fencing club, where I trained with Swiss champion Michel Steininger. I was writing cases for Nestlé in Switzerland and for Philips in Holland, and working in classes composed of an international group of middle managers from all over Europe. Life was unexpectedly rich. The only thing missing was Elaine. She was in New York, teaching and completing her master's degree, but we stayed in very regular touch by letter and phone.

Among my colleagues was a Sicilian mathematician, Angelo Tagliavia, who was paying his doctoral fees at Harvard by gambling according to a statistical system he had created. He was an accomplished bridge and poker player, and when we got our first paycheck, he suggested we go to a casino in the south of France and double it. We were paid $1,300 a month, which was a fortune because it was tax free and our apartments were gratis. And I was still receiving a small stipend from Rheem for occasional work. I had never been so wealthy. Angelo undertook "to show" me Europe and teach me what I could do with my money. We jumped into his car one Friday night and drove to Monte Carlo, where over the next two days he planned to give me a taste of what life really held. On entering the first casino, I was absolutely cowed by the headwaiter and by all the wealthy people. For all my bravado and pretense, I was totally naïve and unprepared for this.

First, there was the language. I just managed to get by in French, drawing on scraps from school, my conversations with Elaine, and a brief liaison early at Harvard with a French girl. Then there was the shock of the whole scene. The minute I got inside, the full horror of my father's propensity for gambling opened up before me. I almost shook. Seeing people gamble with such carelessness reminded me of his horse racing and the impact on the family, even though his bets were tiny compared to what I could see on the tables in front of me. But I fought the urge to leave and spent that first night watching my Sicilian friend play his systems and come out with more money than he'd arrived with. Angelo was a professional

who knew his way around; he was streetwise, confident, and well connected. If he'd told me he was in the Mafia, I would have believed it. He
was the type who could survive anywhere, and I observed him closely,
hoping to learn a few new skills. I placed a few bets to gain some experience, but I had no system or knowledge and was totally naïve. I lost whatever I ventured, and to this day, apart from the stock market, I never
gamble with more than a few dollars in slot machines.

Back at IMEDE I honed my business and finance skills, but the real
value of that period for me was learning my way around Europe and becoming comfortable moving from French- to German- to Dutch-speaking
countries. I formed a real love for Europe, for its history, its culture, and
the diversity of its people. I loved the anonymity of travel. That was the
gift that IMEDE gave me—a chance to look around, learn, reflect, and be
on my own.

While I was enjoying Europe, unbeknownst to me, my father was plotting my return to Australia. At the time, Ord Minnett, a large-share brokerage firm in Sydney, was trying to attract business school graduates from
abroad. A new partner named Ian McFarlane, who had studied at MIT with
Morgan Stanley, was bringing know-how to the fields of corporate finance
and underwriting that were previously undeveloped in Australia. Ords began expanding in these areas and realized it needed more people with similar
expertise. The partners placed an advertisement in the *Australian Financial
Review* for "a Harvard Business School graduate or the equivalent." The
principals of Ords didn't expect that Harvard Business School graduates
would turn up in Sydney, but they thought they might draw out some reasonably qualified people from major companies and government.

Although they received about fifty replies—many from people working with Australian trade unions and businesses who had been sent overseas to earn business degrees—I believe that no one was hired. But they
did get a letter from my father, disputing whether there could be anything
"equivalent" to a Harvard Business School degree. He wrote: "I have a son
who is a graduate of the Harvard Business School and is working in

Switzerland at the postgraduate school, IMEDE. He finishes this tour at the end of the year and I would very much like him to come back to Australia if there were to be an opportunity of sufficient attraction to him."

When Michael Gleeson-White of Ords next passed through Switzerland, he contacted me, and I invited him to the apartment. Michael remembers trying to talk to me over the music of *West Side Story*, which I played throughout our conversation. I explained my commitment to join Rheem International for the following year and said that if the Ords option was still open after that, I would be delighted to consider it. I had also promised to spend a year in New York with Elaine. We were eager to spend more time together and find out whether we were right for each other after more than a year apart.

In Lausanne, I fell in with a group of young people of varied backgrounds and experience. Per Hedblom and his sister Astrid, both from Sweden, and Gisela Buschbeck, from Germany, were to become close and lifelong friends. They constituted my Swiss family and allowed me to have a broad and rich life.

In 1960, I returned to New York full of energy to assume the position of director of growth and development at Rheem International. As I carried my possessions to an apartment in Greenwich Village, I remember feeling greatly challenged because I had to create a new job and define the assignment for the company and for myself. I shared the apartment with my cousin Maurice and anticipated spending very little time there. I imagined I would be setting off around the world to look for investment possibilities for Rheem. But while I was in Switzerland, Rheem had been purchased by City Investing, and I was given back into the charge of Mario Capelli, the executive vice president of Rheem International for whom I had worked during my first summer.

Mario was not concerned that I had learned much about business in the previous two years and found me overeducated, overconfident, and totally lacking in experience. He didn't like my title, either, and decided he'd teach me a quiet lesson. So instead of handing me an immediate high-flying assignment, he ordered me to import a Porsche into the United States for the son of the company's Mexican distributor. He kept me on this task for at least a month, until I was so frustrated I could have screamed. I spent hours and hours dealing with customs people and queuing up in lower Manhattan to try to get the papers stamped. To this day I cannot understand why such a simple exercise took so long, but it did. The weeks I spent going through this exercise seemed interminable, and well below the level that I should enjoy as a graduate of Harvard Business School and a former teacher at IMEDE. What the hell was I doing looking after the car of the son of a rich Mexican? After about four weeks of this, I went to Mario.

"What are you trying to do to me?"

"I'm trying to teach you a lesson, you little bastard," Mario shot back.

Then he explained that I should learn a little humility. The important thing, he said, was how one dealt with people—both inside and outside the office. In international business, he said, you must have good relations with clients. He pointed out that I had very little real experience and had done nothing to make friends with my less-educated colleagues, nor had I shown them adequate respect for their experience. He was right: I was full of myself, and with humility I walked home feeling winded. I sat up very late that night, trying to absorb what he'd said. The next morning, I went into his office at 400 Park Avenue. As soon as I saw him, I said: "Mario, you're right; I would like to start again." Over the course of one month he had managed to deflate my ego, convince me that educational qualifications were the beginning and not the end of the process, and impress upon me that human contact and sensitivity—combined with some measure of modesty—were essential to building a career. It was a vital lesson that changed my entire professional life.

The annoying Porsche was finally cleared, and I was liberated from the New York office. Under Mario's direction, I carefully and modestly planned trips around the world to look for areas of investment interest to Rheem. It was 1960, and many countries were transitioning from colonial to self-rule. They constituted vast undeveloped markets. That year,

I went to India and took the preliminary steps that led to a joint steel-fabricating company. In Greece, I helped to create a joint water heater company, with ISOLA, owned by the Dracos family. When I traveled to Mexico and Latin America, just as in India, I was astonished by the poverty I saw. It was quite different from any kind of poverty I'd seen in Australia, America, or Switzerland. The inequity was so striking that I could hardly absorb what was in front of me. I had known what to expect intellectually, but the reality was a shock. It left an indelible mark that would influence my later life. Mario had the vision, a decade or more ahead of his time, that the developing world would become a major marketplace. He encouraged me to go beyond the traditional markets at a time when nearly everyone was focusing on the developed world.

There was very little American investment in Africa, and Mario guided me to see it as a new frontier to explore, so I planned a trip to Nigeria to set in motion the process of buying land in Lagos to erect a Rheem air-conditioning plant. As it happened, the minister for health had a suitable piece of land for sale, and I jumped at it, thinking the connection might improve our chances of acquiring the development approvals. After meeting with the minister one morning, I went over to the new Parliament building at his suggestion to attend the proceedings and listen to the period known as "Question Time." In my jacket, I had a small Minox "spy" camera, which I had borrowed from Elaine's father, and which I hoped to use to chronicle my travels.

Nigeria had in recent months become independent, and there was great pride in the new Parliament. Inside the new building, I was astonished to see the way all the British paraphernalia had been replicated: The speaker wore a full wig like an English judge, there were black gowns, and a master-at-arms stood ready holding a traditional mace. It was a beautiful chamber. I took out my little camera and began taking photographs. I sat watching and listening to questions and answers. After fifteen minutes or so, a large Nigerian policemen came up and asked if I would mind coming with him. As a guest of the minister, I didn't think twice about the request and stepped outside, thinking one of the ministers needed to see me.

As I walked into the open air of this outside corridor, I could hear people chanting: "Spy! Spy!" There must have been forty or fifty people yelling from the bottom of the steps. I looked around, wondering what on earth was happening and who the spy was, when all of a sudden I realized it must be . . . *me.* My policeman was holding me tightly by the arm and told me that it was illegal to take photographs inside Parliament. My apologies were ignored. I pleaded my ignorance of the law, but that was ignored, too. The policemen reasserted that I was a spy.

"I'm not a spy. I'm here on an industrial mission," I protested.

"Yes, you are! You are a spy, a spy, a spy. . . !" As he began chanting the accusation, the crowd joined him. I was quickly directed inside the building and locked up in the office of the leader of the opposition while he left to decide what to do with me.

Ten or fifteen minutes later, my policeman returned with a photographer and started questioning me. "What were you doing?" he asked. "Are you with an American company? Why do you need photographs inside Parliament?" All I could think of was Rheem's name being blandished across the front of the newspaper. I offered some responses to the questions as they tried to photograph me. I said I would not be photographed. "Yes, you will," they insisted.

Spotting an opportunity, I bolted out the door and ran down a long corridor. With the photographer and policeman in pursuit, it must have looked like a scene from a Charlie Chaplin movie. At the time, though, my heart was thumping. I was desperately trying to find someone in authority, and when I saw a door marked "Prayer Room," I rushed in. It was a Muslim prayer room, and inside a number of members of Parliament were washing themselves and preparing to say their prayers on the mats, which they had already laid out.

"I need asylum, I need asylum," I blurted out. A man who turned out to be a minister in the government, and who also happened to be an Oxford graduate, told me with a cultivated British accent to "calm down." I breathlessly explained my situation. I was frantic. He listened, put on his shoes, took me into the adjoining office of the Speaker of the House, and said he'd be back with help. When he returned, he was accompanied by an Irishman who had remained after independence and headed the Nigerian Security Services, as I later learned. He was polite but not very responsive to my protests and led me down the back way from Parliament House, to a car that took me to the police station, where charges were laid against me. The police had already been to my hotel, searched my room, and collected my passport and other documents. The Irishman clearly knew I wasn't a spy, but he explained:

"Well, the boys have got to have their fun. There's absolutely nothing I can do to stop the process. You may be here for months."

"That's impossible. I can't be." I tried to impress them by dropping names.

"As a matter of fact I am having dinner tonight, arranged by the Rockefeller Foundation, with Judge Louis Mbanefo, who is chief justice of the Western Region. I've never met him, but would he be a good reference?"

"Yes, he would be an excellent one."

As the Irishman watched, I called Judge Mbanefo, whom I was about to meet for the first time. He confirmed our dinner arrangement. Then I told him I had a small problem. I was in jail. He laughed, but he managed to get me released immediately, and a few days later, after writing an apology letter to the Speaker of the House, I was allowed to leave the country. I got off the plane at Idlewild Airport in New York and thrust into Elaine's hands an ivory tusk, two pieces of wooden sculpture, and the local Nigerian newspaper with headlines describing a middle-aged spy being arrested in Parliament House. In the paper was an interview with Jaja Wachuku, who was then foreign minister and who made the astounding claim of having known me when I was a journalist in New York.

This was a good story to recount, but it also gave me an insight into the developing world and the huge gap between cultures. This was the early stage of decolonization, and Nigeria was transitioning from being run by Europeans to self-government. In this role reversal, the indigenous community was learning to run a country that included Europeans. I arrived as this adjustment was being made and presented an opportunity for the Nigerians to exercise their authority over an intrusive white visitor who had broken the law. In later years I would follow the process of ever increasing maturity of governance in Africa, which continues to this day.

*   *   *

During the 1950s it was clear that the locus of international political power had moved from Europe to America. At the same time, communism was expanding, and there was an extraordinarily deep feeling against it. I saw the impact of the U.S. government's attack on communism through Elaine's experiences. Politically, Elaine had been shaken awake by Senator Joseph McCarthy and his witch hunts of the early 1950s, but she was unusual among her peers. Her generation of Americans was extraordinarily apolitical. When she graduated from college in 1958, the press dubbed that year's graduates "the non-generation" because they didn't seem to stand for anything. They were the postwar kids who perceived America as the savior of the world. But when McCarthy began looking for Communists in the early 1950s, having people blacklisted and coercing them to inform on one another, Elaine had been outraged. People were losing their jobs because they refused to say whether they'd ever belonged to the Communist Party. Many who had never had Communist sympathies took the Fifth Amendment on principle. The Red Scare continued to have effects well after McCarthy had been censured by Congress in December 1954. In 1961, Elaine resigned from her teaching job at a private high school in Greenwich, Connecticut, because the school didn't stand up for two of her teaching colleagues who took the Fifth Amendment and fired them instead.

During this turbulent period in my life, daily letters from my father continued to arrive, and I felt mounting pressure to return to Sydney. I was now twenty-eight years old and hadn't seen my parents for nearly four years. I was also eager to test my new skills in the Australian marketplace. By early July 1961, after much churning, I came to a decision. I had to return, and I had to take Elaine with me. Elaine and I were great friends, but we had not talked through plans for marriage or where we would live. Certainly we both felt that marriage was likely. We were in love, but we were both very independent.

The need to return to Australia so I could see my family hastened our decision. In early July, Elaine accepted my proposal of marriage, and several weeks later in Sydney, my parents returned home from work to find a message waiting for them: They should expect a call from New York the next day. When Elaine, her parents, and I called with the news, the line was crackly and it was difficult to hear. We spoke somewhat awkwardly, but my parents seemed happy and wrote to us immediately. My mother's letter was clearly written in a rush of enthusiasm. She addressed us both, apologized that she was too excited to be coherent, and welcomed Elaine into the family. "When," she asked, "would I mail that long-awaited photograph of Elaine?"

My father's letter was quieter. He wished me and Elaine, his "daughter-in-law-elect," a hearty Mazel Tov and predicted both families would be mutually enriched by the marriage.

We were still nervous about our decision to marry and I suppose that neither one of us was certain that we could cope with both marriage and relocation at the same time. In the lead-up to the official announcement, we decided to leave it to fate. The night before the notice of the engagement was to appear in the press, we were driving downtown to get an early issue of the Sunday *New York Times* and made a pact. If the announcement was not in the paper, it would be a sign, and we would not be engaged. We would put the decision off for a while until we were more certain and I had been able to scout out the situation in Australia. Of course, the announcement was there: "Elaine R. Botwinick Engaged to Lawyer," August 13, 1961. We returned to Elaine's parents' house and drank champagne.

With her teaching job over, Elaine had been taking doctorate courses in French literature at Columbia University while her parents planned the wedding reception. We left it almost entirely to them. We visited the Pierre Hotel, which Elaine preferred, but her father said it wasn't big enough and instead chose the Waldorf. Elaine selected the color scheme—blue and white—and that was the extent of her involvement. She didn't care much about the reception, and neither did I. I focused on planning for my parents to fly to New York for the wedding.

From hearing me talk about my parents, Elaine imagined we had the perfect family. Her expectations of meeting them were therefore high and pumped higher by her idealism about poverty and happiness. Very early one morning in November, a few weeks before our wedding, we drove out to collect them at Idlewild Airport on Long Island. We took a wrong turn and got lost, and when we finally rushed into the airport, all Elaine saw was a little old woman and a little old man sitting alone at the end of a big, bleak waiting room. God only knows what was going through their minds. But when we embraced, and they saw I was okay and met Elaine, it was sort of love at first sight. Elaine found them more human than she had anticipated. My closeness with my parents, which she knew had at times been suffocating, had matured into a more balanced relationship after my many years abroad. They found her charming, warm, and grounded, and responded to her intelligence. She was exactly the type of girl they had imagined and hoped for. They also got along well with Elaine's parents; in particular, her mother got along fabulously with my father. We couldn't have scripted a better encounter between the families.

Our wedding was slated for November 26 at Zichron Ephraim, a synagogue in the Moorish Revival style, which would later become the Park East Synagogue. It was an unseasonably warm but beautiful day, and we married at noon because we had tickets for the opera that night. After we had already chosen the date for the wedding, Joan Sutherland had announced that she would sing her debut performance at the Metropolitan Opera on the same evening. We both desperately wanted to go, so we pushed the wedding ceremony back to noon and had a reception followed by a luncheon. For her debut, Sutherland performed *Lucia di Lammermoor,* in which the husband is killed by his wife on their wedding night. Neither of us knew the story, and I felt the blood draining out of my body as the opera progressed.

I was in a particularly vulnerable state and took it very much to heart, so much so that when we went back to the hotel, where we had been given the presidential suite, I became terribly ill. Elaine didn't feel great, either. Neither of us had eaten all day because we were circulating and chatting with the guests. We were both nervous about what married life would mean and although very much in love, we were setting off on an adventure with many unknowns. Australia, for Elaine, was far away from New York, and for me it held new challenges in a field that was far away from Harvard and very different from my earlier work as a lawyer at Allens.

On our honeymoon, we spent a cold week on the beach in Spain—not having realized that we got a great financial deal on the hotel because it was the off season—followed by a glorious week learning to ski in Arosa and then three months in Zurich, where I had a work commitment with Holderbank cement company, arranged for me by our best man and Harvard friend, Tony Schrafl. At the conclusion of our stay, Elaine and I traveled to Pakistan to see Betty, Vij, and their son, Derek. Pakistan was the most important and possibly the most delicate political assignment for an Indian diplomat, and Betty seemed to be managing extraordinarily well in a country she hadn't known much about. She wore saris at official functions, and so far as I could see, she was a perfect partner and diplomatic wife. She opened her house and made a great effort to embrace us. Finally, we continued on to Australia. I was now married, feeling extraordinarily fortunate, and although very nervous, eager to make my mark in my native country.

5

LEARNING MY CRAFT
IN AUSTRALIA

I ALWAYS BELIEVED THAT UNTIL YOU TURN THIRTY YOU CAN MAKE MISTAKES, mess things up, and experiment with your professional life. But when you turn thirty you are on the record. I don't know who planted this notion in my mind, but with less than two years to go before I hit that watershed, I believed it completely. Although life had certainly changed for me and Elaine as we started the serious business of marriage, we still had growing up to do. We arrived in Australia ready to build a life together, but I also felt the full weight of the challenge of launching some sort of professional career that would support us and open the world to us.

It was early 1962 and the Menzies coalition government had recently been reelected with a majority of one. A "credit squeeze" had been introduced more than a year earlier by the treasurer, Harold Holt, and the effects of "Holt's jolt" were being widely felt. Unperturbed by this, I rented 700 square feet of office space in an old building in the city and hired a secretary. I was eager to test my new business skills by opening my own firm. I chose the name "Catena," which means "chain" or "link" in Latin. Catena Australia Ltd. would be both a vehicle for private investing and an advisory service for Australian businesses, and I imagined it as a kind of precursor to international venture capital. Five of my classmates from

Harvard—Timothy Harford, Eric Strathallan, Sandy White, Tony
Schrafl, and Michael Kan—invested about £2,000 ($5,000) each. With
my own contribution, this gave Catena seed capital of £12,000, the
equivalent then of $30,000, which was not a huge amount, but enough to
give me a chance to get started. I proposed to leverage my investment activity through additional fund-raising. In a country with a population just
over 10 million, I confidently and naïvely assumed Catena would make
an impact. I also planned to put out a monthly newsletter for interested
foreigners that reported on what was happening in Australia. My confidence was boosted when I received a contract from the federal government's Department of Trade to write a booklet on export marketing. This
caused a rush of adrenaline, and I knew that I could handle the fee-paying
assignment.

On the investment side, I got off to a rocky start. My first misguided
venture in Sydney was to put a few thousand pounds into an air-compressor
company called Air Products Ltd. The company was developing a compressor that its founder claimed had extraordinary advantages over competitors
in size and capacity. I plunged in without taking the precaution of hiring an
independent engineer to check the design. After Rheem, I figured I knew a
bit about compressors and manufacturing, and when the company sent me
plans, projections, and cash flows, everything looked fine—just like a Harvard Business School case. So I sent along progress payments. For about
eight months I reported on the project to my partners, believing this was
going to be the key to our industrial future. The only problem was that
while the projections and sales figures were perfect, the air compressor did
not exist. I remember well the day I met with the company chief executive
and realized that I had been deceived in the most obvious of ways. It was a
scam. And it had played on my self-esteem and my ignorance.

When the entrepreneur walked into my office, I went into a rage,
threatening legal action. Unmoved by my distress, he calmly shot back:

> You can't possibly sue me because, if you do, people will recognize you
> are really not as bright as you think you are. How would it look, being

the first Harvard MBA coming back to Sydney to set up your own company, then you sue me for taking your money for a nonexistent piece of machinery? You can afford it less than I can. In any case, I'm bankrupt, so what's the point?

I looked at him, my fists clenched in anger, but I knew he was right. I never saw him or the money again.

Around that time, as part of a small joint venture in real estate, I bought two run-down old houses in Sydney's eastern suburb of Randwick. It seemed like a no-brainer, and I made the investment without laying eyes on them at the suggestion of a builder who was to complete the reconstruction. The plan was to renovate and sell them. My friend Tony Schrafl liked the idea and put down some of the money. When he visited Australia several months later, I drove him out to see the houses. Arriving at the first house, we found a local government notice on the door condemning the property as unsafe. I knew the house had been in a terrible state, but there had been no indication it would be condemned. Once again, in an effort to keep my expenses down, I had not sought outside professional help. There was a lone rose in the front garden, which we clipped off before driving back to town. In the end, that rose was all we got from that particular investment; I kept it pressed in a book for years. Tony laughed it off, but I felt like an idiot. We did make a few pounds on the other house, but not enough to recoup the loss.

These early mistakes were valuable lessons that probably saved me substantial amounts of money later in life. Whenever I would consider a potential investment, I would apply the "Air Products Ltd." test. They were cheap mistakes, but they battered my pride and brought me down to earth. I had been in my own business less than a year, but I had already used up more than half the funds with my two bad investments, and my confidence was shaken. I thought nostalgically about my years at business school. How comfortable it had been to make business decisions every day with no risk of real loss, however bad my judgment might have been.

By now it was late 1962, and the United States was in the grip of the Cuban missile crisis. Australia felt like a quiet outpost that only occasionally made international headlines, usually in the sports sections. I was a year closer to thirty and Catena was not looking promising.

A few months later, when Ord Minnett approached me again to become a partner in the firm, the offer looked much more interesting. Elaine and I did not have the $40,000 for a seat on the stock exchange required of all partners, but we did have an offer of help from her father. Ben Botwinick had generously offered to put up $100,000 to help us begin our life in Australia, but after much discussion we decided not to touch it. Instead, I would take the offer of a partnership at Ords and approach the Bank of New South Wales for a loan. Charles Ord, who had previously been a senior official at the bank, introduced me to Bert Henlon, the manager of the Wales House branch.

I walked into Henlon's pristine office in a striking triangular building in downtown Sydney. Henlon was charming and put me immediately at ease. He knew I had come for a loan. "Well, Mr. Wolfensohn, what is your asset position?"

"Sir, I only have a few wedding presents, but I will have a good job and I have good credentials."

"You do?"

"Yes sir. I'm a Harvard Business School graduate, I was a solicitor at Allens, and I'm going to become a partner in Ord Minnett. I may not have any money, but I have got a very good education, and I hope to do very well at Ords."

After some discussion, he agreed to lend me the full value to purchase the seat at the stock exchange. I was surprised and delighted. I only had a small current account at the bank at that time, and here he was, giving me an unsecured loan. I have always thought that Charles Ord may have privately guaranteed the loan—I never found out—but Henlon's gesture was tremendously important, indeed pivotal, in my career because it put me in the mainstream of the emerging financial markets in Australia. It was a generous show of faith that I desperately needed. In return, I would bring the Bank of New South Wales, which in 1982 took over the Commercial Bank of Australia to become Westpac, a great deal of business. In fact, I was to become an adviser to the management many years later when I established my own firm.

In those days, Ords was one of the largest brokerage and underwriting houses in Australia, and when I was appointed, many heads turned. Professionally, Australia was the best possible place I could be, as it allowed me to play in an economy that was small by world standards but had some big-league players and financial needs on a world scale.

At the time, I did not realize what a tremendous opportunity Australia afforded me to grow my skills, but in the end, moving back to Australia would prove to be the cornerstone of my international career. For the first two years, I worked with Michael Gleeson-White, whom I had first met when he visited me in Lausanne. Michael was now the most active partner on the investment banking side, working under chairman Charles Ord. An Englishman who had settled in Australia, he was tall, attractive, and brilliant, and one of the first people in Australia to internationalize the market. He had an instinctive feeling about developing the marketplace. Under his umbrella I tried to fill in some of the lacunae in the financial business in Australia. To work with and compete with Sir Ian Potter, JB Were & Co., and a small handful of other firms, we were creating a whole new industry. It was a unique opportunity that called for and fostered creativity. In addition to working in share trading and brokerage, ably led by my friend and partner Gilles Kryger, Michael and I tried to build the new investment banking side of the business and became involved in mergers, acquisitions, and debt raisings for corporate clients. We were working in a period of enormous change in the international financial world, and many bankers and industrialists from overseas were visiting Australia looking for business ventures of all types, particularly those that would build upon the abundant natural resources.

Initially, I was not very selective about projects and would spend hours on anything that came through the door. But Harvard had given me an edge because at least I knew the international language of finance.

Few people knew about concepts such as present value calculations, ratio analysis, and security analysis, which had been the bread and butter of my MBA course work. There were only a handful of people in Australia who had the corporate analysis training I had. I knew that my knowledge of finance set me apart in a way that would not have been possible had I returned to the practice of law. Beyond all that, Ords gave me the chance to learn about different industries and to participate in an explosion of natural resources in an emerging industrial Australia. I owe a big debt to Michael and Gilles, who helped me to make a limited but effective contribution. I was in my element—stimulated and challenged, reasonably well remunerated, and very happy at home.

*   *   *

I had slipped back into Australia with relative ease, but it was an alienating and tough immersion for Elaine. She had shelved her doctoral studies and could find few people in Sydney who shared her passion for French literature and for the new generation of European and American composers. During our first year, she studied Australian literature at the University of New South Wales, but it did not help much. She felt as if she had almost ceased to exist. Nobody cared who she was or where she came from. We had left the United States during a thrilling time when John F. Kennedy was president. The country was a melting pot of nationalities, and Elaine had loved being part of it. Marooned in white Australia, she missed the diversity and the world of ideas where she had been so at ease. Although she had to struggle at first, she eventually found a few kindred spirits in Sydney. And despite her adjustment trials, she remained a tremendous source of support for me.

When my father took ill, Elaine visited him every day in the hospital, and slowly they became very close. My ever-private father opened himself to her a little. With understanding rather than bitterness, he explained that every time he had been called on to make a decision in life, he seemed to have made the wrong one. Elaine thought he wanted to emphasize how important it was for her to help me make the right decisions. She had the sense that my father wanted me to lead the life that he could have lived, had he made the right choices. Their interactions were touching and also relieving, for I somehow felt my parents' focus on me was made more sustainable with Elaine's help.

When the time came to find somewhere to live, we were fortunate to rent a very small apartment in Sydney's premier neighborhood, on the very tip of Darling Point. Although we lived in the old Lindesay estate, erected in 1834 for the colonial treasurer, we lived in the chauffer quarters. That was the first house built on Darling Point and the first Gothic Revival house in the colony. Our home consisted of three small rooms, a kitchen, and a bathroom, which had been added only fifty years earlier. It didn't matter, though; the spot was wonderful. The lush suburb of Darling Point extended into Sydney Harbour, and every time we walked in the gardens of the main residence we saw water. The view from our apartment was limited to the balcony, but our rooms were bright and our large balcony as well as the beautiful garden of Lindesay compensated for the lack of interior space.

We were anticipating the birth of our first child in late November 1963, but Elaine unexpectedly went into labor eleven weeks early. We rushed to the hospital with no idea what to expect. Four days later, Sara Rachael was born, weighing two pounds. She received mouth-to-mouth resuscitation from obstetrician Malcolm Coppleson, but we did not know if she would live or die. The pediatrician, Wilfred Carey, and Malcolm stayed up all night with our tiny baby, willing her to live. The hospital could not have shown more skill or dedication, and we were enormously grateful. Every day for the following weeks, we would go to the hospital and look through the glass at our tiny child, who had been no larger than two pounds of butter.

The original predictions were that Sara had little or no chance of living. We were terrified that we would lose her, but every day, as I looked through the nursery window, I comforted myself with the knowledge that she was growing. Dr. Carey said there was no medical reason for her survival but something in her wanted to live. Only a baby who had that sort of instinct for survival could have made it against all the problems she faced. When, after six weeks, we were finally able to hold her, I melted into tears. Sara was our miracle baby. She began to thrive, and soon the doctors said she could come home a whole month earlier than her due date.

As anxious new parents, we were unsure about how to care for Sara, and we fretted about her development. We observed and encouraged her far more than necessary. Although she was reaching her milestones late, she was very alert, and instinctively we sensed she was fine. She would look me in the eye and smile, and we knew there was just something "all there" about her. Before she was two, she had closed the gap between her chronological and birth age. We finally relaxed.

Two years later, Elaine unexpectedly went into labor a few weeks early with our second child. We missed the cue because she'd eaten a bag of plums on the beach that afternoon and we thought she had an upset stomach. When it dawned on us that she was having contractions, I flew downstairs to call Mrs. Carter, a nurse who was looking after the Lindesay homestead, grabbed a few things, and we dashed to the hospital.

We'd hardly crossed the threshold before Naomi Roslyn was born, looking healthy and beautiful. The obstetrician teased Elaine, saying, "Surely you should have known you were having a baby." Elaine felt horrible, but I was overjoyed at the normality of the birth, which meant I could have Naomi in my arms immediately. It made me realize what we'd missed with Sara and more so, what Sara had missed. Curiously, Naomi was a more fragile baby, and although she was a normal birth weight, by the time she was two she still hadn't reached twenty pounds. But when we took her home, the nurses commented on how lucky we were; she was unusually serene. And she remained that way.

With these two little girls, our home was transformed. Away at my office every day, my fathering took place during weekends, and while I adored and entertained our daughters, Elaine brought them up daily, giving them values and a structured life. My parents were around in a limited way, but when my mother took to coming in every afternoon to visit the girls, it was too much for Elaine. She started taking them to the park to break that routine.

* * *

I had been throwing all my energy and vigor into work. During my first two years at Ords, it became obvious that I was more adept at corporate finance than at buying and selling shares for clients. Before I arrived at Ords, the firm had decided to follow the British practice of splitting its brokerage activities from its underwriting and investment banking activities and had taken initial steps to form a joint venture with Helbert, Wagg & Co., a London merchant bank. This joint venture was to be called Darling & Company, taking its name from John Darling, who had come on as chairman. At the outset, the shareholding of Darlings was split among the Darling family, Helbert Wagg, Ord Minnett, and the accountancy firm Binder Hamlyn. A short while later, when Helbert Wagg was taken over by Schroders, its one-third interest was passed to the new entity of J. Henry Schroder Wagg & Co., London. This was a very important and innovative move: to combine impeccable reputation and experience in investment banking in London with the exciting but undeveloped markets in Australia.

As Darlings grew and needed more support, I moved from being a partner at Ords to being one of three managing directors at Darlings, where I was in charge of corporate finance. It was an odd structure, with John Darling as chairman and Rupert Burge, John Broinowski, and me, as the most junior, underneath him. At the age of thirty-one, I found myself in the unique position of having the Darling name behind my efforts to build the investment banking business. In Australia, this name has considerable cachet. Darling families had been powerful industrialists in South Australia and educators in Victoria, and now were becoming notable merchant bankers in New South Wales. A flower, a river, a mountain range, suburbs, and rich pastoral and agricultural lands had all been named after the Darlings.

Before we got approval from the Reserve Bank of Australia to use the name, Australia had never had a "merchant bank." So when Darlings became the first merchant bank, many of the American companies seeking something like a U.S. investment bank rather than a brokerage house or an ordinary commercial bank came to us for advice and help. This was a huge advantage, and we found ourselves doing business with a rapidly increasing number of American and European corporations. When the top management of Esso, Alcoa, British Petroleum, or W.R. Grace came to Australia, they came to us. My time at Harvard eased my relationships with these executives, and I had the extraordinary opportunity of working at a very young age with corporate leaders from all over the world. My life-long friendship with David Rockefeller, whom I had met when he visited Harvard, developed when he came to Sydney on behalf of the Chase Bank. With his distinguished heritage and name, and his title at Chase, David was a lofty and admired figure throughout the world. He loved Australia and believed in the future of the country. He made me feel welcome and part of his team.

With the Darling name on my business card, doors opened in Japan, America, and England. We were regarded as a sort of new-breed Australian investment bank, and we received a far better reception than I could ever have expected. Australia was exciting, and we were both a new and a well-known banking name. As my work progressed, I had several assistants whom I trained in financial analysis. I sent a good number of them off to Harvard for their MBAs. I devoted much of my time to recruiting intelligent, energetic people and ran courses for my assistants to bolster their corporate finance skills. Some of my younger colleagues— including David Clark, Mark Johnson, David Block, and Tony Berg— went on to achieve major successes as financial leaders in Australia, while Zeke Solomon went on to Harvard Law School and a great career as a corporate lawyer.

I also began teaching a course at the Business School of the University of New South Wales. I based my course on Hunt, Williams, and Donaldson's *Basic Business Finance: Text and Cases,* which I had studied at Harvard, spicing it up with Australian cases drawn from my experience at Darlings. Every Thursday night, I would rush out to the university in my little Fiat with the textbook open on the passenger seat, a case study in one hand and the steering wheel in the other. It was always a last-minute scramble. This continued for several years and in some ways taught me more about finance than I had learned as a student. Not only was I passing on things I had learned at Harvard, but the process of teaching was embedding the knowledge of finance into my brain. The fact that Australia was a developing market offered me enormous opportunities. The country was just waking up to the possibilities of financing natural resource projects. Previously, mining had been regarded as a highly speculative activity, but by the 1960s, it was replacing agriculture as Australia's strength in domestic and export markets. I found myself giving instruction on how to assess the present value of investments in pipelines and the long-term investments in the mining industry. I worked on the financing of Alcoa's first aluminum facilities, the first iron-ore contracts, and the financing for Savage River, which was a joint project with overseas partners. There is no question but that Darlings pioneered overseas borrowings for Australian companies and offered creative vehicles for investment.

This was new ground for the Australian institutions and the banks, and I spent a good deal of time trying to convince everyone that this was safe lending and that natural resource projects were Australia's future. These first attempts at project financing had me traveling to the United States to try to place shares and raise loans. I got most of my education in financing natural resources projects in New York from the leading investment banking firms White Weld and Donaldson Lufkin & Jenrette. I would fly to the United States, see how natural resource projects and financial structures were assessed and financed, and come home and try to adapt their methods to the Australian market.

Because I was based in a growing Australia that was now opening a new market of opportunity that required funding from overseas, I was receiving an apprenticeship in global banking. I traveled to great financial centers abroad for many different clients, and through this, I was able to build an international network of relationships. I was meeting some of the giants of global investment banking, including Frank Petito of Morgan Stanley, Siegmund Warburg, and Gordon Richardson of Schroders. It felt as if my Harvard case studies were becoming real. I could never have gotten the exposure had I become an associate at Lehman Brothers or Goldman Sachs or at a British merchant bank. I would have had a much more junior position working for senior partners, and I would have had to specialize. In Australia, I had a degree of authority that allowed me to take risks. The situation was developing very quickly, and nobody had done it before. All of a sudden our firm had to find solutions for matters that had previously been handled by foreign, parent companies. I had been thrust into a situation where I could see the whole picture of financing projects and take responsibility well beyond my years.

This was a period of staggering growth in finance, particularly in the development of the Eurodollar market, which was in its infancy. It had been born when the U.S. government announced in July 1963 its intention to place a tax on money borrowed by foreigners in the United States, leading borrowers to look for money overseas.

In the early 1960s, very few American financial firms had any substantial representation in London, but with the prospect of the tax, the market was internationalizing very quickly. Australia was hot. It was a small, politically stable market, close to Asia, where people spoke English. Dick (Gerardus) Dusseldorp, brilliant and charismatic as well as very tough and directed, was chairman of Lend Lease Corporation, the first big Australian client of Darlings that I tried to take into this market. Dick's company was then the premier building and land development corporation in Australia, and Dick himself was an independent, creative character, always pushing the frontiers. Originally from Holland, he decided to remain in Australia and made a historic impact in business. He listened when Viennese-born architect Harry Seidler told him that good design adds no cost, and together they constructed beautiful modern buildings and changed the urban skyline.

One of Dick's innovations was to establish a property trust with the stock held largely by overseas interests. He was probably the first person to try for a substantial issue in the New York and London markets. I went overseas several times to try to make his investment plan a reality. There was a tax advantage for American investors, and everything was on course when, a week before we were due to finalize our first fund, the U.S. government brought down the interest equalization tax, which removed the advantage and killed the issue for us. As disappointing as this was, it didn't impact my relationship with Dick, and we went on to do many borrowings overseas, through the developing Eurodollar market in London.

For about five years, I was in luck and in demand. Mining was booming, resource financing was highly sought after, and I had a role in fighting some of the iconic battles in corporate Australia. I participated in General Foods' acquisition of the soft drink company Cottee's and a transformation in the newspaper business when John Fairfax & Sons, owners of the *Sydney Morning Herald,* acquired controlling interests in Australia's other leading newspaper, Melbourne's *The Age.*

My ambition had no bounds. I could see the bigger house I was going to buy. Perhaps one day I would run for Parliament, maybe even earn a knighthood. We were already living in a larger, rented house in the affluent suburb of Vaucluse to accommodate our family, with direct access to Sydney Harbour. On weekends, Elaine and I would walk down for a swim or lounge in the sun room, watching the boats and enjoying the breeze off the water. We were living right at the edge of our means. Although I was making good money, my phobia about debt meant I constantly checked to make sure we never strayed into the red. Knowing my father-in-law's money was available was my safety net.

*   *   *

By 1967, Elaine had just about reached the end of her patience with me and with Australia. Sara was almost four, Naomi was not yet two, and although Elaine had made many close friends in Australia, she did not want to spend the rest of her life there. I didn't help at all. I was away much of the time, flying all over the world, working nonstop, and feeling pretty full of myself. Even when I was home, I was barely present because something was always happening in business, and I couldn't resist its pull. And we were constantly entertaining overseas visitors.

I began organizing a series of dinners at which a group of young men drawn from finance, industry, and the professions could meet with an invited guest and talk about the problems of Australia and its development. It would be an opportunity for some cross-fertilization of ideas between prominent leaders and perhaps the coming generation of leaders.

I only participated directly in one dinner, but I have never forgotten it. I simply asked the governor-general of Australia, who is simultaneously the queen's representative and the head of state, to join a youthful and talented group for dinner. It was as if a young American businessman called up Barack Obama and invited the president to have dinner with his friends. There was a sense in Australia of incredible movement, a feeling that a new generation was taking over. And this is what enabled a group of movers and shakers to sit at a table with members of the establishment. The young guests at my dinner ranged from Rod Carnegie, my old Harvard colleague and then a partner at McKinsey & Company, the international management consultants; to Alan Greenway, deputy chairman of the Australian National Tourist Commission and chairman of Travelodge Australia; to the architect Harry Seidler; to George Masterman, my barrister friend.

We had no set agenda, so discussions around the table could be lively and free. It was truly a fascinating evening for us all. The next day, the governor-general, Lord Casey, wrote to thank us for the evening: "You and your friends have the ball at your feet, in most important fields, and I envy you the work you are at."

It was an exciting period for me, but Elaine still missed her friends and the excitement of New York. I understood her desire to return to

New York, ideally in time for Sara to start school. We could always return to Australia one day, she said.

Although her desire to leave was strong, Elaine did feel some ambivalence, particularly because she had found an intellectual home at the Rose Bay Convent, where she was teaching French and had good rapport with the nuns. I once asked her to come on a business trip, and she declined because she was preparing her students for a major exam. Surprised and upset, I told her I needed her. Unmoved, she said she couldn't possibly let her students down. We had a huge argument, and eventually I changed my dates. Throughout our marriage Elaine has always been a strong figure, and I learned that tests of strength were not a great idea.

We might never have left Australia—or at least not so soon—had it not been for an unanticipated and ugly episode at Darlings. For a number of years, while simultaneously carrying out my duties at Darlings, I had been chairman and chief executive of Australia's Power Corporation Limited, which had been established by its Canadian parent as an investment and venture-capital company under the leadership of its charismatic chairman, Maurice Strong. That year, Power Corporation in Canada decided, without my help and without my knowledge, to bid for the Queensland copper- and gold-mining company, Mount Morgan. This put me in a tough spot because my fellow managing director at Darlings, John Broinowski, happened to be chairman of Mount Morgan and had no inkling of our intentions.

Foreseeing that this would be an issue, I consulted John Darling about the conflict, suggesting that I could withdraw from participating in the transaction if he thought it advisable. With my experience today I would have seen the possibility of grave problems, but at the time I followed Darling's lead, and he told me to proceed. I also called Gordon Richardson, who had become chairman of Schroder Wagg, London, when Schroders took over Helbert Wagg in 1962. Schroder Wagg held a one-third interest in Darlings, and Gordon and I had become close. Gordon had been a top commercial queen's counsel in London and had had enormous experience. Both Darling and Richardson gave me the green light.

As we made the bid, Broinowski naturally found out and went into a rage. He attacked my most vulnerable spot: my reputation. Broinowski accused me of using inside information that I would have learned at Darling & Company to make the bid—a groundless attack on my personal character. As an investment banker all you really have is your name, and if that is tarnished, you're finished. By then, the management structure at Darlings had changed, with Broinowski elevated to deputy chairman. He was not only senior in rank, but he had the advantage of being much closer to John Darling than I was and was much older and better known in the community. As a young outsider, I began feeling all the insecurity attendant on fighting a formidable man who was twenty years older, a member of all the right clubs, and a pillar of the establishment. I saw my career on the line and went straight to John Darling's office.

"John, I cleared this with you, not once but twice, and you know these allegations are not true."

"I know," he replied, "but I cannot be drawn into a fight between you and my oldest friend."

"But I cleared it with you in advance and with Gordon in London."

"I know, but I am in a difficult position and I cannot take sides. You work it out," he said. I left his office angry and scared.

I was proud of my reputation, and I was determined to defend it. I had seen others tarnished in corporate battles. I knew I had done nothing wrong, and I would fight to the last. Power Corporation was moving directly with Sydney lawyers to proceed with the deal, and when Broinowski had legal papers served on me to go into court the next morning, I flew into action. There was no time to spare. That night, at midnight, I went to the Darling Point apartment of one of our directors, Sir John Dunlop. John was the quintessential member of the establishment and chairman of Colonial Sugar Refining Company, one of Australia's leading companies. He was also a good friend who had been excited by the growth in the corporate finance business that I led. I woke him up after several minutes of banging on the door, and while his wife, Patsy, went to make tea, I told him what had happened.

"John, my life is on the line and maybe the reputation of Darling & Company. This guy is a goddamn liar, and I am going to defend myself with every means at my disposal. I want to countersue him." Dunlop listened, plainly sympathized with me, but clearly advocated a calmer approach. He said that first thing in the morning, he would help me secure the services of Dennis Mahoney, the leading corporate lawyer and queen's counsel. As sleep was out of the question, I spent all night strategizing. John sat up most of the night with me.

At eight the next morning, I was in Mahoney's chambers. Within an hour we had put the papers together, and we managed to serve them on Broinowski by 9:30 AM, half an hour before the case was due to begin. We notified the judge, Justice Laurence Street, who would later become chief justice of New South Wales. Broinowski, never thinking that I would fight him, sought an adjournment. Through Mahoney, he sent a message saying he wanted to talk. I was in no mood for a discussion and sent back a brief message: "There is no reason to talk. Just withdraw the suit and pay my costs. What you have done is unconscionable." He declined, and we went back before Justice Street, who read the papers and told us to go away and settle. I would not budge. I knew the record of the pleadings could harm me. "I'm not withdrawing. I'm going to fight," I told my counsel. By now it was almost 1:00 PM, and the court was about to break for lunch. Street instructed us to have the matter sorted out before court resumed at 2:00 PM.

William Patrick Dean, who had gone to Sydney University with me and was a fellow member of the University Squadron, was the barrister on the other side. I was shocked that he had taken the case against me, as I considered him a good friend. He would later explain that he had been obligated to do so. Of course, barristers are obliged to take "the next cab on the rank," but at the time, I was so furious and vulnerable that I felt it was disloyal. It did not stop Bill's career, however; after becoming a judge and a justice of the High Court of Australia, he became governor-general of Australia. Sadly, our friendship never resumed, although my admiration for his capacities never wavered.

Finally, at 1:55 PM, on the steps of the courthouse, Broinowski's lawyers indicated that he would withdraw the claim and pay my costs. I was vindicated—100 percent in the clear. But the climate had changed. In the aftermath, Peko-Wallsend Limited made a counteroffer, Power Corporation sold off its Mount Morgan holding at a tidy profit, and Mount Morgan became a Peko subsidiary. My dealings with Broinowski went from chilly to icy.

The case had also created inevitable tensions in the office. Darling's image had been affected by the spectacle of two of its managing directors publicly at odds, and the ill feeling was almost palpable. For four years I had poured everything I had into Darlings and helped to shape its business. In retrospect, I should have handled the takeover offer differently and considered more carefully the predictable effects on John Broinowski and our firm. I suppose I was too anxious to do the deal for one of our clients and gave inadequate attention to the effect it would have on our firm or on my personal relations with Broinowski. With more experience and maturity, I might have suggested to Power Corporation that it hire another firm, which would have been the right advice.

The result of my actions was that I no longer felt comfortable at my office. Elaine and I started talking about alternatives. She was nearly as upset as I was. Several months later, toward the end of 1967, I called Gordon Richardson, Schroders being our major shareholder, to say that we had decided to leave Darling & Company, and indeed to leave Australia with our two children.

* * *

A few days later, while in the Queensland port city of Gladstone looking at a mining project, I was called to the phone, which was in a small hut with a corrugated iron roof. Waiting at the other end of the line was the chairman of Schroders. I couldn't believe my ears: Gordon was suggesting I join him in London and become a director of Schroders.

"Gordon, I'll come, but only on one condition."

"What is it?"

"Only if I can get a membership at Annabelle's."

"I don't know that I have ever been there, but I'm sure Lord Chelsea, our manager, will be able to get you in."

Overexcited and unable to absorb the offer, I had made no reference to my gratitude for the offer or for the professional challenge he was offering to me. Instead, I had nervously asked for admission to the hottest nightclub in London. That was my failed attempt at humor in the face of a life-changing opportunity. My chairman must have regarded me as a fool.

When I put the phone down, I looked around the mining site in disbelief. For an Australian merchant banker to become a director of a London merchant bank was unprecedented. I had visited Schroders many times and had been greeted as a friend. I had also hosted many Schroders people in Australia. But it was one thing to be going as a friend from Australia and quite another to be going as a colleague at J. Henry Schroder Wagg & Co., London. I stood by that hut for several minutes, too excited to say a word.

Back in Sydney, I got a call from Siegmund Warburg in London. He'd heard about the incident with Power Corporation from his friend Maurice Strong and knew that I was thinking of leaving Darlings. He was warm and polite, and he invited me to join Warburgs. He wanted me to be a director of Warburg International, rather than a director of the principal bank. He explained that as no one else knew me at the bank, he would have to introduce me in two stages but promised that in a matter of months, I would be a director of the main bank.

I was thrilled and frankly amazed to have these two options but felt unequipped for the decision. I went to London to have interviews with Gordon and Siegmund. Gordon was furious that after four years at Darlings, I would even consider going to Warburgs. I admired Gordon enormously, but Warburgs appealed to me because Siegmund was Jewish and in his lifetime had built probably the most powerful and international investment bank in London. I wasn't sure I wanted to join yet another firm that did not seem to have any Jewish history, and I was bruised, nervous, and not a little insecure after the Power Corporation incident. As it turned out, the Waggs had Jewish blood, and one of the main forces in the Schroder firm in years past, Major Albert Pam, was also Jewish, although that fact was not emphasized. But at the time I felt that going to Siegmund would be like entering a family, whereas at Schroders I would be at risk.

First, I went to stay the night at Gordon's country house. Before dinner, I explained my dilemma to Gordon. I was jet-lagged and jittery, and we had an argument right through the meal. I believe he took offense at the religious references, though he did not deny the possible prejudice that might exist at Schroders. His wife, Peggy, heard what was going on from the other room and came in to tell us we were both being ridiculous. She said it was a cold night, gave us each a hot-water bottle, and dispatched us to our beds. She assured us it would all be easier in the morning. We could talk about it then.

I was upset, and I know Gordon was, too. He was a good twenty years older than I and would later become Lord Richardson and governor of the Bank of England. To him, I probably looked like some little upstart from Australia who couldn't appreciate the value of what he was offering and the enormous risk he was taking on me. But Peggy was right, and the next morning, we were more balanced. After breakfast, Gordon and I walked for over three hours through the beautiful countryside of Gloucestershire, and at the end of our ramble, I said I would join Schroders.

I made the decision on several grounds. There was the loyalty, the years of commitment to the group, to Gordon, and to my Schroder colleagues. I knew the players and had the immediate offer of becoming a managing director. At Warburgs, I would be one step removed and dependent on Siegmund. While I believed completely that he would be true to his word, I didn't want to get into a situation where I didn't know the people and where I had no established reputation.

A couple of days later, I met Siegmund and described my position. He gracefully accepted my decision. But for eighteen months after I joined Schroders, he would never return a phone call. I was upset and hurt. Then one day Siegmund's secretary, Miss Wasserman, called up and asked if I would come to tea. I immediately accepted and rushed into Siegmund's office at 3:00 PM, blurting out, "Why haven't you returned my calls?" He looked at me and said calmly, "I didn't know you'd called." I'd spent eighteen months in purgatory, paying the price for saying no, but now I was readmitted to his presence and the friendship was restored and only grew thereafter.

Having made my decision, I returned to Sydney to close down our affairs and move the family to London. Elaine's feelings were now plainly mixed. She felt regret at leaving her teaching position at the convent as well as some wonderful Australian friends, but exhilaration at leaving the country, even if it was for London, not New York. For my father, there was some ambivalence, too. Although he was clearly sad to lose me again, I could also see his pride and hope as I went on to my new appointment. In his eyes, my going to London to become a partner at a major investment bank meant I would achieve big-city acceptability. This he found deeply satisfying. My mother accepted our decision and said visiting us would be a great excuse to travel. Soon my family and I were on a plane out of Australia. With some trepidation, I felt I was heading to the new world of international finance.

6

꧁꧂

THE EURODOLLAR
REVOLUTION

I ARRIVED IN LONDON IN JANUARY 1968 AND FOUND MYSELF AT THE center of an explosion of creativity in the international markets. Previously, cities such as London, Frankfurt, and Zurich were seen in their own countries as national financial centers that could finance domestic needs as well as trade and investment activities overseas. Now the emerging international marketplace was beginning to unite these distinct national markets into one invisible global market as the U.S. dollar became the international currency. My colleagues and I were witnessing and participating in a major shift from classic London merchant banking in sterling and various local currencies to something totally different.

The main catalyst for this transition was the U.S. interest equalization tax, introduced in 1963 as an attempt to keep money from flowing out of the United States. As a foreigner, if you wanted to borrow in the United States, your interest would be subject to a 15-percent interest equalization tax. This distorted the free market and meant that borrowers tried to find their money elsewhere—in markets not subject to the tax. This led smart people like Siegmund Warburg to establish a financial market in London that was not subject to U.S. law. Siegmund's firm took the U.S. dollar and used it internationally as the currency of transactions made outside the

United States. That move enabled them to deal in those dollars without any U.S. law or tax affecting them.

Thus, the Eurodollar was born. You could lend a non-U.S. entity $100 million for any purpose from London or other non-U.S. centers with no transaction tax. If the same transaction had been entered in New York, it would have been taxed 15 percent. This created the offshore market.

The second major change was technological, with the development of more sophisticated computers and the creation of new financial service providers to clients. The transfer of information, the ability to trade, and the linkage of dealers in markets throughout the world in real time meant that geographic barriers were no longer relevant. By turning on a computer screen, financial service providers and clients could access the market immediately in a way that was never before possible. National boundaries were dissolving, and this change required new skills and created loyalties to international rather than national centers.

New talent was required in the international centers as the London merchant banks began the business of developing the whole range of financial instruments from commercial paper to equity offerings. It was not long before the major U.S., European, and Japanese institutions all set up in "the City." In this way the largest and most efficient international market was born, free of transaction tax and substantial regulations, and ultimately involving many other currencies that could be traded freely on a nontaxed basis. This innovation would revitalize London. Soon a large influx of foreign professionals would turn it into the center it has become today. By the late 1960s, a twenty-four-hour market had developed around the world, unprecedented in scale and flexibility.

My job as a director at Schroders was to help my senior colleagues build the firm into a powerful presence in the complex international markets, drawing on the established reputation of the past, but also launching new services and products for our extended client base. Schroders was the quintessential accepting house—part of the exclusive group of merchant banks that enjoyed privileged status with the Bank of England—and it was trying to create a place for itself at the cutting edge of international banking. Located midway between the Bank of England and St. Paul's Cathedral, the eight-story building sat behind magnificent, modern glass doors, which opened to reveal a mahogany wall above the receptionist's desk. On the wall was mounted a great world clock that recorded the time in Schroders' offices around the globe. This was a bank of contrasts: It was both an international bank—with interests stretching from New York to London and from Latin America to Australia—and an old-line city accepting house. Like other accepting houses, Schroders provided a highly efficient method of financing trade, but it did so in a traditional environment with formally attired butlers greeting visitors.

The modern London house began to emerge at the turn of the nineteenth century, when the Schroder family set up commodity traders and brokers amid the turmoil that followed the American War of Independence. Schroders became a specialist in providing international trade finance and by 1870 was one of the top London-based accepting houses. Over the subsequent decades, it played a major role in dealing with post–World War I financial reconstruction, with its senior partner, Baron Bruno Schroder, acting as an adviser to Montagu Norman, the governor of the Bank of England at the time. But of particular interest to me in this history was the summer of 1919, when in a break with its German and Protestant past, the bank invited Major Albert Pam, a British war hero with enormous expertise in Latin American finance, to join the firm as a partner. Pam, the son of an affluent Jewish merchant, was fluent in German and French, and he became a dominant presence at Schroders from the interwar period and into the late 1940s. Schroders used Pam to win a share of the lucrative business opening up in Latin America at the time, and it would continue to recruit the most talented outsiders, regardless of their religious affiliations.

In a different way, Gordon Richardson was an outsider himself. He had been lured to Schroders from the Industrial and Commercial Finance Corporation, a forerunner of the venture-capital firm 3i that grew up in the 1990s. The son of a Nottingham grocer, Richardson studied law at Cambridge. At the age of forty he switched careers, and on arriving at

Schroders, he was asked by the main shareholder, Helmut Schroder, to undertake a top-to-bottom review of the firm. Although he would acquire all the trappings of the British establishment after becoming governor of the Bank of England in 1973—eventually becoming a lord—when he arrived at Schroders, he was without aristocratic connections.

Gordon undertook a radical reshaping of the company. In the 1950s, he injected Schroders with new financial know-how, organized a buyout of minority shareholders, and brought the American and British operating arms together under the umbrella of Schroders Limited. The holding company Schroders Limited was floated on the London Stock Exchange in 1959 with considerable enthusiasm and a recommendation from the *Daily Mail* to its readers to "Apply Early." But there was an apparent imbalance in the group. Despite the fact that the bank was listed on the London Stock Exchange, the New York arm overshadowed the London operation, accounting for three-fourths of the new holding company's assets (although much less of the earnings). The U.S. board and the U.S.-based management of Schroders were nowhere near as influential at the board level of the London holding company, for whom, quite correctly, the most important business was London based.

As chief executive of the group, Richardson set about deepening the London business. His bold first move was to negotiate the takeover of Helbert, Wagg & Co. In the 1950s, Helbert Wagg had proved a remarkably successful financial house. Under the leadership of self-made banker Lionel Fraser, it had come to dominate the market for new companies undertaking share issues. Wagg relished takeover battles like the famous 1960s "Battle of Long Acre" for control of Oldhams Press, Britain's largest magazine publisher at the time, with newspaper titles including *People* and the *Daily Herald,* then the voice of the Labour Party. In May 1962, Schroders purchased Helbert Wagg for £2.8 million. The result was the city firm J. Henry Schroder Wagg & Co., and the deal brought vigor and growth to the combined group. Richardson became chairman of Schroder Wagg and went on to become chairman of the whole group when Helmut Schroder relinquished his position in 1965.

Under Richardson's stewardship, Schroders advanced itself into a central position in corporate finance activities and advised in an ever-increasing number of mergers and acquisitions. The bank, perhaps ahead of its time, also saw the possibilities of venture capital, an enterprise historically carried out by merchant and investment banks. The firm took equity stakes in growing companies and in ailing or fledgling enterprises that, with the right merchant banking expertise, could be turned around to produce a profit for all the equity holders.

By 1968, Richardson had decided to pursue an expanded international strategy. He recognized that Schroders, with its presence in the Americas, could build on its history. If there was a key opportunity among the London accepting houses, it was that the bank I was joining had a significant domestic presence in the foreign markets—most important of them, New York—and with this base it could gain a lead on its competitors. Its past experience in New York was in activities traditional to a commercial bank engaged in international trade, with much of its business in Latin America. The challenge was to broaden this base and the scale of the operation and, within the confines of U.S. law, to make the New York base more powerful as a balance to London in terms of earnings.

It was clear there were two groups in the firm. There were the traditionalists who saw little need for change and who, in a way, resented it. Then there was Gordon's small team, which was working tirelessly to bring Schroders into the ever-changing world of expanded international business. Gordon quickly assigned me as the junior member of his team, which was led by one of his senior lieutenants, Leslie Murphy, and the group finance director, John Bayley, an early expert in international tax issues and regulation. I later learned that within the firm, our group was known as "Richardson's Court."

It was an intimidating environment, but Gordon immediately made me feel accepted. He and Peggy, his wife, had already become great friends to me and Elaine after several visits between Australia and London. Professionally, Gordon made me feel that I had the kind of fresh blood he was looking for. I also felt supported by my friendship with

Bruno Schroder, scion of the founding family, whom I'd met at Harvard.

At first I shared a double desk with George (Gowi) Mallinckrodt, a nephew of old Schroders hand Gustav von Mallinckrodt. He was married to Helmut Schroder's daughter Charmaine. We kicked a lot of ideas across the desk. I was perceived as entrepreneurial, what with my American education and some new business and managerial experience. Gowi also had some New York experience, but he was steeped in the European markets and tradition, and he taught me a great deal.

Leslie Murphy, a former civil servant turned oilman and industrialist, was my key partner in this new enterprise. Wise and experienced, he had been an outsider who had won his way into a leading position in the firm purely on merit. Gordon liked him and relied on him, but even for Gordon, Leslie was a touch of the new. He was a down-to-earth, pragmatic, brilliant financial man with little interest in social matters. He was an avid golfer and loved to play the piano and the church organ. For a mentor and colleague, I could not have chosen better. Together we would visit the United States many times, seeking Eurobond clients for the firm. Without Leslie I would have made many more mistakes, not just in our creation of new financial instruments, but in particular in my navigation of our London office environment. For various reasons, Leslie had confronted resistance from the more conservative elements in London. Although I made my own mistakes in dealing with London colleagues, Leslie provided me with crucial advice along the way, including holding me back from one aggressive action that might prematurely have terminated my career. He understood that in order to introduce new initiatives into a company as broad and sophisticated as Schroders, it was necessary to lay down the ground, to explain what I was trying to do, and to build support. This was Schroders, not Darling & Company. He was able to manage my relations with the London traditionalists and described our new business efforts as being wholly in line with the highest standards and history of the firm.

John Bayley, a former Cooper Brothers auditor who was in charge of the Schroders balance sheet, was the third man in our partnership. As financial director of the group, he was the rock upon which Gordon Richardson was able to rebuild the financial base of the firm. An eminent tax expert who understood offshore banking and offshore tax havens better than anyone I have ever met, Bayley moved between London, New York, and the Caribbean, organizing a financial and tax structure that was in advance of its time. He was essential in helping Schroders to catch up and even lead in some aspects of the competitive race. Bayley rarely interfered in business decisions but was a masterful adviser on structuring and became indispensable for Leslie and me. Working for Richardson with Leslie and John was the most productive period in the evolution of my investment banking career.

The early days of the Eurodollar revolution were thrilling. I was at the front of the London push, where there was energy, drive, and tremendous innovation. I worked with the leaders of the London-based movement, including David Scholey, who was already a star at Warburgs, where he supported the greatest innovator, Sir Siegmund Warburg himself. I was privileged to work with creative, first-class minds from London and New York—such as Jacob Rothschild, Stanislas Yassukovich, and Michael Von Clemm. These were exhilarating days with new financial products constantly being invented. In the span of a few years, we saw the creation of the whole range of Eurobond issuances, convertible issues, euro-yen lending, and Yankee-bond issues. I worked to create and develop Euro-commercial paper, which allowed corporations to take short-term loans in the international money market, matching the huge commercial paper market that already existed in the United States. Its advantage was its tax-free nature; by keeping it offshore of the United States and designating it initially in U.S. dollars, we allowed corporate treasurers to invest and to borrow on a tax-free basis. This was just one step in the evolution of the global market that exists today, characterized by tax-free transactions, infinite depth and flexibility, and operation twenty-four hours a day.

Although the Euromarket was relatively small at the outset, the major New York houses recognized it had enormous potential for tax-free dollar

financing and were quick to follow. Indeed, it was the Euromarket creation that led so many of the American financial houses to establish subsidiaries in London and in Europe. The market for Eurobond issues began
to grow exponentially. In 1968, $3.5 billion in new Eurobond issues
were announced, compared with $1.2 billion of foreign bond issues on
national markets, an increase of 40 percent and 11 percent, respectively,
over 1967. Today the international presence of the major houses is natural, and in many cases central, to their overall business. When the Euromarket started, their head offices were firmly implanted in New York,
Frankfurt, or Zurich. The Euromarkets created the impetus for this new
phase of globalization of the financial industry. At the time, we sensed
something important was happening, but it was impossible to grasp the
total transition that occurred as a consequence initially of U.S. legislation
and the development of technology. We were witnessing the birth of today's ever-developing global marketplace, the beginning of a vast presence
of internationally held and traded currencies and instruments, and the establishment of European and Asian financial houses now essential to the
functioning of the international system.

When Leslie and I visited the United States in early 1968, we were able
to talk to potential clients about something new. Suddenly we had an un-
regulated, tax-free, tax-exempt way of raising funds for corporate America.
It was fresh, different, and delivered in person by the two of us. We would
arrive at the Ford Motor Company or DuPont, and there would be up to
fifteen executives waiting to hear about the new European U.S.-dollar-based
market. I used to tell the small team working for Leslie and me that we
needed to think of ourselves as shoe salesmen, and each time we made a
presentation, we should have something new to engage our buyer's attention. We had to prove that the establishment city house of Schroders had
something real to offer the American corporate giants. Our offerings
ranged from Eurobond issues to Eurocommercial paper issuance.

Although Richardson's long-term strategy for Schroders was to build a
strong American base, no leading British merchant bank had ever successfully established itself in the United States. Even Warburgs, despite nu-

merous efforts, failed to follow up effectively on its immense lead in the United States after its historic Mobil Oil issue. The same was true of Rothschilds and Hill Samuel. While British houses struggled—and failed—to establish themselves across the Atlantic, American houses such as Goldman Sachs, Morgan Stanley, and Merrill Lynch came to dominate the international scene in London and later in Asia. We dreamed of building an investment banking arm in New York that would offer the salaries and incentives to enable Schroders to buy an American house. I wanted to see an international network based equally in London and New York, with offices in Latin America, Paris, and the Middle East, stronger German and Swiss operations, and improved ties to Australia.

I also hoped to watch the internationalization of the next generation of bankers in Schroders. One Saturday afternoon while playing golf, I tried to persuade my young colleague Win Bischoff, who was working with me and who had a background in Eurobonds in the international department, to go to Hong Kong. We were establishing a joint venture with the Chartered Bank and the Kadoorie family, the great Sephardic banking dynasty that was a dominant player in the Far East. I thought it was a terrific opportunity for a young and promising graduate like Bischoff. He was reluctant to go. "I want no part of it," he told me. Like all his contemporaries, the career path seemed to be in London. But I didn't give up the chase, and I urged, "I want you to read a book by an American academic, and then come back and talk to me." I gave him a copy of Herman Kahn's *The Year 2000*, which forecast that Asia would become the world's fastest-growing region by the year 2000. I had been devouring it, and Hong Kong seemed like one of the most exciting places to be. Bischoff took the volume, read it, and a week or so later came into my office ready to discuss his relocation. He went to Hong Kong, where he remained for twelve years. He would become the head of the Hong Kong office of Schroders, then chairman and chief executive of the whole Schroder Group, and chairman of Citigroup before returning to a leading position in the UK banking scene.

*   *   *

During this time, I was free to devote all of my energy to the new challenges of the international markets. Elaine was bringing up the family pretty much by herself and providing me with everything I needed as a home base on which to build my career. We had settled into a beautiful house at Pelham Crescent, South Kensington, which I had bought just days after arriving in London, to Elaine's chagrin, since she had not seen it. I had paid a large sum for it—£18,000 ($45,000) for the eighteen-year lease—a trivial amount by today's standards but significant for us at the time. The residential neighborhood had good shopping, restaurants, and antique shops that would soon become fashionable. Our tall, narrow Regency townhouse with five floors and seventy-two steps looked out over elegant gardens set back from Fulham Road. It was quiet and light, with a sense of history and generous proportions. With our piano in the drawing room and a communal garden for the children, it became for both of us the house we'd dreamed of.

After the remoteness Elaine experienced in Australia, London felt like home to her. She made new friends, we went to concerts several times a week, and she loved the creativity of pre-primary education in British schools. The whole city was irresistibly alive—and this vitality was contagious. After the dour decades of rationing and shortages that followed World War II, Britain was waking up. It had a vigorous Labour prime minister in Harold Wilson, who had found the language to lift the nation out of its industrial stupor. The "Swinging Sixties" brought a musical and design renaissance. Grayness had given way to brilliant color, the Beatles and Rolling Stones had revolutionized popular music, and Mary Quant and Twiggy had transformed fashion. Being tall and thin, Elaine adopted the new fashions, even if she was slightly uncertain when they first appeared. A bright new generation of painters and classical musicians had put the country at the forefront of contemporary culture. Our shared passion for the children at home and our involvement in the arts helped keep us happy together during a time when I was devoting 90 percent of my energy to work.

We would spend much of the week entertaining my business associates and clients. Because of the breadth of Elaine's interests, none of our entertaining ever had business at its core, and we invited guests from every aspect of our lives to our dinners. People seemed grateful for the chance to mix outside of their normal circles. Where the chemistry was right, we built friendships, and our social events were a clear break from our daily work. Although Elaine would rather have pursued her own career in academia, she never wavered in her support. Torn between the family, her loyalty to me, and her desire for an independent intellectual life, somehow in London she came close to finding a balance.

In London I made a key musical connection that would influence the rest of our lives. In September 1969, the English baritone John Shirley Quirk, whom I knew from Australia, called me and said, "I know you have been a frustrated impresario all your life—now you have your chance." He told me about two young men, Jasper Parrott and Terence Harrison, who then worked for the management firm of Ibbs and Tillett and represented several fine musicians from Europe. They were looking to strike out on their own. They wanted to form a different kind of management agency that gave musicians far greater personal service and attention, and firmer control over their career development rather than having to rely on the lottery of forward bookings with no idea where it would lead.

A few days later, I invited Terry and Jasper to my office. As they explained their ideas and outlined their potential list of artists, I knew I wanted to be part of their enterprise. I immediately told them I was willing to help—and what would they want? But they were just starting in the business, and they didn't have any idea what their financial needs would be. Parrott later told me that they weren't even prepared to say how much financing they would require. In those days, the music management business was, in many ways, financially innocent because costs were low. It was all rather amateurish. My new friends had few resources and were working out of a shared apartment in London, but their venture had potential. Their big starting strength, along with their considerable talent and experience, was their relationship with the brilliant Russian pianist Vladimir Ashkenazy. Their less rigid and far more personal approach would prove attractive to other up-and-coming performers, including the

Romanian pianist Radu Lupu and the Korean violinist Kyung-Wha Chung. Another client was the charismatic conductor André Previn, who was then very much in the ascendancy, having just taken over the London Symphony Orchestra. They clearly had the basis for a new enterprise with a glittering array of classical artists, but they had almost no business framework.

The two young men went away to consider my offer of help. A short while later, they returned with a back-of-the-envelope calculation suggesting they would need a loan of £8,000 ($20,000) to set up office, buy the necessary equipment, and see them through the early days of the agency before the cash from commissions for booking concerts for their clients started to flow in. I suggested that they come over to my house so we could discuss the details of a contract. Amazingly, these two young impresarios gave me a very tough time. They had an ingrained suspicion of city financial experts and what their motives might be in working with people in the artistic community. I had to persuade them that I was on their side. Finally, in exasperation, I asked: "What do you gentlemen want and expect? I'm totally at risk here. I am going to acquire one-third of your business—and put up all the money—you will control it and run it. And you don't even have any business yet!"

To make them feel easier about the deal, I suggested that they write me a letter; they could word it as they liked, and it would be the basis of our contract. Their objective was to draw up something that would allow them to extricate themselves from the fearful Wolfensohn bear hug, should it all go wrong. I was eager to get a look at the inside of the world of the classical music business and happy to accommodate them. We reached agreement and built a lasting friendship.

As a commercial investment, I did not think that the Harrison Parrott relationship was going to make me rich. When a few years later the partners asked for a further tranche of around £4,000 ($10,000), I was only too happy to provide it. With the value of the pound wobbling on the foreign exchanges and much of the agency's business coming from overseas, I decided this time that it would be better if the cash was in Swiss francs.

Within a few years, the company became very successful. I decided that from their point of view, it was time for me to bail out. I told them: "If you don't buy me out sooner or later, you're going to resent the fact that I have a third of your business, on the cheap." Eventually we negotiated an exit price, and I made a modest profit on my investment of £12,000 ($30,000).

Harrison Parrott produced a marvelous and quite different return for Elaine and me as a consequence of our friendship and relationship with the "young lions"—as they then were—of music. We had the privilege of building close and enduring friendships with the great new stars Vladimir Ashkenazy, Daniel Barenboim, Jacqueline du Pré, Radu Lupu, Kyung Wha Chung, Zubin Mehta, Itzhak Perlman, and Pinchas Zukerman, among others. Most of these musicians were in their twenties, and they brought a new sort of vitality to their art and a sense that there were no boundaries in their music. They traveled around the world, full of idealism and full of the love of music, to participate in projects and performances. They were at the core of talent in their generation of musicians, and Elaine and I were lucky to become part of this global family.

Ashkenazy, who defected from the Soviet Union in 1963, lived in Britain until 1968, when he and his Icelandic wife, Thorunn (Dodi) Johannsdóttir, moved to Reykjavik. After a few years, they decided it was time to give something back to the country, and in 1970 they organized the First Icelandic Music Festival, which would become a biennial event. I watched Harrison Parrott put together a fantastic program, which included the London Symphony Orchestra and an array of international artists. It was an unforgettable occasion.

Hekla, the volcano in Iceland, had recently erupted, and I chartered a small plane to fly my friends over it. Hekla was still blasting out incredible amounts of stone, and it was an awe-inspiring sight—though it made the plane bounce around so much that everyone got sick. We hardly slept during the six-day festival. After the formal concerts, we all gathered at the Ashkenazy house, where our friends would play their chamber music repertoire all night. I shall never forget Daniel Barenboim and Vladimir

Ashkenazy sight-reading the repertoire of piano duets well into the early hours of the morning. It was the richest music experience of my life. These friends went on to become like brothers and sisters who would make our home at Pelham Crescent their home away from home when they were in London. My daughter Sara, who was taking her early piano lessons, was inspired and sometimes interrupted in her practice schedule when Radu Lupu or Ashkenazy arrived to practice on our family Steinway. Those occasions reminded me of my boyhood, when music filled our apartment and drifted out of the open windows to the garden.

*   *   *

In 1970, we were in our third happy year in London when Gordon Richardson suggested that we move to New York. He offered me the position of president and chief executive of the J. Henry Schroder Banking Corporation, known as Schrobanco. This offer was not contested in London. I know that some of my partners were probably quite content to see me go. In some ways Leslie Murphy and I were shaking up the London equilibrium as the Eurodollar markets expanded. We were aggressively marketing our services, perhaps more forcefully and less elegantly than the London style. Some of my London colleagues viewed my professional trajectory in the firm as too fast, and we had encountered some resistance to building an international base that was not fully coherent with the existing London structure. It could be argued that I had been inserted in the management structure from the top by Gordon Richardson to work with Leslie Murphy. I was creating a position for myself that might receive premature recognition from the board of directors, and in that way I did not endear myself to the London partnership. I did not do enough to build up bridges with the London-based team, and in the end this was my downfall at Schroders.

But while my proposed new position was something of a non-event in London, at J. Henry Schroder Banking Corporation in New York it turned heads and was certainly not welcomed. I would later learn that

Gordon had unsuccessfully approached a number of distinguished people to take the position before offering it to me. The job was too small to attract Harold Brown, the former U.S. secretary of defense, and others declined because Schroders New York was only a $600-million bank in a world of giants.

But I saw Richardson's offer as an opportunity to meet challenges at a level I had never confronted before. I could not pass it up. It was not an easy choice, and Elaine, who had our third child in her arms, did not want to leave London. Our son, Adam, had been born in April that year. While delighting in our daughters, I was overjoyed to have a healthy son. When Adam came home, Sara and Naomi took him over. I don't think any baby ever received more love than Adam did from his siblings. While they were at school, he slept under the crabapple tree in the garden and when I came home to see him, his sisters were always playing with him. At the time, Elaine was weak. After Adam's birth, she had been discharged from the hospital with serious anemia and Pelham Crescent was an ideal place to recuperate. She hated to think of taking our children to a New York apartment. Both of us felt that this was the time, the place, and the opportunity for us to enjoy a more normal and shared family life in London.

Life in England was a great experience. Six weeks' mandatory holiday each year and weekends at our beloved rental country home at "Little Thakeham" in West Sussex brought our family close together. There were walks in the country, riding lessons for the children, drives to Great Windsor Park and many wonderful English sites, and every Sunday, the friends who rented us our retreat in part of their estate cooked us superb meals. For the first time, our life seemed to have balance, a characteristic of British professional life that I admired greatly.

Despite all that, and after much consideration of the personal costs of moving, the lure of New York was irresistible. Schroders New York was largely a commercial bank, and I would have the unique chance to learn the traditional and complex international banking business from the position of president of a well-respected but small commercial bank. I would also have a seat at the table in London to assist Gordon, Leslie, and John as they created a true international banking business in an unprecedented financial environment. I wanted the challenge.

I told myself and Elaine that though London had started to develop its financial system in wholly new ways and Schroders was well positioned to take advantage of the developments, I was being offered the chance to run a full-scale banking operation in the most powerful country in the world—with the backing of top management 3,000 miles away in London. It was a dream job, especially for someone who had never been part of a commercial bank before.

Elaine wasn't convinced. We'd had our happiest years in London, and she felt the city was just now in its prime. We were comfortable, and the children were thriving. Perhaps she had a premonition of the stresses that lay ahead, of what life in New York would be like and what effect being president of a New York bank, albeit a minor one, would have on my already inflated sense of my place in the world. But with the promise of living near Central Park and close to Elaine's parents and friends, I won the argument. After two and a half years in London, once again we prepared to move.

7

∽∾∽

BECOMING
A BANKER

M Y ARRIVAL AT SCHROBANCO IN LATE 1970 WAS NOT GREETED WITH
unmitigated joy by the executives there. I had the support of the
former chairman, Gerry Beale, as well as that of Chairman Jack Howell,
but most of the American executives saw me as an inexperienced usurper
from London imposed upon them by the ever-restless Gordon Richardson; they felt he distrusted them and doubted their loyalty, even though
this was not the case. Indeed, within a week of my arrival, I was threatened with wholesale resignations.

Two of the vice presidents came to see me and without any ambiguity
told me how they felt. They were unhappy with my being there; they did
not want me to be president; they felt I did not know anything about
commercial banking; and I had neither experience nor stature. On top of
all that, I had not grown up in the firm and I was only thirty-six. I did not
agree publicly, but I had to admit to myself that their analysis was largely
correct and that many of their complaints were legitimate. I braced myself
for a showdown.

Luckily, I had the good sense not to respond that day. I told the two
executives that I'd take them to lunch in two weeks, along with any of
their interested senior colleagues, when we could discuss the whole situation

at length. I needed time to prepare myself for this encounter. I had to make my own appraisal of the challenge and come up with a strategy for facing them.

Two weeks later, I sat down with the top dozen Schroders' executives in a private room in a dining club on Wall Street. I never drank much, but before lunch I ordered my first-ever vodka martini. I remember being asked if I wanted an olive and having no idea what to reply.

Before the main course was served, I took a few sips of the martini and looked around at the twelve faces eyeing me skeptically.

> Look, I just want to say one thing to all of you. I know you're not happy, but I am staying. I know you think I am not properly trained, that I am inexperienced for the job, that I don't have the stature, that I am a poor choice. But I have been chosen, I have been appointed, I am staying, and I am going to make a success of this bank.

Everyone was listening intently, so, determined not to be unnerved, I continued:

> I want all of you to know that I've also learned over the past two weeks that there are a lot of things you do not like about me and, in some cases, about each other. I am, however, prepared to start with a clean sheet of paper on every one of you, but after lunch, if any or all of you wish to leave, come and see me. I assure you there won't be any bad blood, and I'll try and help you get another job.

Then I finished my drink; I really needed it. I listened closely to the concerns of my guests. Their fears were wholly justified from any rational point of departure, but I knew I had to project confidence. I somehow made it through the rest of the lunch, and I went back to my office and waited. Nothing. The next day, one executive came in and said, "I think you are right. We should give this a chance." Then another approached me and said, "I've always supported you." And so it went until all twelve of them were on my side—or at least willing to build on the challenge we had been given by London, even if they remained skeptical. No one left the bank, and we got on with work.

The American business had been very important to the Schroder family, particularly during World War II, when commerce in the City of London ground to a halt. Schrobanco became the linchpin of family interests, providing a shelter for the Schroders' wealth and keeping their financial dynasty strong while many around them were damaged. The Schroders were acutely aware of their German genealogy and the tensions that arose from it during the world wars, so New York was the family's security blanket, and indeed, in the 1950s, 90 percent of the Schroder Group profit was generated by the U.S. operation. The firm could not compete directly in the domestic business with the large American money-center banks, but its reach into Latin America—particularly in Argentina, Brazil, and Venezuela—made Schroders a specialist institution ahead of its time in New York. Its business in foreign markets, in foreign exchange trading, and in the financing of international trade made it unique and served a very real purpose both for American businesses and for the American and foreign commercial banks with whom these businesses worked.

I now had the wonderful opportunity to take control of Schrobanco, assess its strengths and weaknesses, and plan for its future. My goals were to strengthen its specialist capacities, while also introducing the idea that it was part of the worldwide Schroder Group and should look for opportunities with existing and new clients that would benefit from a true global banking business. We had to take advantage of the new, complex, and growing international marketplace. American banking regulations and the provisions of the Glass-Steagall Act meant we could not underwrite and distribute equity or debt offerings and compete with investment banks, but we could unearth clients that could be serviced from London or by subsidiaries of the Schroder Group in places like Hong Kong, Japan, Singapore, and Switzerland.

This expansion to a broader base within the Schroder Group caused some grumbling among my senior colleagues in London. They felt strongly that Schroders New York was a limited specialist organization, and therefore it was in London that the horizons should be stretched. Michael Verey, chairman of Schroder Wagg, saw the family's unwavering interest in North America as a huge distraction and seemed quite happy for me to have the responsibility of running it, so long as I did not seek to impinge in any way on the London-based business. My ally was Gordon Richardson, and he spent an extraordinary amount of time in New York guiding me and leading the effort to meld together a global business, which would simultaneously add to the London-based business.

Because we did not expect our New York sojourn to be more than several years, Elaine and I decided to rent out our house in South Kensington and initially camped in the Stanhope Hotel, opposite the Metropolitan Museum on Fifth Avenue. Having three children in a hotel was not easy, but with Elaine's parents nearby—they had recently moved to the city from New Rochelle—there was plenty of help. Eventually, with the assistance of Schroders, we bought a four-bedroom apartment on Park Avenue. We enrolled the children in the Dalton School, one of the few private co-ed schools in New York.

Some months after our move, I went for a mandatory medical checkup organized by Schroders for its senior executives joining the New York business. Two days later, I found myself in the hospital having major abdominal surgery for a polyp in my colon. The biopsy was positive, but the surgeon told me he had managed to extract the polyp completely and that he anticipated no further problems as long as I came for regular checkups. It felt like a narrow escape. It was disconcerting to think about what would have happened if we had not moved to New York, where executives were required to have regular X-rays and physicals.

Elaine and I decided to tell the world that the growth was benign. In those days a diagnosis of cancer was perceived as a death sentence. The job I'd entered into was not going to be easy, and I didn't need people piling doubts about my physical capacity to do the work on top of existing concerns about my banking experience.

At work, I faced a formidable learning curve. Quite simply, I had to learn or leave. Truly ignorant about the complex regulatory environment in the United States, I was challenged almost immediately by the passage of the new U.S. Bank Holding Company Act of 1970.[1] This was designed to restrict banks' market powers by limiting the expansion of the money-center banks into new areas like investment banking. We quickly realized that this represented a threat to the heart of Schroders. If more than 50 percent of the revenue and capital of the whole Schroder group were held in the United States, then it would be deemed an American bank and the group would be restricted to pure commercial banking operations. Despite the acquisition of Helbert Wagg and the expansion of Schroders globally, the bulk of the bank's capital was still in New York, which meant a real regulatory risk to the whole group. The board considered a number of solutions to the problem, including the sale of the U.S. fund management arm, Schrotrust. But no action was taken. This was fortunate, because in the end, the Federal Reserve—the U.S. central bank—decided to amend the legislation so as to give greater freedom to foreign banks, like ours, that were operating from within the United States.

Although Schrobanco was a very small and specialized entity among New York banks, trying to transform it—with its 600 employees and $600 million in assets—into a more dynamic unit was a substantial task. The company needed both reorganization inside and some redirection in view of the growing challenges from much larger U.S. and foreign banks that were beginning to compete more vigorously for the type of business we were doing. For a time, we worked with and advised new overseas bank entrants coming into the expanding international markets, but that meant we were strengthening a larger competition, and this was especially true of the Japanese banks that were subsequently to become such a force in the international marketplace.

The early 1970s was a high-stress period, but I felt relatively secure because my relationships with Bruno and Gordon were sound. It also helped that unlike my British colleagues, my American colleagues did not regard me as an oddball because I had not come up through the English public school system. Personally, I was in a financially sound position, too, drawing an annual salary of $120,000, which was a reward far in excess of anything I had achieved before. I could feel my perennial fear about financial insecurity beginning to dissipate, and as the months progressed I believe that I actually became quite good at my job.

*   *   *

Because Elaine had not wanted to leave London, and this was not the optimum time to return to New York, which was dangerous and a more difficult environment than South Kensington for raising two young children and a baby, these New York years were a strain on our marriage. I was busy on all fronts; if I wasn't fully absorbed at the office, I was immersed in voluntary work in the community that arose from associations with the business. We were living a life very different than the one we had imagined as students in New York. Being the wife of the president of a small bank in New York was something Elaine never anticipated for herself—any more than I had expected it—and the job of being my spouse in this role was not easy. I couldn't see it then, but I was becoming the typical corporate executive, demanding that we devote ourselves to business and clients rather than to each other and our friends. I am not proud of it as I reflect on my life, but the family came second, though I loved them and cherished them. Simply, I did not give them enough time, as my career was dominant. I regret so much those lost years, which, thankfully, I have been able to make up since that time.

The only exception to my business-centered world was music. Here Elaine and I could combine entertaining clients with attending concerts, and we were able to keep up our friendships with the artists who had become so important to us in London.

Apart from all the entertaining and family responsibilities, Elaine had her own activities, including membership on the board of the New York City Opera and on a committee that read and recommended books on a

broad variety of subjects related to parenting and the family. I was traveling constantly, and when we did see each other, we always seemed to be in
the company of others, entertaining or going out for business or cocktail
parties. We had very little privacy, and a tension grew up between us.
Without articulating it, I expected Elaine to be a corporate wife. I thought
she should be glamorous, urbane, and completely devoted to hostessing.
This was completely unfair. Elaine was cultured and gracious, but she
never wanted to be the married adjunct to an ambitious businessman, and
if she had ever slipped into this role, I probably would have hated it.

Elaine did not have, nor did she aspire to the polish of New York so-
cialites. She wasn't interested in their game; she wasn't interested in accumulating material goods; and she wasn't focused on keeping up with the
latest fashions. She chose instead to devote herself to our family and to
the maintenance of enduring values. I will always be grateful to her for
that, because our children were growing up in a much more privileged environment than I had expected or had ever had. For Elaine, the kids always came first, and she worked hard to ensure that they had a first-class
education and remained grounded, despite their affluent surroundings. At
this time, however, my preoccupations with the office were such that I
found it difficult to give the family—and in particular, our children—the
attention they deserved. In retrospect, I am all the more admiring of
Elaine for keeping her balance and priorities when it was tough for me to
do so. I suppose I was also looking for more lightness and adventure in
my life. I wanted everything. Here I was, the new president of a bank,
given a good salary for the first time in my life, offered club memberships,
chauffeured everywhere, and seated at a good table at most restaurants. It
was pretty heady for me and filled me with my own self-importance. I
could be insufferable, and Elaine wasn't afraid to call me out on it.

Shortly after we arrived in New York, at a time when Elaine was away,
I invited Gayle Rich, a neighbor and friend from Sydney who was in the
city on vacation, to go out to dinner. She and her husband, Steven, had
been very good to us when Sara was born, giving us all their old baby
clothes and furniture. I say we were neighbors, but they had lived in the

grand house close to our chauffeur's quarters on Darling Point. I was eager to impress her. The night before Gayle arrived, I went to Orsini's, which, according to my Schroders colleagues, was the best Italian restaurant in town at that time. I introduced myself to the headwaiter, explaining that I was the new president of Schroders—which I assumed meant very little to him—and asked for a table. I explained that I wanted to get to know the place because the following night I would be bringing somebody special as my guest. I gave him $20, a higher tip than I'd ever given anybody before, and after my dinner reminded him that I wanted the good table in the corner the following night.

The next evening I collected Gayle in the bank's chauffeur-driven Cadillac. As we entered the restaurant, the headwaiter immediately said, "Oh, so nice to see you, Mr. Wolfensohn. Your usual table?" I thought Gayle would be really impressed by this, and we walked to the appointed table, where I asked for two glasses of champagne. I began telling her how well everything was going at Schrobanco. After we ordered our main dishes, the sommelier asked what we'd like to drink, and I answered:

"I would like a bottle of Osso Buco."

He knew I had eaten osso buco, the Italian veal dish, the previous night, and in an effort to make me look less foolish, he said, "But would you like some wine?"

"Yes, please, I'd like a bottle of Osso Buco."

"But Mr. Wolfensohn, you've already ordered chicken."

"I know, but I want a bottle of Osso Buco like I had last night."

"Last night you had Valpolicella!"

I have not eaten osso buco since.

Elaine resisted the glamorous lifestyle. At the time, many of my colleagues were buying houses in the Hamptons or in Westchester County, but neither place appealed to her. She preferred the small retreat we purchased, with borrowed money, in upstate New York. It had an A-frame house on four acres of woodland, beside a lake in Carmel, about an hour's drive from the city. The surrounding community was decidedly middle class, full of firemen, policemen, and many churches. We had some interesting neighbors—writers, artists, and professional men and women—who had no social pretensions. There was something about the quality of these weekends that returned me to reality. There was never any pressure from Elaine to go beyond what we could afford, and this house united us as a family and gave us a chance to relax and grow together without the pressures we were exposed to during the week. Depending on the season, we went swimming, boating, and ice skating next to the house on China Pond. I remember one night when the moon was full, going down to the pond and skating with all our children in the moonlight. As they had during my childhood, Friday nights pulled our family together as we welcomed the Sabbath, and by the end of the weekend, I felt restored and ready to face another Monday at Schrobanco.

In spring 1973, Baron Otto Leithner, the chairman of one of our client companies, requested that I join a small group of advisers to his independent trading and investment company. He invited four bankers and advisers to participate in a meeting with his senior colleagues at Villa d'Este on Lake Como, Italy, where we would each speak about our area of expertise for about an hour. On the first morning, we sat around a green felt-topped table in the villa's meeting room. Laid out for us on the table were writing pads and pens—and a gilded paperweight. Otto gave an introduction and thanked us all for coming but made no indication that we were to receive any fee for our contribution to the day's work. Just being at Villa d'Este was a privilege, but it would be disingenuous of me to say I had not been hoping for a fee.

After the morning's proceedings, as we were ready to adjourn for lunch, I gathered my papers and turned to leave for the dining room when Otto said to me: "I think you should bring your paperweight."

"Well, I thought I would just leave it here on my papers to keep them in order," I replied.

"I think you should bring it with you because, in addition to it being a paperweight, it is a kilo of gold."

Astonished, I picked it up and carried it in my pocket for a few hours. At the end of the day, I decided to deposit it in the hotel safe and said to the manager, "Would you be good enough to look after this gold for me?"

"Certainly, sir."

Then, as an afterthought, I asked, "I have no idea how much this is worth. But if I gave it to you, would it be possible for me to bring my family here for a week with no additional cost?"

He did a quick mental calculation and decided that the kilo of gold would maintain us not only for a week but would cover access to all of the facilities, from tennis to speedboating. I quickly made a deal with him and when I left, he had taken care of my gold, and I was eager to surprise my family with a luxurious Italian holiday during the next school vacation.

Elaine had been to Lake Como with her family twenty years earlier and was happy to return. For the children, it was the first time they had been anyplace so elegant, and they had to behave like little adults. We were there for a wonderful week before Elaine continued on to a suburb near Tel Aviv, where we had rented a house for most of the summer. She had decided it was a good opportunity to expose the children to their Jewish heritage. I joined them there, and it felt like a gift to spend several weeks with Elaine and our children.

That summer, Daniel Barenboim and Zubin Mehta created wonderful concerts in Tel Aviv, Caesaria, and Jerusalem with many of our friends. One night, Naomi slept on Elaine's lap while Daniel conducted Mahler's Fifth Symphony. A week later, while driving to Haifa, we turned on the radio in the middle of an orchestral piece. Naomi said casually, "Oh, that's the Mahler Fifth we heard last week." She was eight years old.

Each of our children had a powerful relationship with music from a very early age; they probably sensed that it was a passion that held their parents together. When Sara was two years old, she could already identify Bach whenever it was playing. As a toddler, Adam became obsessed with listening to Mahler's First Symphony and other music and would himself put records on the phonograph, which was strictly prohibited—because he would inevitably scratch the record with the needle. He would also try to play Naomi's small violin. When he was three, Elaine found Adam his own

violin teacher. The bits of family life that I had were what kept me charged
and to a degree balanced, but the truth was that I was obsessed with my
business life in New York. I was thirty-eight years old, in many ways still a
novice, and the daily challenges of my job demanded my full attention.

*   *   *

The only way I could see Schrobanco prospering and gaining a real international presence was through expansion into noncommercial banking
activities. We were too small to compete against the big money-center
banks in lending. We needed to find niche businesses where skill and international experience would add value. Under John Bayley's direction,
we monitored costs carefully and rented out two of our eleven floors in
the Battery Park headquarters. I appointed as a deputy Mark Maged, a
lawyer with a distinguished background of practice in New York. Mark
became a friend and helped me develop the art of delegating work to others. It was difficult for me at the beginning, but the pressure of work and
my lack of experience led me to delegate far more than I ever had before.
Mark took on much of the day-to-day management, leaving me time to
focus on increasing the income with specific new business initiatives.

   In 1972, we absorbed a group of government securities traders to expand our trading activity. Gordon and the London board showed some
interest in these acquisitions but questioned the high risk involved in government bond trading, which at the time was one of the largest markets in
the world. I countered that the only way to take Schrobanco forward was
to build on the franchise and expand trading activities beyond the traditional work we did in trade finance. I told them that to be recognized as
an international bank, we had to have a broader presence on the ground
in the United States, with special skills in foreign exchange, international
markets, bond trading, and investment management. We were simply too
small to compete for credit lines against the major money-center banks.
We had to focus on smaller, specialized lending, preferably with some international aspect that would grant us higher margins for skill and knowledge.

Latin America seemed like a good place to start expansion, because Schrobanco already had a history in the region and had established representative offices in Argentina and Brazil. We made a breakthrough in 1972 when Schroders Banking Corporation was appointed financial adviser and lead manager for a $23-million syndicated loan to the Brazilian state of Minas Gerais. I used this experience as an opportunity to propose to the board a major expansion into Brazil. After Gordon made a personal visit to Brazil, we formed a joint enterprise with Monteiro Aranha in June 1973, called J Henry Schroder do Brazil. Under the direction of Frederick D. Seeley, an American and a longtime executive of Schrobanco, it provided advice on mergers and acquisitions for Brazilian firms and offshoots of global firms, as well as financial consultancy services to federal and state bodies.

Latin America was also where I developed an approach that would ultimately be copied by banks with far greater reach and expertise than Schroders. In the wake of the Yom Kippur War in October 1973,[2] oil prices had surged to higher levels than ever before as the Organization of Petroleum Exporting Countries (OPEC) increased its pressure on the West. Among the big beneficiaries was Venezuela. The Venezuelan central bank was desperate for help in managing its new and larger cash resources. Schroders' Latin American office picked up on this intelligence and contacted me. I visited the governor of the central bank in Caracas and suggested that we start by training his people for the new challenge. I volunteered to run a seminar for his executives, teaching them the basic financial skills they would need as they began to manage their newfound wealth, which was to begin at $1 billion of reserves.

At the time, I was working closely with a tall, charismatic young British former treasury official, Geoffrey Bell, who had joined the firm as an assistant to Gordon and later would work closely with John Bayley. Bell was a skilled economist with well-developed contacts inside the Bank of England and the Federal Reserve. I put together a team that included Bell and brought in experts from different parts of the group, including Jean Solandt, who had originally trained at Société Générale (SocGen) in

Paris. He had reversed the losses at Schroders' foreign exchange trading in London and was much admired. Erik Gasser, the experienced and effective general manager of Schroders AG in Switzerland, joined the group as well.

I was determined to build a client relationship with the Venezuelans. Our first seminar was slated to take place during December, and we would have to work around the clock with our Venezuelan friends to have them ready to manage the January influx of resources. I offered to buy out those on my team who had already booked and paid for their Christmas (and summer, if in the southern hemisphere) vacations so that we could get down to Caracas and prepare for our first seminar.

This was not the way people in Britain generally behaved or thought, but I had no choice but to be direct and assertive. We had to deliver. I needed to put together a global team in almost no time. We flew down to Caracas, and I chaired the presentation. The effort paid off. We were given the job of training the Venezuelan team jointly with Kuhn, Loeb & Co., a distinguished New York investment bank, which disappeared as an independent firm when it merged with Lehman Brothers. Eventually, Schroders would become the sole adviser to the Venezuelan central bank.

Geoffrey did much of the ongoing work as we developed the Reserve Asset Management Program (RAMP) to advise not only Venezuela but central banks around the globe. I would fly in to Caracas from New York whenever necessary. It was exhausting, but I had promised the governor of the central bank I would be there when they needed me. Typically, I would arrive in time to have dinner with my team and our Venezuelan colleagues. We would review the progress that had been made and, when necessary, adjust my work plan for the following couple of days, when I would meet with the central bank governor and the finance minister to conclude the visit. It was the combined skills and experience of my Schroder colleagues that made the difference, and we kept the relationship with Venezuela for many profitable years.

We had noticed that because of the increased oil price, many central banks were accumulating reserves well beyond their previous levels. Venezuela was an extreme case; during the course of a single month, it accumulated $1 billion of foreign exchange, which had never been seen in its history. Thereafter, we looked for central banks that were accumulating funds but lacked the knowledge of more established European or North American central banks. The triumph of RAMP was Geoffrey's, and he went on to develop his skills throughout his business life in and outside Schroders. RAMP became a world leader in managing reserves of countries with expanding foreign exchange incomes. The moment was right, we had the knowledge and experience, and we were the first to enter the field. In the end, our reach and depth were not as great as such firms as Warburgs, Lehman Brothers, and Lazards, which subsequently entered the business and proved too strong for us.

At one point under Gordon Richardson's leadership, a joint London and New York team considered a far more radical idea for transforming Schrobanco from a hybrid commercial bank into a genuine investment bank. This would mean selling off the commercial bank and its loan book to conform to U.S. banking regulations. It would then put us directly in competition with established American investment banking houses. It was an exciting idea. But it was also daunting, and the process would leave us no base on which to build. The few remaining executives (after the sale of the commercial bank) would not know much about American investment banking or what to do with the proceeds of the sale as we tried to become a U.S. investment bank. We all thought that the established competition was too tough. The idea was rejected.

An alternative was to repeat the Helbert Wagg experience on the other side of the Atlantic and find an investment banking partner, using the proceeds of the commercial bank sale to invest in a partnership with one of the established firms. Gordon was friendly with Paul Miller of First Boston and approached him about buying a substantial interest in that company. When it quickly became clear that the Schroder group was not in a position to secure either a majority ownership or managerial control of this great firm, this too got the thumbs-down from the London board. I was saddened because I felt that a large minority interest in such a great firm would have built a powerful transatlantic alliance.

We then decided to remake Schroders on our own, as best we could, through new initiatives such as reserve asset management. In fact, there was a great deal we could do for ourselves. A group of young men from Brown Brothers Harriman, an old-line New York firm, was brought in to set up our fixed interest expertise and build a management business. We also attracted economists Bill Griggs and Leonard Santow, who quickly developed a reputation for being two of the smartest analysts of the government debt market. They were widely sought after by clients and quoted in the national press for their views. We were also able to develop some important corporate finance relationships, and we became advisers to Hugh McColl when NationsBank was still a small but expanding North Carolina operation. We were in at the ground floor of one of the great banking stories of the late twentieth century as NationsBank extended its reach, many years later effectively taking over Bank of America. In those early days we were important to Hugh. We had great international experience and contacts that we shared with him. He had vision and built resources, so that after some years he was on his way to becoming a legend in the history of banking.

While the flurry of change and activity kept Schroders on the Wall Street map, it was still basically making its money by the time-honored practice of endorsing paper issued by foreign banks. Because of its reputation and knowledge of international markets, Schroders would add its name to obligations issued by lesser-known firms and banks in the international field. By improving the credit of those obligations with the addition of Schroders' promise to pay if the original promissor or issuer did not, the obligations could be financed more cheaply. Schroders would be paid a fee for this endorsement. It seemed crazy to me that we would be paid to add our credit to obligations of Japanese banks such as Mitsubishi and Mitsui in order to allow them better access to this market. But at the time they were a less well known credit in the market of buyers, and they needed the extra promise of an established bank like Schroders—even though they were many times larger than we were.

I was on the road so much that in 1973, I was given my London make-believe title, chairman of Schroders International, as a sort of overseas calling card. Travel was exhilarating and exhausting. I was so drained that on my fortieth birthday in December 1973, I called Elaine to say I did not have the energy to celebrate. In those days, birthdays somehow depressed me, and this one seemed particularly heavy to me. I used my birthdays to reflect on my life, and at the end of four decades I felt confused and in some way unfulfilled. I was too busy on all fronts, frenetic in my approach to life, and certainly without balance or vision. All I wanted to do on this occasion was to hide and go to bed. I got home feeling very low.

My mood changed as I was greeted by a dozen or more of our closest friends, whom Elaine had organized for a surprise birthday party. The children were very excited and, before going to bed, brought in the three cakes that they had prepared for me. When I tried to cut the first cake, I couldn't move the knife. They had iced an upside-down cake tin! They carefully presented a second cake to me, this one beautifully iced in chocolate. On slicing this cake, there was an explosion and bits of chocolate-covered balloon flew all over our lovely living room. By this time I was out of my depression. The third cake was delicious.

*   *   *

These years in New York confirmed my belief, nurtured in London, that to be bearable, a business life must be something more than deal making. A career has to be pursued in a social and cultural context. For me, music was the arena in which I could most easily and frequently mix with both friends and colleagues. I began to find ways to mix business with pleasure and welcomed the opportunity to give back to the community in which we lived.

One of my first jobs at the bank was to oversee the move of Schroders' New York operations from the Cunard Building at 25 Broadway, where the lease had expired, to smart new premises at One State Street, adjacent to Battery Park, at the southernmost tip of Manhattan. This building had been developed and was owned by Zev Wolfson, a successful property developer who would be making his office in the building. Some of my colleagues suggested the space was too large, but I insisted we needed room to expand. I also wanted a different look for our offices, something fresher, more modern. I was fortunate that working as secretary of the corporation in New York was Marion Gilliam. He had a deep knowledge of modern art and a natural eye for design. He and his wife, Olivia, belonged to New York's thriving visual arts scene, and together they transformed the space. With a limited budget of $20,000–$30,000, they chose works of art and modern prints that evoked a sense of quality beyond the price we paid. Thereafter, every year we added an equivalent sum to the budget for artwork and over the years built a fine collection of modern art while supporting young artists.

Rather than throwing a traditional opening party for the new offices, I staged a concert for our clients and guests, including Gordon Richardson and other London colleagues who had flown in for the occasion. Several musician friends joined us, as well as Sol Hurok, the legendary impresario. Some months prior to the opening, I had called Vladimir Ashkenazy and asked: "How would you like to be the first Soviet artist to open a Wall Street bank?" He immediately agreed. It was something of a coup. Schroders was a relatively minor institution without a lot of pull in New York; yet we literally had demands from around the world for invitations to the opening. The event was an absolute success, different from anything I have attended before or since on Wall Street. It took place in the uncompleted banking hall, which we covered in Astroturf and filled with trees to create the impression of spring. We placed a Steinway in our fabricated garden, and after the recital we moved on to dinner in another part of the building, where guests remained until after midnight.

As my life in New York developed, I felt more and more drawn to public service. I wanted professional success in the United States, but I also wanted something beyond it, something that could not be measured in financial terms. I could see that by participating in public service, not only would I contribute to particular causes, but I could broaden my experience and knowledge.

Of course, I understood that as an outsider, public service would help me to integrate into my new society. But as I became involved, I began to recognize the close link between work done for cultural and philanthropic purposes and the responsibility of business as practiced in the United States. This insight changed my whole attitude to life, and it developed in me, and in my family, a whole new approach to setting personal objectives that could not be measured in monetary or egocentric goals alone. I began to believe that business cannot exist without involvement in the community and, indeed, that business has a responsibility to contribute to the strength and quality of the community in which it operates.

My role model was David Rockefeller, who was already playing an important role in my life. Over the years, Elaine and I developed a devoted friendship with him and his remarkable wife, Peggy.

Sometime after my arrival at Schroders, David called and asked if I wanted to join a group of people intent on saving the U.S. Custom House, the great Beaux Arts edifice near Battery Park, designed by Stanford White's assistant, Cass Gilbert. The other committee members—among them John Loeb, Cyrus Vance, Whitney North Seymour, and Gus Levy— were at a level of leadership in Wall Street that was way beyond me. But they needed someone who was willing to roll up his sleeves and who would bring a fresh look to the project because they didn't have the time. It was a good marriage. They were happy to have someone take responsibility for the work, and it was a privilege for me, as a relative newcomer on Wall Street, to work with them. I threw myself into the project, and as I was already involved with Carnegie Hall, I managed to organize concerts similar to the one I'd held at the Schrobanco opening. Somewhere along the way I also picked up the idea that the U.S. Custom House would be a great place for the establishment of a New York branch of the American Indian Museum. The concept took on a life of its own, and later, with the guidance of the late senior senator from New York, Daniel Patrick Moynihan, we managed to secure $20 million in funding from the federal government to save the building from commercial development and designate it as an artistic and cultural center for the downtown area.

My long involvement with Carnegie Hall, which was to become my spiritual home, had its origins in the summer of 1958, when I was a young Australian student and knew almost no one. The lawyer Peter Rosenblatt and his wife, Naomi, had taken me under their wing. They invited me to their apartment in the Beresford in New York, where I met Larry Leeds, whose family owned the Manhattan Shirt Company, and his wife, Dalia. I met Larry again after moving to New York to run Schroders. Knowing of my interest in music, he asked if I would care to join him on the Carnegie Hall board. I was delighted.

As soon as I joined, I discovered that Carnegie Hall was an institution under great strain, with many of its traditional performers leaving for more modern venues like Lincoln Center. It was running at an annual deficit of $60,000–$80,000. Today this seems like a paltry sum, but at the time it was a big problem for the board. Unlike other fashionable New York causes, such as the Metropolitan Opera, Carnegie did not have a Citibank or a JP Morgan as benefactor. It was only the brave work of Isaac Stern, his wife, Vera, and a few civic leaders that stood between that historic venue and the wrecker's ball.

Along with Isaac, at the epicenter of the effort to save the physical and musical life of Carnegie Hall was the experienced administrator Julius Bloom. They needed someone with additional experience and reach in finance and business. This provided a perfect opportunity for me to become a full partner in the enterprise of restoring the hall to its former glory. Isaac and I worked on the project, led by the chairman, Richard Debs. Debs was then the number two man at the New York Federal Reserve under Paul Volcker. He was extraordinarily devoted to the cause, but because of his official position, he was limited in what he could do in fund-raising. It was plain that Carnegie was resting on its laurels. While other venues, including the recently built Lincoln Center for the Performing Arts, were raising large amounts of cash, Carnegie was struggling. Among other things, I was able to advise Ron Gerrity, then controller, on how to produce proper budgets and how to make a presentation to the board that would help its members understand the dire condition of the hall's affairs.

Carnegie was groping for a purpose and essentially counting on being the venue for visiting orchestras and international artists who could not be accommodated at Lincoln Center because of conflicts in the use of the concert hall by the New York Philharmonic, which made its home there. But the trend clearly was downward, and many prominent performers were beginning to go to other venues. Physically, Carnegie Hall was challenged. It was an old building and little had been spent by its private owners on maintenance. It had ancient, creaking elevators, which I always feared would crash to the ground, and a roof that leaked like a sieve each time it rained hard. Its greatest weakness was that in spite of the heroic efforts of Isaac Stern, it was losing its central role in New York's cultural and social life. It was no great coup to find myself in charge of its finances.

Still, while Carnegie may have lost its luster for New Yorkers, for me it represented the essence of quality in music. I relished the chance to be part of a turnaround—if we could manage it. We organized downtown meetings at the impressive offices of Dick Debs, at the Federal Reserve Bank of New York. Isaac loved to sit with his feet up on the desk in Dick's office, where vital decisions about the nation's finances were made. He would make phone calls to friends and associates and tell them that he was in a meeting at the Fed. The work I did with Isaac and Dick gave me two irreplaceable gifts. It gave me a "family" in New York—we were never further away than an almost daily telephone call—and it gave me a cause that would become central to my life and my being, in New York and in the broader world of music and the arts.

But even while I was happy and challenged and could feel myself becoming embedded in New York, somewhere in the back of my mind I had not stopped dreaming about life across the ocean, where the possibility of fulfilling my own—and my father's—aspirations lay. Going back to London and making it to the top in one of the major banking houses would finally bring closure. Unbeknownst to me, the scene was already being set for a future power struggle in London, with Gordon Richardson beginning his journey to the governorship of the Bank of England.

8

———— ⚬⚬⚬ ————

THE OUTSIDER

In July 1973, Elaine and I took a rare break from the mayhem of New York and Schroders. We were sailing on a seventy-two-foot ketch from Panama to the Galapagos as the guests of Dick Dusseldorp, our friend and business colleague from Australia. The voyage was memorable, and the night watches, along with the stars and accompanying dolphins and occasional whales, were an experience never to be forgotten. The only link to the rest of the world was a radiophone, which Dick made clear was only to be used in emergencies. On the seventh day, when we arrived in the islands, my need to be in touch with my other life overwhelmed me. I checked in with New York to ensure that in my absence Schrobanco had not been shut down. As I sat on the stern of the boat, looking out onto the Pacific, I heard the voice of our Swiss-born senior vice president, Martin Witschi.

"How are things going?" I asked.

"Oh, sterling's been devalued by 5 percent," came his calm reply.

This in and of itself was a huge event for Schrobanco; it meant that we had at risk millions of pounds in foreign exchange. It also meant we had already lost a substantial sum on a deal we were doing. But the real shock was still to come.

"And Gordon Richardson has just been made governor of the Bank of England. He's asking where you are," Witschi added casually.

I was stunned. I felt like my world was falling apart. I was thrilled for Gordon that in a financial emergency, the Tory government[1] had turned to him to take charge of the Old Lady of Threadneedle Street, as the bank is known, one of the most important jobs in international finance. But it also meant the loss of the man who had given me freedom and support in Schroders London and then New York to develop a global business. He would no longer be there to promote our shared interests in international expansion.

I had absolutely no idea how the succession at Schroders would pan out, or what it would mean for me. I guessed that Richardson's departure might not be in my long-term interests, but I had no sense of the potential impact it could have on the firm and my position in it. The deep-seated insecurities that had driven me so much of my life began to resurface.

I immediately called Gordon and, at his request, made my way back to London several days later after a brief visit to the islands. It took eighteen hours and difficult flight connections through Ecuador to return to New York, but within the week I was in London, embroiled in talks with Lord Franks, Schroders' senior non-executive director and former British ambassador to the United States. Reorganization was already underway. As was widely expected, Michael Verey, who had been chairman of Schroder Wagg, had been elevated to group chairman. Verey was very much a figure from the bank's establishment past. He was a safe choice, as he had spent four decades banking in the city and had a string of important outside directorships, at British Petroleum, Commercial Union,[2] and Boots. He had been the main dissenter during the 1962 merger with Helbert Wagg & Co. and felt his colleagues had not been fairly treated. There was little love lost between him and the controlling Schroder family, and despite Bruno's support, Verey treated him with disdain. The board made clear to Verey, who was sixty, that he would be expected to retire when he was sixty-five.

Leslie Murphy, who was appointed as deputy chairman at the same time, remembers Verey as having "an extremely valuable nose" that scented the way the wind was blowing on most things. He followed his instincts and was a money maker for the firm. Soon after his appointment, Verey told the *Banker* magazine that his goal was to expand the group's international capability. The reality turned out differently. It seemed he was most comfortable in the confines of London.

The Earl of Airlie, David Ogilvy, who was to become my friend and main rival, was slotted into Verey's old job as chairman of Schroder Wagg. I was reconfirmed as president of Schroders Inc., the holding company for all of the American interests and chief executive of the operating U.S. subsidiaries, Schrobanco (J. Henry Schroder Banking Corporation) and Schrotrust (Schroder Trust Company). The post at Schroders International given to me by Gordon some years earlier was also confirmed in my list of grand-sounding titles. This position lacked substance, but it kept me in the middle of expansion plans for the group. Still, my future was not settled. Unbeknownst to me and much to the annoyance of Verey, Murphy had persuaded the board that within a short period of time, I should return to London with broad group responsibilities.

This initiated a power struggle among all the group entities. Without a clear sense of the hierarchy, or of the scope and reach of each of the Schroder entities, a conflict was bound to emerge. No sooner was Gordon out the door than the traditionalists moved into the ascendancy. They regarded London as the core of the business, and the deft decision to elevate David Ogilvy out of fund management to run Schroder Wagg, the group's central business in London, should have been a flashing red light to me. My London colleagues continued to believe that the American operation had become a "positive liability." They felt that its Latin American lending and ever-weaker position against expanding international and American competition was reducing its competitive position, and that it would never recover its former role. They were also not fully convinced of the profitability and potential of the foreign subsidiaries, the earnings of which were still well below the London business. "Richardson's Court" was in retreat.

Lord Franks, however, gave me hope of greater things to come. We met quietly at the Schroders apartment on Lowndes Square, well away from the prying eyes and city rumor mill. Oliver told me that the board felt it would soon be time for me to return to London to be group chief executive and deputy chairman. My new post would give me an administrative responsibility for all of Schroders' activities, both domestically and around the globe, and a key role in strategy and policy. I questioned Oliver on the scope of the post. It was absolutely clear that Michael Verey was the chairman, and whatever they called me, he was, as he should have been, the number one person in the group. I had seen even so powerful a figure as Gordon challenged as chairman of Schroders by Verey when he ran Schroder Wagg. I knew of Gordon's frustrations in not having all the levers of power. His wife, Peggy, later said that he loved being at the Bank of England, despite the scale of the national crisis he faced. In his position there, people were anxious to find out what he wanted and to help him, which she judged to be in stark contrast to Schroders.

I shared these fears with Lord Franks during our Lowndes Square conversation. If I were to be group chief executive and deputy chairman, I would not have line authority over New York or London because they would each have their own chairman. I would also have Verey sitting above me as group chairman. This was not a good position to go into, as it meant I would have a great title but no levers of power. It would also mean a great deal of personal sacrifice. My children, who had settled well into New York, would have their schooling disrupted again. And to my great surprise, there would be a substantial salary cut. In New York I was earning close to $200,000 a year, whereas in London the salary would be a little more than half of that. Having voiced all of these concerns to Oliver, I asked the crucial question.

"Does this mean I will be chairman after Verey?"

Oliver replied that no decision had yet been made. "But," he said, "there is a fair wind behind the boat," and I could expect to be chairman.

I was elated. Becoming chairman of Schroders would be the pinnacle of my career. It seemed the "brass ring" was within my grasp. It would allow me to bring together under one respected franchise a myriad of ideas to create a world-class investment bank based in London. But I had to make it clear to Franks that the expectation of becoming chairman was the only basis on which I would return to London. I had to be sure that he was speaking as the senior spokesman for the board. It was only on these grounds that I would talk the matter over with Elaine.

"Oliver," I said. "Are you telling me that in asking me to return, you're speaking for the entire board?"

"Yes, Jim. I am conveying to you the sentiment of the board."

With hindsight, I should have been more careful in analyzing what Oliver had said to me. There was a hint of caution in his tone, but at the time, all I heard was the suggestion that I would become chairman after Michael's retirement. Oliver, after all, was a former senior civil servant par excellence. Such people are tutored in the art of obfuscation. Neither the sparse boardroom minutes of Schroders nor its official history provided formal backup for Oliver's offer. It was a casual agreement, and I should have taken nothing for granted. But I went home to Elaine certain we had a move to discuss.

I knew it would not be an easy conversation. Going back to London would mean our fourth major move, with all the usual upheaval, dislocation, and strain on the family. With my endless traveling, Elaine had spent a huge amount of time alone, settling the children into the American school system. She was wary of another move, but in the end we managed to agree that this was an opportunity not to be missed. Notwithstanding our hopes, somehow it did not feel like this would be the last time we moved. So we kept our small house in upstate New York as a base in the United States and began to prepare ourselves for our return to our much-loved house on Pelham Crescent.

*   *   *

Although Elaine and I had sensed London was changing, neither of us fully appreciated how dramatic that change had been when we left New York in September 1975. Culturally and economically, London had become somber, and we barely recognized the city we had enjoyed in the Swinging Sixties. At the Bank of England, Richardson was fighting to maintain financial stability on several fronts. A crisis among Britain's fringe banks had become so serious that at one point it threatened the future of National Westminster, one of the biggest commercial banks in the country. Richardson had to launch a "lifeboat," funded by the biggest banks, to keep the financial system from sinking. Not surprisingly, he turned to his former colleagues for help in organizing the rescue package.

Successive governments had been waging a losing battle to preserve the value of the pound on the foreign exchanges amid fierce selling pressure. The crisis would come to a head in the fall of 1976, when the government of Jim Callaghan[3] would face the humiliation of having to apply to the International Monetary Fund (IMF) for assistance. Industrial relations were in an appalling state, and a confrontation with Edward Heath's Tory government and the power unions had led to the nation working a three-day week.

When our family arrived in London, the gloom over the city was reflected in the sad state of Pelham Crescent. Our diplomat tenants had destroyed the house. We had decorated it simply and elegantly, but none of our work had been saved. They destroyed the walls and so damaged the flooring that the entire house needed to be redone. Elaine fell ill almost as soon as we arrived, and doctors had some difficulty diagnosing the problem. Finally, she had an operation to remove both her appendix and a very large ovarian cyst. She was in the hospital for two weeks, which was terrible for her and frightening for both me and the children.

Our spirits were low, and when friends from the United States started visiting, full of warmth and energy, we began to have second thoughts about the move. For the children, it meant adjusting to yet another school. Although St. Paul's Girls' School had accepted Sara, we decided she should go to Queens College so she would have more time to practice her beloved piano. She was twelve, and it must have been a difficult move for her; this was her fifth school and the fifth time she had to make new friends. Naomi went to Redcliffe School, in Redcliffe Gardens, which was a disappointment after her school in New York. We decided to send Adam, now five years old, to Wetherby, where he was placed with four-year-olds because the British thought Americans did not learn to read until they were six. Adam already read with total fluency and very quickly moved through the first, second, and third class—completing three grades in one year.

On top of these adjustments the children had to make, I immediately had to leave them alone in London with their new nanny. While Elaine was still recuperating from the operation, we went with two couples from Schroders—David Forsyth and his wife, and Anthony and Jenny Loehnis—to work with the Bank of China on the country's first international financing deal.

We traveled to Canton and Peking, as they were then called, and as guests of the Bank of China, we were treated magnificently. Each couple was assigned a car and driver, and it seemed we were the only cars on the road, surrounded by thousands of cyclists of all ages. In those days, the Chinese wore loose-fitting, dull Mao uniforms—except for the children, who were dressed in bright colors. It was an extraordinary time to visit China. Mao and Zhou Enlai were still alive. Driving in the country, we inquired about the many truckloads of cabbages we saw on the road that were stopping at individual houses and unloading their produce. We were told that this was the winter food supply for rural families. The cabbages were stored under the roofs of their tiny cottages or in the small, crowded rooms in which most of the citizens lived.

It was a memorable experience, visiting the largest country in the world—with such a rich culture and history—and seeing the profound effects of its experience with communism, which seemed to make everything dull and without contrast. We were moved by the people in government whom we met and by their desire to make life better for the Chinese people. The business purpose of our visit was to lay the groundwork for a

$130-million financing deal for the purchase of wheat. I think we all felt the latent economic power that existed, but none of us could have conceived the growth that would occur in China in subsequent decades. We sensed that something important was beginning, however, and we learned much from our Chinese government friends about the way their system operated. Later, we were able to implement this initial financing successfully. More important, I think that we were able to aid the Chinese officials in their understanding of the requirements of the international markets in which they were later to play such an important part.

We had a wonderful multilingual guide who had once been a senior official in the foreign ministry but had been demoted during the Cultural Revolution. He was working his way back to respectability and acceptance as a translator. Early in the trip, after we had established a good rapport, he asked me a question.

"Is Jascha Heifetz, your greatest violinist, still alive?"

"Yes, he is living in California," I said. "Actually, there has recently been a reissue of a collection of his greatest recordings."

He looked at me.

"I would be thrilled to send them to you," I continued.

He paled. "Do not do that ever! Ever!" he said firmly, shaking his head.

I realized later that one of the causes of his demotion—and the ransacking of his house, and the destruction of his books and recordings—had been his interest in Western culture. It would endanger him if I sent him the recordings. He was so upset by my gesture that for the next few days he hardly spoke to me, fearing I would do something else inappropriate. It was a sad thing to see.

On the last day, as we were driving to the airport, I leaned over to him in the back of the car and said: "I am so sorry that I scared you with my suggestion. I hope you will forgive me. Please do not worry. I will not do anything silly."

The translator did not respond, but he took my hand and started to sing the opening theme of the final movement of Beethoven's violin concerto. We looked at each other and embraced to say good-bye. I saw tears in his eyes, and I began to cry, too.

*   *   *

When we returned to London, the difficulties of my position at Schroders immediately surfaced. As group chief executive without any clear or definable mandate to give substance to the title, I found myself responsible, among other things, for dealing with the needs of my fellow directors. They approached me constantly about their meager salaries. Would they get a company car? What would their pension be? Most of my London colleagues were living in the country and therefore couldn't stay late at the office. During a day at work, they were offered lunch served from silver trays by well-trained waiters in black jackets and striped trousers, in contrast to the more modest conditions in their homes. The fact that their colleagues in the New York office were far better remunerated was a source of constant dissatisfaction. The truth was that even these British directors, many of whom were my friends, were not under my control. They reported to the chairman of the U.K. business, and there was little I could do to improve their situation. Nonetheless, I became a target for their complaints.

I could not find my feet. On paper, my new job looked important, but in reality it was not. My official job description was "to direct, control, and supervise the activities of Schroders Limited in all parts of the world and co-ordinate the activities of the executive directors of Schroders." Although Mark Maged stepped up to be president of Schrobanco in New York, I retained some hold over the American operation as chairman. Mark reported to me from New York, and Airlie reported from London. But Airlie's lifelong friendship with Verey meant that even though I was in the middle of their document flow, I had no authority. I was never consulted on important decisions. I had all the appurtenances of power—the corner office on the executive floor, access to the best dining rooms, a

Daimler car and chauffeur assigned to me—but I had no real job. I traveled widely. I would be wheeled out for some state occasions and introduced to clients. Everyone made a fuss, but the truth was that I was little more than a figurehead, and not even that for many of my British colleagues.

In the first twelve months, I crossed the Atlantic twenty times, in addition to making trips to Venezuela, the Middle East, and Australia. I told myself that with the world economy and our business changing so rapidly, it was essential to keep in touch, firsthand, with what was happening. But being away meant I was disconnected from what was happening at the heart of the business in London. I was a face to the outside world, particularly the non-British world, and was more involved with policy and strategy for the group than I was in actual business. In any financial organization, the actual transaction of the business is the lifeblood, and my exclusion from our key banking deals should have alerted me to the inherent weakness of my position.

When I found myself not to be part of a big Euromarkets fund-raiser for Imperial Chemical Industries, I became exasperated. ICI was regarded as the bellwether of the London stock market, and where it trod, others would follow. Leslie Murphy had been dispensing financial advice to ICI for many years, and both he and I were kept outside of the transaction. Instead, ICI appropriately talked directly to David Ogilvy as chairman of the London business.

During this tense period, one of the only things that relaxed me and kept me connected to my life outside of work was the cello. Over the years, the relationship Elaine and I had formed with Jacqueline du Pré and Daniel Barenboim at the Reykjavik Festival had deepened into an intimate friendship, and our return to London meant we spent more time together. When we heard, in 1973, that Jackie might have multiple sclerosis, it was a tremendous shock. We were in New York at the time, and she was scheduled to play with Leonard Bernstein in a benefit concert to raise funds for the musicians for the New York Philharmonic Pension Fund. They were to perform the Dvorak Cello Concerto, but during rehearsals she couldn't feel the bow in her hand. Bernstein was upset and could not understand the problem. But it was part of a pattern. Just a week before, Jackie had walked into a lamppost. While doctors tried to find out what was wrong with her, Isaac Stern jumped in that night and played the Brahms Violin Concerto with Lenny, which both of them could do in overdrive. But the cancellation of that appearance was the beginning of the end of her performing career.

Almost two years later, in early 1975, shortly after our return to London, we had dinner with Jackie and Danny at their new house on Rutland Gardens Mews in Knightsbridge, a quiet cul-de-sac on the south side of Hyde Park in London. The previous occupant had been the ballerina Dame Margot Fonteyn, who had adapted the house for wheelchair access after her husband had been paralyzed during an assassination attempt. Jackie had just received confirmation from the consultant neurologist at the London clinic that the severity of her multiple sclerosis would certainly end her concert career. She and Danny were devastated. We sat around the dinner table trying to adjust to this terrifying reality.

"What will I do, what will I do?" Jackie repeated, sobbing. She looked shaken and defeated.

We were silent for a moment. Elaine and I knew there was not much we could do to comfort them, but we wanted to help in some small way. Then I asked Jackie gently, "Why not teach?"

"No one would study with me. I've had some lessons from Bill Pleeth and from Slava. . . . But why would anyone want to study with me?" She had worked with the best teachers—renowned London cellist William Pleeth and Mstislav Rostropovich, the Russian-born cellist, conductor, and pianist.

"Jackie, you are the greatest cellist of your generation. What are you talking about?"

"Oh, no; I could never get students." She shook her head.

"But I would study with you. I can't think of anything more wonderful," I replied.

The following morning, Jackie phoned me at Schroders. Her first words were: "Did you mean what you said yesterday?"

"Of course," I replied.

She clearly had anticipated my reply. "Well, I've found you a cello."

"Shall we meet on Sunday at 3:00 PM?" I suggested.

That Sunday I showed up at her Knightsbridge house with a very inexpensive cello I had acquired from her friend, the great instrument dealer Charles Beare, scion of the Beare family of dealers, famous for restoration of instruments in the violin family.

I had known Jackie as a friend, but having the opportunity to study with someone of her caliber was an unexpected privilege. As we sat down together in her living room, I told her how nervous I was to be there, and I admitted that I was terrified to be studying as a beginner with her. Somehow I was sitting next to one of the world's masters of the cello, with a bow in one hand and a cello in the other. But where would we start? Could I carve out the time and, at the age of forty-one, how would I learn?

Jackie was doing me a tremendous honor, and yet in some ways our lessons would enable me to support her. Before we began, she said that the only condition she set for teaching me was that I must perform in a concert on my fiftieth birthday in 1983. I readily agreed. That was a good eight years away and didn't seem too daunting a challenge or likely ever to happen.

Then she asked what I wanted to play.

"Darling, are you mad? I don't even know how to hold the instrument. What are you talking about?"

"Well, I don't want to teach you unless there is something you really want to play."

"How about Bach's Unaccompanied Cello Suite in G Major?" I offered.

"Fine." And with that she stood up and walked across the room to find the Bach G Major. Placing it on the music stand, she turned to me and said, "Now let's begin."

I must have looked at her in horror. I loved the *idea* of playing the cello. I could read music for the piano and voice, but I had no idea how to translate it for the cello. How did I hold the instrument? Which string was which?

The lessons were always terrible for the first half hour because Jackie insisted that I tune the instrument myself—not an illogical or surprising request. But I could not hear the fifths for tuning between the strings. I'd think that I was on pitch, but by the time I had tuned the A and D strings and was moving on to the G and C, the A would be off pitch. Each time I had to go through this nightmare before she would let me play. I practiced at night and on the weekends, and almost the only things my family heard for the first two years were the "bloody" G Major Suite, scales and exercises, and some of the earliest easy pieces that Jackie's mother had written and illustrated for her when she was three or four years old. But I loved it. Every Sunday afternoon, our family would come back from the country house in West Sussex that we rented for the weekends, and I would go straight to Knightsbridge for my lesson.

Meantime, I was regarded as something of an eccentric in the business world for the way I traveled. On the transatlantic flights, I would arrange to have my cello strapped into the seat next to me. At first I practiced on an undistinguished instrument, which was all I needed. Then one day Charles Beare called again to tell me he had a Guarnerius cello for sale.[4] I managed to find the $60,000 needed to buy it—how I am no longer sure—but it was my greatest purchase, and it is still my pride and joy. In addition, I had the enormous privilege of using Jackie's "Davydov" Stradivarius,[5] which she had asked me to look after for her. I kept her cello in the vault at Schroders, and it was brought up to my office each morning so that I could practice. My office was not entirely soundproof, and I would struggle away with scales before starting my banking day. My colleagues thought this was bizarre, to say the least. I felt guilty for playing in such a primitive way on one of the world's great cellos. This instrument went on to a better life when it was purchased years later by Yo-Yo Ma, who became my good friend and occasional teacher.

*   *   *

Although lost when in the confines of the Schroder London office, I was relaxed and content while traveling. When work took me back to Australia, there was the added bonus of visiting my parents and catching up, however briefly, with my friends. In 1975, at the request of the prime minister of Australia, Gough Whitlam, I flew to Canberra to advise him on what would later become known as the Khemlani Affair. Whitlam's Labour government had been seduced into the astonishing position of trying to borrow billions of dollars with the assistance of a Pakistani loan dealer, Tirath Khemlani. A shadowy figure, Khemlani gained his credibility through working for the respectable London-based commodities firm Dalamai and Sons. He had connections to the Middle East, which was awash with oil money thought to be ready for overseas investment. To me, Khemlani sounded like a con man of the type who would regularly appear, offering fortunes for borrowing or investment if only some fees were paid up front. But miraculously he got the attention of a government grasping at straws. I spent a couple of days trying to talk Whitlam out of working with him and departed feeling very pleased with myself, believing I had succeeded. After I left, Whitlam signed the deal on behalf of the Australian government for a very large borrowing that never transpired. Whitlam was drummed out of office, and Khemlani was revealed as having absolutely no substance.

On this visit in 1975, it seemed only natural to my parents that the prime minister would want to see me. For them, I was the greatest thing that Australia had ever produced; I was their gift to Australian history. This assessment was a source of great amusement to me—and some discomfort—because of the stark contrast to the reality of what was happening to my career in London, despite my lustrous titles.

I had always tried to visit my parents annually, as did Elaine and the children. When I saw my father on that visit, I did not realize how near the end he was, though he was plainly unwell. I had sensed this from his letters, in which his firm handwriting had become shaky. In fact, it would be the last time I ever saw him. My mother was already in and out of a convalescent home, suffering from diabetes. But at last my parents had spent some years during which there was no more financial pressure and they felt at ease with themselves, their friends, and the community. They had me for financial assistance if needed; and for moral and material support, my sister Betty and their grandson, Derek, were living in Sydney. There was a tranquillity and assurance about them now that to some extent made up for the tensions and strains they had experienced throughout so much of their life together. It was in this peaceful condition that I would be able to remember them.

Whenever I returned to Australia, I felt I was coming home. Nothing else could ever replace the feeling in my heart and mind when I walked the streets of Sydney. I loved to retrace my steps along Phillip Street, to walk down Martin Place and visit the location of my first office. I looked at every passerby in the hope of seeing a friend, and amazingly, I could never wander around for long without meeting someone I knew. The small scale of Sydney compared to London or New York gave me a sense of belonging, and the presence of my sister and my parents there naturally made it feel like home. But I had changed as a result of my career, and my mind was not on Australia, even though my heart was still there.

Back in London the temperature at Schroders had dropped several degrees. At best my relationship with Verey was tepid, and I had sensed for some months that he did not want me to follow him as chairman. I was anathema to him, but he put up with me because he was clever enough to recognize that I had helped the group to reposition internationally and to diversify its base. Aside from our different approaches to business, we never connected on a personal level. He was very much a London merchant banker, professional and effective, but our styles and interests were very different. I do not think he appreciated my unconventional behavior—particularly my starting the day with 8:00 AM cello practice. Eventually I heard that Verey was telling colleagues I would only become chairman "over his dead body."

In early December, I received word that my father had died of a heart attack in Sydney. It was a terrible moment. I had only been to one funeral in my life, that of my Uncle Harry in Sydney. Apart from the family, not a soul came to Uncle Harry's interment, and it was a quick and perfunctory affair. I immediately made plans to leave for Australia. I resolved that my father's funeral would be different. I wanted to mourn him in the traditional Jewish way, for seven days. When I arrived at the family apartment, his watch and the few valuables he had owned were gone, though I never discovered who stole them. My mother was now in the convalescent home full-time, and there was no sense of her presence, either. The apartment, which had once been my castle with my toys and records and my life and hopes, had died.

Betty handled all the funeral arrangements with great care and attention. She was the real heroine but allowed me to share fully in everything. Mother was too weak to attend the funeral, and Betty, Derek, and I buried Dad at the Rookwood Cemetery, a few miles from the center of Sydney. Many people came and spoke fondly of my father, including Rabbi Apple, who had recently joined the Great Synagogue, and though he had not known Dad very well, he did his best to sketch his life. For a eulogy, an old family friend, Sir Asher Joel, painted a picture of a man who was charming, almost aristocratic in bearing, and deeply involved in communal life. But no one really captured the texture of my father's life, and none of it touched me. The images that people conjured in their speeches were appropriate for the occasion, but they missed the anguish, struggle, and ultimate severity of his story. In death, the whole great picture of my father's life, full of challenges and missed opportunities and ultimately a level of happiness and well-being, swirled around in my head, seeking some logic or explanation. It struck me that although my father's life had been a disappointment to him, he had always remained an inspiration to me. Apart from driving my ambition, he gave me values that I now hold so dear—education, family, hard work, service, and Judaism. In my eyes, he remained a towering, guiding presence.

I returned to London, planning to take the children to Australia in July to see my mother. But just a few weeks later, we received a call from my old friend in Sydney, Dr. Earl Owen, telling us very simply that we should come sooner if we wished to see her alive, perhaps in March or April. We did, and we had three weeks together. We celebrated the tradi-

tional Passover Seder at the convalescent home. Talkative and in wonderful spirits, my mother rallied for our visit. Two weeks after we left, she
passed away. With a heavy heart and my father's funeral fresh in my mind,
I returned to Australia once again and stood at her graveside. In many
ways, my mother was regarded as the friendlier and more lovable figure in
that marriage, and the funeral was full of admiration and love. I kept
thinking that she would have been proud to hear what was being said.
Again, even as tributes were being made about her public face, I thought
of all the struggles and the sacrifices she made. By the time I flew back to
London, I was emotionally spent.

*   *   *

In June, Lord Franks came into my office to let me know that Michael
Verey would be retiring soon. He indicated that the board wanted a successor who was British, and possibly one with a titled background. I felt
this was a deliberate snub, as indeed it was. True, it was the standard practice to promote the London chairman. But I believed that there had been
a promise strong enough to bring me and the family back to London and
that through that promise, the board had indicated a desire to appoint a
more internationally experienced person.

When Michael Verey informed me later that month that the board
was split on the succession, I was shaken. Franks had promised me a "fair
wind," and I thought the job was mine. I got on a plane and flew to the
United States to our home in Carmel, New York, where Elaine had taken
the children for the summer. After hugging the children, I reported to
her that I did not believe that the chairmanship would come to me, and
that the board of directors would support Airlie, even if the Schroder family and the overseas directors would support my candidacy.

Elaine was upset for me, but level-headed. She had never felt confident that I would get the support of the British board members. So even
though a decision had not yet been reached, we quickly agreed that we
should prepare to leave Schroders for a career elsewhere.

Our conversation soon moved to the practicalities of a return to New York, and we started the old discussion about the impact on the children. I suggested she enroll the children for a September entry in the New York schools. Although I was disappointed, I had the feeling that Elaine was not unhappy. For months she had shared with me the uneasy feeling about our situation in London, and I sensed she wanted to return permanently to New York, where the children could look forward to an undisturbed education—and where we could be more in control of our lives. Still, my gut told me I had at least to put up a fight for the chairmanship as no decision had yet been tendered. Having touched base and prepared my family for the worst, I packed my small bag and went back to London.

The succession battle was complicated. Like so much in Britain, it was conducted behind closed doors. I focused myself and went into the struggle believing that I had a great deal going for me. I represented the expansionist and innovative camp at Schroders. We had carried the group into new areas like the Euromarkets, brought a succession of new clients aboard, rebuilt the New York business so it was no longer solely dependent on commercial banking, and started to establish a global network of activities and offices. We had even managed to do work in China, potentially the world's most valuable future market for financial services.

But my main support was gone. Richardson, once leader of the modernizing camp, made it clear he could not be directly involved. But even without Gordon, I believed that the rest of "Richardson's Court" would be on my side. This included Leslie Murphy, who was soon to leave to join Harold Wilson's National Enterprise Board. Things were tense between Murphy and Verey after Leslie had played a key role in my appointment as group chief executive. Soon after Michael had become chairman, he called Murphy to his office and, according to Leslie, said:

"There's now no job for you. David Airlie is running Schroder Wagg. Jim Wolfensohn is chief executive. What are you going to do? I suggest you become my personal assistant."

Murphy had looked him in the eyes and retorted: "I am deputy chairman of Schroders, and will remain deputy chairman of Schroders until the board decides otherwise." Then he walked out of the room.

My other key supporters included John Bayley and Mark Maged. I believed that Harold Brown and Paul Nitze, the American non-executives who sat on the main Schroders board, were also on my side. Brown later offered a different interpretation of the "fair wind" comment. He saw it as an expectation, not an assurance.

I was certain the Schroder family would not let me down. Bruno and I were still close. Then there was their first cousin John Schroder, who was a shareholder but not in the firm or on the board, and he had never been particularly involved in its affairs. However, Bruno considered John to be a weak link and couldn't guarantee that he could bring his cousin along and muster the 51 percent of the vote necessary to force the board's hand. Bruno wanted to follow the dictum of Lord Asquith, at the turn of the twentieth century, who, when faced with a rebellious House of Lords on a tax bill, merely said he would create more peers until the measure passed. Gowi Mallinckrodt, married to Bruno's sister, Charmaine, and I had become firm friends from the day I arrived in London. But at that time he was not on the main board, and he took the view that the family should steer clear of influencing board deliberations. He later made it clear that he wanted to remain neutral. Bruno felt differently.

In the course of the boardroom schism, Bruno was a tower of strength, a loyal friend who spent many late nights with me at our house on Pelham Crescent as we looked for ways to break the deadlock on my future. Bruno lacked the knockout voting power that could have secured me the chairman's job irrespective of what the rest of the board had thought. I later learned that he resolved that this lack of family control would never happen again.

As with any struggle for power, a number of meetings and cabals were taking place without my knowledge. In the midst of the board debate, Leslie Murphy took a call from Bruno on a Saturday morning in June.

Bruno asked if he and Charmaine could come over for a drink. According to Murphy, he showed them into the living room, where Bruno came directly to the point. He and Charmaine believed I was the best person to succeed Michael. What did he think? As the Schroder family had always seen him as a staunch loyalist, Leslie knew his answer would come as a surprise, and this is what he recalls having said:

> Well, Bruno I would say this to you. Jim's been chief executive for a couple of years. He's had all the opportunity to work with everybody and get them onboard with him. And the one thing that Jim wanted above all else was to be loved. He wanted people to love him, and he wanted prestige. If you appoint him as chairman, as you can clearly do, what will happen to the staff? What will happen to the senior people? A number of them will leave; no doubt about that. You can't run the place, and it is going to be very difficult for Jim against the hostility of the staff. You've got to go along with what the majority of the board wants. As much as I love Jim, I don't think it is a good idea to appoint someone as chairman whom the rest of the board cannot deal with. My advice is to appoint David Airlie, even though I am not sure how well he can do the job.

At the time I had absolutely no idea that Leslie was not supporting me completely, although his judgment might well have been correct. He had been placed in a difficult position. Having worked closely with me for so many years, he had a better appreciation of my skills and character than many others. But as an outsider, drawn from beyond the magic circle, he also recognized the peculiarity of Schroders, the kind of tribal ties that exist inside Britain's establishment.

In the end, when the board came to take a straw vote on the issue, I am told it was seven for me and six for Airlie. Lord Franks, who was running the process, tied up the vote. I was informed that Franks told the board: "Even if there is a one- or two-vote majority, it is not enough."[6] He pointed out that more than half of those in opposition to me were people who ran the businesses—in other words, my support came from the family shareholders and non-executives. That would make it difficult to select me. Bruno, despite his loyalty, was not entirely confident he could deliver the proxies. He was not prepared to risk splitting the family vote and in the process destroy Schroders' independence in the same way that other family-controlled merchants like Flemings and later Morgan Grenfell lost theirs.

I was staying away from the office, camped out in the dining room at Pelham Crescent with a telephone and a sea of papers in front of me. Elaine provided endless cups of tea and food. As the competition reached its climax, my dining room felt like the operations center of a military campaign. The atmosphere was electric. Bruno called often, urging me unrelentingly to carry on the good fight. We were convinced we could still win. Bruno brought in Sir Sydney Templeman, QC, now Lord Templeman and a former lord of appeal, to advise. Templeman also thought the issue could be forced. But by then I had been through enough. I felt totally deflated and couldn't imagine staying on as chief executive and deputy chairman for Airlie. Bruno was greatly distressed when I told him I was giving up and would leave Schroders. He burst into tears in my front hall. It was a moment I would never forget.

Not everyone was as bitterly disappointed. My household had been thrown into a state of upheaval, and my elder daughter, Sara, could sense that the nightmare was coming to an end. Elaine, who by now felt very estranged from everything in London, was relieved and happy to return to New York. What really upset her was that people we had assumed were friends had not supported me. Elaine was stunned by Franks's decision to vote against me and said it had turned her world upside down. She had regarded him as the epitome of integrity, and as a friend, and when he went back on what we considered to be a firm promise, she was so shaken she did not know who to trust anymore.

The words that Franks used when he called me up to inform me of the decision to give Airlie the job still haunt me. "I told you there was a fair wind when I spoke to you after Gordon left. The wind has changed," he said. "It was a fair wind. I never said it was guaranteed."

In retrospect, the choice made by the board does not seem surprising or unreasonable. But at the time, it felt like I'd been punched in the stomach. Although I felt I had been promised the job and had worked diligently to merit the appointment, the core of Schroders was still London based, and the international activities with which I had been identified, while promising, were still to some degree peripheral. The myopia of self-involvement had skewed my vision, and I longed to lead Schroders at a time of historic change in the international financial markets.

There was, to be sure, some personal feeling against me, but basically the board was holding on to an essential conservatism and a desire to ensure that Schroders would maintain its former character. Titles probably weren't the issue. When Oliver and I had that discussion, most likely he was using the British issue as a smokescreen for telling me that David Airlie was going to get the job. They wanted someone who was more in keeping with the history and thrust of the business. Quite simply, I was seen as too big a risk.

The decision to appoint David Airlie turned out to be one of the best things that could have happened to me—and probably to David as well. No longer protected by the comfort of the Schroders environment, no longer served tea on silver platters, no longer recognized because of my position, I was forced to stand on my own two feet. What felt at the time like a major setback was likely the most important moment of my professional life. It undoubtedly allowed me to build a more stable and independent career.

There is nothing like having a mirror set in front of you at a critical stage in life. You might not like what you see, but if you pretend that the image is not there, you are a fool. Elaine and my children softened the image for me and gave me comfort, but the truth of the reflection never left me. I was forty-two years old and had been captured by the professional challenge, and I suppose by the glamour, of the London position. But I had not won the support of my all-important London colleagues. Now, looking in the mirror, I saw an international banker, at a time of profound change in the markets, with a great deal of experience—but with an exalted ego and no job.

My family had already departed for New York, and Elaine was once again scouting for schools and somewhere to live. She wanted the break with London to be clean, so in the middle of the worst British residential property slump in living memory, we sold the remaining leasehold on Pelham Crescent for £18,000 ($40,000). This was contrary to all my instincts never to sell a property. Eighteen months later, the same Pelham Crescent property was sold for £500,000 ($1.25 million). Today it is worth probably $8–$10 million. But we had to cut the cord, and the money from the sale was useful at the time.

Before leaving for New York, I went to see Siegmund Warburg at the Savoy Hotel. On a piece of Savoy letterhead paper, he wrote an aphorism in German that I would keep behind my desk with his photograph wherever I moved: "Those who take disappointments as setbacks don't go further. There are those who treat them as opportunities and profit from them." It was a saying his mother had repeated to him as a child. Siegmund, loyal colleague and friend that he was once he came to accept my early decision to stay with Schroders, immediately asked me to join his bank. He felt it was a mistake for me to have gone to Schroders, a place so alien to my own background and culture. He suggested I become one of the senior people working with my old friend David Scholey at Warburgs. The bank Siegmund had established between the wars had in less than half a century become the City of London's fastest-growing and most sure-footed investment bank. But I was wise enough to recognize that inserting myself into a leadership position alongside David would be a disaster in the making and in all likelihood would destroy a treasured friendship. I thanked Siegmund and declined the offer.

Having given thirteen years of my life to Darlings and to Schroders, I felt I had just been orphaned. On leaving, Schroders gave me $100,000. There was no formal good-bye. Every month thereafter—and to this day—I would receive a £78 ($200) pension, and every time that check arrives it annoys me. But as it turned out, Schroders was my primary school in a business life that was just beginning.

9

⊸⊶⊷

SALOMON BROTHERS AND A NEW YORK-BASED CAREER

IN LOSING THE BATTLE FOR CHAIRMANSHIP OF SCHRODERS IN LONDON, I lost more than a professional dream. My fragile sense of security had been shattered. I had not felt so shaken since childhood. Now I worried that Elaine and the children were the ones anxiously trying to gauge what mood I would be in when I came home. My private hope was to establish my own business with my precious $100,000. But I wasn't ready, and my funds were totally inadequate. Elaine understood this and persuaded me to get some experience in an American financial house. With the help of family and close friends, she gave me enough support to enable me to pick myself up and go about finding a job.

I contacted three people. First, I called Frank Petito, chairman of Morgan Stanley, whom I respected for his important position in the financial community. I had developed a friendship with him during several fishing trips to Alaska, where each of us was the guest of Continental Oil Corporation. Frank could not offer me an immediate partnership at Morgan Stanley, because of a requirement that new aspirants work their passage within the firm for at least twelve months—a rule that was not going to be bent even if he and his partners were to decide that I could contribute. I believed that this was simply his way of letting me down gently. In any case, the door was closed.

Next, I met with David Rockefeller of Chase Manhattan, with whom I had a friendship already more than a decade old. He immediately offered to propose me for a top-level executive post at his bank. David believed that Chase could use my international experience and my contacts, but I felt the offer would take me into commercial banking, when I believed my talents and real interest were more in the field of investment banking. It was the second time Rockefeller had offered me a job. During my Schrobanco stint, he had dangled the top post of Orion Bank in front of me. Orion was one of the new wave of consortium banks focused on international business, but it turned out to be fortunate that I declined. These banks thrived for a while but rapidly exhausted their usefulness as their shareholders entered the business on their own.

Finally, I called Bill Salomon, chairman and senior partner at Salomon Brothers, the dynamic New York investment banking house, at his New York Plaza office. Salomon was a highly tuned trading institution with quick decision-making capabilities. Bill invited me in for a meeting. Although I had never met him before, I knew Bobby Bernhard, a Salomon's partner, through my membership in the Century Country Club, the golf club formed decades before by German-Jewish bankers in New York. Bobby had prepared the ground for me with Bill Salomon, who had earlier doubted that as deputy chairman of Schroders, I would be interested in leaving London to join his firm.

Salomon Brothers was founded in 1910 by three brothers: Arthur, Percy, and Herbert. Initially, Salomon was mainly a brokerage house, matching buyers with sellers and taking a commission and a spread on transactions. It specialized in trading high-quality short-term securities of the kind bought and sold among banks. The brothers were known for their devotion to their work, and when they relocated to 60 Wall Street in 1922, they installed a barber's chair so that they could continue doing business while getting a haircut or a shave. Gradually, the firm became a "discount house," deploying its own resources to buy and sell government and corporate securities. In those days, the firm traded on its conservatism, characterized by its taste in English landscape paintings, Georgian-style chairs, and tables dressed with linens and silver, not unlike the environment at Schroders. Arthur, Percy, and Herbert had watched their father, an established small-scale money broker, separate from their mother, an English-born professional pianist. As a result, in its infancy the firm set great store on the sanctity of marriage and frowned upon divorce.

Percy's son, Bill, joined the bank straight out of prep school in 1933, inheriting many of his early clients from his father. These clients included foreign banks and the stuffier trust companies. In 1957, when he was forty-four, Bill became one of the leading partners in the firm that bore his name and took it upon himself to secure the bank's capital position. He brought in cash-rich, limited partners and in 1964 took on the title of managing partner, effectively becoming the public face of the firm.

Walking into Salomon for the first time, I could see immediately that it was nothing like Schroders. At Salomon there was little patience for ceremony. I entered a huge dealing room, where prices from the New York Stock Exchange and foreign exchanges flashed around the walls. Serried ranks of traders sat with their ears glued to phones and their eyes fixed on their computer screens, buying and selling on behalf of clients and taking risks with the firm's capital. This was the cutting edge of the financial business, and it was new to me.

I was quickly shown into a room with Bill Salomon and his heir apparent, John Gutfreund, who was already running the firm on a day-to-day basis. After about ten minutes of conversation—neither of them liked long meetings—Bill asked if I would like to become one of the firm's managing partners. He suggested the firm needed strengthening in corporate finance activity. Of all the New York investment banks, Salomon held perhaps the preeminent position in trading but needed to develop corporate business, particularly on a global scale. This was an unbelievable offer. Because it did not put me in competition with the existing hierarchy in the firm, it created a win-win situation for us both. Bill suggested that I head the investment banking team and take the additional title of chairman of

Salomon International, yet another fancy title created to give me credibility with international clients. The offer came at the perfect time and simply would not have happened without Bobby Bernhard's support and intervention. He literally changed my life.

Since Salomon was a partnership, I offered to put in my prized $100,000, paid to me by Schroders when I left. By today's standards this may seem a very small sum, but in those days, it was not out of line with severance payments from a U.K. bank, although I admit I thought it quite a small reward for more than a decade with the group. The deal at Salomon was at a totally different level. You made a lot of money, took out what you needed for lifestyle purposes, and left the rest inside the firm to build your capital base. As an incentive to join, I was offered a profit share equivalent to 2 percent of the equity, which was a generous and sizable opportunity if Salomon continued to do as well as it had in the past. In a good year, it would mean I could potentially make several million dollars. I was jumping from a modest U.K. salary to potentially millions of dollars with one leap. This, however, was not an act of charity on the part of Salomon. I was being thrown into the deep end of the toughest business in New York—a business celebrated for its macho culture in Michael Lewis's excoriating 1989 book, *Liar's Poker*. For someone like me who craved financial security, it was a defining moment. The prospect of earning $2–$3 million a year was both scary and exhilarating. I said to Elaine that night, "Darling, I think I'm about to grow up. This is my chance to be in the big leagues. My success or failure will be out there for everyone to see." I felt for the first time that I didn't have a safety net. Whatever I achieved would depend on me alone.

The Salomon partners did not care about my background, my previous job titles, my involvement in Carnegie Hall, or any of my other credentials. They were concerned about my professional competence, how much money I could make for the firm, and how much business I could bring in. This was the end of gentlemanly capitalism for me. I'll never forget my first management meeting. At Schroders, we'd been accustomed to a leisurely 9:30 AM start. We were served tea in our offices by silent, elegant waiters. At Salomon, the managing partners began arriving at 7:30 AM, and by 8:00 AM, the breakfast room was filled with cigar smoke and noise. The waiters, dressed in brown uniforms, served lox and bagels on fine china but were ready to provide any other breakfast a partner desired. Indeed, the kitchen was open all day to meet any request. The room was full of activity. Discussions were always brisk and focused on the decisions to be made at the opening of the markets that morning. There was no time for lengthy analysis or thoughtful debates. These were decision-making meetings; advice was given to the partners concerned, and it was up to them to decide quickly and act. If either Bill or John intervened, his opinion was rarely crossed.

At Salomon you got what you saw. If people thought you were wrong, they would tell you. If they thought you had done badly, they would tell you. And if you did well, they compensated you generously. There was a marvelous directness, and to my surprise, I found that I loved the freedom from the formal environment of London. The firm was a total meritocracy and completely pragmatic. If you wanted to raise $1 billion, the partners would take the risk of a successful fund-raising, price the transaction, and place the issue as quickly as possible. You would choose a course of action in the morning, and in the afternoon, the deal would be on. If you were going after a particular company or fund manager as a client, you gave the word, and the whole machine would kick into gear. There were no long tactical discussions, no board meetings, few committee meetings, no formal papers—just speed, professionalism, and a unique risk-taking capacity. The firm's efforts were entirely directed toward doing good, ethical, profitable business. Bill was the soul of what went on, and John was leader. However, everything was not always smooth and loving. Sometimes there were fights and raised voices, and occasionally bad decisions on trading or the direction of the markets would be made. But there was an inner integrity and real "guts." Everyone stood or fell by the quality of the business done. And it was a real team.

I learned a lot from my partners. John Gutfreund was a trader with nerves of steel but also a man of reflective interest. He was a historian and, in my early days, seemed to do very little socially other than play tennis on the weekends. I never got to know him very well, but I always admired him. I had the impression that he would go home most evenings to read history and literature and come back the next morning to do battle on Wall Street. Many of my Salomon partners were from very ordinary backgrounds; they had more or less come off the Staten Island Ferry with no degree but had made managing partner. It was an incredible group of people, among whom was Mike Bloomberg, a highly educated man who later became the founder of the multibillion-dollar financial information service and news network—and mayor of New York City. Mike was an extraordinary innovator and computer expert who anticipated a whole industry by providing Salomon's traders with the information they needed to make quick and informed decisions.

I also worked with Ira Harris, a Salomon partner from Chicago, who had been doing most of Salomon's corporate finance work before I arrived. Ira was—and still is—unique in his method of doing business. Creative, loyal, and full of ideas, he developed a group of clients who became his business associates and his personal friends. Somehow he managed to amass a wealth of market intelligence from within the firm and from his many contacts outside and, using intuition and experience, seemed to anticipate clear needs of clients and develop and propose solutions. He became an institution in the business.

In my first month at Salomon, the income report came in, and we discovered that we had sustained a loss of some millions of dollars as a result of trading activities. All I could think of was that after this event, my $100,000 was worth less. I asked my partners how such a thing could happen. But I quickly realized that no one was talking about the loss. There are always ups and downs in risk-taking businesses, and the key is staying cool and balanced. I never asked a question like that again. We ended the year with a comfortable profit, and on paper, my share was as predicted, more than $1 million. I took out a generous amount and, with the remainder still in the business, started to build my net worth, for the first time in my life.

The early 1980s was a period of intense rivalry among the New York firms and the first massive accumulation of money by the partners. The competition for business was fierce, and the innovative skill on Wall Street was staggering to me. The firms didn't just beat each other up on an established playing field with established products—banking was changing at a rapid pace and was becoming international in its outreach and complexity. The emerging trading markets throughout the world changed the very nature of American firms, which now had to be global to survive, and the technology and capital were there to allow it to happen. We were seeing the beginning of the era of putting a firm's capital at risk, on a big scale, in order to participate in a global game. Markets were growing at an unprecedented speed, in large part because of new computer technology, which linked all the markets in real time.

My first year in a real Wall Street business was an eye-opener. I was awed by the sheer scale and the tremendous power wielded. I had a great deal to learn about this style of business and about the New York market. In all my years at Schroders in New York, I had hardly touched the surface of the business Salomon was conducting. I now wanted both to learn and to contribute my experience to the growth of my new firm, in investment banking domestically and, in particular, by expanding our client base and funding sources internationally.

*   *   *

On the home front, Elaine and I set about installing ourselves in New York. My investment in Salomon had eaten up all my liquidity, and we needed a place to rent. At the time, Elie and Marion Wiesel, friends from our earlier New York days—and already community and literary leaders—were also looking for an apartment and had seen a place on Eighty-second Street and Fifth Avenue. It did not suit them, but they generously offered it to us. We quickly accepted. Although the address was impeccable, and it was a large apartment with twelve rooms, the building was run-down. Sitting directly opposite the Metropolitan Museum, it was apparently considered too bustling and noisy. Elaine and I loved the fact that it overlooked the Met; the idea that we could walk across the street and see any exhibition we wished made us giddy. And best of all, we did not have to buy it; we could rent. Within a couple of years, the owner of the apartment building decided to turn it into a cooperative, and we had the good luck to be able to buy the apartment for what today seems an unbelievable price: $86,000. As the value of the apartment rose, I calculated that it was more than making up for our loss on Pelham Crescent. In subsequent years, we have taken pride in Elie's reputation in literature and beyond and were delighted when he won the Nobel Prize.

Sara was elated with our return to New York, Naomi was not anxious to return as she was happy at her London school, and Adam was disappointed. He had been born in London and loved it there. It was not easy for any of the children to pick up the pieces again. Through all the moves, however, they did have Elaine as the solid and ever-present center of their lives. I indulged in the occasional flourish of extravagance, but frugality was the order of the day for the children. Although the transition was difficult for them, they were developing their characters in a more complete way. Sara was a sensitive, gifted, and intelligent girl with great musical and artistic talent. Naomi was witty, strong-willed, and extremely intelligent, and school work came very easily to her. Adam was an inquisitive, quick, and balanced young child who was adored by his sisters and brought a great deal of fun to the family. Under Elaine's guidance, we were building a stable family unit because we did not have to think about further geographic dislocations. We were finally settling into New York as our home and felt blessed to have three warm, giving, and lovable children.

At Salomon, I knuckled down to the task of reorganizing and building the corporate finance department. Apart from the singular work done by Ira Harris in Chicago, Salomon was not taken seriously as a corporate advisory firm. I set myself two goals. The first was to use my contacts to build the advisory business. The second was to look at the clients we represented on a trading level to see whether these relationships could be developed for broader activities in issuance of securities or in merger and acquisition work. I put a team together, and we worked to create an approach that would develop existing personal relations with corporate leaders, provide excellent service, and compete with the best investment banking houses.

Ira had understood completely the linkage between corporate finance activities and trading. Over the years, he had established a close friendship and working relationship with another of our New York senior partners, Richard Rosenthal, who ran the trading operations of the firm. Ira and Dick would speak three times a day, and this was the key to the success of our investment banking business in the New York and Chicago offices. Dick was a master at analyzing the markets and at implementing strategies both to trade and to uncover fund-raising and acquisition opportunities for corporations. Together, he and Ira developed the ideas, and then Ira would carry the principal responsibility of selling the ideas to our client.

It was my job to build a more institutional business for the firm and take it beyond these two remarkable people. Working closely with Gutfreund; Dick Schmeelk, the master of the Canadian business; and Henry Kaufman, Salomon's famed chief economist, we gradually built up a client list. Among the most significant clients we brought in was the Hong Kong and Shanghai Banking Corporation. I benefited from having had contacts in Hong Kong for many years, and for a time, Salomon enjoyed the status of being the most important foreign investment bank operating in Hong Kong.

The Hong Kong and Shanghai Banking Corporation, with one of the most developed franchises in the Far East, had a farsighted management that was looking to the end of the British lease on the colony and the transfer of sovereignty back to Beijing. Accordingly, the bank was anxious to secure further geographic sources of income beyond the booming colony. We helped to arrange its first substantial North American foray with the purchase of New York's Marine Midland Bank. We also assisted the Hong Kong Bank in its purchase of an initial stake in Britain's Midland Bank, which needed a new cash-rich shareholder after losing money in an investment in Crocker National Bank in California. The relationship with London's Midland Bank would eventually become the lever that would lead to HSBC, and would move the Asian bank's domicile and regulatory home from Hong Kong to London. The relationship with the Hong Kong Bank also opened the door for us to advise Jardine Matheson, one of the dominant trading firms in the Far East, with tentacles stretching across the globe. For me, this was a return to old friends, as that firm had been a shareholder in Darlings.

To become a leader in corporate finance, we had to be willing to take risks based upon our own capital and our capacity to raise money—and to deal in markets around the world. By any standard, Salomon Brothers was in the first rank of trading and risk taking. The trick was to use this reputation and skill to reach new corporate clients. Our biggest domestic catch as a client was IBM, or Big Blue, regarded as the bellwether of the New York Stock Exchange. One of our most creative partners in the firm, Jon Rotenstreich, came up with the idea of a major fund-raising issue of securities, and Morgan Stanley, which had previously been IBM's main investment banker, rejected the idea of working jointly with us. This was an important turning point, because of Jon's perceptiveness and skill. IBM dropped Morgan Stanley and gave us the business. Salomon was at long last making its mark as a full-range investment bank with a strong corporate advisory business. With our reputation for innovative fund-raising and problem solving, we then won what turned out to be one of the most challenging corporate financial tasks ever undertaken by an investment bank—the reorganization of the near-bankrupt car manufacturer Chrysler.

Months earlier, in the summer of 1979, Chrysler was in crisis. The first public indication of trouble came when the company asked the Carter administration to provide it with $1 billion in federal aid. Chrysler claimed its problems stemmed partly from the burden of government regulation, such as limits on exhaust emissions. That was true, but in reality, the majority of its problems arose from corporate mismanagement on a major scale, grandiose expansion plans that had fizzled, bouts of optimism that were never fulfilled, and sapped confidence among employees and distributors. This was exacerbated by severe gasoline shortages and price increases in the wake of the 1973 Yom Kippur War and the Iranian Revolution. Chrysler's crisis was significant for the company and its shareholders, but it was also extremely important to the image of the U.S. economy internationally. Would the "Big Three" become the "Big Two"?

The business walked through our door in the form of Lee Iacocca, the legendary boss of Chrysler. He came to Bill and John, and they assigned the job to me. Lee was a flamboyant personality and a great marketer with very little time for the financial side of the business. He valued sales, marketing, new design concepts, product quality, and sheer brash leadership. When he was hired to salvage Chrysler in 1978, he confronted a company that had in recent years fired most of its designers and engineers in order to save money. This was not a brilliant strategy. The people on his staff were expert for normal financial market conditions, but understandably they lacked experience in financial workout-type situations. They would learn quickly. Iacocca viewed people like me and his finance director as a necessary evil. But he saw the big picture: the huge power of the automobile in the United States. He also saw the immense political and human implications of Chrysler's going under—both in terms of Detroit and for the country. And he relished the opportunity to demonstrate his individual leadership.

Working with Lee to save Chrysler was a tremendous challenge and a unique experience in modern business and politics. For its time, it would be the most massive government bailout of an industrial corporation in the history of American commerce, and it would involve a global community of lenders, the trade unions, and the U.S. Congress. As an adviser at the hub of Chrysler's restructuring, I found myself working with the Treasury and the global financial leadership, and it was an invaluable experience. At stake were not just billions of dollars, but thousands of jobs in the automobile industry that was one of the pillars of American, and indeed global, business. Also vulnerable were the many companies that were suppliers to the manufacturers and the massive dealership network. The rescue was vital to Carter's Democratic administration, buffeted as it was by an energy crisis, surging inflation, a falling dollar, and the Iranian hostage crisis. Treasury Secretary G. William Miller, like President Carter, was in favor of the rescue. He was particularly conscious of the position of Detroit's mayor, Coleman Young, who feared a huge unemployment problem for blacks. If there was anything Carter could do to prevent it, Chrysler would not go to the wall on his watch.

Working closely with Chrysler's finance director, Gerald Greenwald, and his associate Robert S. (Steve) Miller, I learned the business of the industry. We were a good team, with Gerry and Steve providing expert industry and financial experience, while my Salomon colleagues and I provided market insights, analytical skills, and experience to support both the reorganization and the new fund-raising efforts. The first and most important decision we made was to attempt the rescue of the company outside of the traditional Chapter 11 bankruptcy route. We made the obvious decision that if we went into bankruptcy, the public would stop buying vehicles, and that would be the end of the company. There had never been a reorganization of a company outside of bankruptcy on this scale. We had to feed new money into the enterprise with a mixture of government, bank, and creditor support. This meant I was thrust into a key role, working alongside Treasury Secretary Bill Miller and Paul Volcker, who was then chairman of the Federal Reserve and had been appointed chairman of the Chrysler Loan Guarantee Board.

The odd thing was that Chrysler, while under enormous financial pressure, was not critically injured. It had sales running at $13.6 billion a year, making it the tenth-largest industrial enterprise in the United States. Only thirteen companies in the world were larger; it fit into the category of firms that are too big to fail. But its profits record was highly cyclical. In 1979, as the rescue operation began, the company was predicting record-breaking corporate losses of $1.7 billion. This was a company that was perennially making the wrong strategy calls. When the public was buying gas guzzlers, Chrysler was producing fuel-efficient vehicles. When the customer was demanding smaller cars, Chrysler was building bigger vehicles. And the company had a cost structure considerably worse than its competitors. Suppliers took 68 cents of every dollar that Chrysler earned, compared with 61 cents at rivals Ford and General Motors.

Rootes, one of its subsidiary operations in Britain, bled the company of $200 million between 1967 and 1975—despite $329 million of subsidies pumped in by the British government.

Although there was an upcoming American presidential election and rescuing Chrysler was critical for Jimmy Carter, the case for a federally backed reconstruction was not motivated by politics alone. A series of studies conducted by consulting groups suggested that regulation had indeed played a key role in the company's problems. The studies showed that federal regulatory costs had suffocated the car firm and damaged the long-term competitive structure of the whole automotive industry. The changes affecting Chrysler and the other car companies were considerable. They included the introduction of air bags and an imposition of tough emissions standards as well as a requirement (subsequently relaxed) that by 1985, cars would get at least 27.5 miles to the gallon. These were important regulations, but they did substantial financial damage to Chrysler and created uncertainty among lenders and financiers about the company's future.

My first trip to Chrysler was enlightening. Until that point, I had known little about the world of the car giants, and I was amazed by both the offices and the culture of these firms. The chief executives of the auto companies were like rulers of large but separate kingdoms. To visit them, you had to walk through an elaborate series of halls and waiting rooms before reaching the inner sanctum. It was far grander than anything I could have imagined. Although I had traveled widely, I had never seen anything like the corporate headquarters of the Big Three. I felt as if I were visiting European royalty at the height of its influence. You could just feel the power of the industry. It was clear that I had much to learn about the culture, the importance of engineering, the power of the car unions, and how central the industry was to keeping the American economic machine firing. Years later, my immersion in this industry would open the door for me to advise the Ford Motor Company, the Ford family, and Daimler-Benz, which eventually acquired Chrysler.

Working with Gerry and Steve, we were able to ensure the reorganization outside of Chapter 11. The public had to buy more Chryslers while we were trying to reorganize. We needed simultaneously to convince customers that they were smart to buy the cars, while warning creditors that their only hope for repayment of outstanding debt was to increase their loans and to be very flexible about repayment schedules. This was not an easy task. It has come as a great surprise to me that in 2009, General Motors declared bankruptcy and still sells cars and plans an optimistic future.

For many months at the height of the Chrysler negotiations, I was spending a day a week in Detroit, becoming a regular guest at the spectacular Renaissance Plaza Hotel, the pride of Detroit's urban revival. I spent another day each week in Washington at the U.S. Treasury working with Bill Miller and Paul Volcker, and three days a week working in New York with Manufacturers Hanover Bank as the key creditor bank and trying to organize the 415 banks in thirty-five nations that were serving as lenders to the carmaker. It was the largest reconstruction ever done on a multinational basis, and we eventually managed to secure congressional backing for the legislation. More than any other single thing I had ever done, this put me on the map as a small but recognized figure in U.S. investment banking. It also meant that, three years into my period at Salomon, the Chrysler rescue was occupying 80 percent of my time at the firm. I was so consumed by the job that I failed to register that I was not giving adequate leadership to the corporate finance department. While Bill fully supported what I was doing, many of my other partners felt differently, and they may well have been right.

One of my toughest tasks was bringing the Japanese banks into line. They had become major lenders to Chrysler in recent years, and though they did not have a national incentive to save a U.S. company, they had the best chance of being repaid if they would agree to reorganize their debt. After several trips to Japan, in which I built excellent relationships with my Japanese counterparts both in the government and in the banks, I landed again in Tokyo and went directly to the exquisite guesthouse of the Mitsubishi Bank. When it was time for our meeting, I entered the room and was met with deadly silence. The president of

Mitsubishi Bank, the lead bank, and the presidents of all the Japanese banks involved were sitting around a large table. No one raised his eyes or greeted me. Instead, the spokesman for Mitsubishi rose stiffly and read from a written memorandum that he and his colleagues had agreed upon:

> Heretofore, Mr. Wolfensohn, we have always regarded you as a man of competence, a man of impeccable integrity. You have a long record with Darlings, Schroders, and more recently with Salomon Brothers. We've trusted you as a first-class professional. We're very sad that we have to reappraise that evaluation. We now regard you as the messenger of a running dog.

In some parts of Asia, this is about the worst insult you can throw at anyone. I reeled back in horror. I had no clue what all this was about. I turned to Nakamura-san, who was president of Mitsubishi Bank, and said, "I don't know why it is you think this, but if that is what you think of me, I'll leave right now and return to the United States tomorrow." I turned to the assistant with me and asked him to close the attaché case, as we would be going now. This was an issue of saving face, and if the assault on my character could not be resolved, there was no point in trying to conduct a complex negotiation. I told the bank directors that I would be taking the first flight out the next day, and since my car had already left, I asked for a taxi to be called. The only way that the talks could continue was if the remarks were withdrawn.

Arriving in my room at the recently constructed Okura Hotel opposite the U.S. Embassy residence, I called the United States to find out what the problem was. It turned out that while I was in the air between New York and Tokyo, Iacocca had made a speech that included offensive references to Japan and Pearl Harbor. It would have been inappropriate at any time, but this was the worst possible moment for Lee to make that speech. Unfortunately, it no doubt played well in Detroit, where the huge workforce in automobiles saw the Japanese as one of the prime sources of the American motor industry's difficulties. But not surprisingly, in Japan they felt differently. I went to my room and waited. Soon, a few of my more junior friends from the Japanese banks came to see me. They did not want to lose all their money or see the negotiations stop. Before I left Japan, the Japanese amended their remarks—or at least that is what the translator indicated—but understandably, they remained deeply unhappy about Iacocca's speech. I needed to get him involved.

Back in the United States, I called Lee and visited his office to tell him that he could not go around making statements like the one that had almost cost us the financing in Japan. He was in a belligerent mood. "But you can't trust the Japanese," he retorted. I reminded him that with $600 million in loans from Japanese banks at stake, we needed their support to gain time to reorganize. The Japanese were eager to help us in our efforts, but certainly not if Lee continued to call them names. Lee agreed to adopt a more conciliatory tone. After endless work with the Japanese Finance Ministry and representatives of the ministry and of the Japanese banks in New York, we eventually secured the Japanese part of the deal.

As the Chrysler debt negotiations neared a turning point, my photograph appeared in the *New York Times* as a symbol of the private-sector portion of the reorganization. The June 26, 1980, edition showed a picture of me handing a check for $500 million to Iacocca on behalf of the Treasury and the lenders. I was very proud to be part of the financial team with Gerry Greenwald and Steve Miller of Chrysler, without whom success would not have been possible. They kept the finances of the company running on a daily basis while together we tried to negotiate the overall deal with the banks. Although our work was important, we were only part of a much bigger process in the United States. Lee had done most of the political groundwork, which was essential to obtaining a reorganization package that eventually amounted to a total of $1.5 billion in federal assistance and an additional $400 million from the financing banks. The day we were to meet Vice President Walter "Fritz" Mondale for the vote on the final deal on Capitol Hill, Lee arranged for Chrysler car dealers to come to Washington. Suddenly, the Capitol was filled with people from each state of the union wearing yellow hats with "Chrysler Reorganization" imprinted on them, running around seeking the support of their representatives and senators.

As the Chrysler work for the phase of the reorganization was coming to a conclusion, I was very happy that I could show my colleagues at Salomon that I could also do work for other clients. I took the opportunity to visit Australia after receiving a call on behalf of my friend Neville Wran, the premier of the state of New South Wales. He wanted Salomon's help in the first privatization of a power station in the country. It would be a major transaction with a substantial cost of $1.65 billion, and he wanted to appoint Salomon Brothers as financial adviser and underwriter of both the equity and the Eurodollar debt issue, which constituted $1.2 billion of the total.

This was a large transaction for the time, and vastly complex. As a result of the extraordinary work done by our deal advisers Charles Frank and Kim Santow, and with the support of both the state and federal governments of Australia, we were able to complete this very significant financing and the project was subsequently brought to completion. Regrettably, Elcom, the electricity commission, made its own decision to borrow in U.S. dollars without covering for the foreign-exchange risk, and as the value of the Australian dollar declined, the cost of financing increased considerably, although the deal was successful and hugely important for local development. Had the deal taken place decades later, as the Australian dollar strengthened, the commission would have been smart to borrow in U.S. dollars, but such is the risk of international borrowing.

As the last details were concluded on the Chrysler deal, I began to realize just how strained my relations with my Salomon colleagues had become. I had spent two years trying to save Chrysler. I suspect John Gutfreund thought I had become too big for my boots. I am told that he would say, "Look at this guy; he never does anything for the firm. He's off on another trip for Chrysler." Chrysler was the financial event of the moment and, in some ways, contributed substantially to the making of Salomon's investment banking institution. Beyond the large fee it earned us, I judged the Chrysler transaction to be of central importance to the visibility of the firm. But my colleagues expected me, as head of corporate finance, to spend more than a small portion of my time on developing a broader base of business and a more effective team. In retrospect, I think that they were right. I should have brought in more support from within the firm for the Chrysler effort and spent more time looking for new clients as well as strengthening our team.

There were also rumors that I was plotting to dislodge John Gutfreund as Bill's anointed successor, an aspiration that had never crossed my mind. I recognized that John was running the firm, and unlike him, I had not put in decades of work building the firm. Nor did I have the experience or the competence to run Salomon. Its great strength was built on the trading business, and my skills were in corporate finance. I wanted to focus again on building relationships, on thinking through long-term strategy, and on handling mergers and acquisitions. These areas were important to the firm but not central. I had managed to survive at Salomon because I was doing a nationally visible reorganization of a major company. Chrysler was my raison d'être; it kept me relevant. It was one of the firm's biggest moments of glory up to that time, and yet it also cost me the support of Gutfreund and many of my colleagues.

In some ways I had repeated the Schroders mistake of neglecting office politics. Had I been a real leader of the corporate finance department, I would have diminished my role in Chrysler and spent more time building a broader-based Salomon business. It was a mistake of judgment, and looking back, it is no surprise to me that some of the partners felt I had let them down.

*   *   *

Outside of my work at Salomon, I was building a network of relationships and activities in my new country. It was 1981 and I was now forty-seven years old, but I still felt as if I had no roots. I had been a visitor everywhere I lived, and I yearned to build a stable base in the United States. One day, I had a surprise visit from Robert Roosa, former undersecretary of the

Treasury and senior partner in Brown Brothers, and Steve Smith, husband of Jean Kennedy. The legendary investment banker Andre Meyer of Lazards had recently died, and they were seeking a new trustee for the Kennedy Family Trust.[1] This trust looked after the interests of the late president's children, Caroline and John; Robert Kennedy's widow, Ethel, and their children; and all the other Kennedys and their heirs. I was thrilled by the invitation, but I knew no one in the Kennedy family. What if it wasn't a good match? I felt an impulse to protect both myself and the Kennedy family. In everyone's interests, I wanted to be able to get out if the relationship did not work out. My reaction was, however, utterly inelegant. I said I would accept on three conditions: I would take on the position for two years only, at which point we would all review how the relationship was developing; I would not have to visit the family compound at Hyannis; and I would not be required to engage in political activities to support Ted Kennedy in his possible bid to become president.

A short time later, I received an invitation from Senator Kennedy for a dinner at his McLean, Virginia, home just outside Washington, D.C. It was a major gathering of the clan, and before dinner, Ted spent an hour walking me around the house, pointing out family memorabilia. He showed me notes from family members, including President John F. Kennedy, framed poems exchanged among members of the family at Christmas, and family photographs, many of which are now well known. I was enchanted. I had glimpsed the private world of America's royal family, and I was ready to become a Kennedy acolyte. As I sat next to Teddy during a fine dinner with exceptional French wine, I felt proud to have been invited and elated at the prospect of working with the family.

After dinner, we sat down to discuss the trust. Steve began by saying, "We're thrilled to have Jim here tonight. However, for him it must be a little more difficult because he's only prepared to commit to us for two years, he wants to see whether we are good enough, he doesn't want to come and see us at Hyannis, and he won't work for Teddy to become president." I felt as though I were going to fall through the floor. Steve was smiling. It was a brilliant strategy. It took me a minute to find my voice.

"I know that all sounds a bit absurd," I said, "but all I can say is that I made those conditions before I had a chance to meet all of you." It was an honest but lame excuse for my arrogance. This was a family that was part of the history of the United States, and I was intimidated. Once I got over my insecurity, I saw that being a trustee offered me a chance to join Bob Roosa, Steve Smith, Robert McNamara, and others to strengthen the family, to assist in the management and direction of investments, and to learn more about how America operated. I was grateful for the opportunity, which has led to many enduring friendships within a family that I have come to appreciate for its service and for its loyalty. I became especially close to Senator Kennedy, with whom I worked on many issues within and outside the trust. Elaine and I were greatly saddened by his death and were privileged to pay tribute to him at his funeral.

Around the time that I was asked to be a trustee, I had stepped up my involvement with Carnegie Hall. My role as newly appointed chairman following Richard Debs, then executive vice president of the New York Federal Reserve and who was to become a lifelong friend, was to tackle the physical structure, financial management, and reputation of the hall while Isaac Stern remained the president and the dominant artistic force. One of the first things I did was approach the philanthropist and social leader Brooke Astor, through our director, Schuyler Chapin, of Metropolitan Opera fame. Chapin managed to persuade her to give us $1 million to assess the condition of the building and draw up a blueprint for upgrading the nearly hundred-year-old hall and facilities. It was an extraordinary commitment on her part, and it made our subsequent actions possible.

Without any existing plans for the hall, we had to start from scratch. We did not even have a diagram of the wiring, and there were still safety worries about the original elevators. The whole place was a fire hazard without adequate emergency exits. We would have to reengineer everything. We spent eighteen months working out what had to be done and calculated that we needed $60 million for the restoration. This was way beyond anything Carnegie had raised in the past—until then, we had never raised more than $1 million in a year—but we decided we had to try. We presented our findings to the board, and as chairman, I led the decision to go for the $60 million to restore and rebuild the hall.

Isaac gave me his full support, though he was mystified as to how we would raise the money. He had the artistry, the history, and the relationships with musicians, but he had run Carnegie with an executive director, Julius Bloom, and a small group of supporters and friends. They could handle the annual deficit, but now we needed to move to an entirely different level of funding. There were occasional tensions as we worked together, but Isaac and I shared the common dream of renewing the institution. And we each had something different to contribute. I was no match for Isaac's musical reputation, but he needed me to lead the fight, raise the money, and manage the project. We became a formidable team, and I developed one of the deepest, most trusting, and most fulfilling friendships of my life. I truly loved Isaac. Elaine was constantly by my side during the construction and fund-raising. She and Isaac's wife, Vera, who was and remains a remarkable force in many charitable pursuits, allowed Isaac and me to be the public faces of the project while they made huge contributions behind the scenes.

One of our early ideas for raising money was to host onstage dinners with short pre-dinner concerts. Isaac and I felt confident that by making the quality of these evenings exceptional, we could create a buzz in New York. This meant presenting a creative combination of younger artists with the great old masters, as well as a rich diversity of music. We had goodwill in New York City and a good relationship with donors, but they were used to giving $5,000–$10,000 a year. We needed millions. We decided to capture the interest of Sandy Weill, then president of American Express, who rarely attended classical music concerts. He was my guest at a gala dinner at Carnegie, which opened with a performance by Isaac Stern, Mstislav Rostropovich, and famed pianist Vladimir Horowitz, of the first movement of the great Tchaikovsky trio. It brought tears to Sandy's eyes. He said, giving me a hug, that he had never heard anything like this music, and that we had his support. We made him co-chairman of the fund-raising campaign, and he was able to expand our reach to a whole new group of people. He was a true agent of change, and years later he succeeded me as chairman of Carnegie Hall, a position he occupies with success and vision. We had great support from Lester Morse on the board and from Norton Belknap, Larry Goldman, and the whole of the Carnegie team.

The restoration was all-encompassing, and we were fortunate to have John Tishman to lead the reconstruction carried out in an exemplary way by his company. During the buildup to the renovation, I was often at the hall five times a week. It was not all wine and roses. I was intent on setting a budget we could raise, and as we planned the target, tensions ran high. While preparing for the project, we also ran into our share of unexpected physical challenges. On one occasion, Sandy's guest, Jim Robinson, chairman of American Express, came to a performance with Ed Koch, then the mayor of New York. That night the heavens opened with pouring rain, and the bathroom on the second tier started to leak and coursed down into the light fittings of the box where we sat with the mayor. We managed to laugh that one off. I had to tell Robinson and the mayor that we had arranged the shower as a demonstration of how much cash was needed to bring the building into shape—and in particular, to repair the ancient plumbing.

Beyond the physical state of the building, we had to focus on performance and reputation. We needed to promote the new Carnegie Hall and make money, but we also had to adhere to our traditions, such as admitting students free whenever space was available. Eventually everything came together, and we reopened after twenty-six weeks of construction—exactly on schedule. The place was a blaze of light. The scaffolding had been pulled away, revealing a new bronze canopy, and inside, sipping champagne, was an animated and diverse audience to welcome the New York Philharmonic under the direction of Zubin Mehta.

This great institution linked me to New York and its inhabitants in a way that perhaps no other could have. There was no real wall between my work and my social activities. Elaine and I entertained friends and business associates extensively at Carnegie Hall. As the children became older, it became their home away from home. They could attend performances at any time; we could usually find seats, and on the rare occasions that there were none, we would stand in the director's box or at the back of the hall. The financial pressures were off, my working environment was stimulating, and Elaine and the family were stable and happy. Without the pressure I had felt at Schroders, I was beginning to get to know my children. The Carnegie Hall project gave us an unprecedented opportunity to share experiences.

Although Carnegie was at the center of my interests, other possibilities to work in the community were coming my way. One day, Sylvia Lawry, founder of both the Multiple Sclerosis Foundation in America and the Multiple Sclerosis International Federation, called to ask if I would consider being president of the International Federation. I asked, "How can I be president of a world body when I have never worked a day for multiple sclerosis in my life?"

"You'd be good because you're not American, you have a friend who has multiple sclerosis, Jacqueline du Pré, you're a banker, and you live in New York," she replied. I agreed to consider the invitation and attend an upcoming meeting in the Netherlands.

In Amsterdam, I walked into a huge convention area where some people were on stretchers and in wheelchairs, weakened significantly by MS. Only with Jackie had I seen the disease in a progressed state before, and as I began to meet and talk to people, I knew I wanted to be involved. But I realized I had walked into the middle of a great constitutional fight between the American and non-American factions. Many saw me as a puppet of the Americans, and after much discussion, a spokesman of the board announced that I could become president only if I agreed to a series of restrictions. I could not attend all meetings, nor could I sit on the executive committee. The goal was to cut all the power from the position. The convention turned into a heated debate about my restrictions, and as the discussion drew on, the audience grew angry. I stood up and said something along the following lines:

Before we go any further, I would like you to know that I came here to work for and serve persons with MS, among whom I have a great friend. I am not a politician and I don't mind what you do, but I think you are all eating each other up with politics. So what I would like to do as my first act before considering becoming president is to propose that you adjourn the meeting for thirty minutes so that I can go for a walk around the block. You can decide whether you want to continue with these procedural motions. If you do, I have no problem. I will leave you to your politics, and I will find other ways to help people with MS.

About thirty minutes later, I returned to a different atmosphere. The restrictions were dropped, and I spent six very happy and constructive years as president, helping to pull together the activities of thirty countries and establish new MS institutions.

Not long after I joined the Multiple Sclerosis International Federation, I got a call from Teddy Kollek, the mayor of Jerusalem, and Ruth Cheshin, the director of the Jerusalem Foundation. They wanted me to be a director of the Jerusalem Foundation's U.S. board. The Jerusalem Foundation is an impressive organization that is engaged in the beautification of Jerusalem and in the development of programs for Jews and Arabs in the community. I agreed and at the same time joined the board of the Jerusalem Music Centre, a satellite project that received funding from the Rothschild Foundation in London.

Shortly after my appointment, I attended a luncheon for the Jerusalem Foundation as a new member of the board. It was held in a restaurant overlooking the Old City, and among the guests and members of the board were Isaac Stern, Shimon Peres, and Ruth Cheshin. Sitting next to me was a striking gray-haired woman with beautiful skin, quietly having lunch and obviously the center of attention of the group. She was Dorothy de Rothschild, widow of James de Rothschild.

The Rothschild name was still legendary in my mind. After hearing about the Rothschilds so often from my father, I believe their activities had a significant influence on my aspirations and, in some way, served as a model for me on which to build my life. There was still so much I wanted to know about my father's experience with James de Rothschild in World War I and later in England. I was now sitting next to James's widow, whom my father had admired tremendously. I had many handwritten letters that she had sent him, all with the salutation "Dear Wolfie." Dorothy was still a leading figure in philanthropy and in developing programs and projects in Israel. Among other initiatives, the foundation had financed the building of the Knesset, the Parliament building in Jerusalem, and she was about to finance the new building for the Supreme Court. She did everything quietly and in her own way, and was truly a major and much revered force in the philanthropic community in England and in Israel.

Sitting next to her, I was filled with images of my youth, with questions and uncertainties about my father's past. During the first course, my neighbor and I discussed the weather, school, and other light topics. As the lunch progressed, I could contain myself no longer:

"Mrs. de Rothschild, I really feel as if I know you very well."

She looked at me quizzically. "Oh, my dear. Why is that?"

"Well, my father used to work for you."

"What did you say your name was again?"

"Wolfensohn."

She took a long look at me. "You are Wolfie's son?"

"Yes."

I was overcome by emotion and started crying in the middle of lunch. She put her arms around me, I put my arms around her, and she started crying, too. I can only imagine what everyone else at the table must have thought.

"Your father was a wonderful man," she said.

"But why did he leave you?"

"Oh, my dear, I cannot remember. But that is all history. Your father was a wonderful man."

This brief exchange was a turning point in my life. It was the beginning of a deep friendship with Dolly, as she allowed me to call her. I saw her every time I went to London, and I became involved in helping to implement some of the ideas of her family's charitable organization, the Hanadiv Foundation. I was never more proud than when asked to join the board of this substantial charity, which is now run under the chairmanship of my close friend, Lord Jacob Rothschild. I felt I had closed the circle opened by my father, and I thought he would have been happy. Elaine and I developed further a deep and abiding friendship with Jacob and his wife, Serena. We became close to his sister, renowned economic historian Emma Rothschild, and her husband, the Nobel Laureate Amartya Sen. Later I was able to support the publication of two books about Dorothy's life. This was a symbolic action on my part to express my gratitude for everything the Rothschilds did for my late father and to balance our mutual history in some small way.

My life was evolving in a way that allowed me to balance my business life with my communal and cultural interests.

During my Schroders and Salomon years, and over the nearly fifteen years of my own firm, I built an extraordinary series of relationships in New York that gained a momentum of their own and kept spawning new ones. While at Carnegie Hall, I became a managing director of the Metropolitan Opera Association. My work at the Custom House Institute of New York led to an invitation to join the Population Council and eventually the board of the Rockefeller University. It also led to my becoming a trustee of the New York Landmarks Conservancy, which preserves the buildings and parks of the city. I became a trustee of the Brookings Institution in Washington, D.C., and a member of the board of the governors of the Lauder Institute in Philadelphia, at the request of my friend Leonard Lauder.

My involvement in all these organizations gave me a window into the rich culture of the United States and a chance to meet people with broad interests who were ready to volunteer their time and talent for the benefit of their community. In 1979, I was invited to join the board of the Rockefeller Foundation, where I was in regular contact with Vernon Jordan, Henry Schacht, Bill Moyers, Jay Rockefeller, Lane Kirkland, and others.

These colleagues were true American heroes to me—steeped in their country's history and working selflessly on good causes. The foundation gave me a special insight into the developing world and the issues confronting equitable and sustainable development. I am certain that this activity gave me the passion for development—a passion that later matured into my work at the World Bank. I doubt that I would have received similar invitations in the United Kingdom, where society is less open and where there are fewer philanthropic and social-service-oriented institutions. I was, however, amused when, after all my years at Schroders and after I had relocated in the United States and had become a partner at Salomon Brothers, I was finally invited to join the board of Covent Garden in London. By this point, there were too many other causes I felt passionate about, and I was happy to decline.

Finally, and of tremendous importance to me, I was invited in the late 1970s to join the board of the Institute for Advanced Study at Princeton, founded in 1930 under the direction of Abraham Flexner. It was then under the chairmanship of the renowned Dick Dilworth, who was central to the various Rockefeller activities. This was the home of Albert Einstein, John von Neumann, Erwin Panofsky, Kurt Göder, George Kennan, Hermann Weyl, John Bahcall, and so many others of great distinction. In 1983, I was asked to become chairman, a role that I occupied for twenty-three years. I had the privilege of working with four directors—Harry Wolf, David Goldberg, Phillip Griffiths, and Peter Goddard. I was never more proud of any association. The board was extraordinary and I was especially grateful to my friend Vartan Gregorian for his unfailing support and guidance, as well as to Peter Kann of the *Wall Street Journal*.

My business, social, and cultural activities coalesced, not just locally but throughout the world. As I sought to do business in other cities and countries, there was always a second layer to the business conversation. Music, water shortages, the environment, the rights of women, education—these were the subjects that built the special connections with friends and clients.

In addition to bringing my corporate experiences into the nonprofit sector, I now had enough money to give generously. I set a goal of giving away 20 percent of my income, and by 1990, that meant that I had been able to commit a reasonable amount of resources. Although my donations did not amount to much compared with those of the large charitable institutions, my ability to quietly and speedily make substantial annual donations to many good causes was beyond my wildest hopes.

*   *   *

All these activities crowded my life. Although Elaine and the children were often involved, the family once again suffered. I was not an absent father, but I was a preoccupied one who would sometimes return home in the early hours of the morning. I would see the children on Friday nights or on the weekends that I managed to get to our tiny Carmel cottage. My outside involvements appealed to my sense of duty, and they certainly expanded my horizons. Certainly, if I had it to do all over again, I would have spent much more time at home and with my family.

I did recognize that it was time for change on several fronts. I was in my forties and—dare I say it?—belatedly maturing, at least a little. Once the Chrysler deal had ended, everything had come to a head for me. I'd realized that I'd worked for other people my entire life. I had spent an enormous amount of time thinking about how to get from one position to another. With four and a half years behind me at Salomon and millions of dollars sitting in the partnership, I was starting to feel that if I could have my independence, why not leave and, in accordance with the partnership agreement, eventually get my capital out of the firm?

I returned to the dream of running my own small corporate finance business from a brownstone in New York City. I envisioned a music room on the top floor, where I could practice my cello. I would have no more than ten key clients, for whom I would act as a trusted adviser and friend. After attracting this client base, I imagined that I would never again have to go out soliciting business, claiming, rather arrogantly and probably not correctly, that I could offer better service than Morgan Stanley, Merrill Lynch, or Lehman Brothers because I would do the work myself in conjunction with a small group of partners. My firm would play to my strengths. It would deal with strategic policy issues; it would advise on capital structures, mergers, and acquisitions and deal with human and succession issues at the highest levels. It would allow me to keep at least one-third of my time for the nonbusiness activities that had become such a large part of my life. But above all, it would, I hoped, put the politics of investment banking boardrooms behind me. My name would be on the line, and I would be the boss. If there were successes, they would be mine, and likewise with failures. In many ways, this was a utopian dream, but now I had the confidence and resources to try to make this rather crude vision into a reality.

With my mind at peace, I went to tell Bill Salomon of my decision. I told him, and later John Gutfreund, that I wanted to exit in a quiet and dignified way and with as little disruption as possible. I reminded them that when I joined the firm, I had said I would like the choice of staying five years or forever, but that at five years we would decide. I told them that it was now four and a half years since I had joined. I made it clear I would not be taking any clients with me. I knew that my very experienced partner Dick Schmeelk could take over ownership of the department with support from Harold Tanner and the trust of his partners. I thought everyone would be happy. Bill told me that he was sorry and that he felt that I must be reacting to the criticism of some of my partners. He did not want me to go. Nonetheless, he agreed that I could leave at the end of my five years. My impression was that John was not unhappy.

Within a month of having these confidential conversations, secret discussions began with the big commodity brokerage and trading firm Philip Brothers (or Philbro) about the possibility of a merger or a buyout of Salomon Brothers. As a member of the executive committee, I knew these talks were under way, but I felt it was not right for me, as someone leaving the partnership, to be part of them. So I did not attend the negotiations. At one point, the partners went on a retreat in Greenwich, Connecticut, to discuss the transaction and the share-out of the proceeds of sale. When they returned, we learned that it was a far bigger financial transaction than anyone had imagined. I suggested that because it was such a rich deal, we should each put 10 percent of the cash we would receive into a special fund for Bill Salomon and other former partners. My reasoning was simple: Bill and his colleagues had developed much of the goodwill in the firm, and under the proposed arrangements, they were to get nothing because they no longer had shares in the business. I believe that I was the only one who thought this was equitable, and it never happened. It was the ultimate indignity for Bill, and the experiences of that carve-up never left me. When I left my own firm several years later to join the World Bank, I insisted that my lawyers insert a clause into the contract stating that if the business were sold within five years, I would receive 25 percent of the premium paid by the purchaser. I called this the "Salomon clause."

I turned out to be a big winner at Salomon. My departure date was set for June 30, 1981. The official takeover date by Philbro was July 1 of the same year. Instead of receiving a payout over a period of years of my accumulated capital account—as stipulated in the original shareholder agreement—I was paid out in cash in one immediate transaction coincident with the merger. My Schroders $100,000 had increased an astounding one-hundredfold in five years. For me, it was financial freedom day. Had the firm not been taken over, I would have had to wait many years to see my shareholding redeemed in cash. Suddenly I was independent—and I could barely suppress my joy.

*   *   *

Over the past few years, I had begun to look beyond my life in New York to events in Washington. In 1980, prior to my departure from Salomon, Robert McNamara was planning to step down as president of the World Bank, and President Jimmy Carter wished to submit suggestions to incoming President Ronald Reagan. I had paid close attention to McNamara's inspiring twelve-year reign, during which he had kept the Bank tightly focused on the battle against poverty in the developing world. He was widely regarded as the Bank's most outstanding leader since World War II, and he commanded so much respect in Washington that Carter turned to him for advice on who should be his successor.

I had attended the annual meetings every year since my return to New York in the early 1970s and had been impressed and moved by McNamara's speeches. He not only understood the issues facing the World Bank intellectually, but he also cared passionately about them. Typically, after the speech I would head to a local restaurant with the other people who had no official invitations. Each year, I would sit with Nigel Lawson, then a U.K. journalist and later chancellor of the Exchequer, and other friends, and we would marvel at the speech we'd just heard.

Over the years, I met McNamara a few times in the context of my work with the Kennedy Family Trust, and he was always friendly. But I could not have been more surprised when he asked me to visit him at the World Bank headquarters, just a couple of blocks from the White House. In addition to U.S. candidates, he had drawn up a list of non-Americans he thought should be considered for the post of World Bank president and told me I was on it. The very thought of being involved in the Bank sent my head spinning. He asked me if I would mind if my name were submitted to the Carter White House, and I replied immediately that I would be honored. Still, I knew it was a colossal long shot; for one thing, I was not American.

That was quickly fixed. Soon after McNamara put my name forward, I took a call from the White House. Sarah Weddington, a lawyer and assistant to the president, was on the line. "You know, if you're going to get this job, you have to be an American citizen." I had already established the residency requirements, so she arranged for me to become a naturalized American within the next two weeks.

This was not a step I took lightly. I loved the country of my birth. At that time, there was no possibility of dual citizenship with Australia, so with great reluctance I agreed to apply for American citizenship. I put a call through to Malcolm Fraser, then the Australian prime minister, who was excited at the thought of an Australian heading the World Bank and promised to do whatever he could to advance my case. I explained

that I was relinquishing my Australian citizenship for the job. I would
be grateful, I said, if it were to be noted in my file, in his handwriting,
that if I wanted my citizenship back, I could have it. Malcolm said he
would ask John Stone, who was secretary to the Treasury in Australia at
the time and had worked at the International Monetary Fund, to help
me out. For reasons I do not know, perhaps competitive pique, Stone immediately set about trashing the whole idea of my becoming president.

I worried that my decision might be misconstrued in the media as an
abandonment of my native Australia, but the previously unimaginable
prospect of one day heading the World Bank overwhelmed everything
else. It opened the possibility of new vistas beyond the commercial confines of investment banking. In the end, no one ever commented on my
decision. I was too self-involved to realize that this was not big news in
Australia.

So I pressed ahead. After a weekend of studying the 100-page booklet
on American citizenry, I turned up at the immigration office in downtown New York to take my citizen's test. As I faced a long queue, someone
came looking for me, and I was immediately taken inside. I was asked to
sign my name, and the immigration official then said, "You have passed
your literacy test." She asked me who the first American president was.
Almost before I could get out the words "George Washington," she pro-
nounced, "You have passed your history test. Now we will fill in the final
details." I was disappointed. I had studied and practiced the entire weekend with Elaine and the kids. I wanted to be quizzed on the capitals of
each state and the details of U.S. history. But my request that I be tested
further fell on deaf ears. There were no more questions.

The White House had fast-tracked me, and my name went forward
in nomination to Jimmy Carter, along with several others suggested by
McNamara. But in the run-up to an American presidential election, the
choice for such a sensitive job, which would stretch well into the next administration, needed the approval not just of the president but also of his
Republican successor, Ronald Reagan. Unbeknownst to me, Reagan had

settled on Alden "Tom" Clausen, the architect of the phenomenal growth of California-based Bank of America.

After the election in November, Elaine picked up the morning newspapers at our apartment and scanned the headlines. "It seems you are not going to be World Bank president after all," she said. Though I was disappointed, the selection of Clausen did not come as a great surprise, and I remained honored to have been considered. My ambition to use my banking acumen to give something back to the world had been stirred, but for the moment, I put it out of my mind. The Reagan decision was a good one. Although technically I was proficient, I was not yet anywhere near mature enough to handle the job. I was still too insecure and too preoccupied with my own career path to be able to rise to the demands of such a position. It was time for me to strike out on my own.

10

‱

ON MY OWN

O<small>N OCTOBER 1, 1981, I OPENED THE OFFICES OF JAMES D. WOLFEN-</small>
SOHN Incorporated. This time there was no welcoming concert and
no access onto a trading floor to create a sense of urgency and linkage
with international markets. My old daydream of owning my own business
had become a reality. I was not working for someone else. With my name
over the door, I would not have to contend with office politics or competition for leadership. This newfound independence felt like a great luxury
and a huge opportunity. It had taken me forty-seven years, but finally I
was on my own; success or failure would arise from my decisions alone.

James D. Wolfensohn Inc. would not be about making the biggest
deals or raising the most funds for clients. Rather, my firm would provide
advice to a select group of clients, for an agreed-upon retainer, on the subjects of financing, capital structure, mergers and acquisitions, and management and board issues. We would not compete over the full range of
services with Wall Street or international investment banks. We would not
aggressively pitch for business. Instead, we would try to build special
client relationships and provide the kind of independent, clear-eyed advice
that corporate leaders found hard to come by. Not every deal would be a
must; in fact, we would pride ourselves on our willingness to advise clients

to say no to transactions offered to them if that was the best advice, even though a deal might mean increased fees for us. We would be the people who could challenge, question, and really scrutinize a deal from the point of view of the true interests of the company. We would put the company first and the deal second.

The idea was that companies would pay an advisory fee of $250,000 a year, for which they would receive our undivided attention and advice. My colleagues and I would be available around the clock, and clients could request a meeting or get me on the telephone whenever they liked. I structured it so that the fees would pay the basic rent and salaries. If our clients wanted more, we could perform the investment banking role of negotiation, of drawing up deal documents, completing transactions, and organizing finance. For this extra work, we would receive additional compensation, which would be our profit. Initially, we hoped to build up slowly a small but distinguished set of relationships. As it turned out, with a bit of help from many friends, clients came almost immediately.

Although I was selling my name and record, we still needed a strong, dynamic, and supportive team. My first recruits were Brian Powers, Stuart Ray, Donald Zilkha, and Elliott Slade, who worked diligently with me to build the firm.[1] I also went after Jeff Goldstein, then a brilliant, twenty-seven-year-old Princeton economics professor with a PhD from Yale. This was his first full-time commercial job, and when he came to see me, we spent almost two days discussing plans for the firm. He got onboard immediately and told me he planned to stay for four or five years. About twenty years later, we were still working together at the World Bank and he later held a leading position at the U.S. Treasury as under-secretary. My friend Raymond Golden joined me from Salomon Brothers. He had tremendous experience in all facets of the investment banking business and combined a commercial instinct with great common sense. Without his advice and friendship, the firm could not have made the progress it did.

Even as I mapped out my ambitions for the firm, I was determined to carve out time for music and philanthropic work. My fantasy of a brownstone with a music room on the top floor was thwarted by the New York planning laws governing commercial use. But the space we secured on a small floor in a traditional office building at 425 Park Avenue did just as well. There was no piano or music, but I had a large closet to serve as a home for my cello, which stood as a constant reminder that this life change was not primarily about making my fortune.

Before beginning the enterprise, I had called Siegmund Warburg for advice. By 1981, although he had stopped overseeing the daily operations of S.G. Warburg in London to act as president, he was still the guiding force behind the leadership. He immediately offered to put his own money into my firm and to become a founding director or partner.

"Oh, that would embarrass you. Think of your colleagues," I said.

"Jim, I really want to do this. What you are doing, this is the way merchant banking should be done. I hate the big firms, including my own. It simply has become too large."

Although I never allowed him to invest, he gave me a great deal of practical help assembling a client base, and he made one very special, immediate introduction. He recommended me to Gerhard Prinz, then chairman of Daimler-Benz, Germany's biggest manufacturer. Daimler made everything from cars to trucks to aircraft engines and components. I had never met the formidable Dr. Prinz, but he telephoned me while on a visit to New York just a few weeks after we opened the doors for business.

"This is Dr. Prinz," he informed me. "You have been alerted by our mutual friend Siegmund Warburg that I wish to see you and what you are doing. I would like to come to your offices."

Our "offices" were not set up yet, although we were ready to do business. We were still so unsettled that all we had were some desks, piles of packing cases, a couple of chairs, and a single table. I tried to convince Prinz to meet me in a restaurant, but he insisted on visiting me at the office, so I gave in. We had sandwiches and Cokes at the only table at James D. Wolfensohn Inc., where I explained, as best I could, what I was proposing to do. I was astonished a short while later when Prinz called me back from Germany and said he would like to retain my services as his principal adviser. Thanks to Siegmund, I now had my first European client, and it was one of Europe's largest and most prestigious companies.

Prinz loved the idea of a "boutique" investment bank, and I continued to advise Daimler and Prinz's successors for nearly fifteen years. The concept of personal service appealed to him, as did the absence of conflict in client relationships. There would be security, less risk of the usual leaks, and a team of bright and experienced young people who would dedicate themselves to his account rather than chasing the next fee. In the context of the deal-mad, extravagant 1980s, when mega-mergers, greenmail, junk bonds, inside trading, and other financial detritus dominated the financial newspaper columns, ours was a very different proposition.

In order to carry out our mission, I had to impose a series of rules on the operation immediately. Among the first and most elementary was that I would not take business from Salomon. Having been allowed to lead the investment banking operations, it would have been wrong to walk off with key clients like Chrysler. But one client I had known for a couple of decades insisted on following me. About a year after I opened my firm, I was approached by the Hong Kong and Shanghai Banking Corporation, which I had advised as it sought to diversify and transition from a Far Eastern–based bank to a genuinely global institution. I had helped its chairman, Michael Sandberg, in the original purchase of a stake in Marine Midland Bank, and it seemed I had won his trust.[2] I remember Mike saying, "Look, there are a lot of people trying to screw you on Wall Street. I have played the game. I don't like it. And I'd like you to advise us." After getting Bill Salomon's approval of this exception to my rule of protocol, I told Sandberg that I would love to be his adviser and promised to give him straight advice. "You can trust that I'm not going to push you into deals," I said. It was extremely gratifying to be able to make that promise.

HSBC became a loyal client, and years later, I advised Sandberg's successor, William Purves, on the buyout of the minority shareholders of Marine Midland in 1987. In 1992, I played a key advisory role in the purchase of Britain's Midland Bank, which thrust HSBC into the front line of European banking.[3] With its base strength in Asia, the United States, and the Middle East, HSBC has evolved through mergers into one of the truly great international financial institutions of our time.

In very short order, I had quite a substantial client list. Australians were immediately supportive. I received a call from James Clements of Westpac, the leading financial institution in Australia, who signed up immediately. There followed Lend Lease, the large property development organization run by my old friend and client Dick Dusseldorp; the mining giant Broken Hill Proprietary (BHP); and Westfield, Frank Lowy's Australian shopping-center empire that would become a major international force.

Wolfensohn Inc. grew rapidly. In our first year, our net profit was a few hundred thousand dollars. By the second year, we were making $1 million, then $2 million, and eventually, our total fees hit more than $60 million a year, offering very good compensation for everyone and a substantial profit for my family and for our foundation work. Our team was first-rate, but I felt in those early years that we would benefit enormously by attracting another senior partner to the firm. I was elated when Frank Petito, the retired chairman of Morgan Stanley, agreed to join us. Not only did he provide us with the benefit of his experience, but his involvement was an endorsement of the firm in and of itself. To this day, I am thrilled that I was able to attract him. I suspected that it was due to some internal disturbances at Morgan Stanley, but I never inquired. In any case, it was a great stroke of luck. I was thrilled that Frank, whom I admired immensely, decided to bring his talents to us at a critical time, and the years he spent with us saw not only growth but also the establishment of the ethical principles that ruled our firm.

We were building client lists across diverse markets, from US West in the telecom sector to fashion guru Ralph Lauren to IMG, the manager of sporting events, athletes, and later, musicians. We had neither the ambition nor the capacity to achieve the status of the major underwriting firms. We had no financial capacity to trade in securities, no array of salespeople or analysts. But as a specialist firm giving advice, we were involved in some of the landmark deals of the 1980s. Aside from the work we did for traditional international clients like HSBC, we also advised Nations-Bank, the precursor to Bank of America, as well as American Express and CBS. Many clients from my previous life came to consult with us, including David Newbigging, the taipan of the Hong Kong trading house Jardine Matheson, whose interests ranged from insurance to the Mandarin Oriental Hotel chain and, most important, a staggering 65 percent of the real estate in downtown Hong Kong.

In the early 1980s, the prime minister of Singapore, Lee Kuan Yew, appointed me as an adviser to the Singapore Investment Corporation. We had the opportunity to help shape its structure, and I traveled to the Far East two or three times a year for meetings with Lee Kuan Yew and his team. He had great experience and a powerful intellect. I was never sure why he retained us, because at each meeting, after I had made a few opening comments and was about to present my prepared views, he would interrupt and start speaking, essentially giving a lesson to me and to his whole team on what we should be thinking. I always felt I should have been asking him for advice, not the reverse. Subsequently, I became the adviser to the Government of Singapore Investment Corporation under the inspired leadership of Yong Pung How, who was later to become chief justice of Singapore.

From the outset, I wanted to run the firm as a family-style enterprise. Every Thursday morning, we would have a gathering of all the staff, during which I would go around the table and ask each person to comment on his or her activities. We talked about every single matter in which the firm was involved. The idea was to let everyone know what was going on and to preserve the esprit de corps. First we had five, then ten, and then fifteen associates, and by the end of the third year, there were about thirty professional staff. I loved the informality of it. It made everyone feel like part of the decision-making process.

Before the decade was out, we established a joint venture with Fuji Bank in Japan—called Fuji-Wolfensohn International—to serve clients doing business in Japan, as well as to service some of the special needs of Japanese companies operating in the United States. Under the leadership of Fuji's dynamic president, Toru Hashimoto, and its head of international activities, Toru Kusukawa, we developed a modest business out of New York and made lasting friendships.

While our firm increased its client base and the profits grew substantially, I had a desire to expand into the investment business. In 1983, I put together a high-quality group of advisers to help us invest in high-tech business, including Nobel Prize–winner Joshua Lederberg; Harold Brown, who had been secretary of defense under Jimmy Carter and a board member at Schroders; MIT professor John Deutch, who would later become a high official in the Department of Defense and thereafter director of the Central Intelligence Agency; and Gene Fubini, a former distinguished scientific adviser to the U.S. government. With this outstanding team, I thought we must be onto a winner. I quickly recruited a group of wealthy, high-powered investors. We formed a $90-million joint-venture firm, Wolfensohn Associates, in which many leaders and friends, including David Rockefeller, Fiat chairman Gianni Agnelli, Gordon Getty, Albina du Boisrouvray, the Royal Bank of Canada, HSBC, and Lord Weinstock's GEC in Britain each took a $5-million stake.

It was not a wise decision on my part. The expert panel was great on science, but we quickly discovered that a good technical idea accounts for about one-tenth of what goes into a successful venture-capital company. This was before high tech took off, and the only thing making money was low tech. We did not have the managerial skills to go into companies and provide the direction and financial oversight that is so central to success. Nonetheless, we invested a small portion of the capital and awaited the quarterly results. The lesson was bitter but plain. Don't get into the investment business if your only skills are technical, research oriented, and advisory, and you lack the capacity for management oversight and intervention should it become necessary. In the end, I personally bought everyone out of the fund at their initial cost. Giving them their money back was a no-brainer for me, even though the fund appeared to be losing up to $10 million. I had induced this galaxy of investors to join me, unwittingly overstating my capacities as an investor without the needed management skills. My investors were so amazed to be paid back all their investment despite the losses that I retained their goodwill and at least a reputation for integrity. I would never again enter the business without a management team to monitor and supervise the investments.

Not all of my friendships survived my foray into venture capital. In 1980, when I formed my firm, I went into several small venture-capital investments personally. My old business associate and longtime friend Kerry Packer suggested that he become a shareholder in my business and that in addition, we have an adjunct fifty-fifty partnership, which he would fund substantially to make venture-capital investments. I told him I would not take investors in my advisory firm but that I was eager to do the investment business jointly with him. Over the decades, Kerry had often come to me for financial advice before embarking on new ventures through his main company, Consolidated Press Holdings.

In the 1980s, Kerry found himself facing horrible accusations by the Royal Commission of Australia, which was looking into the Federated Ship Painters and Dockers Union. Several appalling and unsubstantiated allegations were made against him—including involvement in pornography, tax evasion, drugs, corporate fraud, and money laundering. None of the allegations were ever proven, but Kerry's reputation was damaged. He was badly shaken and needed all the friends he could muster. Most of his friends deserted him, and I tried to find a way to help. Not long before the problems started, Kerry had given a $1-million donation to the elite Ascham School for girls in Sydney, where his daughter had been a pupil. The money was used to build a theater, but when it came time for its public opening, Kerry was so out of favor that he thought it would be better if he stayed away. So I flew in from the United States and opened the Packer Theatre on his behalf. I respected him, and I made a point of saying what a good man he was during the opening. Then, to support him publicly, I flew to Australia three or four times during that difficult period. I developed a deep friendship with Kerry and his wonderful wife, Ros. For years, Kerry and I talked on the phone almost daily.

In 1990, Kerry had a heart attack. It was not fatal, but there was another blow to his organization when around the same time his managing director resigned. Because of his illness, he needed to disengage from daily involvement in his many business activities, so he asked American executive Al Dunlap to sort out his business empire. Dunlap had a fearsome reputation that had earned him the nickname "Chainsaw" because of his willingness to cut away layers of corporate management without batting an eyelid. The tycoon Jimmy Goldsmith, an ally of Kerry in the attempt to take over and break up British American Tobacco in 1989, had famously dubbed Dunlap "Rambo in pinstripes." Dunlap was ruthless in his approach, never worrying about costing people their jobs or destroying long-standing loyalties. So perhaps I should not have been surprised when the young man whom Dunlap sent over to look at my partnerships with Kerry announced I was taking Kerry for a ride. Kerry, he said, was not getting his due from our investment relationship, and it was clear that it should end. I was deeply wounded. The rug was about to be pulled out from underneath our business partnership, and Kerry had done nothing to stop it.

The resulting falling-out was extremely painful—both personally and financially. We had a number of joint projects, and I found myself writing personal checks to support the investment portfolio for $250,000 a month. Dunlap was prepared to let these companies go to the wall. But I could not put my reputation at risk by fighting him publicly, and in any case, there was no documentation of our arrangement. I discovered that in a limited liability company, if you are as exposed as I was, there is no real limited liability if you wish to protect your professional reputation. Kerry had left me without a partner, and I was bleeding horribly. It brought an abrupt end to an enduring and special relationship. The whole thing made me sick, but the rift was total. I never spoke to Kerry again, although we were, I believe, both careful not to say anything negative about each other publicly.

Like most powerful men, Kerry was used to people creeping back. I was not one of them. In December 2005, I heard the news that he had passed away. Despite all the bitterness, I was very upset, and I wrote to his wife, Ros, and to their children, James and Gretel. Almost a year later, while in Sydney, Elaine and I met with the family, and we are rebuilding our friendship. It is a source of great sadness to me that Kerry did not reach out to rebuild our relationship, which had meant so much to both of us.

Even beyond the fallout with Kerry, my venture-capital experiment was nerve-wracking. I had invested in a Florida dairy business that we had to close and a dog food business that lost all of our funds. What an awful feeling it is, seeing cash pouring into one failed venture after another. Still, my investment banking business was earning substantial returns and we could keep afloat without risk of failure. Of all my investments, only Southeast Frozen Foods (SEFF), which sells about 5,000 separate products, including a great deal of ice cream, still survives. It was sold to the management and staff in 2007 with a long-term payout to me, I am happy and surprised to say, at a profit, which compensates for the other adventures.

Several years after I started my advisory firm, I arranged for SEFF to buy a used Westwind II aircraft for $2 million, so that I could reach my clients quickly whenever they needed me. This aircraft had only a 2,600-mile range, but with my captain, Howard Holland, it flew me all over the world for nearly twenty years, until I sold it for the same price and bought a more modern, longer-range aircraft. Around the year 2000, as I walked through Teterboro Airport in New Jersey, where I'd housed my old plane, one of the baggage handlers turned to me and said, "Mr. Wolfensohn, I saw you on TV the other night. All this time, I thought you were in the frozen-food business. Just last night, I realized that for the last five years, I've been handling the gear of the president of the World Bank."

*　　*　　*

In December 1982, on my forty-ninth birthday, I received a phone call from Daniel Barenboim.

"First, it's Happy Birthday! Second, where's the concert?"

"What concert?" I asked.

"You promised Jackie you would play a concert on your fiftieth birthday. Well, now she's asking about it. Where will it be?"

"Oh, we can do something at home," I replied happily.

"That's not a concert. A concert is chamber music at Carnegie Hall," he said.

"Are you crazy?" I almost dropped the phone. "I have never played chamber music in my life. And I've certainly never performed anywhere in public."

"Well, you are going to on your fiftieth birthday. I've checked with Carnegie Hall, and it is available on December first."

I was speechless. Elaine was watching and listening to my end of the conversation with an amused look on her face. Finally, I found words to respond.

"But how am I going to get ready for this?"

Danny said that we'd get to that once we knew what I would play and who I would be playing with. He promised to recruit some mutual friends for the concert.

Several days later, he called me back to give me the lineup. He had already recruited Isaac Stern and Vladimir "Vova" Ashkenazy. The whole thing struck me as surreal, but I went along with it.

We decided that I would perform the Haydn C Major Piano Trio, with Isaac playing the violin part and my daughter Sara, who was now in her third year at Juilliard, on piano. We would also perform Schumann's Andante and Variations for two pianos, two cellos, and French horn, so that I could play with Danny and Vova, each of whom would play the piano. Leonard Rose would play the second cello with me, and Phil Myers of the New York Philharmonic agreed, at the request of Zubin Mehta, to play French horn. For Danny Barenboim and Jackie du Pré, playing at Carnegie Hall was nothing new, and I do not think that they had the slightest idea how hard it would be for me. But it was a gift—a challenge that permanently changed and enriched my life.

As I started to practice, I quickly learned that ensemble playing was infinitely more difficult than I had expected. There were two obvious but significant challenges. I had to keep strict time with the other musicians, and I also had to keep on pitch. These were disciplines I had not developed adequately playing on my own, although Jackie and my new teacher in New York kept pressing me to improve my skills. Excitement was quickly eroding into worry. After a few months of lessons with Nate Stutch, a great teacher and cellist in the New York Philharmonic, I called Isaac and asked him if he would mind listening to me play the Haydn. When he arrived at our apartment in New York, I was overcome with panic and could not feel the bow in my hand. My hands were sweaty, and I was shaking. Nonetheless, I started to play the cello with Sara on piano and a friend of hers playing violin. We played for two or three minutes. It was clear that I was off key, unbearably anxious, and making a terrible mess of my performance. My stomach sank as I realized there was no real sound coming from the cello. It was a terrible moment. My great opportunity to play for Maestro Stern was turning into a nightmare. Isaac was blunt: "Look, you know, we really have a problem." I nodded. "The greatest teacher in America is Leonard Rose," he continued. "I will call him and ask him to help you. He could teach a chair to play the cello."

So I began lessons with Leonard, who had once played as a member of the New York Philharmonic and taught at Juilliard. He had a fine career as a soloist and was renowned as a teacher. Every weekend, I visited Leonard in Westchester. He became my teacher and my friend—and he believed in me. Leonard was kind and understanding, but unrelenting in his standards. It was an amazing struggle. Over the next year, as I traveled constantly for business, I practiced cello all over the world, usually at midnight or six o'clock in the morning. I received complaints from almost every hotel where I stayed until I discovered the practice mute, which kept down the sound and allowed me to play during the edges of my workday without disturbing my neighbors.

As my fiftieth birthday approached, I still felt unprepared. Two months before the performance, I hired a half dozen students from Juilliard. We agreed they would be prepared to play with me at any hour of the day or night when I was able to practice. In the two or three weeks before the performance, we played for several hours every day. I can hardly imagine what they thought about my efforts, but they were gentle and kind and extraordinarily supportive. The talent and capacity of those young musicians never failed to amaze me. Throughout all of this, Elaine and my children were valiant in their support. They never made fun of me, never did anything but encourage me. In fact, they always treated my efforts as "normal." I remain awed by Elaine's ability to create normalcy even as I was consumed in such a crazy and egocentric exercise.

On the day of the concert, the stage was set aside for rehearsal. Incredibly, I was about to play onstage at Carnegie Hall with some of the greatest musicians in the world. That evening I would appear before more than four hundred people—family, friends, and colleagues whom I had invited to witness this Walter Mitty–ish event. Danny Kaye would have been proud of me. Looking back, I am astounded at the gamble I was taking. What if I had frozen up? Fortunately, at the time I was so wrapped up in the music, the months of preparation, and the logistics of performing that I didn't think about the risks.

The daylong rehearsal onstage made vivid the gap between me and these leaders in the musical world. They simply walked onto the stage, picked up the music, and played. No nerves. No questions. Just instant mastery of their craft. And then there was me. It was my first time on any stage, and it was Carnegie Hall. There was nowhere to hide. It was too late to back out or improve the quality of what I was about to do. I was going to make music or look and sound like a fool. It was surreal. It was also the culmination of twelve months of hard work, and I was completely focused. Now was the moment.

When I walked onto the stage that night for the concert, my friends in the audience gave me an ovation. I was immensely grateful for it, not knowing what would happen after I played. But the evening progressed as planned, and I got through the concert—if not with distinction, then at least with some skill. When I finished, I saw hundreds of smiling faces and noticed roses around the hall wherever I looked. The audience responded wonderfully, both to the Haydn trio and to the Schumann. Since then, I have listened to the tape of the performance many times. My performance was not perfect, but it was acceptable. It was a first-time chamber music performance with artists of distinction, and there were no critics present. I had survived my premiere performance, and I was elated. I had met Jackie's condition that I play on my fiftieth birthday. Afterward, Elaine put on a fantastic reception and dinner onstage and right in the hall.

The sadness of the evening was that Jackie could not be there. Her multiple sclerosis had advanced to the point where she could not travel. It was for that reason that I recorded the performance. Had she been there, she would have given me her encouragement. After the performance, she would have been very loving—and moderately acclaiming. She never extended the truth. I don't think she ever told me what she thought of the tape I sent her. But in inspiring me to play and bring all those people together, she had given me the gift of a lifetime.

This evening established a tradition for me. On my sixtieth and seventieth birthdays I gave concerts at Carnegie Hall and the Library of Congress. I was joined by an incredible group of friends, including my initial guests Yo-Yo Ma, Jaime Laredo, Sharon Robinson, Vladimir Feltsman, Joseph Kalichstein, Itzhak Perlman, and Radu Lupu. At the last concert in Washington, Bono joined us. We also invited young Arab and Israeli artists to fill out a small chamber orchestra. I hope that I will have the strength, and that my friends will have the endurance, to attend my eightieth birthday concert.

My fiftieth birthday was a moment of reflection for me. The children were becoming grounded, accomplished adults. Sara was doing well at Juilliard, and Naomi had recently started Princeton. The previous April, we had celebrated Adam's Bar Mitzvah. His beautiful soprano chanting evoked memories of my past in Sydney. My business was on the rise, and I was enjoying both my work and my relationships with my colleagues. Life was good to us, and after half a century, I had reason to be thankful.

*   *   *

Despite this pause for reflection, I remained in perpetual overdrive through the late 1980s and had more restless nights than were good for me. Every car, plane, or train ride was used by my colleagues to brief me on the latest transaction or an upcoming meeting. Jeff Goldstein describes me in those days as "a sponge." He remembers one occasion when he met me at the Concorde to take me to a boardroom presentation in midtown Manhattan. He had been living with the material solidly for two weeks, and during the half-hour drive from the airport to the city, he briefed me so that I could go in and make the presentation. This kind of approach was routine. I would use the human resources of the firm to leverage my experience and take it to the next stage. I gave my colleagues and assistants as much rope as they could handle, and I simply would not have been able to function without them. Special strength was added with the contribution of Glen Lewy, a great lawyer. He has gone on to build a fine career in investment banking and public service. Any success we had was based on the work of our leadership. Nonetheless, I had some useful and complementary skills: I could learn quickly and I could absorb and present complicated issues in a simple and direct way. We were a good team.

The first giant merger that we advised was the $4.75-billion hostile takeover of Sperry Corporation by Burroughs in 1986. We played a role in merging the two companies to create the electronics and computer company Unisys Corporation. That same year, Lou Gerstner, chairman and CEO of IBM, joined our client list soon after he joined the board of the New York Times Company in 1986. With no prior warning, he called me on behalf of the New York Times Company to ask if I would assist them in the purchase of the *Boston Globe*. I felt proud that he had picked us from among all the Wall Street firms, not because I had approached him but because of our reputation for skill and integrity. With the help of our distinguished neighbor and friend, Arthur ("Punch") Sulzberger, the chairman and publisher of the *New York Times*, and his immensely competent team, we made a successful transaction.

This was a time of intense reorganization in the business world. It was a boom period for buyers and for acquisition work. We were there at the right time, with the right team. Our firm was small but very effective, and we had made a remarkable entry into the investment banking world. We worked on several major retail deals in 1986. We helped to take New York's landmark department store R. H. Macy and Company private, and we worked to ease the financial burden on the buyout executives by arranging the $500-million sale of three shopping centers and a tract of land to my Australian friends at Westfield. We also advised Kmart on a series of mergers, which took the firm into the warehouse club business with the acquisition of several companies, including Sports Authority.

When Frank Petito stepped down from our firm in 1988 to return to the Morgan Stanley family, we needed someone talented to fill his shoes. I set out to attract as my new chairman the powerful and formidable former chairman of the Federal Reserve Board, Paul Volcker. Paul and I first met through Geoffrey Bell, the colleague at Schroders in New York with whom I had worked on the Venezuelan central bank management initiative. Paul came to know me better during the Chrysler rescue, when he was the chair of the government body supervising the financial rescue, the Chrysler Loan Guarantee Board. Paul was an icon. He was brilliant, capable, and expert in running the economy but had very limited commercial transaction experience. I knew, however, that his advice on economic and strategic matters would be invaluable to our major clients and that his name and reputation would add much to the firm.

Attracting Paul was not easy. We talked at length, but he vacillated for many weeks. Finally, I gave him an ultimatum. I asked him on a Monday to give me his decision by 5:00 PM the next Friday or the offer would be withdrawn. That did the trick. With minutes to spare, we signed a contract, which consisted of one typed page full of standard legal jargon attached to thirty or more pages of handwritten notes on a yellow legal pad.

My father, circa 1917

With my sister Betty at Watson's Bay, Sydney, 1938

Ivan Lund, Keith Hackshall, Hil Van Dijk and me—Australian Épée Team, Olympic Games, Melbourne, 1956

Fencing display hitting Michael Diamond at Air Force demonstration, Sydney, 1956

With my parents at my wedding in New York, 1961

Elaine with her parents at our wedding, 1961

With Sara, one year old, Sydney, 1964

With Former Australian Prime Minister Robert Gordon Menzies, at a Harvard Club Dinner, Sydney, 1966

Sara and Naomi, at
"Little Thakeham"
West Sussex, 1968

With Elaine in Jerusalem, 1971

Daniel Barenboim,
Radu Lupu, and Pinchas
Zukerman on Naomi's
violin, New York, 1972

Sara, Adam, and Naomi
during a visit to
Australia, 1972

Fishing with Adam in Alaska, 1979

Fishing with Senator Ted Kennedy in Alaska, 1983

With Vartan Gregorian when we each received an award from International Centre, New York, 1984

Giving Pinchas Zukerman a New York Award, 1985

With Vernon Jordan, a friend for forty years, 1987

Mayor Ed Koch, Isaac Stern, and me at groundbreaking of building adjacent to Carnegie Hall, 1987

With the family—Naomi, Elaine, Me, Adam, and Sara—at the Kennedy Center, 1990

With Chairman Paul Volcker at the tenth birthday of
Wolfensohn Incorporated, 1991

With Director Phillip Griffiths
outside Wolfensohn Hall
at the Institute for Advanced Study
at Princeton, 1993

With Brooke Astor at Carnegie Hall birthday concert, January 1994

With Elaine on a World Bank trip to Haiti, 1995

Dancing with women's group in Bamako, Mali in 1995—my first trip to Africa as World Bank president

With Village Chief in Korokoro, Mali, June 1995—The village birthing center was named after Elaine and a little girl born that day was named Elaine

With President Museveni in Uganda, June 1995

My first G8 meeting in Lyon, France, 1996

With Michel Camdessus, managing director of the IMF, and President Kim Dae Jung of South Korea, 1998

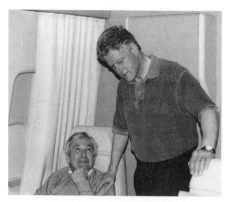

Flying to Jordan for funeral of King Hussein with
President Clinton on Air Force One, 1999

Visit to Bethlehem with Sara and Adam, meeting
President Arafat and Shimon Peres, 2000

With President Putin and Bank Executive Director Andrei Bougrov in Moscow, 2000

With Elaine, Alan Greenspan, and Andrea Mitchell at our home in
Jackson, WY, during our annual holiday, August 2000

With Elaine at Catherine's Palace while doing
work for the World Bank in St. Petersburg,
Russia, October 2000

With General Lebed (far right) and my first kill in
Northern Siberia, near the Arctic Circle, July 2001

Our fortieth wedding anniversary celebration with Jen Small, Adam, Sara, Sharon Rockefeller, Elaine, Senator Jay Rockefeller, me, Naomi Wolfensohn, and Valerie Rockefeller, November 26, 2001

At the United Nations with Kofi Annan and President and Mrs. Fox of Mexico, 2001

With President and Mrs. Toledo in Peru, 2002

With Lord Nicholas Stern, meeting in Beijing with President Jiang Zemin, 2002

Meeting with Premier Zhu Rongji, Beijing, May 2002

With expanded G8 meeting in Evian, France, 2003

With Afsaneh Beschloss, Jim Lehrer, Michael Beschloss, Don Graham, Kate Lehrer, and Mary Graham
at Carnegie Hall birthday concert, 2003

Bono performing in Washington with Yo-Yo Ma, me, and orchestra, 2003

With President Akayev in Kyrgyzstan, 2004

With the King of the Ashantis in Ghana, 2004

Meeting in late 2005 with President Bush, Vice President Cheney, and advisers discussing Gaza withdrawal

Meeting with Secretary of State Clinton, 2008

After the deed had been done, Paul and I grabbed a cab and went for a glass of champagne at Paul's apartment, where Elaine and his wife, Barbara, had been waiting for two hours. During the cab ride, Paul said, "Now I am chairman, and I never even asked you who else is on the board."

Taken slightly aback I replied, "Well, it's my wife and me, but if you would like your wife, Barbara, to join, she can." I thought he might jump out of the car. He had just come from the Federal Reserve and was used to working with the most prominent people in the world. Now he was in a small family business.

It was something of a coup. There had been huge speculation in the business media about what Paul would do after he left the Fed. This was his first commercial appointment after a lifetime of public service. If anything was to put James D. Wolfensohn Inc. on the global map as the boutique investment bank to watch, it was this.

On March 3, the *Wall Street Journal* reported that Paul would become chairman of our firm under the headline "The Great Volcker Sweepstakes Is Over." *Forbes* reported that in his new post, Volcker was likely to be earning ten times the $89,500 he picked up for managing the American economy at the Federal Reserve. Paul's arrival ratcheted up our public profile. I believe that because of the prominence he brought, I made it to the cover of *Forbes* with the tagline "When he talks, the corporate mighty listen." The piece noted my independence and "aversion to the quick buck."[4] I was proud. It was gratifying to see my mission for the firm recognized, and I wished that my parents had been around to see it.

It was, without doubt, a very difficult transition for Paul. He had a comfortable office, but no army of economists and assistants, no security guards, and no sense of being at the center of global economic power. He also had to adjust to the brash language of Wall Street. I would rush into his office and say, "What do you think about interest rates? Are they going up or down?" "Well," he would muse, "it could be that they will move either way; the economic situation is difficult to read." This was known as "Fed-speak," and I would make fun of him for it. Paul simply had limited experience in the business world, and the experience he did have was

decades old. It was like learning a new language for him. He was in no
sense an aggressive salesman. But gradually he became interested, involved, and very proficient, lending strength and leadership to our team.

It also took Paul quite some time to learn to give his opinion to our
clients. I remember William Purves, HSBC chairman, saying to me, "I
think you have got a lemon in Paul. You ask him a question, he doesn't tell
you anything. You hold someone out as an expert, and then he doesn't
give you an opinion." But in that early period, Paul had not yet adjusted
to his new role outside the Fed. He was there to provide advice to our existing clients and, even more important, to give me and my colleagues the
benefit of expertise on global and national economics. We all cherished
his judgment and, eventually, his friendship. Paul was especially important with clients like Chase, which wanted his overview of the commercial
banking business. I am sure that Chase came to us because of Paul, as did
several others, including Fannie Mae.[5] All of us in the firm were proud to
have Paul with us as a colleague with his unique capacity and values, and I
am happy that our close relationship exists to this day.

Because we were the house investment banker to our many clients,
other firms would bring in the deals to the clients and we would provide
advice to the board, the chief executive, or the chairman as to whether
and how to proceed. We also came to handle some of the deals ourselves
when they were generated by our clients without another investment
bank, and we became a useful source of income for the legal community.
If the deal needed public financing, we would bring in another, more established investment banking firm with the larger underwriting and
placement capacity that we lacked.

Our deals became more prominent, creative, and important. We assisted one of my oldest clients, DuPont, in repurchasing shares owned in
DuPont by the Canadian Bronfman family. It was a spectacular deal. We
arranged a multibillion-share buyback operation, the proceeds of which
allowed the Bronfmans, through Seagrams, to diversify out of DuPont
and into a new portfolio of activities in the entertainment industry. Quite
separately, Paul Volcker and Jeff Goldstein were monitoring what the Fed-

eral Reserve Board and Congress were planning; Paul and Jeff were preparing for the day when interstate banking barriers and the remnants of the Roosevelt-era financial laws imposed under the Glass-Steagall Act would melt away in the United States.

As our client list grew longer and the size of transactions increased, my informal style of running the firm inevitably changed. After ten years, we had grown into a firm with more than fifty-five professionals, and we were still expanding. We had almost too much work to do, and my personal financial matters and social life were in a mess almost all the time. However, the leadership of Paul, Jeff, Ray, and Glen kept the firm moving forward. My long-standing secretary and close confidante, Emily Ostrowski, supported me, kept my private life in order, and dealt with the clients. I occasionally raised my voice, but she never raised hers. She was calm, no matter what the crisis. Indeed, I trusted her so entirely that over the period of more than twenty years that she worked with me, I would supply her with a pile of blank, signed checks, which she would write on my behalf as required, examining, assessing, and negotiating whenever there was some error. Never once did I look at my records other than to ask how much money remained in my account.

*   *   *

"Out of the question," I said in 1989, when James Evans, vice chairman of the Kennedy Center for the Performing Arts phoned to ask if I would become the center's chairman. Of course, I was familiar with the Kennedy Center and respected its mission. I was flattered by the offer. But it did not seem humanly possible. Serving as chairman would mean going to Washington two or three days a week, and I was already consumed by my business and an almost absurd number of public activities, of which the most personal and important cultural activity to me was being the chair of Carnegie Hall. Nonetheless, Evans continued to pursue me, explaining that the Kennedy Center faced serious problems. He said that it needed some fresh blood.

I knew Evans from his work at the Union Pacific Railroad. He and his talented wife, Mary, were friends of President George H. W. Bush, who was concerned about the conditions of the cultural center of Washington. I felt I at least owed Evans a visit to assess the situation, and in truth, the offer was too tempting to dismiss out of hand. I thought there might be some way in which I could assist without taking on a formal role.

When I arrived in Washington and met with some members of the board, I could see that the organization faced substantial problems. The Kennedy Center was losing several million dollars in a good year and needed to be completely overhauled. It had been created in 1971 at a time when America's capital city was a cultural embarrassment. It was built to house a theater, an opera house, an orchestral hall, and two smaller performance spaces. With the support of the Kennedy family, it was intended to be both a monument to the late President John F. Kennedy and a center for the performing arts at the highest level.

There were problems. First, the location had difficult physical access. The beautiful site was slightly off center on the city map, overlooking the Potomac River, but difficult for many people to reach. The nearest subway station was at least a five-minute walk away, so visitors usually came by car or bus. Second, it lacked clear sponsorship from a high level of government. The National Park Service, which is responsible for many of Washington's monuments, maintained the center's grounds and public spaces, while a cumbersome public board, appointed by the president, oversaw the financing and the output of the theaters and the related educational programs. Funding for the physical support of the building was limited and had to be approved by Congress. Finally, there was inadequate public support for the programming and cultural content of the institution. Because of a long-standing belief that the government should pay, fund-raising in Washington was not fully developed for local institutions.

In Washington, the board reiterated the offer that Jim Evans had made to me. However, my schedule was simply too full, and it seemed irresponsible to take on a project of this magnitude. Yet I could feel the

Washington pull. I had come close to Washington during the Chrysler crisis, and I was intrigued and flattered to be asked to take on this new challenge. I agreed to conduct a study of the center personally during the coming three weeks.

At the end of the three weeks, I submitted a hard-hitting report to a board that included Senators Ted Kennedy, James McClure, and George Mitchell.[6] I emphasized that despite the genius and energy of its founder, Roger Stevens, the Kennedy Center suffered from a lack of artistic direction. I insisted that for there to be any hope of continuity, the government must address the big hole in the balance sheet. I recommended several immediate measures, including $15 million in federal money to wipe out the larger part of the deficit and a further $30 million to repair the leaking garage and dilapidated infrastructure. Unless urgent steps were taken, the place might as well be closed down.

The report struck a chord. The board again urged me to take the job, for two days per week. I was tempted, but it was madness. I declined. Evans kept the pressure on. He invited me to lunch and told me how much I was needed, notwithstanding anything else I was doing. He added that this would be a national platform and a chance to see how Washington worked.

"There is absolutely no way I can join you now," I answered. "I'm putting in so much time at my business and at Carnegie that I barely sleep, and Elaine and the children need more of my time. It is simply impossible."

But he was a good salesman, and I agreed to go down to D.C. for the annual presentation of the Kennedy Center Honors in December. A group of five artists had been selected for recognition in the presence of the president and a black-tie audience that would fill the Opera House.

On the evening of the performance, Evans invited Elaine and me to the White House for the presentation of awards to the chosen artists. Evans had told me that President and Mrs. Bush were eager to discuss my views on why the Kennedy Center was hemorrhaging so much cash and what needed to be done to put it back on its feet. We had only once before been to the White House, and that was for Vladimir Feltsman's private piano recital during the Reagan presidency. We were delighted and honored to be invited, and I was also curious to see what kind of reception I would receive from the Republican president, as my closest friends in American politics were Democrats. Bush greeted me warmly in the East Room, where he was shaking hands with guests while the White House photographer snapped away. His opening remark was: "Jim, we hope for our country's sake you will agree to think about becoming chairman of the Kennedy Center." The president had clearly been well prepared by Evans. It worked.

I was in the White House, speaking to the president of the United States, and he had addressed me as "Jim," like an old friend. I thought I had died and gone to heaven. Envisioning the eagle at the top of my bed and the American flag flying outside my house, like a fool, I later said yes, but this was only after seeing the magnificent honors program, then directed by George Stevens Jr., and Nick Vanoff, which impressed us both so much. There is something almost intoxicating about presidential power when you meet it for the first time. President Bush and his wife, Barbara, used it with respect and with a friendly manner. I found them irresistible. Behind the dazzle, I also had a sense that doing something of consequence in Washington was important. I loved my business and my philanthropic efforts in New York, but Washington would open a door for me to learn more about how the government worked and, possibly, give me the chance to make a national contribution.

Of course, finding time for the Kennedy Center would still be a logistical nightmare. It took three months before the details were worked out. First, there was the matter of Wolfensohn Inc. I just couldn't oversee it on a daily basis. So Paul remained as chairman, while Ray Golden, my colleague from Salomon; Jeff Goldstein; and a very talented corporate lawyer, Glen Lewy, took the responsibility of day-to-day running of the firm.

*   *   *

Meanwhile, an issue of seismic proportions was happening at home. Elaine had been diagnosed with breast cancer and was undergoing treatment. The very day that I had agreed to become chairman of the Kennedy Center, she had started chemotherapy. When it was time to make a decision, she said, "This is going to be a very difficult year for me. If you could put it off a year—you are so busy, anyway—it would help me a lot."

It pained me to think of what Elaine would have to go through over the coming months, but there was no way I could put off the Kennedy Center for a year, the situation was so dangerous. So we agreed on a compromise that would keep me available in New York on the critical days of the chemotherapy and allow me to take quick trips to Washington in the periods between treatments. Looking back, I think I was running away from the reality of Elaine's condition. I was scared of losing her and could not imagine our family without her. She showed enormous courage, although she was weakened and debilitated by the treatment. She not only survived but emerged strengthened.

The Kennedy Center was Washington's white elephant, and it quickly became clear that directing it would require a great deal of hard work and a full-time management team. I was constantly commuting between Washington and New York. At least two nights a week, I would attend performances at the center and either stay over in an apartment at the nearby Watergate Hotel or leave after 10:00 PM and get back to New York around midnight.

I had the trip down to a science. I would take a car to National Airport, where the plane would already be warmed up, and we would fly to Teterboro, where a car would meet me, and I would be home in ninety minutes, door-to-door. I saw it as part of my job each night to visit all five performance houses and spend time backstage. I had to see everything and everyone. The title of chairman was a misnomer. I was actually a chief executive, very involved in the day-to-day workings of the Kennedy Center, working directly with its talented and experienced staff.

It quickly became apparent after one year that I could not keep my role at Carnegie Hall. I could sense resentment in New York over my attempts to do both jobs. Sometimes, the pressure was so great that I would fly into New York in the evening and go directly to my office to work until the early hours of the morning. With little time to play my cello or focus adequately on Carnegie, I decided to step down and make way for Sandy Weill, who became chairman in May 1991. He had become increasingly involved and was well positioned to work with Isaac Stern and the management team to take Carnegie to the next level. He was the right man at the right time, and to this day, his record is extraordinary. I still feel a sense of loss over leaving Carnegie Hall, though, of course, it has developed wonderfully without me. Isaac and the hall were part of me, and I felt heavy with guilt when I left. It was to be an important transition for me, giving me my first exposure to the national scene in Washington, but it was bittersweet.

At the Kennedy Center, I set out with two goals. The first was to improve the quality of performances, and the second was to put the finances on a sound footing. But this was a far more complex world than the one I'd experienced through Carnegie. To start with, Carnegie was predominantly a hall for classical music. The Kennedy Center showcased all aspects of the performing arts and film. Because Washington in 1990 was significantly a black city with white suburbs, there were enormous sensitivities to matters of gender and race. The center had to offer material that would appeal to the whole community. More than just financing concerts and performances, the challenge was to build the institution as a local as well as a national arts center.

There is an assumption in the arts world that the Kennedy Center can put on more challenging material than commercial theaters because it receives government funding. In fact, the biggest problem I faced was trying to raise money. As a major visitor attraction, the center was obliged to keep its doors open 365 days a year, and it enticed almost as many tourists as the Smithsonian Air and Space Museum. Despite this allure, government cash was hard to get. Like Carnegie Hall when I arrived, the

Kennedy Center building was in dire need of an infrastructure upgrade. Despite being just twenty-two years old, the air-conditioning system was inadequate and antiquated in a city where summer humidity and heat can be unbearable. The rigging, lighting, sound systems, curtains, and acoustics were in need of updating in all of the center's theaters. During construction, the center's walls had been wrapped in a veneer of marble, bonded onto the concrete exterior, but Washington's extreme temperatures had caused it to crack. And the ceilings leaked.

My first task was to extract cash from Congress. In this, the Chrysler experience and the immense amount of lobbying, entertaining, and stroking required by that deal held me in good stead. Fortunately, I had cross-party support with the members of the board drawn from Congress. Bush had appointed me as chairman, but I had a good relationship with Senator Kennedy; his sister, board member Jean Kennedy Smith; and the rest of the family, all of whom wanted to ensure that the center, as a monument to John F. Kennedy, was in good shape. Teddy made himself fully available. When I called for help, he could make anything happen. He became my partner and my link to the family. I also had the ever-present advice and hugely competent assistance provided by his associate Kathy Kruse. The 2009 death of Senator Kennedy had a deep impact on me and on my family. He was truly a great and human figure on the American scene, and he will be missed.

Still, working with Congress is immensely difficult. When it is in session, members are in constant motion. Often, the only time you can grab someone is during the ten minutes it takes a member of Congress to walk from his or her office to a committee meeting or congressional session. For most, the center was at the margins of their interests. In many cases, they neither fully comprehended nor accepted the importance of the issues I was describing. Few members of Congress even read our briefs. I asserted that we were dealing with the future of the children of America and racial and cultural diversity. We were not just an arts center; we had an obligation to make the arts available and understandable to all segments of our society throughout the country. Although my request for funding had a glittering cast of bipartisan senators as supporters, including Kennedy, Wyoming's Alan Simpson, Oregon's Mark Hatfield, and New York's Daniel Patrick Moynihan, the fund-raising process was slow and awkward.

After several months of frenetic lobbying, I managed to secure authorization from Congress to inject $45 million into the institution and to provide $10–$15 million annually for capital improvements. But we still required the appropriations of the funds, and this too was a challenge. In the end, all the funding came through, and we succeeded in turning the center around physically and in achieving more diverse programs at a higher and more interesting level of performance.

During this time, I confronted truculent unions and claims that the center was antiwomen, antiblack, and uninterested in reaching out to ethnic minorities. A common view was that the Kennedy Center was inaccessible to the people in its own neighborhood. No one went there unless they were middle-class white and had a car. I was more than aware of this danger in a city where even a minor slight could be blown up into a lawsuit. The center was also criticized as middle-brow and unadventurous. I was lucky to have my assistant, Dinah Smith, to represent me whenever I had to be in New York. She knew how to recognize issues before they arose, and she alerted me to problems, finding ways to deftly protect the center in its new mission.

We worked hard at building up an alternative repertoire to classical tastes. The major change came with the appointment of Lawrence Wilker, who settled in as the chief executive and brought professionalism and knowledge to our efforts. We imported such popular musicals as *Cats* and *The Phantom of the Opera*, we commissioned six American dance companies, set up the Fund for New American Plays, and strengthened the center's commitment to education. We began to see a new spirit coalesce, which resulted largely from Mickey Berra's informal leadership of the stage team, a remarkable and talented group of professionals who keep the center operating. We tried to engage local artists through a community board designed to encourage diversity. Our belief was that the arts should not be optional or extracurricular for American children. The arts are a fundamental part of education because they open up the possibility for creativity: They allow children to dream and to develop their imagination. We commissioned children's opera and constantly lobbied members of Congress to make the arts a centerpiece of the educational agenda.

Many of these efforts were not recognized by the public, and there was always criticism. There were many stories about my threatening to resign in frustration when I did not get my way. I never considered resigning, nor did I ever threaten to do so. Despite the strike threats, the clashes about diversity, and the other difficulties, I felt that the challenge was worthwhile. And I had the full support of my board and our dedicated staff. I believe that, working with Larry Wilker, we made the Kennedy Center a more accessible and exciting place.

Although my five years at the Kennedy Center had a terrible effect on my health, my temper, and my peace of mind, it gave both Elaine and me a unique opportunity to learn about the Washington scene in an apolitical way. I was able to meet the people who lived and worked in Washington, inside and outside politics and on both sides of the aisle. At the Kennedy Center Honors each year, we found ourselves chaperoning presidents— first, George H. W. Bush and his wife, Barbara, and after the 1992 election, Bill and Hillary Clinton, whom I didn't know before their arrival in Washington. I became close to Clinton's chief of staff, Thomas F. "Mac" McLarty, and met at least half the cabinet, as well as senators and representatives. I learned where the levers of power were located and got to know the diplomatic community. In 1995, I was notified by Buckingham Palace that I was to receive an "honorary knighthood," a KBE, from Her Majesty the Queen for my services to the arts. My father would have been delighted.

After Elaine's recovery, although I was traveling constantly and hardly saw the children during the working week, I did manage to talk to them most days and made an effort to be with them on the weekends. For a time, I was putting more energy into the Kennedy Center than into my family, but after some months, I was able to restore a better balance. By the end of my tenure, Elaine had been in recovery for some time, and over several years, she was able to join me on many visits to Washington and enjoy much of what the Kennedy Center had to offer. We made many new friendships that have remained very important in our lives, and this experience gave us a common interest and enriched our life together at a crucial time.

*   *   *

An important aspect of my frenetic Washington years came to be our vacation time in Wyoming. In the summer of 1987, before my Washington adventure commenced, Elaine and I went to visit our friends Senator Roy Goodman and his wife, Barbara, in Jackson Hole, Wyoming, when the New York Philharmonic was performing there. As I descended from the plane, I looked around me, took in the view, and said to Roy spontaneously and rather surprisingly, "This is where I want to die. Let's go find some land while the ladies go on to your home." I felt instantly connected to my surroundings, the light, the mountains, the sagebrush, and the river. Over the course of a very few weeks, I did some research and with Roy's help found a piece of land that I could pay off over ten years. It cost about $100,000, and we decided to put a prefabricated log cabin on the site. Back in New York, the renowned architect Cesar Pelli was working with us to put up a new building adjacent to Carnegie Hall. I asked him to choose a prefab design for my house. He told me that I could not have a prefab log cabin. He would design and build me a house for the same price. Obviously, I didn't know what I was getting into. After Pelli and my son, Adam, visited Jackson Hole, instead of building on our ten-acre property, I ended up buying a hundred acres for cash and over time constructing four houses on the property. Pelli, despite the cost overruns, did a brilliant job, insisting that the house have cathedral ceilings and more than thirty massive tree trunks, which measured over forty-two feet high, as columns. His talent, his taste, and his devotion to his craft were unique. It was the best investment I have ever made.

Beginning in 1990, Wyoming was the place where I saw the children most frequently, and it provided the balance to my Kennedy Center activities. At first, Adam and I took a few polo lessons nearby, but we quickly decided that the sport was beyond us and spent our time together fishing in the river or playing tennis. I also enjoyed the golf courses. In winter, the whole family gathered there to ski. We all loved being in Jackson with our magnificent location, the Snake River rushing through our backyard, and the peaks of the Tetons in the distance. Our property contained a lake filled with trout and a wildflower meadow in summer. We saw moose, elk, and deer, sometimes a lone coyote, and very occasionally, a bear. We were very lucky to have this property as part of our lives, and eventually it became our main home as a family. It continues to provide us a closeness to nature and a respite from the pressure of work, for which I am ever grateful.

I believe I really got to know more of my busy adult children during the time we spent together in Wyoming. We tried to spend all the holidays together and often included Elaine's parents, who were very close to all three children. Sara had become a fine pianist and was managed by International Creative Management. She played in many concerts in Europe and Latin America during the year, and though she was sometimes nervous, she always performed with professionalism and acclaim. Naomi had studied history at Princeton and was working for a small publishing company. She had a great time writing and editing books for teenagers and young adults, but decided to go to law school so that she could have a more meaningful career and support herself. Meanwhile, Adam was at Princeton, majoring in music and directing a singing group. As I watched his hair growing ever longer, I bit my tongue and hoped that this stage would pass quickly. When we fished together in Jackson and Alaska, he was a free spirit, idealistic and fostering a love for nature that was to become his life's work. I was at last establishing a deeper set of relationships with my more mature children and spending more time with them. For more than a decade I took Naomi, Adam, and a dozen friends fishing in

Alaska, which helped us know each other better while developing lifelong friendships with our guests.

Meanwhile, after a fifteen-year absence from the London banking scene, I returned to form a joint venture with my friend Jacob Rothschild. We called our enterprise J. Rothschild, Wolfensohn & Co., and our aim was to deliver our own personal brand of investment banking across Europe and in the newly opened markets of the former Soviet Union and Eastern Europe. As a business venture, J. Rothschild, Wolfensohn & Co. never really took off. The firm earned some fees, did some deals in Russia, and eventually turned a profit, but we dissolved the London partnership in 1995, when I joined the World Bank. If our venture achieved nothing else, for me its existence alone was significant. My connection and deep friendship with Jacob lives on, and he and his wife, Serena, remain part of our lives. Today I share offices with Jacob in London, and he with me in New York.

I couldn't know it at the time, but in 1994 my career in independent banking was coming to an end. At the age of sixty-one, when many Wall Street bankers think about scaling down their horizons, a whole new vista was about to open up for me in the world of public service.

11

———— ∞∞∞ ————

THE ROAD TO
THE WORLD BANK

ON THE EVENING OF DECEMBER 4, 1994, IN THE PARKING LOT OF A
convention center on the Miami River in Florida, I got word that
my life might be about to change. I was hurrying to a cocktail party when
Roberto Dañino, a Peruvian lawyer from Washington, stopped me. "Jim!"
he said. "I see you may be the next president of the World Bank." I had
no inkling what he was talking about. The World Bank had not been in
the front of my mind for years, and Lew Preston, the president, was in the
middle of his term. "I read it in the *Financial Times* this morning,"
Roberto explained.

The rumor sent my head spinning, though all I could do for the moment was try to put the thought aside. The cocktail party was the prelude
to the Concert of the Americas, a musical extravaganza that the Kennedy
Center was set to stage the following night at the behest of the White
House. The concert was meant to be the grace note of the Summit of the
Americas being held at the convention center that week. To entertain and
inspire heads of state and delegates from thirty-four countries, we'd assembled a glittering array of North American and Latin American performers, from salsa stars to gospel singers, with Tito Puente, Bob Marley's
widow, Liza Minnelli, and the poet Maya Angelou. I'd pitched the idea

for the concert many months before as a way to showcase the Kennedy Center, but the green light had come only in October—giving us less than two months to create a major cultural event. I knew that possibly the only person who could make it happen was Quincy Jones, the impresario who had put on a memorable concert at the Lincoln Memorial for Clinton's inauguration. When I called Quincy, he balked at the time frame, but he and his business partner David Salzman proceeded to amaze us all. They quickly pulled together a spectacular production that would ordinarily have taken many months to plan and implement.

I did not actually see the *Financial Times* item until I got back to Washington two days later. Titled "Summers' Bright Day?" it reported that the brusque and brilliant Lawrence Summers, a forty-year-old international economist and former Harvard professor who was now deputy secretary of the Treasury, was "jostling" for the top spot at the World Bank. But, the story went on to say, Summers might lack the necessary diplomatic skills and contacts—and the person "to fit the bill" might be me, though I lacked his government experience.

Larry Summers's star was on the rise. He had been the Bank's chief economist before joining the Clinton administration. He and Robert Rubin, who became secretary of the Treasury on January 10, 1995, achieved dazzling success by coping with the Mexican monetary crisis in 1995, which threatened to throw the global financial system into disarray. This was the first of a series of feats of diplomacy and successful deal making for which *Time* magazine would ultimately name them and Federal Reserve Chairman Alan Greenspan "the Committee to Save the World." So it didn't surprise me that Summers might want to head the World Bank. What did surprise me was that the job might be open at all—and that I was being talked about as well. The story even described me as the preferred candidate of Wall Street, backed by "powerful allies" like my business partner, Paul Volcker.

I did not know how much credence to give this rumor, but my mind started racing. I had pushed the dream of leading the World Bank to the back of my mind after having been passed over for the job fourteen years earlier. I still tried to attend the Bank's annual meetings, but the president's speech was no longer the inspiration it had been during the thirteen years of Bob McNamara's tenure. After Bob left in 1981, his successors, although capable, seemed to me to lack his farsightedness and passion. I would go when I could, meet many regular attendees from Africa and Asia, and gain fresh insight into the issues facing the developing world. My interest in the subject of development more generally was not limited to the annual meetings. My work at the Rockefeller Foundation and the Population Council had given me a deep and abiding concern for poverty and gender issues, and notwithstanding the pressure of my professional life, I continued to take time to read about these issues. I never gave any thought to the possibility of running the Bank, and yet, hearing the rumor, I knew I would jump at the opportunity if it was real.

Elaine responded the same way. It was obvious that taking the job would stand our lives on end: It would demand total commitment and incessant travel from us both. I was sixty-one, and Elaine almost fifty-eight. Our children were grown and out of the house. We had worked hard to build a balanced life, in which making money was the facilitator, never the goal—and we certainly had enough. I had reached a point where my time was devoted about 50 percent to business and 50 percent to charities and public service, and we were looking forward to spending more time in Wyoming. I was the master of my own small universe. Now the question was whether to give up this hard-won and carefully crafted life and throw ourselves 100 percent into an old dream.

Elaine was, if anything, two steps ahead of me. She knew me and recognized that this would be the culmination of all my hopes. For my part, I had run my firm now for fourteen years; it was doing well and I was happy with it. Still, building a successful banking business was not a cause. I had also turned around the Kennedy Center in my five years as chairman. This had been a service and a pleasure, but it was not a long-term aspiration.

The possibility of working to end global poverty was of quite a different order. It would be the biggest challenge I had ever faced and was something

I cared about deeply. And it would allow us both to give back to society some of what we had gained and learned. So the conversation between Elaine and me was entirely pragmatic. We started discussing how to find out whether the job was really open and whether I truly was a candidate.

My first call was to Vernon Jordan, my close friend of twenty years, whom I had met when we worked together on the Rockefeller Foundation board. Vernon was now working as a lawyer in Washington and had a unique, trusting relationship with Bill Clinton. My friend was in and out of the White House on a regular basis, and I knew that if he thought it appropriate, he could ask the president directly what was going on. I believe he spoke to the president to advance my cause, but he never spoke to me about his conversation, if it indeed took place. Next, I called Donna Shalala, Clinton's Health and Human Services secretary. I'd come to know her from the Kennedy Center board. I knew she, too, would be able to get me straight answers. She did some checking and confirmed that there was a search under way and that many names, including mine, were being thrown into the ring. I told Donna that I was seriously interested but made it clear I did not want my interest to become public knowledge. My business depended on my personal involvement. It would cause real trouble if I were seen to be looking for another job at a time when we were trying to get new assignments from our clients. From Vernon and Donna it was clear to me that a search was on and that my name was on the list, but either they were unable or did not wish to give me an assessment of my chances.

After several weeks, which seemed like years, there had still been no announcement that Lew was retiring, so officially nothing was happening. Yet word got around that he was ill and there might be a vacancy. By February, the uncertainty and the growing rumors were starting to cast a shadow on my business. The chairman of the HSBC called to ask if it was true that I was leaving for the World Bank. I called Vernon and Donna and asked if they could convey to the administration that I needed an early decision within a week or I would have to remove my name from contention. I explained the delicacy of my position: "The worst thing would be for me to be publicly discussed as a candidate, lose my clients at the firm, and then discover I do not have the job." This was not gamesmanship—although in a business setting, a deadline is often the way to close a deal. In this case, it was reality forcing my hand.

I needed a distraction and thought it would be better if I was out of town and apparently disinterested. So I decided to go ahead with a scheduled business trip and touch base with some clients in Europe. The first stop on my itinerary was Berlin, where I was to attend a concert of the Berlin Philharmonic celebrating the one hundred twenty-fifth anniversary of the Deutsche Bank. I'd reached London, on my way to Germany, when a call came from Jan Piercy, the U.S. executive director of the World Bank, who was involved in the search process. She asked that I come back to Washington immediately if I wished to be considered further. I told her that I would be available the next day at the Watergate Hotel, but that I could stay only one day before having to return to Germany for the Deutsche Bank event and for other meetings. Jan's comments led me to think that this would be the big moment, the start of the final round of talks that would see my candidacy rise or fall. But when she arrived the next morning at my Watergate suite in the company of two White House colleagues, I quickly understood that this was something rather different.

The team standing before my hotel room door surprised me. The officials Jan had brought with her were a midlevel personnel officer and a junior lawyer in his first days on the job at the White House—hardly the players who would be dispatched to vet a serious contender. I had the feeling that Summers had the appointment already in his hands. That feeling grew stronger as I listened to what they had to say. They were there not to tell me I was the leading candidate for the job but to tie me up with red tape.

They started out by declaring that any hope of my appointment's being done—if it was to be approved—within the week was ridiculous. They explained to me that the process was complicated and that I had to get congressional clearances. This came as a surprise to me; I knew that the nomination for World Bank president is not subject to approval by

Congress. In order to apply for congressional approval, they continued, I would need to provide a log of all my exits from and entries into the United States over the last decade.

"I haven't the slightest idea how many trips I've made—it must be hundreds!" I said. "And I haven't a clue where my old passports are." But they were insistent. "You have to do it; these are the rules." I argued that this was not an appointment by the United States, subject to congressional approval, but a recommendation by the president to the World Bank's board. But they insisted this was not the case.

While I was arguing with these visitors and trying mightily to hide my anger, the phone rang, and I picked it up. On the line was Vice President Al Gore's chief of staff, Jack Quinn. The staffer was a stranger to me, and though I had met Gore at the original Stockholm United Nations Conference on the Human Environment in 1972, I hardly knew him, either. But the vice president was at the forefront of many of Clinton's initiatives, and he had a special interest in development and the environment and, consequently, in the World Bank appointment.

"I know what is happening there," Quinn said quietly. "Don't get upset. There's a lot going on. Get rid of them and come over to the White House at one. You have an appointment with the vice president at two and the president at three. The vice president wants to run through where you stand on various issues and what sorts of things the president might ask you. Then you'll have your meeting with the president." Quinn added, "For God's sake, don't say anything there about this call."

Feeling a lot more confident about dealing with my guests, who, I now understood, had come to sidetrack me, I became conciliatory. I wrote down all the questions they posed to me. Yes, I said, I would try to provide some answers as soon as possible. I even managed to convey my enthusiasm for the Bank and the work I thought it should be doing and to thank them for their interest.

As agreed, I met Jack Quinn at the White House at 1:00 PM, and he reviewed the afternoon's agenda before taking me in to see the vice president. Gore and I spent nearly an hour running through the questions President Clinton might ask, touching on the environment, the managerial challenges at the World Bank, the role of women in the Bank, and how I intended to deal with the rash of vocal Bank critics from all sides.

Vice President Gore really knew the issues. I was very impressed with the depth of his understanding of the problems the Bank was facing. He had a deep, personal commitment to the environmental challenges in particular but understood that the single factor having the most impact on the environment was, in fact, poverty. I was deeply disappointed when Al Gore did not become president of the United States in 2000.

At the end of the hour with Gore, I was ushered into the Oval Office, where I was greeted by President Clinton. He looked amazingly relaxed. I had been in various White House reception rooms and offices before, and Elaine and I knew the Clintons socially from the first Washington dinner that Ann and Vernon Jordan had given president-elect Clinton in 1992, as well as from the Kennedy Center Honors, where as chairman of the center, I, along with Elaine, would sit with President and Mrs. Clinton in their box. He and Hillary had visited our home in Jackson Hole during their summer vacation, and we had given him a birthday party at our house. But this was my first time in the inner sanctum, and my first meeting where there was a substantial issue to be discussed. He showed me some photographs and objects in his office, poured me a cup of coffee, and asked me to sit down. How was it that I was sitting in the Oval Office in an armchair next to the most powerful person in the world? I was as nervous as I had ever been, but I tried not to show it.

Very little of the material I had rehearsed with the vice president came up. Instead, the president started by asking what I'd heard people say in London and Germany about the handling of Mexico's financial crisis. Then the conversation meandered through music and the Kennedy Center before moving on to global politics. The president did most of the talking. He was sipping a Coke and seemed perfectly at ease. He spoke of global issues not in a distant way but with urgency, somehow conveying that they were part of his responsibility. There was implied power in the way he spoke, but he never seemed threatening to me. He engaged me as someone who was already helping to make the world a better place.

I never had a sense that I was being interviewed. Erskine Bowles, Clinton's deputy White House chief of staff, sat in the room with us, watching the whole thing, taking notes. But he never said a word.

Finally we got around to the World Bank. "Well, what would you like to do at the Bank?" Clinton asked.

"Mr. President, I really think I should talk first about myself just for a minute," I said, "because you've always regarded me as a sort of cultural fixture in Washington and a really bad golfer."

"No, no," he said. "I know more about you than that. I may know everything about you. So forget talking about yourself, just tell me what you'll do at the Bank."

So I told him I thought the world was in a difficult state, that poverty and development were clearly fulcrum issues, that in hot spots in Latin America, Africa, Gaza, and Bosnia, the presence of a long-term agency like the World Bank that could work on infrastructure and economic development was absolutely crucial. I said that the growing disparity between rich and poor was real and accelerating, and that the increasing discussion of the environment was no longer a fringe issue but a vital debate that would shape our children's lives. I said that women's rights, sustainable development, and the extension of health care and education were all issues the Bank had to address. I also told him that the Bank seemed very inward-looking and tied up in bureaucracy. I acknowledged that Lew Preston had tried to address these challenges and shake the place up, but he was caught in midflight. Ever since Bob McNamara, it seemed that there had been no real burning dream in the institution, and not enough passion. I told him that Bob's last speech had brought tears to my eyes. I said that I would like to get people at the Bank crying and smiling again and to rebuild their confidence. I ended by saying, "If you give me the job, I won't let you down."

"I know you won't," he said. And there was a little silence.

The next words out of my mouth were practical and mundane. I told the president that I was in a bind with timing. "I know that you're considering a number of people for this job, and I don't want to put you or your administration under pressure," I said. "But for me not to damage my business, I need a decision quickly. But even leaving me out of it—it's critical for you and for the Bank that this thing not drag on. And if I'm obliged to go through four or five weeks of security checks before you announce your choice, frankly, that just makes it too difficult and I will have to withdraw." President Clinton simply said, "I know, I know. I know." With that, our hour ended, and I was ushered out. I was amazed he had given me so much time.

Dazed but hopeful, I rushed to the airport and returned to Germany for the Deutsche Bank concert and anniversary celebration the next afternoon. Before the event, I met Fritz Metzler for a drink in his office at the Metzler Bank AG, Germany's oldest private bank. My old friend George "Gowi" Mallinckrodt of Schroders joined us. As we chatted away, a secretary came in and announced, "There's a call for Mr. Wolfensohn from the White House." They say that the White House switchboard can find anyone, anywhere in the world in a matter of minutes, and indeed it had discovered me in one of Europe's most exclusive banking parlors. I was extremely nervous, but before my banking friends, I acted as if this were an everyday occurrence.

It was Jack Quinn on the line. "I just want to let you know that the president had a meeting last night after you had gone, and you have been selected as his nominee." Quinn cautioned that the FBI would conduct a preliminary check by noon the following day to ensure that there was no problem, and he confirmed that there was no need to go through the congressional procedures. This was all I needed to hear. I was elated. Although this was to be secret until I was cleared, I could not contain myself. I immediately told Fritz and Gowi, insisting that they not tell anyone else, and then I called Elaine. We drank champagne to celebrate the news, even though it was not yet official. Later that afternoon, I heard one of my favorite orchestras, but I have almost no memory of it. My mind was 3,000 miles away.

I later learned that the president had called his lieutenants into the Oval Office on the evening of our meeting and asked them to give him their views on the candidates. I was told by one of Clinton's assistants that there was a lengthy discussion of the possible choices and that he had asked them one straightforward question: "Which of the candidates will be distressed the most if he screws up the Bank job?" I was told that the majority of people in the room had picked me and that the president said, "I agree. Let's nominate him, then."

With the information from Quinn, I believed that I as good as had the job. Technically speaking, the World Bank appointment is not made by the United States but by the Bank's executive board. In the recent past, high-level appointments to senior global jobs at the International Monetary Fund (IMF) and World Trade Organization (WTO) have become global political wrangles. But at the time of my nomination, President Clinton was at the height of his popularity worldwide, and it was clear that his choice, especially in a case where he had taken such an active interest, would be supported.

I never asked President Clinton why he chose me, the dark horse, over Larry Summers, the inside candidate. I later put together the following picture. Clinton and Gore wanted a candidate who had, among other things, a deep interest in the environment. But there may have been other reasons. Summers was a brilliant economist and already in an important job at the Treasury. My skills lay in making people work well together. Clinton knew I was a poor kid from Australia who had made a success in the global investment banking business and had money enough to devote years to public service. Moreover, I had not been exposed to the rigid organizational structure that most civil servants, including my soon-to-be colleagues at the Bank, had become accustomed to. I had no institutional baggage, and I was beholden to nobody. I also believe that

Summers was seen as a highly important member of the Treasury team, and Clinton did not want to lose him. As Larry later became secretary of the Treasury, it all may have worked out for the best.

I wanted to prove that Clinton and Gore had made the right choice. I felt as if everything I had done in my life was preparation for this challenge. I was just over sixty years old, and here I was being given the extraordinary opportunity to summon all my experience and skills and apply them to what I considered the world's best job. The World Bank presidency brought with it prestige, influence, and the capacity to act, but my goal was not ego gratification—it was to use the presidency to bring about positive change in the lives of people in the developing world. My responsibility was not only the financial bottom line, and my contributions would be measured in human terms.

*   *   *

The hardest thing I now had to do was tell my partners and staff in New York. On my return, I immediately called them together and described my conversation with the White House, explaining that it would mean giving up my role in the firm, and ownership, so there could be no possibility of conflict of interest. Sitting at the end of a long table at our Lexington Avenue offices, with about seventy-five people, including Paul Volcker, crowded into the room, I tried to describe the importance of the World Bank job and the mission ahead. But when I looked around the room, saw my colleagues, and realized that they had become like family to me, emotion got the better of me, tears came to my eyes, and I could not continue.

Eventually, I regained my composure. I remember thinking as I spoke that all my explanations were logical and coherent. The truth was that I was making a personal decision to leave the firm to pursue a life's dream. But after creating a business and building it up for fourteen years, the moment of abandoning it was very hard.

The announcement was a shock to my colleagues. But they handled it with grace and encouragement—despite the fact that the firm had my name on the door.

My departure would be rushed, and there was little time to negotiate with my partners on the terms of my separation. They feared that the business would suffer, but they did not know by how much. I assured them we had built something permanent. They suggested that because I was seen as the principal source of business for the company, my withdrawal would put it all at risk. They felt I was taking away the goodwill. So my partners offered to buy the firm only for its book value of approximately $10 million, which represented my investment. I agreed, although I admit I felt that the business was worth much more than the "cash in the bank" and that as founder I should have received a higher valuation. Instead, I was leaving the business after fourteen years with just the money that had been retained over the years.

But I had no real bargaining power. And I felt that I was abandoning my colleagues. So I didn't fight over the price. I confined myself to asking that the contract include what I called the "Salomon clause." I wanted to make sure that if my partners were ever to merge or sell the firm, I would receive my fair share of the proceeds—as Billy Salomon never had upon the sale of Salomon Brothers. The arrangement we agreed upon was that if James D. Wolfensohn Inc. were sold within five years of my departure, I would be entitled to 25 percent of whatever the purchaser paid over and above the firm's capital.

Once the contract was signed, I never thought about it again; I became fully immersed in the World Bank. Just over a year later, I was in Vietnam, a world away from the concerns of New York investment banking, when my former partners called to say they had sold the business to Bankers Trust. The price was $210 million, out of which the Salomon clause delivered me $45 million in Bankers Trust stock. I immediately gave half of the stock to the foundation that Elaine and I had established in 1982 to support our donations to our activities in the arts, culture, and health care. I am happy to say that to this day the Wolfensohn Family Foundation continues to be active in many fields and is now run by my children and one staff member, with a little help from Elaine and me.

*   *   *

I had a gap of approximately two months before I would officially take over the presidency. During that time, I threw myself into understanding as much as I could about the Bank and its contribution to development. I quickly relocated to Washington, where, with the permission of Lew Preston, I roamed the Bank corridors and spoke to staff at all levels. Simply walking up to the impressive Bank headquarters building, two blocks from the White House, was enough to remind me that the challenge facing me was more complex, more formidable, and more important than anything I had attempted before.

To say the headquarters occupies an entire block is an understatement. It is actually a complex of seven buildings, where 9,000 of the Bank's employees work. Another 3,000 employees are spread among over a hundred locations in various countries. The headquarters complex includes a separate building for the International Finance Corporation (IFC), which devotes itself to private-sector activities in the developing world. But the centerpiece is a grandiose edifice of Reagan-era white concrete and glass, started by Preston's predecessor, well-known former congressman Barber Conable, and plagued by a $100-million cost overrun upon its completion in 1993. Emblazoned next to the main entry is the motto, "Our dream is a world without poverty," which cynics like to mock, but which, I would learn, accurately describes the goal of most of the people who work at the Bank.

The World Bank arose from the embers of World War II. Along with the International Monetary Fund, it was created at the Bretton Woods conference in New Hampshire in 1944. The IMF was intended to act as a global central bank providing financial advice, liquidity, and short-term loans to nations with inadequate resources and balance-of-payment difficulties. The International Bank for Reconstruction and Development, which became known as the World Bank, was charged with providing expertise and loans to support postwar reconstruction and economic development—first to war-torn Europe, and later across the globe. Over the decades, its task became more complex and diverse. During his thirteen-year tenure as president, Robert McNamara greatly expanded the Bank to speed up development in scores of newly independent countries and to focus on poverty alleviation infrastructure and the provision of basic needs. The Bank became the principal point of contact on economic matters between wealthy nations, which supplied most of the Bank's capital and donated additional funds, and poorer developing countries, which received loans and grants and tapped its expertise.

As international banks go, the World Bank is only midsized. The assets of the leading commercial banking groups dwarf the $275 billion held by the World Bank in 2009. But its size understates its importance. Unlike the major commercial banks, the World Bank is a cooperative. Its capital comes from the treasuries of its member countries; governments, not wealthy individuals or pension funds, are the owners of the World Bank. Nearly every nation in the world belongs, rich and poor alike, 185 at last count. All members subscribe to purchase shares in rough proportion to the size of their economy, so that the bulk of the funding comes from so-called Part 1 countries—the rich, developed countries of the world. Given that the shares are only partly paid up, the owners of the shares are obligated to subscribe additional capital when it is needed.

Therein lies the Bank's unique strength. In effect, its financial stability is guaranteed by the full faith and credit of all the rich nations. This gives the Bank the ability to borrow on capital markets by issuing its AAA bonds at the lowest prevailing interest rates—and to funnel those borrowings as loans to the developing world at that time on the order of $15–$20 billion a year. In addition, the Bank raises billions more annually directly from the donor governments for outright grants and interest-free loans through the International Development Association (IDA). Every three years, the Bank management seeks a replenishment of the IDA funding. The private-sector side of the work is in the hands of the IFC and its thousand-person group of specialists with a deep knowledge of all aspects of business and banking. Finally, the Bank group also includes the Multilateral Investment Guarantee Agency (MIGA), which provides guarantees for borrowing for developing countries, and the International Center for the Settlement of Investment Disputes (ICSID), an agency established to settle commercial disagreements arising in member countries.

By the time I became president, the Bank faced many challenges that had been building for years. Under McNamara and his three single-term successors, the Bank's strategies had been affected by swings in the American political pendulum. Energy shortages became an important passion while Jimmy Carter was in the White House, and the Bank plunged headlong into large-scale power development projects across the world, from dams in India and China to power plants in Latin America. It was a central player in infrastructure projects throughout the world, as well as on some softer issues such as governance, health, and education. When the environmental movement started to take hold in the 1980s, the Bank took a leading role by inserting environmental criteria and biodiversity considerations into its projects. When Thatcherism and Reaganism became all the rage in the 1980s, the Bank's emphasis on economic planning came under heavy fire. Ronald Reagan himself opened the annual meetings in Washington by lecturing on "the magic of the marketplace." In one speech, he declared that the best way out of poverty was to follow the route he had taken: He urged developing countries to "pull themselves up by their bootstraps." This statement produced a standing ovation.

In the 1990s, when Bill Clinton first took office, the Bank was still promoting market solutions to development problems, such as the privatization of national assets and enterprises, even though the practice was often an open invitation to corruption. Clinton wanted to emphasize the importance of including the developing world in the growing market-place of the future. Wave upon wave of development thinking influenced the operations of the Bank, and each wave seemed to leave behind it another layer of bureaucracy. And during the long years of the Cold War, the Bank was often pulled into supporting regimes friendly to the West, even if they had a poor development record and less-than-clear financial practices, lest they fall into the Soviet orbit.

Despite the many efforts to please its richest member, the Bank found its support in Washington ebbing away. Successive Bank presidents felt that the Bank's operations were under constant threat of reduced funding. By the time I arrived, the globalization of trade and international finance was advancing at a rapid pace. Increased access to capital markets was enabling governments in developing coutries to tap into the flow of finance, making many nations in Asia and Latin America less dependent on the World Bank. By 1995, net private-capital flows to developing countries were nearing the $250-billion-a-year mark, dwarfing the $20 billion provided by the Bank, but the poorer countries without natural resources generally did not benefit. Critics on the right and on Capitol Hill often cited such data to argue that the Bank was becoming less and less relevant and perhaps should be phased out or substantially reduced.

Critics on the left had reached the same conclusion for different reasons. Because of its insularity, the Bank was increasingly seen among activists as the problem rather than the solution to the issue of poverty. It was deemed to be slow, clumsy, and maddeningly inept at addressing poverty and the environment. Some suggested that management appeared more concerned with preserving a top rating for its bonds than with the quality and effectiveness of the loans it was making.

The fiercest critics were the nongovernmental organizations (NGOs). With the end of the Cold War and the spread of globalization, organizations like Oxfam, CARE, Friends of the Earth, Doctors Without Borders, Amnesty International, and Human Rights Watch were gaining moral force. In some instances, they saw themselves as the conscience of government, bringing pressure to bear on world leaders, encouraging them to look beyond their borders and national politics to consider the human needs of the planet.

To get a measure of the antagonism toward the Bank, I read the material prepared by our major critics among the NGOs. Typically, they argued that the Bank's projects were doing more harm than good. The growing consensus was that the Bank had outlived its usefulness. Oxfam claimed that the Bank was not paying enough attention to poverty and that the efforts it did make were not effective. This NGO was particularly aggressive in its criticism, clashing with the World Bank and other multilateral banks over the reluctance of the financial establishment to consider debt forgiveness, which had become a hot-button issue. Worse, argued many NGOs, much of the funding that the Bank provided to client countries was not even being used to better the lot of the poor. Like consumers with maxed-out credit cards, these nations were using most of their borrowings to repay existing debt. Friends of the Earth complained that many of the Bank's major projects—for example, financing the building of dams and roads without taking steps to prevent the clearing of cropland and forests—were hurting the environment. Transparency International asserted that the Bank turned a blind eye to corruption and graft.

The Bank tended to ignore all such critiques. I could understand the impatience of the typical World Bank rural development professional, just back from six years in the field in Brazil or Cameroon, having to listen to Hollywood luminaries hold forth on the displacement of native peoples. But the Bank was making no apparent effort to distinguish between serious organizations with knowledgeable people in the field and well-intentioned but ignorant and naïve dreamers.

An organization might send the Bank a long, detailed report bearing hundreds of signatures and, in response, get a standard two-paragraph form letter thanking them for their concern. Rarely was there follow-up or dialogue. In poorer nations, some NGOs were closer to the problems of communities assisted by the World Bank than the Bank itself. And yet Bank experts tended to dismiss all such organizations—a defensiveness that made them seem arrogant and elitist. Whether they advocated debt reduction or micro-development projects, the NGOs were largely excluded and seen as troublemakers seeking to undermine the Bank's work. Instead of engaging in a dialogue with them, the Bank closed in on itself, believing that the soundness of its plans and solutions and its own long experience would suffice. Yet the widespread criticism was indeed having an impact. Inside the organization, it hurt morale, to the point where at senior management retreats, veteran World Bankers would debate whether the Bank was indeed becoming a "sunset institution."

The critics were getting politicians' attention as well. Lew Preston found himself under increasing pressure from his own directors to tighten the Bank's budgets and downsize the Bank's programs aimed at the poorest countries. There was serious talk about cutting funding for the IDA, the arm of the Bank that gave grants to the world's poorest countries. These grants were of enormous value and should have been preserved at all costs. Plainly, I was entering an institution that had reached a crossroads.

*   *   *

In early April 1995, I visited Lew Preston at his home. He was only sixty-eight, but he was very ill with late-stage cancer, and it was clear to him that he would not be able to complete his work at the Bank. President George H. W. Bush had appointed him just three years before, as Lew was winding up a stellar career as CEO of JP Morgan Bank, the legendary and powerful New York financial institution. Lew's first focus as World Bank president had been to impose internal discipline. The Bank's budgets were notoriously out of control after the huge overspending on the headquarters project. Lew tackled these by putting in place state-of-the-art financial controls imported from JP Morgan and increasing the degree of accountability up and down the ranks. He focused on what he knew best, in the belief that if the Bank became a more efficient, reformed organization, it would be better able to fend off its critics and achieve more in the field.

Lew was a quiet, private man who was most effective working behind the scenes. Even as the Bank battled its critics, a great deal of internal reappraisal and soul-searching went on during his tenure. Senior managers on retreats actually had serious discussions about whether, now that the Cold War was over, the Bank should phase itself out, battered as it was by critics from both sides. Meanwhile, to defend the Bank's image and help articulate its positions, Lew recruited Mark Malloch Brown, a British public-relations troubleshooter with a background in development at the United Nations. Mark, as ferocious as Preston was mild, was unwilling to take criticism of the Bank lying down. During the annual general meeting of the Bank in Madrid in 1994, there were vigorous protests against Bank policies. An attending NGO held a press conference in which two Nepalese condemned a World Bank–funded power plant project. In response, Mark made sure a Nepalese official appeared before the cameras. Each side claimed the other had its facts wrong.

Had Lew been well, I would have treasured the possibility of flying around the globe with him, learning from him the president's business firsthand. I would have enjoyed walking the halls of headquarters with him to get to know the staff, and I certainly would have benefited from spending hours in private briefings with him and calling upon his wisdom and experience. But his illness did not permit those things, and I knew that my visit at his home might be all the time we would have. I wanted to convey how much I respected his work and all that he had achieved, so I decided to keep my questions to a minimum and hear whatever advice he chose to give.

The main thing he wanted me to understand was how incredibly difficult the organization was to run. Once you get to know the Bank, he said, you realize that the invisible internal structures—the hierarchies and networks and fiefdoms that had solidified over the years—are every bit as massive and immovable as the expensive new headquarters edifice. He didn't have to tell me that this meant trouble for any would-be leader. When you inherit an entrenched bureaucracy, you have to decide whether you'll be a figurehead or a real boss. If you don't impose yourself on the institution starting the minute you arrive, you never will.

"Now," he said, "let me tell you what I've done for you." The news he had was that Ernie Stern, a thirty-year veteran who was acting president in Lew's absence, would be retiring from the Bank to join JP Morgan. Lew had engineered this transition, which, he told me, was more significant than I probably realized. For years under McNamara and his immediate successor, Stern had been the senior vice president in charge of the Bank's operations, which he had run with a strong hand and unmatched control. In time, Stern had become the person who was truly in charge. Working with a tight-knit group of senior colleagues, he was the de facto chief executive. Every decision and every piece of paper, including documents flagged for the president's eyes only, landed on Ernie's desk. I am told that even the executive directors, the representatives of the governments that owned the Bank, felt the need to run every idea past him before taking it to the board.

During the Reagan era, Bank president Barber Conable had tried to break Ernie's hold. In a 1987 reorganization, he swapped senior vice presidents, sending Ernie to run finance and naming as chief of operations Moeen Qureshi, who later became prime minister of Pakistan. But Ernie's influence and network remained dominant. Lew had tried to dilute his power in 1991 by creating three new posts of managing director, which made Ernie one of the three people supervising the Bank's nineteen vice presidents. But Ernie still chaired the all-important loan committee, which oversaw operations.

Without question, Ernie was skillful, well informed, and highly motivated by the mission of the Bank. Clearly Lew respected him, as Ernie joined Lew's home, JP Morgan, for his commercial career. But Ernie was also like a feudal king, divvying power among the vice presidents, who, in exchange for loyalty, were allowed to build independent fiefdoms of their own. By the time Lew arrived, he explained to me, the Bank resembled a federation of feudal states. Each vice president ran his own department with almost no overall sense of direction. He said that Ernie's departure "gives you the opportunity to truly be chief executive."

While I was still trying to take this in, Lew turned the conversation to the future direction of the Bank. He had one other major piece of advice: I should not allow the interests of the United States to unduly influence the Bank's decision making. To be sure, the United States remained the largest single contributor to the Bank, accounting for 16 percent of its capital. But during Lew's tenure, membership in the Bank had expanded enormously as many former Communist bloc countries had joined; they and other developing nations deserved an active voice, he said. Beyond that, China, India, Brazil, and other rapidly developing countries, particularly in Africa, were increasingly dissatisfied with the way the Bank was governed. Possibly the most serious challenge at Madrid had come not from NGOs but from the finance ministers of developing nations. They had actually convened a meeting on the outskirts of the city to protest the dominance of the G7 wealthy nations and to demand a greater say in multilateral finance. Part of my job, he said, would be to work with other major shareholders of the Bank to develop an effective counterweight to the influence of the United States.

*   *   *

My meeting with my predecessor seemed to support the tentative conclusions I had reached. I was convinced that the Bank had an extraordinary global resource of talented people who were committed to achieving change in the world. I felt tremendously fortunate to be given the opportunity to work with such people. Yes, there was ample and not entirely groundless criticism from NGOs and other interest groups. And yes, the rapidly developing nations deserved more of a say. But the Bank represented a unique vehicle for bringing about more equitable economic and social development. The World Bank, in the view of many, had gone woefully out of tune, but it was surely the right instrument to play.

Taken as a whole, the world had never been richer. With the Cold War ended, the global economy was on a roll. The standard of living was rapidly on the rise for hundreds of millions of people around the Pacific Rim. We had seen the boom of Korea, Malaysia, and Thailand, and now India and China were on the rise. Latin America, too, was showing significant economic growth, though at a slower pace. On a global scale, poverty was in retreat, but still not at a sufficient pace, and Africa was making only limited progress.

Yet the aggregate numbers disclosed serious problems: intractable poverty, wildly uneven development, a degrading environment, continuing hardships for women, and a growing divide between rich and poor. Half of humankind was still at the very bottom of the world economy— 3 billion people living on less than $2 a day, with more than 1 billion of these people subsisting on less than $1 a day. This was not just another statistic. As I read more and learned more, the enormity of this reality struck home. The Bank's mission—now my mission—was to bring this gigantic issue to the attention of the world and to do something about it.

On May 31, 1995, the eve of starting my five-year term as president of the Bank, I was full of heady optimism. I was convinced that change could be achieved during my tenure, and I imagined that my ability to communicate, which had served me so well in business, would enable me to overcome the Bank's dysfunction. Yes, the mission was daunting, but I could not let myself entertain any doubt. My family and I had dinner that evening at the British Embassy, where Ambassador Sir Robin Renwick invested me with an honorary knighthood, a KBE, for my work in the arts. We were surrounded by friends. I commented in my remarks that in a way the evening represented, for Elaine and me, the end of our old life and the beginning of a new one.

The press release with which Mark Malloch Brown's PR department greeted my appointment gave an inkling of struggles to come. Presenting me to the media as a "Renaissance banker," it applauded my accomplishments as an investment banker, my success as chairman of Carnegie Hall and the

Kennedy Center, and even my skills as an amateur cellist. But to me, what was conspicuous about the release was that it lacked any reference to my interest in and knowledge of development through my extensive work at the Rockefeller Foundation, the Population Council, and many other relevant organizations. I had been called a Renaissance man before, but in the charged atmosphere of the World Bank, it was a backhanded compliment. I knew what it really meant. The staff was used to running the institution. I suspected that Mark and others inside the Bank thought that if they positioned me as an ivory-tower character—a charming deal maker with an eye and ear for the fine arts—they could continue running things. They were in for a big surprise.

12

A DIFFICULT ENTRY

THERE WAS A SOMBER MOOD AT THE BANK. I COULD SEE THE STRAIN and apprehension in people's faces as I stood to address several hundred employees on my second day as president on June 2, 1995. Not only was their institution beleaguered by outside critics, but their popular leader, Lew Preston, had been wrenched from them after a scant three years. Now they faced having to adjust to me—an idealistic interloper from Wall Street who was known to them mainly for heading Washington's Kennedy Center and for playing amateur cello at his own birthday party at Carnegie Hall. Gossip in the newspapers before my appointment hadn't helped. The media had reported I was campaigning for the job by proposing major staff cuts and resignations of vice presidents. The rumors were untrue. In fact, most of them had originated in the Bank, reflecting the anxiety and crisis of morale that awaited me there.

The previous day, I sent the entire staff an open letter with a simple message. I wanted their help. We needed to transform the Bank into an organization that, while conscious of financial management, was motivated and explicitly driven by ideals. I wanted the Bank to face outward, not inward, and to make poverty the core of the agenda. I wanted us to think of our mission in terms of people first, not numbers, although it was essential that we lend prudently and work to keep the Bank profitable. "We all work at the Bank because we care about the world," I had written. "We care about poverty, the environment, social justice and the other issues that make up the dreams of this institution. These should be our guiding lights."

Now, as I spoke before the staff, I could see my mild jokes were being met with weak smiles, and I could sense the chill in the air. I was well aware that I was throwing a grenade into an entrenched culture. But I thought it important to get my initial ideas out into the open and ignite a debate. I was going to have my say, and I could see no point in trying to sugarcoat the message.

I turned first to the malaise affecting the Bank. Point-blank, I asked the staff to quit bad-mouthing the institution to their families, their friends, and the press. I wanted to encourage change within, not fuel the attacks from outside. I pointed out that there was a poisonous atmosphere within the Bank. Just one day into the job, I had received nasty anonymous letters complaining of individuals and systems. "I have no problem with vigorous internal criticism," I said, "but I have a big problem with anonymous criticism." Then I said, "Whoever is writing me those anonymous letters may be very smart, but if I find them, they'll be out of here in thirty seconds."

I was unambiguous and direct, and it got their attention. I attacked the complacency and insularity I had been finding in the Bank with an appeal to the staff's better professional selves:

What is needed is a sense of mission, which I'm sure each of you has, and a dream and a sense of something on the outside. There are those among you who live in the ecosystem of the Bank. You have found out that you can exist in the Bank with no sense of the outside world. There are procedures, there are personnel manuals, there's health service, there's catering, there are rumors that there's sex—there's everything you need inside the ecosystem. I don't think that's a particularly useful concept. And I hope that soon no one will have that view.

Finally, I spoke about the rumors of mass firings that had been circulating. I said that the reports were false. On the issues of staffing, strategy, and budget cuts, I explained, my intent was to suspend judgment for at least six months. In the meantime, I would visit the field to talk to our colleagues and clients.

> My objective is to get a sense for myself of what we're doing well, what . . . we can improve, where we should put our resources. . . . When I know that, I'll tell you the right size of this institution. The one thing I do know is that when we have the objectives clear and when we know the resources, we'll have the right number of people. And they'll be people who care and they'll be people who are proud to be here.

These remarks did not go over well, to put it mildly. Some people found the tough talk repellent and even vulgar. Some thought my idealism was naïve—that I was going over ground that had been traversed many times. And, of course, I had made some people fear for their comfortable jobs. Many of my colleagues, especially senior colleagues, felt they already understood the Bank's mission and were engaged in tackling the important issues every working day. They knew how to go about it, no help needed from an enthusiastic new chief.

I knew what was expected of me: I should be a figurehead, a presentable emissary to the many officials and heads of state I would meet, while the Bank went about its business as usual. After the staff meeting, Mark Malloch Brown, my vice president in charge of communications, told me bluntly that I had gone "off-message"; in this day and age, the World Bank president ought to be talking not about the needs of the poor but about market-based reforms.

But I was very conscious of what I was doing. I wanted to infuse the Bank with a sense of passion before I decided upon a specific course of action. I knew that most of the people working for the Bank had a deep sense of mission and wished to make a difference, and I wanted to tap into this reservoir. I wanted more humanity in what we were doing, and less of a feeling that we were a bureaucratic machine. And perhaps more than anything else, I had to become the leader of the management team and not an appointed figurehead.

In the chaos of those first ten days, I barely slept, cramming each day full of meetings and speaking to as many colleagues as possible. I knew I was not coming through well to the staff, and as much as possible, I wanted to remedy that. I sought out younger and more junior people in particular, as I sensed in them more willingness to deviate from accepted practice. This was rare in the Bank's upper echelon, and often when I tried to bring the conversation with senior staff people around to the over-whelming priority we should give to the fight against poverty, most of my colleagues would look at me as if I were from another planet. Poverty reduction was already their objective, they would respond. They did not want me to review and change the well-established practices of the institution.

Being in charge of a massive organization of more than ten thousand people was new to me, and I struggled to adjust. My own firm of a hundred people was a minnow compared with the World Bank. Though I had toiled for many years in substantial but still modest-sized investment banks and worked with and advised giant multinational corporations, I had never run one. Within each of the separate institutions that compose the World Bank group, powerful fiefdoms had evolved. Within the Bank itself, each regional division had its own vision, approach, experts, and staff. And each was presided over by a regional vice president. Other de-partments at headquarters worked almost autonomously under powerful bosses to conduct research and develop expertise in specific areas such as education, health care, infrastructure, the environment, macroeconomics, and trade. With scores of experts on every region and discipline, some of them world renowned, the Bank group was by far the largest development institution in the world, dwarfing not only in numbers of people but also in depth of expertise other multilaterals like the United Nations Develop-ment Programme (UNDP) and regional banks such as the Asian Devel-opment Bank, the Inter-American Development Bank, the African

Development Bank, and the more recently established European Bank for Reconstruction and Development.

The World Bank had taken on the issues of poverty and development in the broadest sense. But to my eyes, it seemed to approach these challenges in a technocratic way, with language clothed in jargon and devoid of emotion. The Bank never talked about social justice, although the issue was no doubt a present consideration. Sanitized and quantified official project proposals were what defined business as usual. And the culture of numbers and project proposals dominated, better adapted to the time when the Bank was financing power plants, dams, and roads than in its current expanded role, which included financing policy reforms, improved governance, and human development.

Atop all this bureaucracy were the president and not just one oversight body, but two. If you were to design a way not to govern a company efficiently, you would have the World Bank. Its top board, the Board of Governors, consisted of the ministers of finance or ministers of development from all the member nations—185 of them. It convened only at the annual meeting in the fall. In addition, there was the Board of Executive Directors, the twenty-four-member working board of the main bank, appointed by the governors. Members of this board, each of whom served for a limited period of years, also acted as executive directors of the International Development Association, and the Bank's other institutions, the International Finance Corporation (IFC) and the Multilateral Investment Guarantee Corporation (MIGA).

These executive directors functioned like no corporate board I had ever encountered. Whereas a corporate board typically convenes perhaps once a month, the board of the World Bank is a resident board. And though the president is the chair of the board, the executive directors supervise the president day-to-day. With offices in the main building and their own extensive staff, which is drawn from the nationals of the countries they represent, executive directors were always present on the premises in Washington, meeting daily in committees, and formally as a board at 10:00 AM every Tuesday and Thursday in sessions that sometimes ran until late afternoon or early evening. I quickly learned that I was expected to chair every one of those meetings. The cost of the executive directors and their offices amounts to tens of millions of dollars each year, and the demands they make on staff time are substantial. I only hope that our shareholders feel that the costs are justified by better results in lending.

In time I came to respect the board; its members could be very supportive and constructive if I was open with them and kept them informed. I worked closely with the successive deans of the board, Ibrahim Al-Assaf, Evelyn Herfkens, Jean-Daniel Gerber, Andreï Bugrov, Franco Passacantando, and Yahya Alyahya, relying on their advice and guidance on many occasions when we faced delicate issues.

But initially I found a major disconnect between the board, the Bank, and me. The institution was run by the permanent staff, which is to say, the vice presidents in their individual fiefdoms. They, in turn, did not talk much to each other; there were few management meetings, and those that took place were not forums for open exchanges. The senior managers did share one very important understanding, which was to keep the board and the president out of it: "Tell the board as little as possible, in very lengthy presentations, and get what you want" seemed to me to be the mantra of the vice presidential cadre. They had seen presidents and executive directors come and go; as career bureaucrats, they knew they could always outlast the appointees. So there was little accountability to the board or president other than when the projects had to be approved by the board.

The project-oriented culture played neatly into this. Presidents were appointed for five years, and directors normally for two to five years. But a typical project—building a road in the Andes, let's say—would take several years to put together, with all the preliminary work negotiated with the relevant government or authority in order to develop a proposal setting forth its purpose, its cost, and the management framework. The proposal would go before the board, which would vote and approve the project, and then it would take another several years to see the road built. By that time, the membership of the board would have turned over once or twice, and the president would probably have changed as well. Even if the project fell miserably short of its original goals or had to be adapted and changed, there was no one on hand to hold the officials in charge of Latin America accountable for the performance.

I did not know how I would ever get my arms around this juggernaut, but I was determined to make a start. The institution was seen as bureaucratic, yet hundreds of the staff members I was meeting had a better understanding and deeper, more informed feelings about combating poverty than were publicly recognized. I concluded that we needed two things. First, there had to be a consensus inside the institution regarding our main goals and a larger concept of our role. And this had to include the IFC and MIGA. Second, we needed a much more aggressive program to project to our shareholders and critics, a forceful and clear vision for our institution.

*   *   *

Whatever the remedies for the Bank group's defects were, I was sure I would never find them in Washington. I had to understand the true scope and complexity of the problems facing poor nations, and to do that, I had to see them for myself. Most importantly, I had to find out whether my early impressions of Bank activities were anywhere near correct. Traveling was in my DNA. I had never hesitated to jump on a plane to provide advice to my business clients, to close a deal, or simply to be part of a meeting. I also had made many overseas visits with the Rockefeller Foundation and the Population Council. Thanks to those trips, I had already spent enough time in developing countries to know that the rich world did not spend nearly enough to support development and that what it did spend was not always being used effectively.

Fifteen days after I became president of the Bank, Elaine and I left to visit five nations in sub-Saharan Africa. The staff had scrambled to put this trip together. The word was already out that I was different, and they were struggling to adjust. I had made their task doubly difficult by insisting that I actually expected to get work done during the trip. I had learned that after McNamara, Bank presidents were generally more hands-off than I hoped to be. Country visits by World Bank presidents and their wives tended to be ceremonial. I was told they would fly in, meet the head of state and relevant ministers, inspect a few selected projects, visit a village or two, attend a cultural event, and give a pep talk to the local staff and a reception for the local development community. I made it clear that I cared less about formal events than about getting into the field to review projects and meet our real clients.

Elaine had worked in education for years, and she offered to give me substantive help. Even without an official title, she was my adviser on human development, and her input was invaluable as I tried to understand the Bank's challenges. We hoped to see for ourselves what worked and what did not. When the itinerary said turn right, I warned the staff that occasionally we were going to turn left. We wanted to learn from all levels of our local staff, and we wanted to engage directly with those we served.

In my mind, this would be the first of scores or even hundreds of country visits with two initial objectives. First, I would make poverty the Bank's focus. And second, I would not rely on intermediaries to understand the issues on the ground. Of course, I met with leaders in every country, with government officials and with others working in the development field. But, I tried always to do this after my field visits. This pattern gave me a sense of the issues at hand that I could speak about when I did meet with the leaders. It also was quite discomforting to some of them.

In Africa, my real education began. On a sunbaked June day in Mali, I found myself sitting under a tree in Korokoro, a small roadside village. We had already been greeted with warm hospitality by the officials. We marveled at their pride in Mali's history. I was now sitting among the people the Bank was meant to help. I saw Elaine chatting animatedly with the women in the group. I sat on the ground with the old village chief, who had given me the traditional welcoming gifts of salt and flour, and I felt an immediate kinship. He described the challenges his people were facing: the lack of water, the long walks women had to undertake to find firewood, the poor facilities for education and health. It was humbling to listen to him and clear to me that he knew what his village needed. From then on, I tried to seek the input of our village hosts. I was also given the traditional gift of a goat. I asked the chief to look after the goat for me and to find him a home, maybe in a zoo. Despite some support for the idea from my local colleagues, I suspect that in the end, "my goat" provided a meal in the village.

We also visited Amadou Toumani Touré (affectionately known as ATT), the general who had led the overthrow of a long-standing dictator a few years earlier and who, up to that time, had kept his word that he would step down and permit a democratic transition. When I told him I was struck by the poverty in Mali, he replied: "We are not poor; there are no homeless people here. Our culture, our traditions, our history, and our solidarity are our wealth. And we know what we want."

And yet there was grinding poverty. Mali then had the second-lowest per-capita income in the world; its 10 million people lived with a GDP per capita half that of India. What ATT illuminated for me was that income was not the only dimension that mattered. Understanding the context and the culture of each country and its state of development was essential in order to make judgments about a country's needs and to be effective in designing programs to meet them. The first step had to be listening to the people whose lives were affected. And the second was to try to understand the local history and the governance structure in which they were living. Cultural sensitivity was essential. I learned quickly not to judge a situation by my standards but to dig deep to get a sense of the local values and history and only then to try to make some preliminary judgments about what the community needed.

I soon discovered that the Bank resident representative in Mali, a young American economist named Linda McGinnis, had jumped at the chance to have me visit—not because the World Bank's efforts were succeeding so well, but to call my attention to the country's plight. She was one of a generation of younger, hardworking, devoted development officers. While she had become a confidante and a trusted adviser to the

Malian president and to senior government officials, she was equally comfortable in villages. She projected a very positive image—of a caring and
listening Bank, with little technocratic arrogance. I saw her as the kind of
person who could build the future of our institution.

I was traveling with Edward "Kim" Jaycox, the experienced and
knowledgeable vice president for the region. A tall, ruddy, heavyset American, Kim had been at the Bank nearly thirty years, and his well-known
passion for the development of the continent had earned him the nickname "Mr. Africa." Elaine attended a lunch with Kim and a small group
of Malian women leaders and found he had ample insight into their needs
and a personal vision of some of the solutions for Africa. Indeed, Kim was
considered a reformer who had tried to change the Bank to bring it closer
to its clients. But he was also one of the Bank's real barons, used to operating autonomously. Though he greeted me politely and accompanied us
on our tour, he was clearly on his guard and concerned about my lack of
knowledge.

Mali's poverty dismayed us. In Korokoro's health center, we visited the
birthing room—a mud hut containing a wooden table without stirrups or
other supplies. There was no running water, just a few buckets. The windows had no glass panes, only burlap. A baby had been born just as we arrived; she and her mother rested on a canvas cot outside the door. Elaine
and I both knew that the odds were stacked terribly against this child. She
faced the prospect of stunted growth from malnutrition. Her chance of
going to school was one in four. At an early age, she was likely to un-
dergo genital mutilation. She would probably marry young and face a
one-in-twenty chance of dying in childbirth. It was heart-wrenching.

When we were about to leave, I asked Elaine to make a donation to
fund a better birthing facility. After some persuasion, she reached into her
handbag and took out some money, which the village chief accepted with
a look of embarrassment. Later, Linda McGinnis took me aside to have a
quiet word. "Be careful," she told me. "You can't fix world poverty that
way. You'll be a poor man and it sets a terrible precedent. It's human, but
it's not smart." She was right, of course. I learned to restrain myself from

such impulsive actions in the future, though the urge was often there. The broader impact of this incident was to point me in the general direction of trying to improve the lot of women. I would learn that in many cultures, they carried the bulk of the workload but all too often were seen more as chattels than people. In the years that followed, I would work to keep this issue at the forefront of our efforts.

We spent time with Mali's president, Alpha Oumar Konaré. A Europe-educated poet and historian, he was a very gentle man of integrity and vision. He had come to power democratically, through the transition process that ATT had supervised. We met at his palace, which was not at all palatial, and talked of the country's heritage. Mali was the nation of Timbuktu—the Pearl of the Desert—a legendary stop on a major trade route in the fifteenth and sixteenth centuries, when that city already boasted a large and important university. While we conversed, the president showed me some of the beautiful beads for which Mali was once known. It was a country with a tradition of scholarship and reverence for ancestors, but it had lost its empire and fallen on the hardest of times. No one really cared about Mali now, except for France, which kept an interest in its former colonies. Yet the culture had maintained its deep respect for family and for elders, and Malians expressed a joy about life, even though they had very little in the way of material goods.

Soumaila Cissé, the finance minister, had prepared a long wish list for his meeting with me, which he read aloud. I was startled to hear him talk about debt as one of the crushing problems his country faced. At about $3 billion, with roughly one-third owed to the World Bank, the external debt of Mali at the time was slightly larger than its total GDP. And in spite of numerous debt rescheduling agreements, debt service payments continued to limit not only the country's ability to invest in its future but also the freedom of the government to set its priorities, especially on education, one of President Konaré's top objectives. Could this be right? *"Je vais m'en occuper,"* I told him—"I'm going to work on that."

The economics of debt came up again two days later, when we moved south to visit neighboring Côte d'Ivoire. In the Riviera district of Abidjan, we met with an imam who wore a flowing white robe and who turned out to be well versed in his government's dealings with the World Bank. He gave me a simple but profound lesson in the impoverishment of nations.

"My people tell me that there is money coming into our country," he said. "But what they tell me is that the money comes in this pocket," he gestured to the right-hand side of his robe. "And that is the new loans."

"But," he went on, reaching for the other side of the robe, "out of this pocket, they have to repay a similar amount for the old loans." He brought his hands together. "What's left in the middle is nothing. Can you explain that to me?"

Côte d'Ivoire, Mali, and many other poor countries were choking on what economists call overhanging debt. They began borrowing heavily in the early 1970s on the theory that by developing their economies and selling commodities to the industrialized world, they could raise their standard of living and later repay the debts. The collapse of commodity prices in the late 1970s and early 1980s, combined with currency depreciations and fiscal ill-discipline, had destroyed that model. Country after country defaulted on its obligations and had to be refinanced by new loans; inflation exploded, and poverty spread. In the 1980s, both the IMF and the World Bank responded with "structural adjustment programs" designed to restore fiscal and monetary discipline and to fight inflation by implementing free-market policies. This was the age of Thatcher and Reagan. By balancing their budgets and allowing market forces to set prices, the theory went, debtor nations could regain stability, attract foreign investment, and reignite growth. But in many cases, the imposition of economic austerity only made the lot of the poor worse; for political reasons, the expenditures most likely to be cut were those funding the already limited health and education services to the voiceless poor. Meanwhile, the struggling economies remained mired in debt. Far from learning to be more responsible in running their affairs, many African leaders came to see the structural adjustment programs as millstones around their necks, and some used these programs as an excuse for not fighting poverty with vigor.

By the time I arrived at the Bank, the poor nations owed so much money that much of their new borrowing was eaten up by the need to make payments on the loans they already had. They were like households whose breadwinners have lost their jobs and maxed out their credit cards—and in these nations, the drain on funds meant that the powerless poor were the ones most badly hurt. In Côte d'Ivoire, policy makers had long opposed currency devaluation, as the currency had been on a fixed parity with the French franc for fifty years. The 1994 currency devaluation had begun to restore competitiveness and stability to the economy. Nevertheless, as the imam had told me, debt service remained an overwhelming burden for the poor.

My encounters with the ministers and the imam struck a chord in me. In my previous life, I had played a central role in reorganizing the debt of corporations in crisis such as Chrysler and Burma Oil. If this could be done in the private sector, what was different about the public sector? I was a newcomer and had never been involved in lending to poor African nations, but from an economic perspective, the situation seemed absurd. We had reached a point where in some countries, almost the sole purpose of the new lending was to repay old debt.

When we met President Henri Konan Bédié of Côte d'Ivoire, it was a striking contrast to the situation in Mali. Clearly, the well-being of the citizens was the last thing on his mind. He gave us a lavish dinner in his sumptuous palace in Abidjan. We sipped champagne under crystal chandeliers, and the food and wine were superb. Bédié boasted that he had obtained his chef from the Élysée Palace. The ministers and courtiers in his entourage wore expensive gold watches. A few wore Légion d'Honneur boutonnieres awarded by the French government. Elaine and I could not get out of our minds the abject poverty we had witnessed in the countryside that very day. By the time dessert was served, I was livid.

I confronted Kim Jaycox after we were out the door. "Where is the Bank's money going?" I demanded. It certainly wasn't flowing into education or health care or anything we could see. What was the point in granting Côte d'Ivoire money for projects if the government was simply using the funds to make payments on old loans and using whatever was left over to support a lavish lifestyle for the leadership?

My indignation must have galled Kim, and he fought to keep his cool. He explained—with a little too much patience, I thought—that we were in the business of "adjustment." There was a finite amount of help the World Bank could provide, and in this case, all the Bank could do was refill the country's budget. "That's idiotic!" I said. "It's crazy to pretend that the weakest countries can cope with this kind of debt." The argument escalated from there. Kim stood his ground, citing policies of not forgiving debt owed to the World Bank—policies that had been worked out over many years. "You have to understand . . . ," he kept saying, describing all the ways in which the Bank and other donors had tinkered with the debt issue without ever confronting it squarely.

Clearly, he was affronted to hear me challenge the accumulated wisdom of the Bank and other development institutions. "I know you have more knowledge of Africa in your little finger than I will ever have," I said. In truth, Kim had been fighting the French to stop "defensive lending," jargon for making new loans to repay old ones. But this was not generating results. I said that I felt there was something fundamentally wrong with our approach if all we did was lend money for projects we designed with the governments and then, at the same time, demand that the government pay us back an equivalent amount on old loans. The imam's words had affected me deeply.

*   *   *

Uganda, our next stop, brought an unexpected respite. President Yoweri Museveni took Elaine and me to his beautiful farm in the hills, where he introduced us to his longhorn cattle—great Ankole-Watusi cows and bulls, each with a long pedigree going back to Egyptian times, which the president recited. The Musevenis treated us to a special performance of dance and music in the Ugandan tradition. We met people from the nearby village, Katwe, including illiterate parents whose faces lit up with pride as they showed us photographs of their children, who were studying for degrees at universities in Uganda and for doctorates abroad. Thereafter, we met a series of small business entrepreneurs. I vividly remember a woman who was converting banana peels into charcoal using a simple furnace and some molds to make briquettes. She used the proceeds of her sales to improve the life of her family and the community. With all the pride of a CEO of a multinational company, she shared with us her pencil-written records. This was our first glimpse of an upwardly mobile Africa.

Yet the specter of poverty and AIDS was always present. In a slum in Kampala, I visited a factory that produced coffins, in all shapes and sizes, for victims of AIDS—a vision that will never leave my mind. Dismayingly, this was Uganda's fastest-growing business.

Our next stop was Malawi, a country where 40 percent of the urban expectant mothers were HIV positive and where women lawyers were already ringing alarm bells about the feminization of the AIDS pandemic and the need to empower women by giving them the means to protect themselves, often from promiscuous husbands. Elaine visited a hospital in Blantyre, where she saw AIDS victims with advanced tuberculosis and other symptoms of disease.

During our brief final stop in South Africa, we attended the World Cup Rugby finals with our friends Irene and Clive Menell and experienced the roar of the stadium crowd—blacks and whites together. When Nelson Mandela came to the match wearing the green jersey of the Springboks, the entire crowd joined in singing the anti-apartheid anthem. That moment was full of an optimistic sense of South Africa's potential strength to unite and lead the continent to a better future. Later we rejoiced with our South African friends as their team beat the favored New Zealand.

During this first overseas trip, I broke World Bank precedent and began meeting with people from NGOs. This was a much bigger deal than it may now seem. Feelings were still raw within the Bank after some of the NGOs had disrupted the 1994 annual meetings in Madrid. Colleagues in the Bank and many government officials in rich and poor countries alike questioned their legitimacy, pointing out that the NGOs had no electorate at all. Why should they have a voice in World Bank affairs?

It's true that some of these organizations were nothing more than extremist groups bent on opposing the Bank, no matter what it did, but many were serious organizations doing good work in the field. They had earned the guarded respect of some of the development professionals within our institution. But previous attempts at dialogue by the Bank had led nowhere. The NGOs preferred to pressure the Bank by playing the media and lobbying politicians directly. For me as president, it was risky to meet with them because it raised their visibility still more. There was a possibility that any encounter might be used against me. And, after years of being mostly scorned by the professional elite of the Bank, the NGOs were suspicious of interactions with this institution, too.

For all these reasons, I needed to act with care. I held my first meeting with several NGOs in Uganda. To lower the risk of publicity for each side, we met in the evening and avoided the hotel lobby. My staff met my NGO visitors outside and brought them up the back stairs to my hotel room. After greeting them, I explained that I wanted them to have access to me, but only if they were willing to keep our conversations private. I did not wish to turn on the TV the next day and see our meetings being used against me. I needed to hear directly what was on the minds of civil society leaders, to understand their concerns, to hear their advice, and to try to build an atmosphere in which we could work together.

My session with Tony Burdon, the head of Oxfam in Uganda, was one of my most difficult. Oxfam had been founded during World War II as the Oxford Committee for Famine Relief by a group of British academics, social activists, and Quakers to collect food for war-ravaged Europe. Like the Bank, it had expanded over the years; it now helped supply food aid to many parts of the developing world, along with identifying and addressing a host of other development problems. Tony, an economist, had been with Oxfam for years. He embodied the anger that many in the NGO community felt toward the Bank. "For once," he told me, "I'd like to see the Bank stop pontificating and listen to what we have to say." As he and his colleagues talked, I began to think they had a point. They seemed to have at least as strong a grasp of the development process as did many of my staff. One of the most startling facts they threw out was that the Ugandan government was spending $3 per citizen per year on health care and approximately $17 per citizen per year on paying back debt. I thought again about the imam. I said to myself, *This is the economics of the madhouse!* It was a debtor's prison. Our World Bank loans were dragging down the very nations we wanted to help.

I returned from Africa exhausted but with my education begun and with a greater sense of purpose. The trip had accomplished what I had hoped. I felt I had taken my first steps to feel less like a newly appointed bureaucrat and more like a leader of this institution that was essential to combat poverty. It gave me a growing sense of confidence that I was starting, just starting, to grasp at least some of the issues. I also developed a growing respect for the Bank people I saw in action on the ground. They struck me as a force to be nurtured and supported for their development expertise, experience, and deep commitment. I immediately set in motion plans for more travel. I wanted to see what we were doing in Latin America, China, and India as soon as possible. I also wished to call on ministers of the major developed countries who served as governors of the Bank, to get their advice and to assess the extent to which they were prepared to entertain change.

On the long flight back from Africa, I had made up my mind about three things. First, the confrontation between the Bank and independent aid groups had to cease. I wanted organizations like Oxfam to be our partners rather than our foes. They would remain independent and critical, but we had to find a way to work together. Second, the Bank needed to get closer to the people it served and allow more decision making to happen in the field. Finally, debt relief, even more than corruption, was the issue to be addressed most urgently. As soon as I got back to Washington, I set up a small team, working outside the formal bureaucracy, to come up with ideas about how to help poor nations mired in debt.

*   *   *

The most visible and important occasion for any World Bank president is his speech at the annual meeting held in September or October. It is the moment when the Board of Governors convenes, bringing together the finance and development ministers from around the world. It is also the moment for the president to address many of the important people in international development and international finance—the heads of the central banks, top investment and commercial bankers, development experts, and several hundred journalists and broadcasters from around the globe. The session rarely produces fireworks. Delegates flit in and out of the main hall, their minds on private meetings in offices and hotel lobbies. And if the president's speech drags, people yawn and even doze. Despite this, the president's annual speeches along with the speeches of the managing director of the IMF are dissected and analyzed in finance ministries and newsrooms. Any speech by an incoming or a departing Bank president is bound to receive particularly close scrutiny.

I knew from having watched Robert McNamara and his successors that this annual event provided a great bully pulpit, a platform for raising major issues and putting new initiatives before the world community. I had heard McNamara do this with the subject of basic human needs. In his 1973 Nairobi speech, he coined the term "absolute poverty," a condition of deprivation that "falls below any rational definition of human decency." This call to action in the fight against poverty still rings in many people's ears. In every subsequent speech that I attended, there was always a message for the future in addition to a report on the past year, always a direction to follow, and words to inspire. Now that I had my chance, I wanted to give my audience something fresh and meaningful to hold on to. As we pulled the speech together, I repeatedly told Mark Malloch Brown and the rest of the team that I was aiming for a minimum of yawning and dozing. We must not burden the speech with "World Bank–speak," I insisted.

Again, I wanted the primary message to be human, not bureaucratic. I'd spent seven of my first twenty weeks traveling to our borrowing and lending member countries, and when I got up to speak, I tried to convey to our shareholders and to those in the audience the nobility and capacity of the people we were trying to assist. I spoke of slum dwellers we'd met in the Brazilian city of Salvador who were working with the World Bank to install water and sewer systems in their neighborhood. I described villagers we had visited in Gansu, China, who had pooled their resources to build new fields, roads, and schools and a World Bank–funded aqueduct that delivered the water they needed to end a chronic drought. "Development can be measured not by the bureaucratic approval process but by the smile on a child's face when a project is successful," I told my audience. Some people thought this was corny sentiment, but I intended it as a challenge. We had to cut through the murky layers of bureaucratic obstruction and concentrate on the human aspect of our work.

I went on to sound many of the themes that inspired my presidency: fighting poverty, using technology and education to document and spread knowledge, protecting the environment, and revitalizing the Bank. But my listeners really started paying attention when I zeroed in on debt relief. "For a small number of countries, the debt overhang remains just too great," I said. "And as it grows, new lending becomes less effective." As mild and tentative as this may now sound, it riveted the audience's attention. The president of the World Bank, holder of $165 billion in loans at the time, was calling on his shareholders to consider whether the poorest debtor nations could be relieved of some of their obligations. The ministers and bankers knew that this was a challenge to the status quo, especially on Capitol Hill, at the U.S. Treasury, and in Japan, where there was strong resistance to changing the rules governing the repayment of sovereign debt.

My speech was generally well received, but gaining sympathy was one thing; turning the audience members into advocates for debt relief was quite another. I knew I needed to develop my ideas more clearly before I could count on these people for support. The World Bank had considerable financial strength, but not enough for it to afford unilaterally to write off the debts of all the poorest countries.

Unlike most commercial financial institutions, the Bank has no bad-debt provision in its accounts. The Bank had operated on the understanding that every country was obligated to repay debt, with no provision for unusual circumstances that would make repayment impossible. To change this understanding risked weakening the balance sheet of our institution, hurting our ability to sell tens of billions of dollars' worth of bonds each year in the public markets, and thereby jeopardizing the funding for all of our loans and grants. Had we decided on an immediate and broad debt forgiveness program we would have been forced to strengthen the capital of the Bank by calling on its unpaid equity and increasing its capital base, which would have been a dramatic and unwelcome event for many of its principal government shareholders. To avoid this cascade of ill effects, I reasoned that we would have to raise new money specifically for debt relief—in large measure outside the Bank—and we'd have to take write-offs of the Banks' claims on borrowers only to the extent that reducing our capital would not weaken our credit rating. This meant going, hat in hand, to the governments of the world's wealthy nations to ask them to forgive debts that they had never wished to write off, even though they would never be repaid. As I would discover, this was difficult to sell to the rich nations of the world.

For the rest of that week, I used every opportunity to bend delegates' ears about debt relief. Officials from the German Bundesbank and the Japanese Ministry of Finance, two of the Bank's biggest stakeholders, were loath even to discuss the issue. In their view, any debt forgiveness by the Bank could endanger the entire Bretton Woods system of multilateral finance. To justify this argument, they evoked the venerable banking doctrine of "moral hazard." Let any debtor off the hook, the thinking went, and all your other borrowers would start losing their incentive to pay off their loans.

This orthodoxy failed to acknowledge that we had already crossed the Rubicon. More than a decade earlier, during the Latin American debt crisis of 1982, the IMF and global banks had agreed to "reschedule" tens of billions of dollars in loans to Mexico and Argentina. Although not writing off the debt, the institutions effectively "reduced the burden of debt" under a different name. But the truth was that there had been no write-offs. The difference between the Latin American debt crisis and the problem of overhanging debt in the other poorest nations was that much of the Latin American debt had been owed to Western commercial banks, and there had been a great deal of private investment at stake. Among the poorest countries of Africa, which would be the principal beneficiaries of debt relief, there were few such commercial interests; most of the countries' debts were to governments and aid agencies. In both cases, the borrowers clearly could never repay the loans without replacing them with new loans.

The adverse response of the Germans and Japanese meshed with the so-called Washington Consensus, a neoliberal approach for dealing with third world economies that had come into its own during the late 1980s. It stood for a constellation of Reaganite and Thatcherite policies that reformist Polish finance minister Grzegorz Kolodko summed up in 1988: "Liberalize as much as you can, privatize as fast as you can, and be tough in monetary and fiscal matters." Although such policies had proved effective in rapidly developing countries such as Poland and Hungary, the Washington Consensus did little to address the menace of deep poverty in Africa.

Yet not all of the rich nations viewed development this way. Ministers from some Western democracies were even eager to discuss the debt problem. The British minister, Kenneth Clarke, chancellor of the Exchequer, was one of them. Plainly, with John Major having succeeded Margaret Thatcher as prime minister, England's Tory government had become considerably less doctrinaire. Clarke's support, and that of ministers from Holland, Norway, Sweden, Denmark, and Finland, encouraged me and gave us a base on which to build.

My hope was that debt relief would prove a rallying point for World Bank staff. I thought that surely they must be frustrated to see the benefits of money provided for health, education, and other projects being offset by similar amounts of money from the treasury of the assisted country being used to pay back loans. I also hoped that debt relief would be an issue on which the Bank and its critics among the mainstream NGOs could find common ground. The bottom line was that if I could marshal debt relief into a common cause, then maybe, just maybe, we could create enough of a groundswell of popular and political support to overcome those who wished to see no change in the status quo.

Launching the project, which we called the Debt Initiative for Heavily Indebted Poor Countries (HIPC), was a nightmare. It meant cutting across decades of history within the Bank. As my staff worked overtime to formulate proposals, my plan to include the NGOs became a hot-button issue. Some of my colleagues accused me of being autocratic and too eager to look outside the Bank while giving short shrift to our own experts, who often knew more and had broader perspective. This was absolutely not the case. I had enormous respect for most of our Bank staff working on the front line of development. I also thought that the majority of lenders, including the Bank, were caught in an unreal and unsustainable trap. How, I reasoned, could you have a lending business to borrowers of low credit and then pretend that you would be repaid 100 percent of every loan? I thought that any system that relied on this logic was doomed.

Despite the initial resistance, as the initiative evolved, it gained government support. Further momentum was gained from 1997 onward with the appointment of Clare Short as Britain's first secretary of state for international development, a position with full cabinet status. Through encouragement and guidance, she persuaded Oxfam International to do much of the early arithmetic on debt relief. Clare was an effective and vigorous social activist and often a fierce critic of NGOs, both in public and in private. But she also knew how to work with them. Look beyond their rhetoric, she taught me, listen to their criticism, and try to agree on relief measures that can be sold to the governments and the voters of the developed world.

The debt relief initiative would affect about thirty countries, including Benin, Bolivia, Burkina Faso, Côte d'Ivoire, Guinea-Bissau, Guyana, Mali, Mozambique, Senegal, and Uganda. These countries were charac-

terized by basic criteria: low GDP, a heavy debt burden, and efforts to improve economic management in a sustainable manner as demonstrated
by the presence of an active program with the IMF. The total debt owed
by the HIPC group was about 10 percent of the debt owed by all developing countries, but it put a disproportionate burden on the HIPC countries' economies. At the time, our best estimate of what we needed to end
this ugly dilemma was about $20 billion. The cost would be between $6
and $9 billion for the Bank, depending on the number of countries and
their debt profile and on the evolution of commodity prices, given their
impact on the export earnings of many of the HIPC countries.

The HIPC initiative was envisioned as a joint project of the Bank and
the International Monetary Fund. Without the IMF, which had always
been the monitor of each nation's financial situation, it would be difficult,
if not impossible, to get the agreement of the ministers who served on
both our boards. And to gain the support of the IMF, I had to win over
my counterpart, Michel Camdessus. The brilliant Parisian economist
was very much a leader among international civil servants. Everybody
warned that Michel would be difficult. He had trained at France's elite
civil-service schools, and though he was soft-spoken and gentlemanly in
conversation, he had a reputation for being tough and unyielding. Before
1987, when he was chosen to be the IMF's managing director, he had
been France's central banker, the governor of the august Banque de
France. He was far more experienced than I and had a much deeper understanding of the workings of the international financial community.

I had called Michel as soon as I became president of the Bank, asking
for his guidance and cooperation. Every two or three weeks, Michel and I
would have lunch, alternating between the Bank and the IMF. The conversation was always cordial, sometimes in English, often in French,
which was a test of my language skills, and during the first year we worked
together, I always brought up *l'allégement de la dette*—debt relief.

Initially Michel was skeptical, but he understood the logic of our case
and kept an open mind. He always listened carefully to my arguments,
sometimes offering insights and criticism. I would use his feedback to

refine my argument and come back at him. For his part, he would fill me in on what was happening at the IMF and, much more importantly, give me his outlook on the global economy and his views on the problems he and I might face in the period ahead.

As the months went by, Michel warmed to the idea of debt relief, never enough to become an avid proponent, but enough to act as my ally in encouraging teams from the IMF and the World Bank to agree on a plan. By working with me, he was able to influence the shape of the program and ensure that it would be consistent with the principles espoused by the IMF. I have immense regard for Michel and his wisdom, experience, and friendship. Ultimately, we launched this project together.

The campaign to gather support among governments gained immeasurably from the fact that we had caught a popular wave. Outside the United States, a social movement was taking hold with the goal of forgiving the debt of poor nations by 2000, the millennium year. Jubilee, as this movement was called, had sprung up in the most unlikely way. In 1994, in an apostolic letter, Pope John Paul II had floated the idea of canceling international debt. His inspiration was a passage in the Old Testament book of Leviticus, which prescribes that after seven agricultural cycles of seven years each, there should be a "jubilee" year in which all land lies fallow and all debts are absolved. Activists at Oxford picked up on the idea and christened the movement Jubilee, and it was rapidly gaining support. Church groups, NGOs, entertainers, and celebrities all felt its appeal; accordingly, politicians around the world took notice, and the members of the World Bank board began to come around to my point of view.

President Jacques Chirac hosted the G7 meetings in Lyon, and for the first time, he invited the leaders of the IMF, WTO, UN, and the World Bank—Camdessus, Renato Ruggiero, Boutros Boutros-Ghali, and me—to attend and participate. It was an important recognition of our institutions, and I was surprised and delighted to be in such company. Even more crucially, it presented an opportunity for us to push our ideas on debt relief. I was not disappointed. The G7 issued a communiqué endorsing the goal of creating a comprehensive, international exit strategy for debt relief. I had proposed to my board that the Bank set aside $500 million from its own surpluses to provide seed money for a special trust for debt relief, to which the world's richer countries could contribute directly. Crucially, the G7 recognized that debt relief would only be possible if bilateral creditors and multilateral institutions coordinated their efforts and committed to a much more aggressive action plan than what was in place. The meeting was truly the breakthrough I was seeking.

On the final day of the summit, we were photographed in the Parc de la Tête d'Or. I remember the photo for two reasons. First, I had recently been stricken with Bell's palsy, so my face was contorted. Second, being unaware of protocol, I accepted President Clinton's invitation to stand next to him, which put me in the front row of the photograph. I realized that on all similar occasions thereafter, my appropriate place was at the back or the side of photographs.

In November 1996, shortly after the second annual meeting in Washington, D.C., debt relief became real when the Bank's executive directors approved the allocation of $500 million for a debt relief trust fund. The guidelines for dispensing the money, laboriously hammered out by the World Bank and IMF staffs, were far more stringent than I had wished. Michel had deferred to purists on his staff who demanded tight restrictions on the choice of eligible countries and the conditions they had to meet to qualify for debt relief. These criteria were so strict that most of Africa had no chance of quickly qualifying. It was not until 1999 that the eligibility criteria were relaxed to provide faster and deeper debt relief, and the pace accelerated somewhat.

This meant that at the time of its introduction, rather than being hailed from the rooftops, the initial HIPC initiative became a target for critics who called it narrow, mean-spirited, and ineffectual. It actually helped fuel the Jubilee movement. But even though the critics were not willing to recognize it, the HIPC initiative represented an enormous breakthrough in thinking about poverty. The dam had been cracked. Debt relief would have a prominent place on the global financial and political agenda for years to come. And from now on, the debate would be about details—the speed of delivery and conditions of eligibility—rather than the principle. Finally, the World Bank could be seen as any other bank: It would have bad loans that needed to be written off. Thanks in part to the world economic boom that was beginning, by 2000 global lenders would succeed in writing off between $30 billion and $50 billion of poor-country debt, and by the end of 2006, the debt stock of the thirty-one HIPC countries had been reduced from $106 billion to $40 billion, with the corresponding savings in debt service invested largely in education and health.

The night the HIPC program was approved by our board, I invited people from Oxfam and other NGOs to our house in Washington to celebrate. There would be rocky days ahead, but we were slowly banishing the old antagonisms. I told my guests: "I feel privileged to be doing this and am thrilled by your congratulations. But I am absolutely certain that within two weeks, you will be coming back and beating me up for not having done enough." Indeed, many of my guests that night soon redoubled their pressure on the Bank. But that wasn't entirely bad. We had learned to work as partners, we were building initial trust, and the inevitable frictions were now producing not just heat, but also light.

*   *   *

NGO support was crucial in our next major initiative, attacking corruption. The problem was endemic in the countries we worked with, and it undermined development at least as much as such accepted problems as illiteracy, malnutrition, and poor infrastructure, which were often exacerbated by the very fact of corruption.

Everyone I worked with had seen it. We had all been entertained in the lavish homes and palaces of certain political leaders. After my first visit to Côte d'Ivoire, I developed the practice of looking at government officials' watches. Were they gold? Were they Patek Philippe or Rolex? If an official wrote with a gold pen, if his spouse wore designer dresses, and if the couple talked about vacationing in the south of France or the Alps, it was a good bet that something was wrong.

I had witnessed the signs of corruption in virtually every country I had visited and heard tales of much more that did not immediately meet the eye. Corruption took many forms: It came in the form of promoting one's children or family members; concealing agency fees; or grossly inflating the cost of equipment, raw materials, and labor, enabling those in authority positions to skim profits from a project. In some cases it was simply stealing. In many places, the poor reported having to pay managers, hooligans, and the police "protection" money to save themselves from harassment, theft, and abuse.

At the World Bank, I gave up trying to count the forms corruption can take. The creativity of people in devising ways to steal money is almost beyond imagination, and we had to be vigilant about fighting it. When I had visited Nigeria as a young businessman in 1960, the scam was for each minister to offer prospective foreign investors land that he had previously directed from government ownership to himself by fiat and at little or no cost. This enabled the ministers to make huge capital gains on property values in ways that looked perfectly aboveboard, but which in most cases were simply a concealed payment for government officials to gain their support.

You learn to sense corruption even if you cannot put your finger on it, from clues such as a community's failure to thrive despite financial help or the behavior of its leaders. On my first trip to Haiti in July 1995, I visited President Jean-Bertrand Aristide. He found out I was going to La Saline, the slum in Port-au-Prince where he had been the parish priest. He had not gone back there for more than five years, and he used my presence and the availability of police protection as a pretext to visit again.

At that time, Aristide was a bit of a hero for us all. In Washington, he had a reputation as a change agent and a tireless advocate for the poor. After being elected in 1991, he'd been deposed by a military coup, and

President Clinton had restored him to power by sending in U.S. troops. Aristide's close supporters included Colin Powell and Senator Sam Nunn.

We saw the strength of his appeal back in his old parish. At the day's end, we went to a ceremony where it seemed to me as though the entire population of the neighborhood had turned out. People nearly threw themselves at Aristide's feet, shouting his name. But instead of reaching out to his people by discussing the importance of educating their children or conveying his empathy for their plight, he squandered the moment with a speech full of slogans. His self-aggrandizing statements were greeted by cheers from the crowd, but they contained little, if any, substance and certainly no call to action to improve the lives of his sad and impoverished people.

This apathy was mystifying to me. Elaine was also shocked, and she said something to an old friend of Aristide's who was accompanying us. He acknowledged the hollowness of the performance and said to her, "But he once did care. He is not the person that he was."

Power and its privileges had transformed the hero of La Saline into an indifferent, showman president, at a huge cost to the people who had given him their trust. What I saw in Haiti depressed and angered me. Nothing Aristide or his cabinet members told us was compelling or convincing. Over the years, the World Bank had poured in over half a billion dollars in loans and grants, yet it seemed that almost no aid was reaching the people.

Back in Washington, I expressed to my colleagues how deeply concerned I was about the impact of what we were doing in Haiti. It was clear to me that this country, despite its many educated people, had disintegrated as a modern state and that corruption had become endemic. We began keeping a much tighter rein on our money in Haiti and later stopped all lending other than for humanitarian purposes.

In light of experiences like this, I was perplexed that corruption seemed to be nowhere on the Bank's official agenda, despite a good number of passionate anticorruption advocates on the staff. I checked past speeches from annual meetings; I checked the minutes of the Development Committee, a powerful Board of Governors working group that is supposed to review the Bank's programs twice a year. The term *corruption* simply did not appear. The only time I ever heard the subject discussed was in private gatherings in people's homes. There was a wall of silence surrounding this critical issue.

"What is going on here?" I kept asking my staff. Finally, Ibrahim Shihata, the Bank's experienced and intelligent general counsel and a friend I greatly admired, took me into the hall outside my office. Looking over his shoulder, as if someone might hear, he warned that in the Bank, there was no room to discuss the "C-word." "It would be offensive to our shareholders and risk political repercussions," he said. Attacking corruption, he made me understand, would insult some of the executive directors who represented countries where corruption reached the highest levels. It would also insult some of the rich countries that were well aware of the problem but used it to their advantage. In some developed countries, including some of the major European countries, corrupt payments made by corporations in search of new business were deductible as a legitimate expense for tax purposes.

I pondered his words and concluded that there was no way I could accept or condone corruption. How could effective development proceed unless corruption was attacked simultaneously? It was so obviously a disease within the system. We had to diagnose it, confront it, and find appropriate measures to eradicate it.

First, we had to clean our own house. In June 1996, we instituted independent audits of selected projects—detailed spot checks designed to monitor what was happening to the money under our control.

At the second annual meeting in Washington in October 1996, I took the issue public. I said to the audience: "Let's not mince words; we need to deal with the cancer of corruption."

In country after country, I said, the people were demanding action on this issue. They knew that corruption diverted resources from the poor to the rich and powerful, deterred foreign investors, and created a barrier to equitable development. Solutions, though, had to be homegrown.

National leaders had to take a stand, and civil society had to play a key role as well. The Bank Group, I explained, could not intervene in the political affairs of our member countries. But we could advise and support governments willing to fight corruption, and they would, over time, be rewarded with more investment. I made it clear that the Bank would not tolerate corruption in the programs we supported, and I announced we were taking steps to ensure the integrity within our own projects and activities.

This broke the wall of silence—the hidden C-word was now out in the daylight, and for the first time ever at a World Bank gathering, corruption was acknowledged as a central development issue. Soon my ministerial colleagues began putting it openly on their own agendas, and we were able to speak about corruption at our meetings. The impact of my message that day colored my ensuing years at the Bank.

It also made people angry. In early 1997, I met with the Indonesian President Suharto, in Jakarta. The president asked me, after he had given a speech to open a conference at which I had been invited to speak, what I was doing raising the subject of corruption as a serious issue. I told him we couldn't talk about development without addressing corruption. He replied, "Well, you come out here from Washington with these high ideas to tell us about corruption. But what you call 'corruption,' I call 'family values.'" This characterization brought home to me the enormous gulf that existed between my understanding of corruption and the reality of political life in many countries.

Nonetheless, within the Bank, we began work on new approaches to measure corruption and combat it in the field. Today, the Bank works closely with Transparency International, the world's premier corruption watchdog, which was founded in 1993 by former Bank director Peter Eigen. This constructive partnership is one of the key achievements of the anticorruption campaign.

*   *   *

What drove me at the Bank—and what drove other people crazy, particularly at headquarters—was my willingness to break eggs in the service of our mission. I was ready and anxious to take on the issues that were obvious and difficult, even if solutions would take time. I felt that we had to listen to our critics and appraise their criticism, and if we found them to be valid, confront them rather than trying to hide.

I reached out to friends with experience in changing organizations and in managing effectively. One of the most important moves I made was an effort to learn from chief executives of global corporations. I recruited from the business world hard-driving change agents to be my corporate advisers. There were too many to list here, but among others, Percy Barnevik of Asea Brown Boveri in Switzerland, Sir William Purves of Hongkong and Shanghai Banking Corporation, Minoru Makihara of Mitsubishi Corporation in Japan, Jérôme Monod of Suez Lyonnaise des Eaux, and Rupert Murdoch of NewsCorp all generously agreed to serve as my informal advisory board.[1]

Their names never appeared in our annual report, and we were not officially a board. But we met every twelve or fifteen months until I retired. Being able to ask questions and hear suggestions from these leaders of huge organizations helped offset my inexperience and gave me a much-needed touchstone outside the Bank. We would begin with a private dinner at my home, and the next day, I would organize sessions where these advisers could discuss selected issues with my Bank executives. We would have lunch with a larger number of my colleagues, and the day would conclude with another private session, where my friends would give me their criticism and advice. They offered me the best advice any person could hope for and gave generously of their time over many years.

One of the many initiatives that these meetings sparked was my effort to convince my colleagues to think of ourselves as a "learning organization," where successful practices and not-so-successful initiatives could be recorded and made available to all. The idea was to establish a digital information bank that would grow and service staff members and governments on development practices and experience. We dramatically improved our computer facilities and our means of communication and accessing information. We also linked all our offices with videoconferencing facilities that allowed us to discuss and learn from regional and global initiatives. Mohamed Mushin led these efforts on information sharing and conference linkage with great skill and selflessness, and he and his team produced first-rate innovations. We became the leaders in the field among all other international agencies.

We also established a groupwide private sector development team to pull together all our strengths and make them available to the private sector—and to foster synergy among different private sector activities from which we hoped to learn about entrepreneurship and risk taking. Richard Frank guided its beginnings with the help of Jannik Lindbaek, the most effective head of IFC.

All of the initiatives that we introduced depended on the success and hard work of my leadership group and on the quality of our staff. Lew Preston had left me an experienced and dedicated senior cadre of managing directors who knew the Bank group well. I came to rely on their advice on how best to push change inside the Bank. Sven Sandstrom, Gautam Kaji, and Richard Frank made an effective team. To give me more time to focus on the outside world, I added Caio Koch Weser and Jessica Einhorn—the latter being the first woman to become a managing director—to the senior management. Together they pushed the internal program of renewal that I had launched. Among many achievements in 1997 was the raising of $22 billion for the International Development Association (IDA) to cover the next three years, thanks in a large part to Sven's work as chair of the negotiations.

The Bank had a reputation for providing very generous benefits to its employees, many of whom are paid on a tax-free basis. They often travel business class and, occasionally, first class. Their salaries and benefits certainly far exceed those at most NGOs. But on this issue, I had to defend the Bank. It drew to its portals the best and the brightest development experts from more than 140 countries, including more PhDs than many of the world's great universities. Many of our professionals had skills that would have been highly marketable in the commercial world. It was essential for us to attract and retain such talent. The strength of the World Bank resides in the quality of our team. Employees come for the unique opportunity, but also for job security and benefits and, for some, the chance to make the United States their base. For most of the staff, the job is about devoting their lives to improving the world, working long hours, and spending weeks and months of the year away from their families to develop projects in the field. Our best people showed extraordinary skill and devotion. Their compensation was often well below what they merited. And always in the back of my mind was the thought that on Wall Street, people got paid a whole lot more for doing work that was a whole lot less important.

Nevertheless, there were problems to address. Life at the Bank, in my judgment, was too comfortable at headquarters and often very hard in the field. And yet the way to move up seemed to be to get a headquarters job. This had to be turned on its head. "If you want to become a vice president, go out into the field," I told people. I put in place policies to reinforce this message. I had been astonished to learn that many country directors—the people overseeing operations in our client countries—were actually based in Washington. We ordered many of them into the field, and we decentralized decision making. Starting in 1996, any senior staff person who wanted a shot at becoming a top manager had to take a resident post in the developing world for at least two years. By 1999, we had more than 3,000 people stationed in client countries—including 25 high-level decision makers—up from 1,700 when I joined the Bank. The number for the whole Bank group would grow to more than 4,500 by the end of my second term.

These changes provoked strong reactions, both positive and negative. Several vice presidents at headquarters actually gave up their titles to go manage programs abroad. I was very grateful to them, and everyone benefited. When these managers returned to Washington, they were much stronger agents of change. Others, particularly at headquarters, dug in their heels. A great problem I had, and one that my CEO advisers certainly did not share and did not envy, was that I could not fire people at will. Although I came to have great respect for the competence and commitment of the great majority of our staff, not all of them met the professional standards of a normal commercial market or provided what was needed within the Bank. Many of our best managers in the Bank were all too aware of this problem. Yet putting someone on notice to leave the Bank gave rise to a mind-bending array of appeal procedures that were lengthy and extraordinarily disruptive for coworkers. Colleagues and superiors would be called upon by a tribunal to air their criticism of the employee concerned, with the added painful knowledge that in most cases, the person fired would immediately lose his or her visa to work in the United States and, with the person's family, have to return home. The result is that there has always been within the World Bank and, dare I say, within the United Nations and other international institutions, an inability to operate tough, first-rate standards of management while benefiting from the many nationalities represented.

I also struggled to boost the effectiveness of the Board of Governors, my ultimate boss. The full group of governors, with more than 185 members, was far too unwieldy to take an active advisory role. But I had hopes for its 24-member subset, the Development Committee, which met twice a year to review our programs. Nominally, the Development Committee included some of the world's most powerful finance and development ministers, but it had been allowed to stagnate. When I arrived, the meetings were perfunctory. Most of the governors did not bother to attend in person, other than occasionally to read a ten-minute statement and then leave, with their seat being taken by a lower-level official or by one of the executive directors of the Bank. I felt it important that these sessions become a forum for strategic decision making and for serious in-depth discussions with ministers on global issues and particular challenges facing the Bank.

It was equally important that Bank staff understand that we worked for the shareholder countries, and not the other way around. A dialogue that engaged these countries' sense of ownership could only benefit our work and ensure their ongoing support, in terms of both cooperation and dollars. I worked to turn past practice around, establishing new substantive agendas for our biannual meetings and cutting down the time allotted for prepared statements by ministers so that we could actually discuss issues. I encouraged the participation of the successive chief economists of the Bank, which never failed to spark important discussions. Michael Bruno, who died tragically and prematurely soon after my arrival; Joseph Stiglitz, who won the Nobel Prize after leaving the Bank; Nicholas Stern (later, Lord Stern), who wrote the pathbreaking *Stern Review* on the economics of climate change; and François Bourguignon not only gave distinguished leadership to our economic research but also helped me to make the meetings more meaningful. Their hard-hitting presentations greatly improved the attendance of key ministers, who now found the gatherings useful.

Despite some successes in my first two years, many at the Bank saw me as a force for chaos. I was constantly traveling, meeting with people, cramming in up to a dozen meetings a day, and breaking taboos. I listened to the NGOs and would talk to anyone who showed respect for the Bank, even if the person was highly critical of aspects of our work. Despite the whirlwind, I felt I was learning precious lessons. But some people thought I was crazy.

One way I gauged my impact in my early years was by reading the newspapers. There was a steady stream of leaks, particularly to the *Financial Times*, the *New York Times*, and the *Washington Post*, by staffers recounting my real and imagined failures. I remember with gratitude my dear late friend R. W. "Johnny" Apple Jr., the Washington bureau chief of the *New York Times*, who called me whenever more than the usual number of complaints rolled in. One time, he called when in one week, there had been more than five negative reports that had pointed to my management deficiencies and my lack of experience. He would check out the allegations with me and give me the chance to respond or put forward a different case. Never once did he write an article that I thought was unfair.

I'm sure there was some truth in the criticism, but I was on a steep learning curve, and I felt my direction was right. In a way, the media attention kept me from becoming overconfident. What the newspapers printed typically had balance, and although I was criticized frequently, support came from key stakeholders among the rich countries, from many groups in civil society, from a growing number of staff inside the Bank, and most important, from the poorest countries that I was endeavoring to empower. To survive bureaucratic infighting, you have to know how to deflect criticism as well as to sustain it—and to benefit from it. I was managing to stay slightly ahead of the game.

*   *   *

In February 1997, Elaine and I paid our third visit to Africa. This time we started in Senegal, meeting with our representatives from Benin, Côte d'Ivoire, Guinea, and Togo and the staff of the Banque Centrale des États de l'Afrique de l'Ouest (BCEAO). We visited communities in the Dakar slums, where a street in the poor neighborhood of Pikine had been named after Elaine because of her commitment to education in Africa. We also visited rural areas, where we spoke to farmers and their families. I was delighted and honored to spend time with President Abdou Diouf, who was one of the significant and constructive African leaders of my time at the Bank. Next we went to Ghana and then to South Africa, where I was eager to visit a township to get a sense of what life there was really like. We were hosted by Finance Minister Trevor Manuel, who was an effective and imaginative economic leader of his country and who remained so for more than a decade. We spent five hours in Khayelitsha township outside Cape Town. Though it was an impoverished area, there was a palpable feeling of hope—expectation, even—that things would get better under the new leadership of President Nelson Mandela.

For me, the luminous recollection of that trip was our meeting with President Mandela. It was a special honor to sit with this truly great man and to absorb, after just a few minutes, the integrity, beauty, and wisdom that characterized him. He put Elaine and me immediately at ease. It was the beginning of a treasured relationship with him and, later, his wife, Graça Machel. I know of no other example of one man who made so great a difference in his country—and throughout the world—while maintaining integrity and human values in building a more balanced society. We are fortunate that he has lived in our time.

My trip concluded with a visit to see President Joaquim Chissano in Mozambique and a round table with representatives from government, civil society, the private sector, and academia. We could not have been other than impressed by Chissano's leadership and vision. Mozambique since then has been an example for Africa.

During this time, I was also expanding our efforts in other regions, notably in the Middle East. The Bank had long played a major role in addressing the Israeli-Palestinian conflict, and my colleagues worked vigorously to assist the Palestinians in the West Bank and in Gaza. The Bank staffers were a useful buffer in discussions, and the Israeli administration took some note of our views as we pressed for better living conditions for the Palestinians in terms of work, education, and health care. As the years progressed, I became more and more involved in the region. I met frequently with the leaders of the Arab world, building upon the Bank's standing and the resourcefulness and dedication of my colleagues. We not only established trust with many of these leaders, but for a time we were of material help in easing tensions and improving the lives of the Palestinians.

By the spring of 1997, however, the Bank and Syria had reached a stage where we were not talking. Syria owed the Bank in excess of $300 million and was paying neither interest nor principal. I was urged to meet with President Hafez Assad to see if the matter could be resolved. With the help of the Syrian ambassador in Washington, Walid Moallem, now the foreign minister and deputy prime minister, a visit was arranged for June.

When I arrived in Damascus, the finance minister and several ministerial colleagues held a lengthy dinner to welcome me and, more importantly, to brief me for the meeting. I took notes as they gave me detailed economic and political arguments to put to President Assad. The meeting was scheduled for 10:00 AM the next morning, and I was told that it would last for four hours. Henry Kissinger had advised me in advance to drink very little at breakfast so that I would be able to sit through the whole period in comfort!

The next day, promptly at 10:00 AM, I entered the palace and walked up the very long and imposing staircase to the president's office. Assad and I met in private, accompanied by a translator. We talked nonstop about politics, religion, family, health, education, and the history of Syria. It was one of the most fascinating encounters of my presidency. After three hours and fifty-nine minutes, I heard the helicopter that was to fly me from Damascus to Lebanon for a meeting. I told the president that I must leave and thanked him. He said that he was very pleased to have met me and asked me to visit again with my family as his guest to see the historic sites throughout his country.

As we were walking to the door, he took my arm and asked, "What about the debt?" I replied, "I thought you would take care of that, sir." He smiled, and I said good-bye. At the bottom of the stairs, a worried-looking finance minister asked me what I had said about the debt. "Nothing," I replied. "Did he say anything?" he asked anxiously. I explained that I had not raised the subject, but that as I bid him farewell, I got the impression that he would do something. The finance minister almost threw me onto the helicopter; I had followed none of his advice. Two weeks later, President Assad approved a repayment schedule, which was followed until the debt was repaid. I had followed my instinct, which, contrary to my advice the previous evening, told me first to create a relationship before discussing the issue of debt.

Later, I did return to Syria with my son Adam. We visited archeological sites that were breathtaking in their beauty, and I met President Assad again. At the time, he was suffering from a bad back. After talking for several hours, I offered to show him some exercises that had eased my own back problems. I stood up, took off my coat, got down on the floor, and demonstrated the exercises for the president and his assistant, pulling my legs up to my chest and going through the whole routine. President Assad could barely stop laughing, proclaiming that this was the first time any visitor had lain on the floor doing exercises in his presence. As I left his office, he embraced me.

The last time I saw him was in February 1999 at the funeral of King Hussein in Jordan. I was walking up the street with President Clinton and President Chirac beside the mosque where the Muslim invitees were saying prayers. A car pulled up beside us, and out stepped President Assad in a coat and a beret. He walked to me and, without any acknowledgment of my more distinguished neighbors, gave me a warm greeting and a big hug, then returned to his car and drove off. My companions were very surprised at this abrupt visit and departure and asked me what on earth I had done for the president. "I gave him back exercises!" I explained.

*   *   *

The 1997 annual meetings of the World Bank and the IMF took place in late September in Hong Kong. The government of China and the Hong Kong authorities did a remarkable job of organization. By the time of that meeting, I was beginning to have a much clearer insight into the development process and what I wished to do at the Bank.

I spoke of "the challenge of inclusion" as the key development challenge of our time. I wanted it to be understood that we could not have two worlds, with one for the rich and one for the poor. "Whether you broach it from the social or the economic or the moral perspective," I said, "this is a challenge we cannot afford to ignore. There are not two worlds, there is one world. We breathe the same air. We degrade the same environment. We share the same financial system. We have the same health problems. AIDS is not a problem that stops at borders. Crime does not stop at borders. Drugs do not stop at borders. Terrorism, war, and famine do not stop at borders."

I emphasized that development was not an issue for attention by institutions like the World Bank alone. I argued that it was essential to conceive the attack on poverty with the governments and the people of developing countries in the driver's seat. We had to bring together all the players and coordinate efforts to avoid replication and waste. Our partnerships must involve bilateral and multilaterals, the United Nations, the European Union, regional organizations, the World Trade Organization, labor organizations, NGOs, foundations, and the private sector. Only with each of us playing to our respective strengths in coordinated interventions could we leverage up the entire development effort and avoid duplication and waste.

Finally, I noted that the countries we were seeking to help bore a heavy responsibility as well. "We should offer our assistance to all countries in need. But we must be selective in how we use our resources. There is no escaping the hard fact: More people will be lifted out of poverty if we concentrate our assistance on countries with good policies than if we allocate irrespective of the policies pursued. Recent studies confirm what we already knew intuitively—that in a good policy environment, development assistance improves growth prospects and social conditions, but in a poor policy environment, it can actually retard progress by reducing the need for change and by creating dependency."

To ensure that within the Bank we could meet the challenges and bring about institutional change, we had launched the "Strategic Compact" to renew our values and commitment to development and seek to improve the Bank's practices and effectiveness. To make this happen, we were decentralizing aggressively in the field. I noted that we now had eighteen of our forty-eight country directors with decision-making authority based in the countries they served compared with only three a year earlier. We had also created a Knowledge Bank that would draw from experience inside our institution, record it, and make it available to all our officers.

Perhaps the most important lesson that I had learned in my first two years at the Bank was that we did not exist to dream up initiatives and solutions in Washington to impose on our client countries. I had visited nearly sixty countries by September 1997, meeting with governments and

business and nongovernmental groups, and it was the people—the poor
and disadvantaged—who made the biggest impression on me. We needed
to listen and learn and combine messages from the field with our unique
experience. These poor did not seek charity; they sought opportunity.
They did not want to be lectured to; they wanted to be listened to. They
wanted partnership. "They do not want my culture or yours," I said.
"They want their own. They want a future enriched by the inheritance of
their past." It was critical that we at the Bank respect the people, their cultures, and their traditions—and encourage them to develop from within.
People have an inherent dignity, and we had to honor their history, beliefs, and aspirations. Without respect for cultural continuity and for social institutions, I felt certain, there could be no true development.

13

CREATIVITY AND
CHANGE DURING
THE CLINTON YEARS

As an investment banker, I had spent countless nights at the ready—waiting for the urgent call when a deal was in the offing, a board was split down the middle, or a corporation teetered on the brink of collapse. I loved this aspect of the job and was often first on the plane when our clients ran into trouble or were confronted with a rare opportunity. But that was the world of the private sector.

The culture and function of the World Bank was different. It was, after all, intended for "reconstruction and development" and not crisis intervention. When I arrived, the Bank was rarely the first on the scene in a humanitarian disaster or an active participant in restoring peace soon after conflict—even though there were many reasons for early entry into tough situations. During such crises as the civil wars in Sierra Leone and Liberia or after an earthquake or a devastating tornado, the Bank sat on the sidelines, waiting to intervene until a modicum of peace was restored or until the emergency UN agencies, the Red Cross, or NGOs such as Doctors Without Borders had distributed food and provided emergency assistance to displaced persons and refugees. If a civil war broke out or a country's economy tanked, there was no expectation that the World Bank would act immediately.

The Bank's task was to prepare and implement medium- and long-term projects, to focus on rebuilding society. Because the loan approval process was so rigorous, with careful checks and balances built into our procedures, we rarely were able to move with immediate impact, even under our streamlined procedures. Our contribution was essential, but it came in the later phases of any emergency. Even so, some member nations felt that the Bank got more involved than it should in the actual crises as they evolved. Such involvement was the consequence of my colleagues' being on the ground when problems arose. They had the natural reaction of wanting to help their clients who were in trouble. There had been strong pressure on my predecessors to limit the kinds of intervention the Bank would undertake. The board, and the Bank as an institution, shied away from anything that smacked of politics. This attitude also helped remove the Bank from emergencies around the world. There was no confidence inside or outside the institution in our ability to be fast moving and immediately relevant.

In contrast to our practice, the International Monetary Fund had a track record of acting quickly and decisively when it was needed. And to be fair, in any comparison of the two Bretton Woods institutions, this advantage had been built into the IMF—its ability to respond quickly to financial crises was an essential part of its mission. In 1976, it had swooped in to rescue Britain during its sterling crisis. In the early 1980s, it had played a central role in aiding Mexico and the rest of Latin America when the entire global banking system looked to be on the verge of collapse. IMF teams swarmed across Eastern Europe and the former Soviet Union when the Iron Curtain disintegrated, working toward rapid economic transformation. Even today, the IMF role in solving the problems of Greece and other European countries is critical.

Because of the high visibility and immediacy of financial issues, IMF concerns usually dominated our joint annual and semiannual meetings, overshadowing questions of development. The meetings were seen as the place to review global financial stability and economic performance, to discuss interventions in financial hot spots, and to identify emerging financial problems and opportunities. All of this was the purview of the IMF, not the World Bank, and there was no doubt about which meetings the ministers regarded as more important.

Finance ministers and central bankers of member nations regarded themselves as directly responsible for the activities of the IMF and for meeting any challenges to the stability of the financial system. By contrast, responsibility for working with the Bank was often shared with the development ministries. Whereas the finance ministers felt married to the IMF, many of them looked on the World Bank as a distant relative. I tried to attract the attention and interest of the finance ministers by scheduling at least some discussions on items of immediate interest for our meetings with the IMF. My management team and I also decided that it was desirable and even essential that we get to a crisis early, so that we could understand the causes of disturbance and lay the groundwork for future reconstruction efforts. This opportunity was provided to us by our increasing involvement in conflict situations around the world. Very often, crises occurred in countries where we had existing programs. The big breakthrough was in Bosnia-Herzegovina, where an entirely new strategy emerged for our postconflict work.

In the summer of 1995, just after my arrival at the Bank, Bosnia-Herzegovina was a landscape of destruction following more than three years of bitter and intense civil war. The fighting had begun when Bosnia-Herzegovina declared independence from Yugoslavia on October 16, 1991. That war, darkened by the appalling shadow of ethnic cleansing and genocide, would see more than 100,000 dead or missing and populations forced off lands that they had inhabited for generations. Bosnia-Herzegovina's real GDP plummeted by 80 percent. More than 2 million people—nearly half the prewar population—became refugees. Although this type of human and physical crisis had been seen before in Africa, this time it was occurring closer to Western Europe and was therefore of greater concern to the European powers.

The trigger for the Bank's involvement was an accident on Mount Igman, near Sarajevo, in August 1995. Peace envoys from the United States were making their way down the mountain on a narrow, muddy road, heading for the besieged town of Sarajevo, when their armored vehicle slid off the road and plunged down a ravine. Three of the envoys died. My friend Richard Holbrooke, the leader of the American team who was trying to broker peace, was on the scene and badly shaken.

President Bill Clinton and Hillary Clinton were both vacationing in Jackson Hole at the time, as was I. The president had been briefed in the early hours that morning by his staff. I met with him later in the day, and he sketched out in general terms what had happened. He was clearly horrified. His own representatives had been killed, and this gave the issue in Bosnia-Herzegovina a personal urgency. I immediately called my staff at the Bank. The Bank had been preparing to mount a reconstruction effort in the region. Led by the dynamic Turkish economist Kemal Dervis, who later became finance minister of Turkey and thereafter head of UNDP, our team on the ground had attended donors' meetings and built political support for the Bank to take a role in planning and implementing an assistance program. Staff members in Washington were anxious to go over and help this team. But our board had been reluctant to see us go into a war zone, feeling strongly that our focus should be limited to reconstruction and development after the fighting had stopped.

This board resistance to crisis intervention reflected not only policy differences but also political divisions among the developed nations. Western intervention in Bosnia was largely an Anglo-American affair, and the prospect of Americans on Eastern European soil was not widely applauded in the chanceries of Germany and France. Our argument to the board—that in order to launch reconstruction and development, the Bank had to get in early—had stalled as a result of all this. Despite the months we had spent getting the board to allow us some flexibility, there had been little movement.

For a change of policy, we needed a trigger. Now we had one. After the death of the peace envoys, with shock and sadness in the atmosphere, we enlisted the support of the secretary of the U.S. Treasury and other ministries of finance of leading countries to break the board's resistance. The argument was simple: We needed to be on the ground early to prepare for our work, to make contacts, and to understand the emerging challenges. If we could learn the issues during the crisis, and even intervene modestly, we could give better-directed and better-informed assistance during the reconstruction phase.

When I pressed the green button, the Bank team responded spectacularly, moving into Sarajevo so quickly that in some neighborhoods, bullets were still flying. Led by Kemal Dervis and Christine Wallich, our first country director for Bosnia-Herzegovina, the team quickly assessed the immediate human and structural needs. The involvement of the World Bank made the reconstruction a multinational project, keeping it from being labeled a U.S.-British affair. This in turn helped facilitate the peace conference that President Clinton hosted in Dayton, Ohio, in November 1995. The resulting accord, signed in Paris in December of that year, ended three and a half years of conflict and set up a series of agreements on military, diplomatic, and governance aspects that came to be known as the Dayton Agreement.

By showing effectiveness in Bosnia-Herzegovina, the Bank demonstrated that it could be an important player in a crisis. We were able to play a leading role in the "Peace Implementation" conference in London that December, during which we dealt not with broad concepts but with real challenges on the ground. Speaking there, I stressed immediate priorities. We needed to restore food production and agricultural distribution, and rebuild roads, schools, and hospitals. It was urgent that we provide resources for the return of teachers and medical staff and get shops, factories, and power plants running again. We also had to deal with the personal tragedy of divided families. So widespread was the destruction of Bosnian life by their Serb neighbors that we would literally have to import animal stock so that the Bosnian Muslims could start regaining self-sufficiency. The complexity of these challenges helped reinforce the argument for an early integrated and cooperative response by donors,

NGOs, and other aid agencies. It also helped strengthen the political partnerships the Bank needed for its core antipoverty work.

None of this could happen, however, until Bosnia had cleaned the
slate of past debts. On February 23, 1996, the board approved the creation of the Bosnia-Herzegovina Trust Fund. In March 1996, we persuaded the executive board to provide Bosnia and Herzegovina with
expedited membership in the Bank. Then the board approved the first
emergency reconstruction project for the country. This allowed us to clear
past arrears and refinance the borrowings. The project was designed to
help meet some of the most urgent priority needs, including institution
building, and to finance critical imports to jump-start production and repair infrastructure. A month later at a joint donor conference with the
European Union in Brussels, we announced that we had assembled nearly
$1.3 billion in assistance from donor countries and agencies for the coun-
try for the coming year. This meant we could take advantage of the summer months to accelerate reconstruction so that the Bosnian people could
see there was hope for a better life. We had to address the immediate challenge of creating employment for 300,000 soldiers who would soon be
demobilized and would be looking for a life of dignity and purpose. This
was not simply charity. It made good economic sense and was essential for
stability and peace.

On a visit to Bosnia in April 1996, I saw firsthand that everything I
had hoped the Bank might accomplish in regions devastated by war was
indeed possible and that we could make a concrete and measurable difference in alleviating misery at an early stage in a crisis situation. We succeeded
because we were ready to act and got there quickly, but also because we
figured out how to cooperate with the people we sought to assist.

Above all, we did not try to compete with the emergency agencies or
NGOs. We knew that we needed to help Bosnia's citizens create societal
structures to replace those that the war had destroyed. We began with the
physical rebuilding of the supreme court. Although some may have thought
this a luxury, we thought it essential to have a functioning institution that
protected rights. Simultaneously, we worked with the IMF to create an ef-

fective financial system. Establishing a central bank for Bosnia became a cause célèbre, as it raised many technical issues about the advisability of a currency board model and political issues about who, among the members of the federation, would be in control of regulating the financial system.

Perhaps the most dramatic and visible legacy of our Bosnia work was the reconstruction of the Mostar Bridge. Built in the middle of the sixteenth century, this beautiful landmark had managed to survive the devastation of two world wars. It connected Mostar's Bosnian and Serbian neighborhoods and was the pride of the city, the image on all the postcards. But in the bitter fighting of 1993, it was destroyed. The Bank provided one-third of the $12 million required to rebuild this valued cultural icon. The project became a symbol for the people's reconnecting with each other after a period of savage violence.

Meanwhile, our colleague Djordjija Petkoski was creating programs in Bosnia-Herzegovina and other countries in the region to involve families and communities in a public debate to relieve tensions and to help make constructive decisions for the future. Believing that good governance should be inclusive and collaborative, he encouraged programs that would build consensus. He even reached out to children as young as six years old, asking them to express their vision of the future through art. The children's insight and hope was inspiring to their communities as well as to all those who saw the traveling exhibition that was created out of their artwork.

Bosnia-Herzegovina was a turning point for the Bank. Our participation sent the message to Washington and to our other shareholder countries that we could respond swiftly and efficiently in an emergency without going beyond our mandate. It became clear that we had excellent people in the field who were close to their clients in the developing countries and who understood the urgency of the moment and could prepare early for the reconstruction phase. Through our work in this crisis, we resolved many of the administrative complications that had prevented the Bank from staging a nimble response. It also made us more relevant. Thereafter, we would have teams and procedures that enabled us to respond to crises quickly, and with the board's consent and support.

Bosnia also taught me a lesson in management very early in my tenure. I realized that while I had to make sure that the Bank functioned according to its rules, it was even more important to establish relationships with my board colleagues so that, when I needed to, I could use the board's support to move quickly and preemptively. The succession of corporate secretaries throughout my tenure—Tim Thahane, Shengman Zhang, Cheikh Fall, Ngozi Okonjo-Iweala, and Paatii Ofosu-Amaah— were invaluable allies in facilitating my relationship with the board.

I also realized I needed to strengthen our political support at the ministerial level. It was a good thing for the board to understand that we had to lift the profile of the Bank so it would be seen as a major player when issues arose around the world and so it could obtain the necessary backing and financial support when needed. This could only happen if the Bank were perceived as active and not bureaucratically constrained.

To give our efforts the final push, I made informing and gaining the interest of world leaders a big part of my job. Unlike my predecessors, who had limited their contact to occasional visits with heads of state and government, I met frequently with leaders around the world and engaged them on issues in which the Bank was involved. The challenge was to convince them that development, though a long-term activity, was essential to the stability of the global system. To the extent that I succeeded, I lifted the status of the Bank to become more relevant in immediate political and humanitarian issues as they arose, and not months later, after the crisis period had passed. Michel Camdessus at the IMF supported this shift of emphasis. Together we convinced the leaders of the Group of 8 industrial nations that we could make a real difference on immediate crises.

*   *   *

In the summer of 1999, the Bank faced another emergency, this time in East Timor. After voting for independence from Indonesia in August, this little country was ravaged by violent departing Indonesian occupiers and destructive militia groups. An estimated 1,400 of East Timor's less than

1 million citizens were killed, 75 percent were displaced, and nearly 70 percent of all buildings, homes, and schools were destroyed. The embryonic nation was practically dead at birth. As soon as the UN-created International Force for East Timor (INTERFET) restored peace, the Bank set out to help rebuild the infrastructure and get the economy functioning again.

My colleagues focused first on the agricultural system, which, like Bosnia's, had nearly been destroyed. The departing Indonesians had killed nearly all the livestock in a coordinated act of anger. Within days, we imported new oxen to pull the plows. We helped the East Timorese vaccinate the small number of cattle that remained and distributed 71,000 chickens to 14,000 families over succeeding weeks. Working with the East Timorese, we helped to restore the school system, eventually rebuilding hundreds of classrooms, providing textbooks, and raising enrollment levels. We made sure that children under five received vaccinations. Some 1,300 soldiers were demobilized and trained for useful civilian jobs. The Bank was also at the center of helping the executive leadership get back on its feet and conduct new elections.

Our leader in the effort was Sarah Cliffe, one of the most remarkable executives at the Bank. She combined great organizing ability with empathy and understanding of the local people and the conditions in which they lived. Unlike relief workers from the United Nations, who were housed in ships moored next to the port, our teams had no place to stay. So Sarah, after a period when her staff camped in tents in the sports arena, decided we should rent space to live with local families in their houses—and when necessary, help build an extra room onto the house, which would be a valuable asset for the local hosts when the team left. In this way, we could provide income to families and help them rebuild their lives in the wake of the devastation. I have never felt more proud of my colleagues than when I witnessed their humanity and their quiet achievements when Kofi Annan and I visited the area.

Our Bosnia and East Timor accomplishments went a long way toward awakening the board and some of my colleagues to the importance of moving into conflict zones early. In 1997, we brought together our experienced colleagues into a special post-conflict unit, which set out the rationale and guidelines for the Bank's involvement in a wide range of situations. With this, the Bank's focus broadened into new areas such as demobilization and reintegration of soldiers, especially child soldiers, land-mine clearance, and the rehabilitation of state institutions. We now had the confidence to try to help with immediate needs whenever there was a conflict anywhere in the world and, just as important, to get immediate and long-term development issues on the table while peace settlements were being negotiated.

As our work in these stressed countries became more complex and more costly, we came to realize that we had to take yet one more step in expanding our mandate. Rather than participating only in postconflict reconstruction, we also needed to focus on prevention. Economic and social issues were often at the root of conflict; if we could confront them early enough, there would be greater hope for peace. In other words, if we could prevent the destruction, we could avoid the need for reconstruction. In 1999, the Bank's research arm, under Paul Collier, opened a global debate on the economic causes and consequences of conflict. It was clear that poverty was both a cause and a consequence. Again, this led us to clarify the Bank's mission. In 2001, we adopted an operating policy known as Development Cooperation and Conflict, under which we extended aid to conflict-affected and conflict-prone areas, not just postconflict countries.

*   *   *

While we were expanding our mandate in the area of reconstruction and development, we had to be careful not to be drawn into the issues in the IMF's purview. The financial crisis that rocked Asia in July 1997 posed such a challenge. The turmoil began in Thailand after the Thai baht, previously pegged to the dollar, was allowed to float. Within less than six months, the country's currency collapsed, losing half of its value. The currencies of the Philippines, Malaysia, Indonesia, Taiwan, and South Korea followed suit, and the ensuing crisis devastated banking and corporate sectors throughout Asia. Financial systems in some parts of the region were already vulnerable because of political cronyism, corruption, and poor regulatory and lending practices. Poverty and social distress exploded, with Indonesia also stricken by ethnic violence.

Except for Malaysia, which blamed speculators for its troubles and resorted to capital controls, most affected countries asked for IMF support. The challenge facing the IMF and its "firefighters" was possibly unprecedented, given the sheer scope of the financial distress and the economic dislocations. In the year following the collapse of the Thai baht, the value of the most affected east Asian currencies fell 35–80 percent against the U.S. dollar and the most serious stock market declines were as great as 40–60 percent in dollar terms. As it soon became clear, there was no easy solution: The IMF's effort to impose its traditional remedy of fiscal and monetary discipline—though it ultimately did restore currency stability— was widely blamed for making a bad social situation worse and for delaying economic recovery. Joseph Stiglitz, the Bank's chief economist, was one of the most outspoken critics of the IMF's tough approach. "This creates a lot of resentment on the other end of the world," he said, his comment causing considerable irritation in the U.S. Treasury and at the IMF.

The IMF eventually responded by softening its stance. Upon its request, we worked closely with the IMF staff to restructure the region's bankrupt financial systems and alleviate the social effects of the crisis. Still, Joe's criticism was seen as representative of a view that was widely held among Bank staff. Many people had come to feel that the IMF's economic orthodoxy was heartless and that greater humanitarian and development assistance was necessary to balance it. I attempted to keep the Bank out of the debate. I did not feel that we were expert in this area, nor was it appropriate for us to take a public position.

Russia provided another test of the limits of our intervention in financial crises. In Moscow, the ruble was also linked to the American dollar. For several years, the Russian government had been financing severe budget deficits by issuing vast quantities of short-term, high-yield,

dollar-denominated debt instruments known as GKOs that were tempting to foreign investors. But by mid-1998, the Russian treasury was running out of dollar reserves to back its growing debt. Speculators began
betting that the value of the ruble would plunge and that the IMF, which
had made large commitments to help stabilize the former Soviet Union,
would have no choice but to stage a bailout.

In August 1998, yields on the GKOs hit an astonishing average of
106 percent, with a peak at 148 percent on August 13, eventually forcing
the government to default on its interest payments on August 17, just as the
speculators had foreseen. Inflation was already at high levels, and the Russian economy was in recession. It became clear that in order to stabilize its
markets, Russia would need more funding. Yet the United States and other
Western powers, wanting to keep their distance from Russia's problems,
were reluctant to intervene directly. So the heat was on the IMF to step in.

In late August, I took a call from Deputy Secretary Lawrence Summers at the U.S. Treasury. It was 11:00 PM, and without any preamble, he
said that he had been talking to the IMF and to the Russians, and they
needed cash immediately. He explained that the IMF was putting a rescue
package together and said bluntly that the Bank needed to commit $6 bil-
lion immediately as part of the financing. If we did not agree, he continued, we would break the whole deal and he was certain that the World
Bank would be blamed for the collapse.

I was appalled. Financial bailouts were a job for the IMF and not, I
believed, for us. I had not been consulted about any of this; nor had I attended any of the crisis meetings. I had no details beyond what I had
seen in the press and what Larry had just told me. Neither I nor any of
my colleagues had been involved in a single negotiation with the Russians. "We are not firefighters, Larry," I said. "This isn't how the system
was set up." I was angry. Such a demand was a direct affront to the integrity of our work at the Bank. Worse than that, we had no executive
mechanism to put together such funds at short notice. I certainly did not
see our role as jumping to salute at the U.S. Treasury's order. I was already dealing with a divided executive board, and getting a $6-billion

decision overnight would be extraordinarily tough. But I realized that Summers would not be calling without President Clinton's support. Although Larry's brusqueness offended me, now was not the time to start a battle. I told him that if he wanted us to help, I would put it to our board the next morning, but that in order to make a positive decision more likely, our focus had to be on reconstruction and that certainly I needed more precise information concerning the situation so that I could lay out the issues in a clear way.

As I soon discovered, word had already reached the members of my board. While Summers was talking to me, the IMF executive directors and their finance ministries from several Western nations were making phone calls to their counterparts at the Bank. So at the emergency board meeting I called the next morning, the ground had been prepared. My executive directors from the wealthy countries were very simply instructed on how to vote. The poorer, developing countries were shocked by the amount of money requested and were resistant to the idea, but the rich member countries that were the dominant shareholders voted to say yes. The market needed to believe that the plunge of the ruble and the drain on Russia's dollar reserves would not be allowed to break the Russian central bank. It was important for public confidence that the IMF announce a huge amount of assistance available for the rescue package. So the resolution passed.

As it turned out, the IMF never called on the Bank for a single dollar of the billions we had promised. After Moscow received an initial installment of close to $5 billion from the IMF and confidence had been somewhat restored, the Russian Parliament rejected the economic and financial policy conditions the IMF had set forth for the rescue, and the IMF cut off further funds. Although the initial crisis passed, the Russian economy for the near term remained in disarray and the financial ripple effects spread to other markets, culminating in the collapse of the hedge fund Long-Term Capital Management in 1998, which shook Wall Street. We at the Bank continued to support Russia with project loans at an increased scale. Under the leadership of President Vladimir Putin and his cabinet, and with the increase in commodity prices, especially hydrocarbons, Russia made a significant recovery to gain financial independence.

The financial crises of 1997–1998 brought to mind Lew Preston's admonition when I took over the reins at the Bank. He had warned that despite the frequent pressure I was bound to feel, I should not allow the interests of the United States to unduly influence the Bank's decision making. It was a line that had been crossed many times, and I felt it had just been crossed again. The struggle between the Bank and the U.S. Treasury traced back almost to the Bank's inception. Because of it, the very first World Bank president, Eugene Meyer, had lasted only six months. He had thought he was going to run the show, but the Treasury had its own ideas, and rather than clash with the Truman administration, Meyer elected to resign. The Treasury has always had a paternalistic view of the Bank and had intervened many times over the years. Although when I arrived the United States owned just 18 percent of the equity of the Bank, a proportion well below its global weight in economic terms, the nation was still the largest shareholder and contributor, not to mention the host to the headquarters of the institution. The U.S. executive director of the Bank, unlike other directors whose capitals were far away, could walk down the street as needed to attend top-level Treasury meetings, then return and exert a very strong influence on the Bank president and in the boardroom. This proximity brings power.

During my time at the Bank, the influence of the Treasury became more modulated, though not because of my efforts. After the creation of the euro, the European Union gained clout, and as a bloc, it represented about 30 percent of the Bank's ownership. The EU nations did not always act in unison, but beginning in the late 1990s, they began to move in that direction. The emerging-market nations were also changing the balance. As new economic powers in their own right, Brazil, China, India, Russia, and South Africa were no longer simply clients of the Bank. They now sought to exercise an important role in the direction of the institution.

I tried always to cultivate a working relationship with the Treasury so that I could hear what administration officials had to say. At the same time, I tried to keep them at arm's length when there were major decisions to make. My relationship with the administration was far from perfect, but as long as President Clinton was in office, there was always an open door. I grew accustomed to frequent calls from Clinton's staff. Elaine and I were regular guests at White House functions for foreign dignitaries, and we developed a relationship with the president and Hillary Clinton that was cemented by their visits to Jackson Hole during two summer holidays. I had been Clinton's choice for the Bank, and I had a natural affinity for many of his other appointees. Former secretary of the Treasury Bob Rubin was always extraordinarily gracious with me, even though I was not his pick for the job. It took a little longer for me to build a working relationship with Larry Summers, but I grew to like and respect him greatly. Notwithstanding our interaction during Russia's financial crisis, by the time he became secretary of the Treasury, we rarely had any problems. Eventually, a firm and enduring friendship developed, and I was delighted when he later took on a prominent role on President Obama's economic team. While Clinton was president, I felt I was dealing with supportive friends in the Democratic administration, even if we sometimes disagreed.

*   *   *

During my time at the Bank, I learned that many of our battles were largely public-relations related. One of them involved an unexpected firestorm surrounding a project in the mountain regions of China, the so-called Western China Poverty Reduction Project.

In June 1999, the Bank board approved a project aimed at bringing 58,000 very poor people, including 3,500 Tibetans, down from high mountains in the western Chinese province of Qinghai to a better-irrigated region of foothills, where they would have access to land they could develop for farming. We expected the project to raise the income of the farmers from just 20 cents a day to a sustainable level. And their relocation would be voluntary.

Qinghai, unfortunately for the Bank, borders the Tibet Autonomous Region, which has long been of intense interest to human rights activists. The Bank's project manager, Jemal-ud-din Kassum, vice president for east Asia and the Pacific, believed that the scheme would benefit tens of thousands of struggling Chinese farmers by moving some of them to more fertile lower ground. The reasoning went that even those remaining behind in the upper levels would benefit because they would not have to share the land with as many people. Just months after taking up the post, however, Kassum learned that the foothills area was being claimed by Tibetan support groups as ancestral lands. Within days, the Bank found itself at the center of a maelstrom, the main objection being that the Bank project would aid a Chinese policy of diluting Tibetan culture. The Tibet Information Network, based in London, put out a newsletter asserting that moving Chinese into a culturally Tibetan area would "dramatically affect the demography" of Qinghai. This claim, in my judgment, turned out to be baseless upon close scrutiny: The foothills in question had never been claimed or populated by Tibetans, although from time to time, Tibetan nomads would move through the area. But a tiger had been unleashed.

The fact that we had already helped to raise the incomes of 2–3 million people in the immediate region through similar relocation and development projects went totally ignored. So was the fact that we were carefully monitoring the project's impact on the 276 nomadic herders who were the only Tibetans living nearby. Although it was mostly Chinese farmers who were being relocated, the Bank had been very careful to make sure no Tibetan community would be disrupted. None of this made any difference. Before we knew it, the protesters were out, a consortium of NGOs had labeled our project anti-Tibetan, and our enemies on Capitol Hill joined the attack.

A group of anti-Bank legislators led by California Republican Christopher Cox mobilized opposition in Congress and introduced the Ecosystem and Indigenous Peoples Protection Act. It proposed reducing Bank funding for the International Development Association, the Bank agency that serves the world's poorest countries, by $8 million. This was equivalent to the U.S. share of the Qinghai project costs. All the work we had done on building partnerships with NGOs, legislators, public figures, and even the White House was in danger of being undermined. The Bank had become public enemy number one. "The Bank is helping China to dominate Tibet!" were the cries.

We believed that the project would not change the balance between Tibet and China; instead it would help both Chinese and Tibetans, mainly very poor people wanting to live a better life. But however good the project was, Congress was on our back, and so was the general public. Harrison Ford and his wife, screenwriter Melissa Mathison, friends of ours from Wyoming, stood at the front of the protests. Congresswoman Nancy Pelosi, another good friend and subsequently the Speaker of the House, gave me hell. Among her constituents in California were the groups that were most pro-Tibetan and anti-Chinese, and none of them would listen to our explanations.

Under extreme pressure, I eventually submitted the matter to the Bank's inspection panel, a three-member standing committee established by the executive directors in 1993. Its primary purpose is to address the concerns of people who may be affected by Bank projects and to ensure that the Bank adheres fully to its operational procedures. The Inspection Panel findings, delivered to management in April 2000, made it impossible for us to carry on. Despite the project's many virtues, the Bank had failed to follow some of its own applicable procedural regulations governing project preparation.

The Bank board became deadlocked on how to proceed. A couple of directors felt we should scrap the project and start again from scratch. A second contingent suggested we do additional studies that the panel had requested and then make a decision. A third group argued that we should carry on, making changes as we went. Jemal Kassum and his colleagues worked with me and tried to find a way to continue the project, but sadly, we failed. I had no choice but to postpone the project for fifteen months and in the intervening period call for a deeper environmental review.

The reaction of the Chinese government was immediate: On July 7, 2000, it announced that it was withdrawing its loan application to the Bank. China wanted no more help and would use its own resources to press ahead with the relocations in Qinghai. Zhu Xian, the Bank's Chinese executive director, decried the "politicization" of the Bank's lending project:

> It is unacceptable to my authorities that other Bank shareholders would insist on imposing additional conditions on the management's recommendations, namely, coming back to the board for approval again for a project already approved last year. China will therefore turn to its own resources to implement the Qinghai component of the project. We regret that because of political opposition from some shareholders the World Bank has lost a good opportunity to assist some of the poorest people in China.[1]

The Free Tibet Campaign lost no time in declaring victory, calling the inspection report "a damning critique of policy failures" and "institutional inadequacies."[2] It was a stinging defeat for me and for the Bank—and one of my lowest points during my ten years there. The Bank's public image had been damaged, and partnerships that I had worked so hard to develop with the NGOs and the U.S. Congress had failed to give us support. I eventually concluded that even if we could do business with many of the moderate NGOs, we would never satisfy those whose special interests are more important to them than all other concerns. There would on occasion be more radical elements that would come back and punch us in the nose.

We had made mistakes. The Bank often lacked political sensitivity to its activities, and this time, we had fallen into a trap. Even though the claims of the pro-Tibetan activists were almost entirely unfounded, they had sufficient popular and political support to undermine the entire project. Jemal-ud-din Kassum showed enormous patience and courage throughout the ordeal. I was full of admiration for him and his team and deeply saddened by the result. Because our screening process for political risk had failed to flag this problem, we decided to institute a new approach in our internal screening process. We did not want to be caught off guard again.

This had been a frustrating mess. It was easy for NGOs operating from the comfort zone of London and Hollywood and for politicians in Washington to place obstacles in our way. But the Bank's expulsion from the project left Beijing free to do as it liked without any of the safeguards and planning that accompanied all our work. I believe that our opponents had won a Pyrrhic victory. In the end, the real losers were the farmers earning 20 cents a day.

*   *   *

While we did much work in those years to establish the main lines of activity for the Bank group, there were also some less central but inspiring initiatives that had a profound impact on the way we carried out our development functions. Nearly all of them emerged because of the creativity and enthusiasm of members of our staff. The initiatives were not the result of directives for our top management, but rather from the efforts of members of our team to add quality and effectiveness to our efforts.

For instance, early in my tenure, in 1997, a group of young Bank executives, all around the age of thirty or younger, requested that I meet with them to seek ways in which the Bank could benefit from new and fresh ideas. This exercise was originally intended to give everyone a chance to influence the direction of the institution regardless of age or position. I saw it as an opportunity to unlock the creativity that existed within.

This young group came up with the idea of the Development Marketplace. After a false start, the small team came up with the idea to ask Bank staff on the front lines—and eventually, anyone else involved in development—for their best ideas for fighting poverty. People were asked to bring their ideas to the Bank and participate in an open competition. The funds were originally set aside for innovation in the strategic compact that I proposed to the board in 1997. I sought a small amount, $10 million over three years in a budget that averaged $1.2 billion per year at the time, so perhaps it was no surprise when nobody noticed that the funds were entrusted to a small and untested strategy unit run by a young and entrepreneurial staff.

It was revolutionary. It was also a series of firsts: The first time any president of the Bank had asked every staff member and everyone in the development community—not just senior managers of the Bank—for good ideas to fight poverty; the first time the beautiful atrium of the new Bank building was thrown open to a large public; the first time award decisions were made within twenty-four hours by a collaborative group of our young executives bringing together aid experts, NGOs, and the private sector. In other words, it was the first truly global and public effort to use the wisdom of simple practitioners to innovate in the fight against poverty. *Crowdsourcing*, as this has come to be known in the age of Wikipedia, was then a novel and unusual idea, especially for the staid World Bank.

What came out of the Development Marketplaces, as the events were named, was a series of ideas—ranging from the AIDS vaccine initiative to Roll Back Malaria to an ingenious merry-go-round that village children could ride, driving rainwater through a pump to a tower above the village square (eventually, the tower featured advertisements combating AIDS). Some of these ideas succeeded and scaled significantly, others provided significant lessons, and others failed. But the Development Marketplace went on to be held on a regional and country basis in over fifty instances. Ultimately, the original environment nurtured innovation by allowing participants to try and fail, and the initiative provided many lessons. Dennis Whittle and Mari Kuraishi—the young innovative managers of the small strategy group—went on to create Global Giving, a successful online site where people can provide financial support to innovative projects across the globe and follow the progress of the activities to which they donate.

*   *   *

On a trip in early 2001, one of the Bank's representatives in India showed me how quickly technology takes hold. As a continuation of the "Hole-in-the-Wall" experiment pioneered by the software-education company NIIT, a local group headed by technology entrepreneurs had installed a computer monitor with a built-in touch pad under glass on a wall in a slum in Mumbai. The idea was to make a computer available to the people in the slum to see what they would do with it. No information was given on how to use it. The group installed a camera nearby, to record what would happen. Would the computer—programmed in English rather than the local language—have any impact? And how and when would it be used?

In the first few days of the installation, children—mostly boys but also a few girls—ranging in age from six to twelve approached the computer. Then came the sixteen-year-olds. Next, we saw boxes. Why boxes? So that the little kids could stand on them and reach the touch pad. The parents, at least the women, never came near. But after a week, the children had developed their own language to describe the cursor and had learned to use it. A few children who knew some English got together and pooled their knowledge. Within a month, they were using the computer to access the Disney Channel and logging on to information channels and computer games in a language that was almost unknown to most of them. The children with English knowledge took the lead, but the other children quickly adapted. At that time, InfoDev, the World Bank's Information for Development Program, was working with local entrepreneurs, replicating the project around India to test its impact. It quickly became clear that there was enormous potential for computers to serve as teaching devices and central sources of information in villages.

On one of my early trips to a plantation in Côte d'Ivoire, I had a similarly memorable experience. In a village ceremony full of tradition and warmth, I was made a chief as a sign of gratitude to the Bank for all our work in the community. Shortly afterward, wearing a beautiful robe, I sat with my brother chiefs in a hut. "Would you like to see our computers?" they asked. They took me along a dirt road to visit with two young Ivorians working in a hut with a thatched roof. One was weighing and testing the quality of coffee and cocoa being brought in and registering the results on the computer. The other was using a computer and a modem to get information from Reuters on prices being paid in global centers. These numbers were then sent out on cell phones or inexpensive pagers to people in the local communities, so they would have price information when selling their coffee to the buyers who visited their individual farms and cooperatives.

Another remarkable story came from a colleague after a trip to Ethiopia. He had gone to discuss e-commerce with a group of village leaders and to see what help the Bank could offer in the area of computer technology.

"I suppose none of you knows what an Internet site is," he said.

Someone put up his hand: "I do. I sell goats on the Internet."

"How do you do that?" our representative asked.

"There are Ethiopian taxi drivers in Chicago, New York, and Washington, and it is our tradition for them to buy goats for their families in Ethiopia at festival times. So I sell goats on the Internet from a cyber-café here in Addis and I have them delivered on behalf of distant relatives in the United States. I have a great business going."

We launched several initiatives to use the Internet for development during my tenure. One of these projects, World Links, aimed to link schools in the rich world with those in poor countries to foster exchanges and mutual understanding on issues of common interest. What started as a pilot experiment between a school in Wyoming and one in Uganda grew into a useful tool for training teachers and improving the quality of their work. It was also used to launch joint research programs. The project is doing particularly well in the Arab region, where the needs for such improvements are significant.

We also launched the Development Gateway, a set of Internet tools that provide practitioners in the field of development with easy access to information: an up-to-date listing of development activities, portals for countries to present themselves to the world, e-procurement to increase transparency and reduce costs, Internet sites where communities of practice can exchange experience and learn from one another, and, more recently, a tool for countries to manage the flow of their aid resources. After their incubation within the World Bank, both World Links and the Development Gateway were spun off, with all the excitement and angst of start-ups making their way into the world of development. Today they are permanently staffed, and they represent real achievements of the young people in the Bank who created them.

We also harnessed the power of computers through the World Bank Institute. Originally called the Economic Development Institute, it was established in 1955 to train government officials from developing countries in general development as well as economic analysis and implementation of development projects and programs. Over the years, the scope of its subjects and the type and number of clients expanded greatly. In 2000, it was renamed the World Bank Institute and continues to offer courses, seminars, and other knowledge-sharing activities on subjects as various as economic management and poverty reduction, environmental and socially sustainable development, private sector investment, human development, infrastructure, and governance. In June 2000, we created Global Distance Learning Network, which links 120 distance learning affiliates in eighty countries with high-speed communication technologies, interactive video conferencing, and e-learning facilities. I consider it one of the greatest achievements during my presidency, and my colleagues at the Bank remain at the forefront of using computer technology to enhance development.

The pace of information transfer and the impact of technology on lives have triggered a revolution in development. Computer programming and computer-aided services are an enormous part of business in India. China's advance would not have been nearly as fast without technology. Although knowledge can be a source of conflict, I believe that on the whole, information builds aspirations and is a powerful motivating force. The truth is that with or without outside help, the e-revolution will take place and have a significant impact on the developing world. It can be a source of good or a source of evil. Ultimately, the benefits that technology can provide in knowledge and access to the world represent one of the miracles of development in the twentieth and twenty-first centuries. Technology and information deserve to be introduced as widely as possible by international institutions, and this technology may turn out to be the most important development tool ever known in history.

14

A FRESH LOOK
AT DEVELOPMENT

FROM MY VISITS TO PROJECTS IN AFRICA TO THE MIDDLE EAST, FROM Asia to Latin America to the transition countries of Eastern Europe, and from my discussions with leaders of governments and with family, I had gained sufficient experience to have the confidence to envision how a model for successful development could be conceived. Over my Christmas break at the end of 1998, I sat in my library in Jackson Hole, Wyoming, and drew up a document outlining the direction I thought the Bank should take. I had now been president for three and a half years, and I had spent much of this time learning how the Bank functioned and how it was perceived by its clients. Now I thought back over the accomplishments and difficulties of those years in search of common threads in policies and projects that would make us more effective in the future.

Of greatest importance was the fact that we had moved away from the doctrine of structural adjustment toward an antipoverty focus. Debt relief—essential if we were to have any chance of supporting human development at the level that was needed—was now firmly on the global agenda, even if progress was painfully slow. We had won additional resources for development in the poorest countries from the wealthy countries and had emphasized the importance of reforming international trade rules to level the playing field. We had begun to establish aid, trade, and debt relief as the three pillars of development and poverty reduction. We were openly discussing—and fighting—corruption. We had started to think more deeply and systematically about the changes needed in the institutional structures within our client countries and, in particular, the challenges of education for boys and girls alike. Our own approach to project proposals had become more rigorous and comprehensive, and we had opened discussions with other aid agencies in an effort to avoid duplication and waste. Finally, the Bank had thrown open its doors to NGOs and was building bridges with regional development banks, the United Nations, and interfaith leaders previously excluded from our deliberations.

Nonetheless, I felt that we lacked an overall framework to unify this disparate set of reforms, something that would bind together all these positive steps and our broader policy initiatives. Nor did we have an adequate system to assess the progress we were making. The document that the Bank used to guide a country's economic and social development for both the national authorities and their development partners was the dry and technocratic policy framework paper (PFP). This blueprint for each case was focused on macroeconomic policies and was written in Washington by staff of the IMF and the Bank. It was then "adopted" by a particular country as a prerequisite for getting aid. The process for conceptualizing a development strategy, outlining an effective operating plan, and conducting a fruitful and interactive dialogue with the countries was in urgent need of repair.

During 1997 and 1998, the IMF had overshadowed the Bank on the world stage. It had fought to contain the "Asian contagion," when an epidemic of currency collapses crippled Korea, Thailand, Indonesia, and other fast-developing economies and threatened the growth of world trade. The Bank had played a supporting role, offering billions of dollars in loans to help stabilize and rebuild the stricken economies. But now, as those crises eased, my colleagues and I sensed a need to reassert the Bank's antipoverty mission and emphasize what made us different from the IMF.

By now, I believed that our interventions should be addressed in a comprehensive way. If poverty reduction was to be restored as the central purpose of the Bank, development had to be rooted in a long-term vision of a country's need, not fragmented in narrow and unrelated initiatives geared to crisis intervention. The Bank's strategy had to emphasize results, rather than simply the amount of money being invested in a project. We needed to think long-term and build cohesive programs, not just operate contribution by contribution. And to set ourselves apart dramatically from the IMF, we needed to look beyond macroeconomics and focus on social policy as well.

So I took up a pen and my legal pad and got to work. The basic idea was simple. We had to look beyond just being a financial institution to focus on the whole issue of human development. I emphasized the inter-dependence of all elements of development—social, infrastructural, im-plementational, cultural, legal, environmental, economic, and financial. To have any chance of long-term success, the framework had to harness all these factors, not just on a project-by-project basis, but in accordance with an overall vision or plan. Merely to understand development in all its aspects is a hugely complex task. There is no single solution for change. You have to take into account differences in countries' state of economic development, culture, history, economics, and levels of education. You cannot even hope for successful individual projects without looking care-fully at the total structure of the society, the way it operates, and the avail-able human and natural resources.

Yet I had seen that at the Bank and at other development institutions, all too many projects were undertaken without regard to the total frame-work that would make them sustainable. The many regions and depart-ments of our client governments rarely integrated their efforts or shared insights. And worse, in some cases we were alienating or confusing the very people we meant to help. For the Bank's projects to succeed, the re-cipient country or community needed a sense of ownership in those proj-ects, rather than feeling that the initiatives had been imposed from without.

There was little point in starting a school, for example, if we were simply going to place a new building in the community without working with the authorities to ensure that it could function as an educational institution and be adopted by the community over time.

I recalled that in 1997, Elaine and I had visited a small primary school in a rural part of Ghana. The school had been built several years earlier with funds from the Bank. It was barely functional. All of the light bulbs had been removed, much of the furniture was gone, and the building was on its way to becoming an empty shell. The Bank had provided the cash, but we had failed to work with the government to establish the conditions that the school needed to succeed. This school was a forceful reminder of the futility of installing physical facilities without engaging the community to support a program that would sustain them.

The image of this school showed us that for education, physical facilities are only a beginning. Of course, for a school to succeed, you must have teachers and curricula, teaching materials and books. In many developing societies, girls are vulnerable, and to attract female students to class, you have to be able to get them to and from school safely. You have to make sure there are separate toilets for boys and girls and, where possible, water. Of course, it is helpful to have electricity, and a computer or two, though for most schools, this is only a dream. In some communities, you must provide payments to the parents as compensation for the agricultural work the children might have been doing had they not been allowed to go to school. If you do not make health services available and do not provide adequate nutrition and some early childhood development programs for the children you hope to educate, then many students will enter school weakened by inadequate physical and mental development and will remain behind. In Africa, teachers are among the groups most vulnerable to AIDS, so it is important to address AIDS prevention and treatment to have any chance of an effective education system. If you do not provide continuity through teachers and assure community involvement, then five years after the school is built, you are likely to find that it has been turned into a storeroom or a stable. Or the local community itself may ravage the school.

Governments alone cannot create a successful school; parents, teachers, the village council, and the local agricultural cooperative must also contribute to its planning and administration. In that village in Ghana, there were a handful of well-intentioned secular and church groups seeking to help educate girls, but the groups were not working in harmony. I knew that experienced Bank colleagues believed that we needed to be more involved in the overall education system planning process before agreeing to construct schools, but often we did not have the necessary leverage.

There was an additional problem that I encountered. Even the most brilliant staffers at the World Bank were at risk of becoming victims of its bureaucracy. It was common enough for them to spend years devising programs to win the board's approval, in a process that almost forced them to simplify proposals to move forward. By the time a project was approved, it would often be so formalized and constrained by red tape that the passion that had originally inspired it was lost. Worse, the projects that emerged from this bureaucratic gauntlet sometimes made little sense to the people they were meant to help. This failure doomed some projects in advance, for the simple reason that village elders often had more say over a project's real prospects than did the entire World Bank board. The best-intentioned and most brilliant plans drawn in Washington without local support could never have the impact and the traction needed to change lives. If we listened more to the people in the slums and villages, and to their leaders as well as their emerging civil societies, we could vastly improve the effectiveness of our interventions.

I was not the only one to identify this failing in our development strategy. In January 1998, I had met with African leaders in Kampala. They identified a mass of constraints plaguing African development: There was too much emphasis on economic growth and too little on human development. Education and health needs were not being addressed adequately, and when help was given, there was little attempt either by the authorities or by the donors to coordinate interventions. More thought had to go into practical aspects of education like teaching quality, textbook creation, and culturally sensitive curriculum development. Programs were burdened by bureaucracy and ineptitude.

The economic obstacles faced by many African governments were daunting. Unfavorable terms of trade and limited access to Western markets were paralyzing their economies. Infrastructure was woefully inadequate to deliver services and to allow their economies to compete. Their debt burden was still enormous. Development programs suffered from a lack of entrepreneurship, a lack of research, and a failure to capitalize on the limited number of experienced administrators. Finally, we were seeing no meaningful partnership between African leaders, civil servants, and donors.[1] Government officials felt that aid agencies did not ask and did not listen.

I thought that to some extent, the leaders were blaming developed countries for mistakes that were also African. Yet their larger point resonated with me. Africa's problems were not one-dimensional. Neither infrastructure nor debt relief alone was the magic bullet, any more than was market liberalization or privatization. All of these factors needed to be taken into account in an overarching poverty-reduction strategy before individual projects could be undertaken with a chance for success. They had to be developed and adopted by the countries concerned, in partnership with aid agencies and donors. The Bank, as the world's biggest source of development expertise, had an opportunity and an obligation to orchestrate this process and to help recipient governments develop a strategy that they owned and were willing to operate consistently over a period of years. Once the plan was established, individual new projects could be designed and implemented consistent with and part of a long-term program.

Over several days in Wyoming, I tried to harness this thinking into a plan that we could adopt at the Bank. I called my approach the New Development Framework and meant it to be a guide for the Bank's future direction—and an inspiration. Not everything in the NDF, as it became known, was original, of course. It drew together ideas gleaned from my time in the field; from conversations with government officials, teachers, and administrators; from discussions with my senior Bank colleagues and staff; and from my experiences with people in the broader development community.

The Bank's chief economist, Joseph Stiglitz, had been particularly helpful to me as I tried to map out a more inclusive approach. Joe had been chairman of the Council of Economic Advisers under President Clinton for the two years before coming to the Bank in 1997 and was known for jolting Wall Street and the banking world with his outspoken criticism of neoliberal ideology. As explained earlier, this thinking was called the Washington Consensus. It held that the ultimate one-size-fits-all answer to global development was the privatization of state-owned enterprises and the opening up of trade and capital markets. Yet for many of our poorest clients, unleashing the private sector and encouraging market competition had little relevance. These were nations where institutions were unformed, managers scarce, workers almost always undereducated, and the rule of law so weak that it was very difficult to conduct business or protect people's rights. In my view, the Washington Consensus made little sense within the context of most of the countries we were trying to help.

There were difficulties within the Bank as well. Getting people to work together meant overcoming divisions that were deeply entrenched. Like most international aid institutions, the Bank was compartmentalized by specialty and region. In this kind of structure, health specialists might recommend that a medical clinic be established in a village. In making their case, they would probably look beyond the clinic's physical structure and consider the difficulties associated with staffing. Even so, the plan would rest on assumptions that might or might not be true and that could make all the difference to the project's success. Someone had to ask: Is there electricity? Is there clean water? Is the culture such that women in the community can be examined by male health workers? Do people have a way to travel to the center? And at the more general level, do the village elders approve? Who will control the clinic? Who will attend to the payments? How much money is involved, and can the community afford to keep the clinic open? Will there be adequate housing for those working in the center? What if the health workers themselves get sick?

The list of key questions could go on and on. The most experienced members of our staff fully understood many of these logical questions, but because they sought approval for each project from the board, the central issue was getting immediate approval for a particular proposal. Extended consideration of longer-term issues was rare. The NDF attempted to provide a checklist of the issues that in one way or another confronted every project. It was meant to force planners to view each project in a broader context, so that they could take into account the key surrounding factors even as they assessed an individual project's nuts and bolts.

*   *   *

In January 1999, as soon as I returned to H Street, I circulated my draft to a few selected members of the board and to top staffers at the Bank. I did not expect the NDF to be embraced unconditionally, but I felt that much of what the draft contained would be music to the ears of anyone who cared about development. Instead, I found myself thrust into a new battle.

I tried to explain my thinking: "We have to look at countries and their futures as a totality," I would say. "If we don't, then individual projects may not succeed." We had to examine the overall context within which a project operated, and assess all the other relevant projects that were being contemplated or implemented at the same time. "We've probably wasted a lot of money by not looking at the context and circumstances of the projects we launch," I said.

"If you make it so complex, we'll never get the projects done," was an immediate response.

The aversion to change inherent in every large organization was compounded by the Bank's horrendously entangled budgeting process, which kept people so busy accounting for time spent on individual projects that they resisted anything that might involve more work and complicate the

approval process. Worse, I was proposing to hold people more accountable for their projects' outcomes. This was a major challenge, because in
many parts of the Bank, the tradition had been to bring out the champagne the moment a project was approved by the board. Considering the
years it took to put a project together, that was only human. But it still
seemed inappropriate. The real celebration should not have come upon
surviving the board approval process but upon actually building the
schools or roads or water systems, which might take another three to five
years, and then making sure that they worked and would continue to
function. Another internal bureaucratic problem was that before a project
had run its course, the Bank's priorities would change, or funding would
shift, or managers and staff members would move on, or the division chief
would be succeeded by a new one with different passions. This was another thorny set of issues that affected all aid agencies, not just the World
Bank, but I was determined to try to address it.

A central idea behind my proposal was that development must not be
imposed from the outside. We had to listen to and support local initiatives
built around positive aspects of history and culture. Our long-standing
practice had been exactly the opposite: To hammer out the details of
antipoverty programs, we would convene meetings of the poor countries
and their development partners in Paris or Geneva or some other world
capital. "Why don't we have the meeting in the country we are discussing?" I asked. "If the project is in Mali, let's go there. We should at
least have one session on the ground in a country that we are trying to
help." People immediately objected: "It can be a long way," they said.
"It will cost time and money." No one minded jumping on a plane to
Paris, but even when my Bank colleagues were prepared to take the extra
time to go to the country they were discussing, they thought it unlikely
that there would be an adequate representation of our colleagues in our
shareholder group and other institutions. I felt that this was an echo of
colonial attitudes, so I insisted.

My years at the Bank had taught me that the first reaction to any new
idea I proposed was that it was "not new." The immediate response would

be that it had been around for years, and the staff and management already knew all about it. And indeed, holistic thinking about development was very much in the air. "It takes a village to raise a child" had been Hillary Clinton's mantra since 1996. The vice president of Bolivia had developed a well-integrated approach for his own nation's antipoverty efforts. So when I came up with the NDF, I figured I could count on critics' accusing me of reinventing the wheel.

Many people thought the very title "New Development Framework" was grandiose. Some said that the concept was so obvious that it did not need stating. When I refused to stop promoting the idea, my colleagues were forced to examine it in detail. Thus began phase two of their resistance. I began to hear suggestions for better ways to achieve what I had suggested. Although I was grateful for constructive criticism, often these suggestions were really aimed at killing the idea. It is a clever bureaucratic gambit: Tell the boss that his or her concept is brilliant, and then help "improve" it in such a way that it becomes impossible to implement. This strategy both impressed and infuriated me, because sometimes it was dismayingly effective.

But the cynicism and foot-dragging only emboldened me. My experience over the previous decades told me that unless you shout an idea from the rooftops, drive it forward as hard as possible, listen to the criticisms and make appropriate amendments, and engage as many people as you can in debate, nothing will happen. So I hammered away, making my arguments over and over. I was determined not to let this proposal get mired in the Bank's "glutinous layer." Every big idea is made up of many little pieces that touch many different people, thus conflicting with all sorts of agendas. I wanted to stick with the big idea long enough to get through the criticisms. By keeping at it, at least I could open up the discussion about a broader, more integrated long-term strategy for each country.

The executive board was even less receptive than the staff. The members were satisfied with the time-honored project approach, which was well adapted to the board approval process. They agreed that there should be policy discussions to set directions, but they thought that my insistence that we evaluate an overall integrated strategy before approving individual projects was grandiose, and moreover, they believed, it was not our job.

Their resistance disappointed me, but I understood it. I invited the board members, one by one or in small groups, into my office to convince them to support the idea or at least to keep an open mind. I wanted the executive directors on my side. It had to be a team effort. This campaigning gained me some support. But I don't think many directors saw my proposal as being as different or constructive as I thought it was. After three previous years of seeking to refocus the Bank on the core issue of poverty reduction, I had naïvely assumed that our vast bureaucracy and executive board would finally rally to my side. I thought they would be ready to experiment with me and show support for my ideas because I had proven myself in other areas. Looking back, I think that my self-image was ahead of my external image. There was no way that I could count on uncritical support.

One bright spot to encourage me was Jorge Quiroga, the vice president of Bolivia, who had developed a well-integrated approach for his own nation's antipoverty efforts. It differed from my proposal in the details, but conceptually, it was absolutely on the same path in its prioritization of an overall framework for development first. His work encouraged me, and I had him visit the Bank to help me sell my program to the management and the board by telling his story. I suppose, had I thought of it, I should also have brought in the Chinese to explain their five-year planning cycle and to show how they put all the pieces together, to establish priorities and sequences for implementation. Looking back, I could say I was trying to extend best practice to the Bank's programs. There seems to be nothing revolutionary now in calling for a long-term, integrated vision before starting on individual projects, but at the time, few of my institutional colleagues wanted to hear the idea. They felt that the individual project approval process worked well. This was a debate I had to win.

One man who understood both my ambition and my frustration was Robert McNamara. Our paths only crossed occasionally, typically at parties in Washington or at occasional public gatherings, but we stayed in touch and I respected him greatly. I did not ask him to involve himself in the details of the problems facing the Bank, but I sought him out and explained my ideas to him, and he backed the direction I had chosen. Publicly, this support meant less than one might think; former World Bank presidents, even one as distinguished as Bob, quickly lose their sway. I have certainly learned this lesson myself. But privately, it was enormously important to me. When the bureaucrats ground me down and I needed reassurance, he gave me encouragement and legitimacy, for which I will always be grateful.

*　　*　　*

It took until late 1999 to put the new architecture firmly into place. By the time I announced it at the annual meeting that September, the scheme had been hammered at, refined, and pilot tested in a dozen nations throughout the developing world, including Bolivia, Uganda, Vietnam, and Romania, as well as in Gaza and the West Bank. The NDF had by then acquired a new name, even more generic than the first: the Comprehensive Development Framework (CDF). But what encouraged me, and many others in the development community, was the growing evidence that we had created a process for achieving development based on a comprehensive and inclusive approach with measurable long-term results, with the recipient nation in the driver's seat, and in partnership with international institutions, NGOs, and the private sector. I regard this change in approach to comprehensive planning as one of my most important legacies.

I also used that September 1999 annual meeting to unveil the results of a separate initiative, an ambitious World Bank study called Voices for the Poor and led by my remarkable colleague Deepa Narayan. In the course of two years, she and her team interviewed sixty thousand people from sixty countries in an effort to understand the Bank's "clients" as individuals, by listening to what they had to say. This was no mere exercise in public relations, but rather a serious piece of research that became a watershed in international development. The lesson that emerged was that poverty, in the experience of those suffering from it, is much more than a matter of income. In fact, money was usually the last thing that poor people mentioned. The individuals whom the team interviewed sought a sense of well-being. They wished to have a voice in their own future and to participate in setting priorities in relation to housing, health services, community services, and personal safety. They sought choice and freedom, as well as the opportunity to work for a steady income. And their deepest concern was for the future of their children.

A middle-aged man in Eastern Europe told us, "To be well is to know what will happen to me tomorrow." A young man in the Middle East said, "Nobody is able to communicate our problems. Who represents us? Nobody." A woman in a South American slum asked the researchers whom she should trust—the police or the criminals? These were strong, sophisticated voices, voices of dignity. At the annual meeting, I expressed my view that impoverished people are assets, not objects of charity: "They are seeking control over their lives. They are talking about security, a better life for their children, peace, family, and freedom from anxiety and fear."

I ended my annual meeting address by quoting Bashiranbibi, an agricultural laborer from South Asia who had benefited from a microfinance program for women. She had told us, "At first I was afraid of everyone and everything: my husband, the village, the police. Today I fear no one. I have my own bank account. I am the leader of my village's savings group. I tell my sisters about our movement." We had to commit ourselves to bringing about the day when all the poor of the world will be able to say, "Today I fear no one," and ensure that they are listened to as priorities are established.

For me and thousands of others at the Bank, unveiling both Voices for the Poor and the CDF were proud occasions. They signaled to the world that the World Bank was no longer a project shop. We had clarified our mission and had made the reforms needed to confront poverty effectively in the context of globalization and the impending millennium. I also believed, even though I did not say so, that we had decisively refuted "Fifty Years Is Enough," the criticism that had appeared on the 1994 NGO protest signs in Madrid and had so plagued our organization. In fact, many of the NGOs that had led the protests were now more our partners than our foes.

*   *   *

As a direct result of the work on the CDF, which was intended to produce programs tailored to the particular country concerned, all of us at the Bank became more sensitive to local conditions and history. In pushing the initiative, I constantly stressed the importance of preserving poor nations' cultural wealth—not as an optional bonus but as an essential element of the development process. The importance of this had become clear to me when Elaine visited Timbuktu during our second trip to Mali, and she told me that she had listened to her hosts describe the intellectual and trading center it had been in sixteenth century. As a child, I had always thought that Timbuktu was a figment of my father's imagination and not a real place. Whenever he wanted to get rid of me, he'd say, "Go to Timbuktu." But Timbuktu had once been the center of an empire that stretched from the Atlantic all the way to Egypt. For young Malians, this ancient past was their birthright and their strength, something to build on, even though economically they were now among the poorest people on earth.

But pride was not the message they were being given. On our first visit to Mali, Elaine and I had visited a first-grade class in Bamako, the capital. At least one hundred children sat crowded on long benches in a dark classroom. The teacher had the only textbook provided by the French Ministry of Education, which showed a picture of an ambulance arriving at the scene of an accident, where a car had hit a fire hydrant. One of the children in the illustration was calling for help: "*Au secours!*" But these kids in Mali had never seen an ambulance or a fire hydrant. French, while part of the colonial heritage, is hardly universal in Mali today, and they understood very little. I was not surprised to learn that the dropout rate in Mali's primary schools was astronomically high. How different the system would have been if the textbooks had been built around Mali's culture and history, using local languages in addition to French.

A similar realization occurred on a trip to Guatemala in 1998. I had sat with a group of Mayan elders who explained their belief that long before the West "invented" astronomy, mathematics, and engineering, their ancestors had developed large instruments to study the stars and had cultivated their own science and sophisticated philosophy. Dramatically weakened, this Mayan culture was now struggling to survive. Near where we sat, the Bank was in the process of building a school. I was hugely ashamed to note that with its red bricks and tiled roof, it looked like a school in any Southern California suburb. The design made no allusion whatsoever to Mayan culture. Yet with a little sensitivity and at no additional cost, we could have linked the design of that educational institution with Mayan architecture, history, and tradition.

Building on the knowledge and experience of the past, my colleagues and I learned other basic lessons about conveying a sense of ownership to the nations we wanted to help. Meeting on-site in the countries with which we were working brought a wealth of benefits. It brought the national leadership prominence as the host; typically, the meeting was cochaired by the minister of finance or minister of development. Local antipoverty groups and church groups did not have to scrape up funds to travel abroad in order to have their voices heard. And the meetings attracted a great deal more local media attention, automatically raising the visibility and often boosting the popularity of the programs and the likelihood that they would be implemented successfully.

We learned to consult not only the top government executives of developing countries but also the legislatures, including leaders of the opposition. Whenever I attended one of these gatherings, I tried to speak to parliamentary bodies and take questions. This sometimes led to fireworks. But it increased the chance that the antipoverty program would take hold, and it showed the appropriate respect to the local instruments of government. Nations that were just beginning to open up to the world sometimes regarded our inclusive approach as too liberal. Government officials frequently regarded NGOs as adversaries, so it could be a struggle to get officials into the same room with representatives from NGOs. Members of parliament said to us: "We are the elected representatives of the people. Why do we have to talk to them?" In Vietnam, after a tough exploratory session involving the Bank, the government, and three NGOs, one of the NGO representatives openly sobbed. I spoke with her outside when the meeting was over. She told me that this was the first time in all her years of work that the government had given her any recognition and included her in an official meeting. On a subsequent occasion in Morocco, the renowned writer and scholar Fatima Menissi told us that this was the first occasion she had seen the Royal Court, government, and civil society meet together to discuss the future priorities of the nation.

Finally, we won local support from civil society when, in every country we visited, we would raise the question of corruption. This was difficult in many countries, of course, but most leaders whom I challenged felt compelled to agree that this was a serious issue and to indicate a willingness to address this problem. Nevertheless, I had to navigate the subject carefully, and sometimes I failed. I tried for several years to influence President Daniel Arap Moi of Kenya to bring about changes. We met secretly every six months or so in London to discuss the steps he would take. But eventually it became clear to me that this was all a tactic to keep me quiet. When he retired, he had changed nothing.

As we refined the CDF, we also learned to make continuity of policy a priority. With changing governments, changing personnel in international organizations, and changing global economic trends, a country would need an overall program for development that was accepted and recorded, so that a change in government would not mean having to reinvent the wheel. In developing countries, where institutions are fragile and governments often not accountable, the existence of a written, integrated program was very important; the Bank could help provide continuity and act as a stabilizing force. Of course, in some countries there was no need for such intervention. China was a notable example of economic success achieved through disciplined and systematic policy initiatives driven from within and publicly announced at the party congresses. Its leaders made the brilliant decision to emphasize planning, education, infrastructure, and research, while at the same time never losing sight of China's dependence on the people in its towns and communes.

Having benefited so greatly from bringing in the NGOs, we began to reach out even more by cultivating partnerships with other multilateral institutions. The United Nations was at the top of the list. Although technically the Bank and the IMF are agencies of the UN, they are not like UNDP, UNICEF, UNESCO, and the other UN agencies in that they do not report to the secretary-general or to the General Assembly. The Bank and the IMF have their own boards of governors, voting structures, and funding, and they have always been careful to operate at arm's length to the UN. At times this caused competition and resentment, in particular between the Bank and the UN Development Programme, which did important work in many of the areas within the Bank's mandate, but with smaller financial resources.

Nevertheless, I believed the problems we faced were too big for partnership not to be the rule. I had laid the foundation very early in my tenure by reaching out to Secretary-General Boutros Boutros-Ghali. He immediately agreed that it was ridiculous that two related institutions should be striving to improve living conditions around the world without their leaders talking to each other. In the summer of 1996, Boutros and his wife, Leia, came as guests to Jackson Hole, along with Michel Camdessus and his wife, Brigitte. We quickly saw the mutual benefit to be gained from working together. Boutros began inviting Michel and me to attend the UN's biannual meetings with his agency chiefs. Each night before the meeting, the three of us would meet for dinner and off-the-record discussions at the home of the secretary-general in the company of our wives. These social encounters built a trust that made all our efforts more effective. We took to calling each other Boutros-Boutros, Michel-Michel, and Jim-Jim.

The three-way dinners continued with Kofi Annan and his remarkable wife, Nane, after he succeeded Boutros in 1997, and they expanded to include Renato Ruggiero, the director-general of the World Trade

Organization, and his successors, Mike Moore and Supachai Panitch-pakdi. Kofi and I almost instantly became close friends. He was extraordinarily open with me and made himself available at any time. If I telephoned him, unless he was overseas, it was rarely more than an hour or two before he called back, and I strove to do the same for him.

I was truly sorry when, in February 1999, Michel Camdessus retired after years of extraordinary leadership. We had developed a deep working relationship and a great personal friendship. I had—and still have—unbounded admiration for Michel and was privileged to work with him and to learn from him. Horst Köhler, who later became president of Germany, replaced Michel at the IMF and brought extraordinary skills to his position. Elaine and I also became good friends with Horst and his wife, Eva. Horst had a very constructive and open attitude and a desire for enhanced partnership with the World Bank. Together we demonstrated and maintained the close relationship between the two Bretton Woods institutions with the shared objective of improving quality of life and reducing poverty through sustainable and equitable growth. He remained interested in development in his role as president of Germany. Sadly, he resigned before completing his second term of office.

*   *   *

Despite its slow start, the World Bank's new comprehensive approach began to take hold. In 1999, the staffs of the Bank and the IMF finally agreed on a joint planning methodology that stood the old way of planning on its head. And at the September 1999 annual meetings of the World Bank group and the IMF, the ministers endorsed the proposal that country-owned, comprehensive poverty-reduction strategies would provide the basis of our lending and guide the use of resources, which in addition would be facilitated by debt relief under the enhanced Highly Indebted Poor Country (HIPC) Initiative.

Instead of dictating programs to recipient nations, we now called on these nations to set their own poverty-reduction plans, which would then be assessed and responded to jointly by the Bank and the IMF. We had come a long way from the top-down macroeconomic focus of the policy framework paper dictated by the Bretton Woods institution. The new strategy emphasized the Poverty Reduction Strategy Paper (PRSP) prepared by the governments and citizens of the country concerned. This institutionalized the key tenets of the CDF: putting the recipient nation in the driver's seat; asking its government to develop a long-term vision in consultation with NGOs and other development partners; integrating macroeconomic, social, and cultural policies; and laying out goals that it would own and that could be monitored and assessed. All of this involved a great deal more red tape than I had envisioned in my original plan. But I was willing to tolerate a certain amount of bureaucratization as long as the fundamental course of the generally accepted approach to development changed.

In late 1999, we convinced Mamphela Ramphele to join the Bank as managing director after a lifetime of struggle for justice and equality in her native South Africa. For me this was a real sign that the world was beginning to perceive the World Bank differently, and her role in the organization helped bolster these changing perceptions.

Three days before my 1999 annual meeting speech and after more than four years in the job, the Clinton administration announced that it was nominating me for a second term. The word was delivered to the Board of Governors by my onetime rival and now friend, Larry Summers, secretary of the Treasury. The reappointment came despite the fact that under my leadership, the Bank and the Clinton administration had not always seen eye to eye.

Yet the Bank, the IMF, and the Treasury had worked together effectively on many projects, and my pushiness and idealism seemed to have earned approval within the administration. I felt proud to become only the third president in the history of the Bank to serve two or more terms. The others were Eugene Black, who led the Bank throughout the 1950s, and of course my role model, Bob McNamara. I welcomed the prospect of another five years, as did Elaine. In no way was my work even halfway done. The reappointment gave me the opportunity to continue to implement the CDF as the best means to achieve poverty reduction with local ownership and support.

In January 2000, just before President Clinton left office, I made an appearance before the UN Security Council in New York, under the chairmanship of Vice President Al Gore. The subject was the war on AIDS, and this venue gave me the unprecedented opportunity to speak of the challenge, particularly in Africa, of the fight against this disease, which had already claimed 13 million African lives and orphaned 10 million children. At the time, 23 million people were living with HIV/AIDS in Africa. I told the audience that we faced a major development crisis and, more than that, a security crisis. Without economics and social hope, we could not have peace, and I said, "AIDS surely undermines both."

Although other institutions contributed more funds, the Bank was at that time the leader in making the fight against HIV/AIDS a development issue—and not simply a health issue. It made a difference at the community level and in particular exercised a parallel influence on governments through the work of the Joint United Nations Programme on HIV/AIDS (UNAIDS). We organized adult and school education programs in vulnerable areas using every means at our disposal, including a remarkable set of dramatic performances done by local artists and held in public squares and marketplaces throughout selected African cities. There is much work still to be done, and today only relatively small numbers of AIDS victims are being treated with drugs to delay or to counter the disease. The Bank remains active and committed in support of the work of UNAIDS. The world must also thank President Clinton and Bill Gates for their extraordinary contribution to the fight.

The event at the United Nations was a fitting end to the Clinton-Gore era. It underlined a global issue of great importance that had received strong support from the administration. It was, however, a moment of sadness for me, losing my friends in the Democratic leadership combined with a sense of uncertainty about how a new Republican administration would view the Bank and a president that they could not change for another four years.

Looking back on the last couple of years, however, I felt that we had permanently changed the approach of the Bank to development and that no U.S. administration would be able to change the impact of the Comprehensive Development Framework with its focus on developing a holistic approach and a clear, long-term vision for solving development problems and, above all, on eradicating poverty. As I entered the new millennium, I felt that we had the right direction, an extraordinary team to guide our institution, and certainly abundant challenges to face.

There were signs of progress. Extreme poverty in developing nations was falling. China and India had succeeded in lifting hundreds of millions of their people out of destitution. Global poverty was expected to decline to 10 percent by 2015, which the United Nations rightly indicated would be called a striking success.

Even so, too many people were excluded from education because of poverty, poor policies, and corruption. Disparities of wealth were widening on a vast scale between the richest and the poorest nations. Of the world's 6 billion people, the 1 billion who lived in the developed, or rich, world accounted for more than 80 percent of global income. The 5 billion people of the developing world accounted for less than 20 percent. Fully 3 billion of those people were scraping by on less than $2 a day, and 1 billion—a number equal to the entire population of the developed world—lived and died in extreme poverty on less than $1 a day. They lived mostly in sub-Saharan Africa and East and South Asia, where they remained trapped by disease, lack of education, natural-resource depletion, environmental degradation, corruption, and war. Globally, 125 million children were still out of school, and nearly 1 billion were illiterate—the majority girls and women. We still had a long way to go.

In April 2000 at our semiannual meetings, thousands of demonstrators flooded into the Mall in Washington, urging the World Bank and IMF to dump poor countries' debt. This time, I was not vilified, and I even got some modest acclaim for the leadership role that the Bank was taking with Jubilee 2000. I saluted the Jubilee coalition for bringing debt relief to the world's attention and cited HIPC as the first comprehensive approach to debt relief in the World's poorest heavily indebted countries. At that point, the combination of the HIPC initiative and traditional debt cancellation meant that we were on a path to eliminating unsustainable debt in more than thirty countries.

It became clear that the World Bank's new way of working had caught a wave. In September, the UN adopted the Millennium Development Goals, a set of eight great ambitions, the first of which was to halve extreme poverty and hunger, all to be achieved by 2015:

THE MILLENNIUM DEVELOPMENT GOALS
1. Halve extreme poverty and hunger
2. Achieve universal primary education
3. Promote gender equality and empower women
4. Reduce child mortality
5. Improve maternal health
6. Combat HIV and AIDS, malaria, and other diseases
7. Ensure environmental sustainability
8. Develop a global partnership for development

These goals were inspiring, but like many people who were devoted to fighting poverty, I felt uneasy about them as well. Had the UN overpromised? It had promulgated its list without any explicit agreement on how to fund efforts to reach the goals. In fact, as many on my staff were quick to point out, it hadn't even done a thorough economic analysis. Many worried that if the UN were to fall short on the Millennium Development Goals, the resulting disappointment would foster cynicism and actually set back the global struggle against poverty. Notwithstanding these risks, however, I believe that the goals provided necessary focus to international efforts, and they continue to serve as a reminder to the world's rich countries of the obligations they have undertaken.

*　　*　　*

I like to think that the Comprehensive Development Framework will be the most lasting legacy of my presidency. In an age when the world's eyes, and those of young people in particular, are more focused on the poor of the world than ever before, the CDF and models developed from it offer real hope. It is a practical tool for bridging the gaps between culture, religion, governance, economics, and finance within the context of each nation's resources and stage of development. Its most important contribution, however, is that it gives poor nations ownership of their fate and introduces the notion of the longer-term planning so essential to real change. The World Bank can bring vast experience, knowledge, and funds to many problems. But development must grow out of the personal involvement and commitment of a country's inhabitants and leaders. No made-in-Washington plan, no matter how well intentioned or how grand, ever works as well as one that is locally owned and developed.

My first five years as president were crucial in making the World Bank a more effective organization to fight poverty. Debt relief, the fight against corruption, and forceful advocacy for the opening of rich countries' markets to exports from developing nations had redefined the parameters of the development dialogue. The CDF was enshrined in the way the international community was approaching its work. Poverty had been put front and center on the agenda, partnerships had been developed, and the Bank was seen as more open and less arrogant. Finally, we were working hard to ensure that poor people's voices were heard and that they became the agents of change for their own future. I was very proud, too, of the role of the IFC in supporting private sector developments more aggressively than before. I was privileged to have Jannik Lindbaek and Peter Woicke working with me.

The instrument I took over in 1995 had been retuned. The unknown factor for me was the new administration and how it would deal with us. But I was determined that my second term would be fully devoted to the mission and the dream that brought me to the Bank. As the world refocused on the Millennium Development Goals, and as Bank staff rallied behind my vision, I would fight to use my position to implement our new policies and programs to serve the poor.

15

⚭

THE BUSH YEARS

MY SECOND FIVE-YEAR TERM AT THE BANK BEGAN IN JUNE 2000. The first term had been turbulent but very productive, but by now I felt greatly supported by the management that I had put in place at the headquarters and by the many country directors and their teams in the field offices. I had survived the testing period of the first five years. The image and authority of the Bank had changed for the better. With greater knowledge and experience, I was a much more effective leader of the institution. We were now about business and not about reorganizing the structure or setting the objectives of our institution. Moving forward, we would focus on implementing the many initiatives that we had launched. I was privileged to have the executive team and the staff of the Bank carry out our plans. I had no doubt that my success would be dependent upon their work.

With the electoral victory of President George W. Bush at the end of 2000, life changed for me. I was a Clinton appointee and had more than five years to run in my presidency. My appointment was secure; it was based on the votes of all the member countries and could not be changed by a new American president. But the closeness that Elaine and I had enjoyed with the White House disappeared with the arrival of the new president.

To George W. Bush, I was an inherited international civil servant whom he could not remove. After his administration had settled in, I made a courtesy call on President Bush. He was gracious to me, but in the year that followed, my relationship with both the White House and the Treasury Department cooled. Both President Bush and Treasury Secretary Paul O'Neill paid much more attention to the IMF than to the Bank because the IMF dealt with those economic crises that could have an immediate impact on the United States. Issues of international development were longer term, and they did not seem to interest President Bush, at least in his early years, to the same degree they had preoccupied Clinton.

Treasury Secretary O'Neill seemed skeptical of me from day one. That surprised me, as in my early career, I had worked with his predecessors in Alcoa, a company he led before coming to Washington. He put a lot of stock in a 2000 report about the Bank that had been written by Carnegie Mellon economics professor Allan Meltzer and which was inspired by hostile Republican thinking on Capitol Hill. The report took a cleaver to the Bank's activities. It called for our withdrawal from Asia and Latin America and urged the replacement of loans to poor countries with grants. Unfortunately, O'Neill and I never had the sort of open discussion that might have cleared the air. I never accepted Meltzer's arguments, because I found them impractical, and yet the Meltzer criticism endured for the remainder of my presidency.

It was only when John Snow took over from O'Neill in early 2003 that my relationship with the Bush Treasury improved, though I still had to deal with the critical attitude of John Taylor, the Treasury undersecretary for international affairs and the official most directly involved with the Bank. John was always fair with me, but there were areas of policy where we clearly disagreed. Relations with the Bush White House, however, never improved. Despite my efforts to reach out to members of the Republican administration, there was never any intimacy between the Bush administration and me, although Elaine and I were friends with several leading Republican senators. It may seem superficial, but in contrast to the Clinton years, when we were included in social occasions as a member of their team, Elaine and I received from the Bush White House only two invitations, both after I left the Bank. One was a retirement dinner for our friend Federal Reserve Chairman Alan Greenspan, which Elaine attended alone because I was overseas. The other was a farewell dinner for Kofi Annan and his wife Nane, when he retired from the UN.

Whatever was happening at the White House, within the Bank we were much stronger. I had a first-rate senior management team, led by members of the executive committee: my great friend and former colleague Jeffrey Goldstein, Mamphela Ramphele, Sven Sandstrom, Peter Woicke, and Shengman Zhang. The management team divided responsibility for supervising our reform initiatives while simultaneously running the institution on a daily basis. Mamphela, with the assistance of our only senior vice president, Jean-Louis Sarbib, directed the projects related to education, health, and human development. Shengman Zhang supervised projects around the world and oversaw the presentation of new proposals to the board. Jeffrey did a first-rate job on the banking and finance sectors and on directing the controls and financial management of the institution. In the portfolio work of the Bank and in the funding of the institution, he was assisted by a world-class team of executives under the fine leadership of Treasurer Afsaneh Beschloss. Sven Sandstrom, the most senior of my colleagues, took an overall part in the activities of the institution and was a source of strength and support because of his long service and experience. I was privileged to have effective and hardworking colleagues. They gave me support and helpful criticism. They also freed me to visit our clients to stay on top of our country strategies and promote the more critical work of our institution with our shareholders and leaders of the international development community.

Meanwhile, the International Finance Corporation was ably run by Peter Woicke, who brought efficient and imaginative leadership to the work of his organization and expanded the scale and range of the business. The Multilateral Investment Guarantee Agency was building up its business under the direction of Motomichi Ikawa. I was fortunate to have the support of the board, and with few exceptions, the board and the management agreed on policy.

I think that my management team was grateful that I was not creating any serious new initiatives; we all felt that we had already launched a sufficient number of changes in the previous five years of my presidency and were eager to be focusing on implementation and obtaining better results in the field.

In order to set an agenda for my second term and to focus my own mind, I set down a brief list of the initiatives we had already launched. These were my handwritten notes from January 2000:

1. *Poverty alleviation*: ensure that it remains the central mission of the institution, together with the overriding goal of human development
2. *Debt relief*: complete our forgiveness program of overhanging debt for qualified borrower countries
3. *Corruption*: continue the fight against the scourge in all countries in all our initiatives and activities
4. *Comprehensive Development Framework*: further develop the implementation of this approach in the interested borrowing countries and to ensure local ownership of their programs
5. *AIDS*: a growing development and human challenge—continue the fight in conjunction with other organizations, local and international
6. *Technology*: take advantage of the major breakthrough of recent decades, which transforms information exchange, education, and implementation of projects
7. *Outreach*: continue to work with the official institutions, global, regional, and local, and with NGOs and civil society in its broadest extent
8. *Local representation*: assure continuity of efforts to put decision making in the field and to pursue local ownership of programs by local government and civil society
9. *Enhancement of resources*: continue efforts to build resource base, financial and human, to permit quicker and deeper initiatives

10. *Pre- and Post-conflict work*: continue efforts both to avoid conflict and, where it occurs, to operate speedily to mitigate damage and rebuild society

11. *Outreach to private sector*: build relationships with private sector and join with them to improve economic growth and job creation and, in particular, to build emerging field of micro-credit facilities

12. *Women's inclusion*: work universally for gender equity and social justice and the utilization of the skills that women have

13. *Youth initiative*: reach out to youth to help them early with education and health care; engage them and listen to them as part of the development process

14. *Environment*: through the CDF pay special attention to this common challenge to all who inhabit the planet

This was a daunting list of issues for us to confront in my remaining five years. But if we could make progress with them, I had no doubt that my whole team would be richly rewarded for their efforts. I also felt that if, at the conclusion of my ten-year term in May 2005, I could point to progress on all these fronts, I would be satisfied.

I would soon learn that thinking strategically and carefully to follow a five-year plan would not constitute the core activity of my second term. There were too many daily crises and tectonic shifts on the horizon, and the global balance would soon be shaken in ways that I did not anticipate.

At the 2000 annual meetings in September in Prague, there were renewed protests about the IMF and the World Bank. Over 9,000 demonstrators were estimated to have vowed to halt the meetings, continuing the antiglobalization drive that had disrupted trade talks in Seattle the previous year and had prompted violence in London in May. My security detail would not permit me to witness the violence or vandalism, but I learned that Molotov cocktails, bricks, and rocks were thrown at the police and at some officials. Czech President Václav Havel, a former dissident himself, appealed for calm. After nightfall on the first day, 200 anarchists moved through the streets, smashing bank windows and demolishing two McDonald's outlets and a Kentucky Fried Chicken shop. According to the police, more than 34 people were arrested.

This set of incidents reflected a swelling tide of resentment against the Bank and the IMF. Dissidents argued that the IMF and the World Bank were worsening the plight of the world's 3 billion poor and that debt relief was proceeding far too slowly. We were accused yet again of spoiling the environment and propping up dictators. The demonstrations depressed me, but there was little that I could do beyond indicating to the protesters that they raised many legitimate questions, showing that we fully understood the issues they were raising, and indicating my willingness to continue to work with them to fight poverty. I received tremendous support from the governors, including our chairman, Finance Minister Trevor Manuel of South Africa, who commented that the demonstrators were making a huge mistake in trying to turn back globalization.

In my speech, I noted that we could not turn back the tide, but that our challenge was to "make globalization an instrument of opportunity and inclusion—not fear and insecurity." For many in the world, the optimistic economic outlook was still a mirage. I pointed to the dangers. "We live in a world scarred by inequality. Something is wrong when the richest 20 percent of the global population receives more than 80 percent of the global income. Something is wrong when 10 percent of the population receives half of the national income—as happens in far too many countries today. Something is wrong when the average income for the richest 20 countries is 37 times the average for the poorest 20—a gap that has more than doubled in the past 40 years. Something is wrong when 1.2 billion people still live on less than a dollar a day and 2.8 billion still live on less than two dollars a day."

I went on to emphasize the theme that had become natural for me: It was time to recognize that "we live together in one world, not two." I added that "the fight against poverty is the fight for global peace and security." I do not know how many times I repeated these themes, but I felt that I was gradually getting through to a broader audience and engendering support at a level beyond my directors and shareholders.

We made commitments in Prague to put Africa at the center of our efforts. In February 2001, Horst Köhler and I, together with Elaine and Köhler's wife, Eva, visited Africa on a joint mission. As far as we knew, it was the first time that the two institutional leaders had taken a trip together. We made stops in Mali, Nigeria, Tanzania, and Kenya.

On the whole, the trip was a success in focusing attention not just on the problems of Africa but on the steps necessary to bring about change. We developed with the African leaders a set of common goals to measure and sustain growth rates to above 7 percent for ten years, to double Africa's share of world trade every five years, and to accelerate the attainment of the Millennium Development Goals in poverty reduction, wealth, and education. All this was to be included in the leaders' own African redevelopment proposal, a Millennium Africa Renaissance Program, or MAP, which they hoped to extend to at least twenty African countries.

The African leaders outlined the key challenges confronting their countries. First, they had to address conflict and weak governance. The leaders stressed the importance of confronting corruption and building an effective state with a strong civil service. Second, they recognized that progress would not be possible without a stronger human base, which required greater investment in education and health as well as confronting the problem of AIDS. Third, they emphasized the need for stronger African cooperation and planning to maximize local resources and avoid duplication. Finally, they noted the importance of better understanding the international institutions and the support they could give as well as the emergency program of debt reduction offered to them.

These observations and goals could as easily apply today in 2010. My hope is that one day soon, the fifty-three African countries will come together and achieve as a continent the results they deserve. Though not discussed often when all the emphasis is on China and India, Africa will by 2050 contain close to 2 billion people and nearly 25 percent of the population of the world. It will, however, account for less than 2 percent of global income.

*   *   *

On the brilliantly clear morning of September 11, 2001, my daughter Sara was walking to a meeting on Broadway in Lower Manhattan's financial district. She heard a plane flying overhead at very low altitude—and looked up to see it crash into the World Trade Center. She rushed to a pay phone and called Elaine, who caught me just as I was going into a management meeting at our Washington headquarters. Seconds later, inside the Bank buildings, as in almost every office across the world, people gathered around TV sets and watched in horror as another plane slammed into the second Twin Tower. Before I could gather my thoughts, there was a shudder just across the Potomac, and from my twelfth-floor office I saw smoke billowing from the Pentagon.

America was under siege. After speaking to our Bank security team, which was in touch with the U.S. administration, I believed we were likely to be clear of danger, although I could not be certain. The Bank was not far from the White House, and if there were to be another attack, we were in the danger zone. I knew that all of my colleagues would be concerned about their children and families.

Like most international institutions resident in the United States, at that time the Bank had no arrangements to handle the attack of September 11 or anything like it. We were, however, prepared for normal emergencies, and our security staff displayed admirable coolness. From our emergency room at headquarters, I addressed all the staff through the public information system. I explained that they could leave the building if they wished, but advised that rushing into the streets was probably not a great idea; the streets around the Bank were jammed with cars, anyway. During the ensuing hours, we regularly updated the staff, and when it appeared that the immediate danger was over and the roads were cleared, we organized an orderly set of departures from the building throughout the afternoon. I was the last to leave, after 6:00 PM, and I went home a tired, shaken, and very sad man.

A few days later, our entire staff gathered in the glass atrium for a brief memorial. The U.S. executive director, Carole Brookins, spoke movingly for the Bush administration and the American people. I followed, on behalf of the Bank. "It is time to tell our host country and its citizens that we are with them. We share their grief. We need to join together," I said, before asking everyone to link hands for a minute of quiet contemplation and remembrance of the lives lost. In that moment, the throng of different nations before me was a single people united.

The feeling in the atrium that day reinforced my belief that the Bank's work was not peripheral to the world but central. The themes of poverty, peace, and security were closely linked, and if our lives had any meaning, it was to carry forward this message. "Poverty itself," I said, "does not lead to terrorism. Yet we know that exclusion can breed conflict and that conflict-torn countries become safe havens for terrorists." Post-9/11, the need for the Bank to tackle issues of poverty, illiteracy, and disease in a multilateral way was more important than ever, and it was my hope that this would become clearer to our leaders.

The U.S. government responded to the 9/11 attacks by declaring a war on terror. The first target would be Afghanistan, the "terrorist state" said to be harboring Osama bin Laden. From that point on, the intense focus on Afghanistan and Iraq, countries outside the World Bank's sphere of influence in the past few decades, would test our crisis management and postconflict systems to the limits. Both the Bank and the IMF quickly came under heavy pressure in the United States and other G8 countries to enforce stricter anti-money-laundering standards in our client countries. The sources of funding to terrorist organizations had to be cut.

But the proposed new rules had not been developed with the client countries' participation, and to ram them into place would have caused havoc in weakly regulated financial systems. Not surprisingly, our clients—the poorer countries of the world—were angry at any attempt to intrude on their domestic banking systems without full consultation.

The World Bank and IMF boards agreed that precipitous action was not the way to go and granted us the time to work with the G8 treasuries and with the developing nations so that we could forge a more cooperative and, ultimately, effective approach to dealing with this problem.

The Bush administration also demanded that we jump straight in to provide support in Afghanistan and Iraq in the wake of the U.S.-led invasions. Clearly, there would be a great need for rebuilding infrastructure and assisting communities. Although I recognized the importance of our involvement, I would not let the Bank be bullied into premature action. "We are not going in on the backs of tanks," I told my staff. Such a move would not only risk the lives of my colleagues and potentially waste valuable resources, but would also undermine the Bank's credibility as a multilateral organization with high standards when it came to both our emergency responses and our projects.

Instead, we threw our weight behind a truly international effort to organize relief. In January 2002, ministers from sixty-one countries and twenty-one international organizations attended the Tokyo International Conference on Reconstruction Assistance to Afghanistan. Cochaired by Japan, the United States, the European Union, and Saudi Arabia, the conference raised $1.8 billion for reconstruction projects in 2002 and gave the Bank joint responsibility with the United Nations Development Programme, the Asian Development Bank, and the Islamic Development Bank to assist the Kabul government with the allocation of expenditures.

In May 2002, the Bank established its first office on the ground in Kabul since suspension of its presence there in 1979. I traveled there to open the office and to get a firsthand look at the local conditions. What I saw remains seared in my memory. The destruction was overwhelming. Everywhere, I saw rock piles, rubble, and skeletons of houses in varying degrees of decay. Not only was the nation in ruins, but the drug business was already recovering. Hamid Karzai, then chairman of the Afghan Interim Administration, and subsequently president of Afghanistan, struck me as a man with a finely tuned sense of his country and his people. He was just coming to understand the problems he would face and the special difficulties in governing under such turbulent conditions. At the time, he had very limited government experience, but he was articulate, and he was ready to throw himself into the job.

The Bank was fast off the mark in backing four projects, valued at $100 million, less than six months after the donor meeting. One of our first tasks was to help President Karzai by assisting the government in installing expert financial management. We believed that corruption would be an enormous issue. I said frankly to Karzai and his colleagues that all would be well if the cash were used to the benefit of the people. If it were to be stolen, it was unlikely that international support would continue. It is sad to think that as of 2010, conflict across Afghanistan continues and the country's drug economy still thrives. In 2009, the export value of Afghanistan's opium crops was $2.8 billion, according to the UN Office on Drugs and Crime. The Bank and the international agencies certainly cannot count Afghanistan as one of their postconflict successes, and I fear that Karzai did not live up to expectations.

To the challenge in Afghanistan, we soon added an equally complex problem in Iraq. During the period leading up to the Iraq War, I listened to leaders throughout the Middle East explain why the United States should not invade Iraq. At our dinner table in Washington, Vice President Cheney, as well as friends from the Department of Defense, were certainly exposed to open discussions about the reasons to stay out of Iraq. Clearly we had no influence. Once the decision was made to enter Iraq, however, we sought to provide Bank services to meet the needs of the civilian population in situations where damage was devastating.

President Bush entrusted Defense Secretary Donald Rumsfeld and his team, including Deputy Secretary Paul Wolfowitz, with the task of executing the war. Unfathomably, he also put them in charge of the peace. Whatever expertise the Pentagon had, it was not in postconflict reconstruction. I suspect the president had in mind the precedent of General Douglas MacArthur's iron rule in post–World War II Japan when Bush

signed a national security directive setting up the new Office of Reconstruction and Humanitarian Assistance in the Department of Defense.
Yes, the reconstruction effort would be dangerous for everyone involved.
Still, President Bush's decision to entrust the Pentagon with this critical
mission baffled all of us in the development community.

From the moment the occupation of Iraq commenced, it was clear
that the reconstruction plans were at best inadequate, at worst nonexistent.
As economic and humanitarian chaos descended on the country, I took
an urgent call from John Taylor at the Treasury, who demanded that the
World Bank get involved. I pushed back. I felt we should play an important role, but I wanted to gain a little time to study the situation more
with my colleagues. I responded that Iraq owed the Bank a great deal of
money. The country was in default on its payments, and legally we were
not permitted to lend further monies until the debt issue was resolved.
My second point was more direct: We could not act until the Bank and
our shareholder governments, many of which were, to say the least, not
thrilled about America's unilateralist approach to the war, could get experts on the ground and make a full assessment of Iraq's needs. Then I
would seek board approval to put a team on the ground. Finally, our information was woefully out of date. I assured Taylor, however, that work
was under way to rebuild our knowledge, and we were proceeding with all
possible haste, given the chaos on the ground.

This call was hardly the end of the matter. The pressure was on, and
the Bush team clearly wanted us involved to add legitimacy to the occupation and the reconstruction efforts. Given the Bank's complicated dependency on the United States, we were obliged to speed up our response.
Working closely with the United Nations Development Programme, and
with board approval, we established an office in Baghdad in the early
summer of 2003, just weeks after the invasion. Our joint goal was to produce an assessment of Iraq's needs by the end of the summer.

While the administration's May 1 declaration that year noted that
"major combat operations" had ended, the fighting continued. Unlike

American aid workers, who were sequestered behind huge concrete barriers in what came to be called the Green Zone, World Bank and UN staffers were allowed to move about freely inside and had some limited flexibility outside the zone. I was very concerned for their safety. In late July, I visited Baghdad to see the situation for myself. I flew in on a military aircraft, and with a full security escort, and all of us wearing flak jackets, we drove a heavily guarded route to reach the Green Zone from Baghdad Airport. The following day, a car was blown up on the same road, killing the occupants.

Our staff had faced danger many times in postconflict countries, but Iraq proved more lethal than anything we had encountered before. On the afternoon of August 19, less than a month after my visit, a cement truck packed with explosives detonated outside the UN and World Bank offices in Baghdad, killing twenty-two people and wounding dozens. The blast left a six-foot crater in the street and blew off the facade of the Canal Hotel, which was serving as our base. Tragically, one of those killed was the top UN envoy, Sergio Vieira de Mello, whom I knew from our work together in East Timor. Just a few weeks before, I had visited him in the very office where he died, and we had engaged in a long discussion over lunch. Sergio was a brave, capable, effective, and well-informed international civil servant. His death was an immeasurable loss for his family and for the world community he served. Also among those killed was a Bank official, Alya Sousa, an Iraqi who had been helping to set up and run the Baghdad office for the Bank since July. These deaths devastated me.

If anything, frustration among Iraq's population that led to such indiscriminate violence made it all the more imperative that we carry on with our mission. But I could not let Bank employees become pawns in Iraq's strife, and I could not endanger their lives. I immediately ordered the evacuation of our staff to Amman, Jordan. They could carry on the reconstruction assessment from there, with visits to Iraq as necessary to complete their work. The Bank's work in Iraq gave new meaning to the phrase in our name "Bank for reconstruction and development." This challenge was much more difficult as we worked while destruction was still taking place.

Notwithstanding the special challenges of these pressing conflicts, the main activities of the Bank were in the countries ravaged by poverty, and it was to these places and to international meetings addressing these special needs that I traveled extensively in my second term.

16

————— ∞∞∞ —————

TRAVEL AS PART
OF THE JOB

D URING MY DECADE AT THE WORLD BANK, MY VISITS TO OVER 120 client countries affected me more profoundly than anything else. This chapter will read a bit like a diary, and I have debated with myself as to whether I should simply offer my conclusions. But I do not believe that I can provide a flavor of my work at the Bank without including something of a travelogue. Without feeling the urgency and confronting the stark reality of the issues facing us on the ground, I could not have provided the leadership that was required of me.

At the same time, it is important to recognize that my trips were a small part of running the Bank. The institution functioned because teams worked every day to prepare and review projects and to implement initiatives already approved by the board. The top executives of the Bank, IFC, and MIGA were fully in charge of the business of the institution. I had delegated to them the authority and they displayed extraordinary skill in carrying out our mission. For my heavy personal commitments, I relied on my office staff, headed by Jane Holden and supported by Deana Punsulan Canlas, Minerva Patena, Dianne Lust, Lai Foong Goh, Allison Tsatsakis, Maree Aniba, Araceli Tria, and Matekwor Ofori. Without their intelligent and devoted support my job would have been impossible.

Elaine accompanied me on the majority of my visits to developing countries. She was an enormous help to me both in assessing the leadership of these countries and in the development work we were supporting. More than that, however, she gave me a unique and professional insight into issues involving women, early child development, and especially education.

Let me then simply start my brief review in 2002 and give a very selective account of what my travel was like in the period to the end of my term, in May 2005.

In March 2002, I participated in the UN International Conference on Financing for Development, which was held in Monterrey, Mexico. There I joined Kofi Annan; Horst Köhler; Supachai Panitchpakdi; ministers of finance, foreign affairs, development, and trade; business and NGO leaders; and another international leaders. The challenge was to realize the Millennium Development Goals—in particular, to halve global poverty by 2015—by increasing foreign aid and investing in development projects. In the days leading up to the conference, pledges of hundreds of millions of dollars of increases in overseas developments assistance were made by the United States and European Union.

Although the word *financing* was in the very title of the conference, we wanted to make sure the meeting looked beyond just dollars and cents. Naturally, we needed to win more money from rich countries and increase the level of aid, but it was naïve to think that handouts alone would suffice. The balance between rich nations and developing ones had to shift, and the responsibility for development had to be shared.

The Monterrey conference marked a turning point in how the world viewed development, and I was proud to see that the World Bank's Comprehensive Development Framework had a decisive effect on the debate. The CDF provided the conceptual scaffolding for a landmark agreement that came to be known as the Monterrey Consensus, an allusion to the Washington Consensus it displaced. What united the signatories, in essence, was the idea of reciprocal obligations between rich and poor. Under the terms of the Monterrey Consensus, the poor countries would drive their own development and adopt policies to reduce poverty, fight corruption, and maintain good governance. The rich countries would open their markets for trade and fill the financing gap through debt relief and increased aid. The consensus reflected a shared understanding that the leaders of the developing and developed world are united by global responsibility based on ethics, experience, and self-interest.

Although some progress has been made, sadly, as of 2010, many of the initiatives launched in Monterrey are falling short of their targets. Apart from India and China, which have made excellent progress in combating poverty, vast problems remain, particularly in Africa. Nonetheless, international development is altogether more cohesive and comprehensive today than under the Washington Consensus and prior regimes. I only wish that the enthusiasm of the time of Monterrey would have been carried through with the same passion in the ensuing years.

After Monterrey, Elaine and I visited Moscow, where I met with President Vladimir Putin before embarking on an eight-day visit to five countries in Central Asia—Kazakhstan, the Kyrgyz Republic, Tajikistan, Turkmenistan, and Uzbekistan. These countries had been given little attention in the West, but undoubtedly, they would be important in the future. The distribution of natural resources varied among these countries, but as a group, they were extraordinarily well endowed and situated in a pivotal location between West and East. Populated by 55 million people, they had large resources of oil, gas, and hydro power, as well as enormous agricultural potential. Although they had close ties to Russia and Europe, they were increasing their trade and involvement with China and India. Clearly they would constitute a very important economic force in the years ahead.

In Almaty, Kazakhstan's largest city, I had the first of many encounters with President Nursultan Nazarbayev. We discussed the goal of reducing his country's overdependence on hydrocarbons and of broadening the economic base of Kazakhstan and the region. Our talks led naturally into the Eurasia Economics Summit attended by the leaders of four of the central Asian republics and Jean Lemierre, president of the European Bank for Reconstruction and Development.

In the Kyrgyz Republic, I met with President Askar Akaev, and we discussed the progress he was making on implementing reforms built upon the CDF. A scientist by training, Akaev adopted readily our suggested program. Until 2005, when he was forced from power during the Tulip Revolution, he lent great support to basic agricultural, health, and educational programs in his country.

After meeting with President Rahmonov in Tajikistan, we moved on to Turkmenistan. Like Tajikistan, Turkmenistan was endowed with a wealth of hydrocarbons. Its leader, President Saparmurad Niyazov, who gave himself the name Turkmenbashi, meaning "the Head of All Turkmen," had an unusual style, to say the least. He had, for example, renamed the days of the week after his family. Statues of the president abounded, including a gold statue supported by a column that rotated hundreds of feet in the air in the capital city of Ashgabat. During my visit, Niyazov took me to a cabinet meeting where he sat on a chair that was higher and set apart from the others. When the ministers were allowed to speak, they stood at attention while doing so.

I concluded my brief tour of Central Asia with a visit to President Islam Karimov in Tashkent, Uzbekistan. We discussed the much-needed reform programs in his country, including the establishment of a single currency exchange rate, and we signed an historic agreement for the Bukhara and Samarkand Water Supply Project.

My visit to this varied region gave me crucial insights into the extraordinary culture and rich natural endowments of Central Asia. It was also my first realization of the political importance of this region that is strategically situated between Europe and Asia and that was destined to play an important role in the years to come.

In July 2002, at the invitation of recently installed King Mohammed VI, Elaine and I visited Morocco. The king was eager to discuss his views on his country and the region. I was impressed by his efforts to enhance social inclusion, but I pointed out that lowering unemployment and poverty would require a revamping of policies conducive to higher growth in the country. The king in the successive years has proved to be an able and sensitive leader for his nation and has recently celebrated the tenth anniversary of his reign.

Later in the year, Elaine and I visited Mongolia, where I was impressed by my meetings with Prime Minister Nambaryn Enkhbayar and his cabinet colleagues. Mongolia is a beautiful country, with a deep sense of religion as well as a great history. Unfortunately, on my visit, I got food poisoning. I was treated by a Harvard-educated Mongolian doctor who, to my great surprise, punctured my stomach and inserted a rubber tube to relieve the pressure and rehydrate me. Somehow, Elaine and I managed to continue most of our scheduled activities, attending the Besreg Naadam, an ancient festival of horse racing, wrestling, archery, music, and dance—an unforgettable display of cultural richness.

May 20 marked the independence of East Timor after decades of occupation by Indonesia and nearly three years of UN rule, and Elaine and I attended the celebrations with Kofi and Nane Annan. I had worked during the preceding year with President-elect Xanana Gusmão, who received us most warmly. Thousands of people attended the simple but moving ceremonies, with the thirteen districts of East Timor represented.

Following East Timor, we undertook our fourth trip to China for an eight-day visit to review a number of development projects supported by the Bank in Yunnan, Sichuan, and Shanghai. I was anxious to see the earthquake reconstruction program in Yunnan, a collaboration between the local residents and my colleagues in the Bank. Throughout the trip, I was moved by the commitment of the Chinese in seeking to build a better life in both rural and urban parts of the country. The leadership of President Jiang Zemin and Premier Zhu Rongji was inspiring, and both men were generous in giving time to me and my colleagues to share their plans and to exchange ideas. It is no surprise to me that the pace of Chinese development has been so great in recent years. It is hard to believe that at the time, the $3 billion value of projects approved each year by the Bank was important to the Chinese leadership when today China has more than $2.4 trillion in foreign-exchange reserves.

One of my goals in this early part of my second term was to focus on the 10 percent of the people on our planet who have special needs arising from some form of disability. In many of the developing countries, little is done for them, and some of these individuals can become forgotten by society. With my own background of work in disabilities and multiple sclerosis, I was determined to expand the activities of our Human Development Network to address this issue.

In 2002, I appointed Judy Heumann as the Bank's first advisor on disability and development. She had served in the Department of Education during the Clinton administration, supervising more than three hundred employees and a budget of many billion dollars. One part of her early addresses at the Bank stuck with me: "People can become disabled at any point in their life as a result of injuries from industry, land mines or rebel conflicts, or conditions such as HIV/AIDS, river blindness, or malnourishment. Poverty is a leading cause of disability. As a result, people with disabilities are disproportionately represented among the poor." I was very proud to give her support, but I also learned how difficult it is to engage public support on a continuing basis for efforts relating to disabilities; much more remains to be done in this area.

*   *   *

Every year in June, my colleagues at the IMF and WTO and I were invited to meet with the finance ministers of the G8 and then with the G8 leadership and the heads of the UN and the European Union. These occasions were remarkable in giving us the opportunity to engage personally with the world's leaders and to learn from them the political problems they faced. These meetings gave us a chance to clarify and to present some of our own activities, to respond to issues raised and to identify the help that we could give both in analysis and action. Given that the G8 and more recently the G20 have no permanent secretariat, the international institutions are an important source of information as well as tools for action for global leadership.

The annual meetings in September 2002 gave me an opportunity to point to encouraging progress over the previous year. In November 2001, the Doha Development Round had been initiated with the goal of lifting poorer countries out of poverty by increasing global trade. It recognized that agricultural subsidies of $1 billion per day in rich countries squandered resources and profoundly damaged the opportunities of poor countries to invest in their own development. The idea was that rich countries would open their markets and cut subsidies for agriculture, and in exchange, wealthier developing countries, such as India and Brazil, would cut industrial tariffs. In March 2002, the Monterrey Conference had produced financial commitments to meet the goal of halving the number of people in poverty by 2015. And at the UN World Summit for Sustainable Development, held in Johannesburg in August 2002, world leaders had pledged to support development that would not damage the environment. The development community was thus confirming the Millennium Development Goals.

These efforts to make the global agreements effective were ambitious and inspiring. But what perhaps was most important to me was that leaders of developing countries had asserted publicly that the responsibility for their futures was in their hands. They had acknowledged that they must drive their own development and create a constructive environment to encourage growth that would be equitable and just. Developed countries agreed to work in partnership with the developing countries and put behind them, as far as possible, old colonial attitudes.

In my address that September, I tried to focus my listeners beyond 2015, which I called a "staging post on a much longer journey." By 2050, we would see the population of the world grow from 6 to 9 billion people, with more than 90 percent of that increase going to the developing world. Food needs would double, and the annual output of carbon dioxide would triple unless steps were taken to avert environmental disaster. And for the first time, more people would live in cities than in rural areas, placing an enormous strain on infrastructure and the environment.

I was setting a challenge for the ministers who were listening. The president of the World Bank cannot mandate a world order, but it was essential that I sound the alarm: Unless dramatic steps were taken, the future of our planet was almost certainly very grim. It saddened me when the Copenhagen Conference of December 2009 made it clear that our leaders are not yet ready to act in a purposeful way.

*   *   *

While it was important that I spend time with our institution in Washington, Elaine and I kept up a parallel travel schedule, which occupied about a third of the year. In October 2002, she and I visited Egypt, both to discuss domestic issues with President Hosni Mubarak and his team and to meet with the impressive secretary-general of the Arab League, Amr Moussa. We were privileged to attend a unique performance of *Aida* at the Pyramids, an event that no opera house will ever be able to match.

The following day, we went to Alexandria to visit the newly reconstructed library, which would be opened officially several days after my departure. It was a particularly meaningful visit because the director of the library, Ismail Serageldin, had worked with me formerly as a vice president of the Bank. He and his colleagues had made the library a spectacular center for the exchange of cultures and knowledge—and a haven for tolerance and dialogue. It had the latest telecommunications capacities and represented a truly global resource in a country that once boasted the great libraries and research centers of the world.

After a period back in Washington, Elaine and I set off to travel again, this time to Brazil, Peru, and the Eastern Caribbean islands of Saint Kitts and Nevis. The purpose of the trip was to signal our continued support to the region, which confronted substantial challenges, and to demonstrate, particularly in Brazil, the breadth of the Bank's assistance. We landed in Brazil's northern city of Belém, in the Amazon region, and began by visiting the jungle community of Ponte de Pedras. There I met with various community leaders and observed a project run by a local NGO in which residents made car seats from fibers drawn from coconut husks. For me it was amazing that these were later to be used in Daimler-Benz cars manufactured in Germany. It seemed like internationalism gone wild: products being created in the Amazon for the most luxurious of vehicles.

In Belém, I chaired a meeting of representatives of government and civil society to discuss the Brazilian strategy for sustainable management of the Amazon region. This was the first meeting ever held with northern governors and tribal leaders by the president of the World Bank, and I was warmly received. Given the region's rich history and resources, it was critical that plans be laid to preserve the environment and provide a future for those who lived in the Brazilian rainforest. Thereafter, we visited the northeast region town of Garanhuns and then the port city of Recife to meet with Governor Tasso Jereissati and sixteen other current elected governors of all the northeastern states. Finally, we went to Rio de Janeiro for productive meetings with Governor Benedita da Silva and other members of civil society.

On my last day in Brazil, I met for several hours with President-elect Luiz Inácio Lula da Silva ("Lula") and handed him a copy of the Brazil policy notes that we had prepared especially for him. We were joined by members of his transition team for another hour of discussions and then arranged for a full-day return visit two weeks later to the president's country house. This proved extremely valuable in helping the president-elect to develop confidence in the Bank's contributions, but it did more than that. I brought with me a half dozen of my more experienced colleagues, and we ran what amounted to a seminar on the experiences of new governments around the world as we had observed them, on the issues Brazil was likely to face, on the organizational lessons we had learned, and, in particular, on key challenges for the first hundred days. The president-elect went out of his way to express his desire to work in partnership with the Bank, which would include financial support, but even more importantly to accept the support of the Bank's development experience. Lula struck me as a visionary and a social reformer who demonstrated fiscal responsibility—a fantastic combination. Certainly, his record since that time has justified my observation.

My farewell visit with then-President Fernando Henrique Cardoso took place at a launch of the National Center for Information and Reference for Afro-Brazilian Culture. I had developed immense respect for President Cardoso and his wife. I was honored when, during a private ceremony in his home, he conferred on me on behalf of the Bank the Cruzeiro do Sul, Brazil's highest order of merit, as a generous act of recognition of our work in Brazil over decades.

The following morning, we set out for the Aguas Calientes and Machu Picchu sites in Peru. Successful developments had been made in the area to take advantage of the unique archeological and ecological value of the region, while preserving the indigenous communities around them. Elaine and I were stunned by the early-morning beauty of the Machu Picchu sites and overwhelmed by the mysticism and sense of history of the region. The next day, we met with President Alejandro Toledo and First Lady Eliane Karp in the Urubamba Valley and spent half a day with the indigenous leaders from Bolivia, Colombia, Ecuador, Guatemala, and Peru. We launched a Capacity Building Program for the indigenous leaders. The program had been initiated through the World Bank Institute and proposed a plan that would expand the offerings of the Development Gateway.

It was a shock to confront a very different challenge the next day, when we met with the Truth Commission, which had been playing a vital role in Peru's steady emergence from two decades of internal violent conflict waged largely by the Shining Path guerilla movement. Composed of fifteen respected Peruvians, the commission had a mandate to find mechanisms to help the affected populations heal their wounds and to start their lives anew. I met with Afro-Peruvian representatives and discussed their focus on health care, sanitation, and education services. Above all, they wanted to give a better start to the younger generation than they had received.

The trip ended with a visit to the two-island nation of Saint Kitts and Nevis to meet with the leaders of the Eastern Caribbean states and the governor of the Caribbean Central Bank. Our host, Prime Minister Denzil Douglas, was a strong advocate for his region. We discussed the nations' challenge, as disparate island states, in reaching competitive levels that would allow them to transform geographically disbursed educational facilities, overhaul antiquated production systems, and confront international competition. They also needed to increase their interconnectivity, which was now possible through information technology. The Eastern Caribbean states launched a program to cooperate in developing competitive industries and to share educational and other resources with each other.

But perhaps the most memorable part of the trip was the previous day in Lima when I met with my local staff and a group of people in their late teens and early twenties. These were local students and young professionals who had come together as Voces Nuevas, or New Voices—and they were working without outside assistance. I immediately invited them to come to Washington to show my colleagues what young people could accomplish by reaching out to others in their community to help them in the development process. If we could engage the youth of countries in the resolution of their challenges, then we would be engaging those people whose futures depended most heavily on creative solutions. I was delighted when this group of young people visited Washington and presented their innovative work to my colleagues from all geographic areas at the Bank. It was another reminder that so often, the solution to development problems can be found in the regions themselves and not within international institutions.

*   *   *

The year 2003 began with a meeting of the World Social Forum in Porto Alegre, Brazil. Created as an alternative to the World Economic Forum in Davos, Switzerland, it was expected to draw over 100,000 people from 157 countries, many of the attendees antiglobalization activists. I could not attend the meeting, but I wrote an op-ed that appeared in several publications, emphasizing the need for those concerned about development to work together and not to destroy each other in the process. I voiced a theme that had become important to me, that poverty anywhere is poverty everywhere, and emphasized our collective demand for a global system based on equity, human rights, and social justice. I am told that the article had some resonance, but the World Bank was still a whipping boy for civil society, and during the conference, we came into a fair amount of criticism.

During the month of February, I met with President Jacques Chirac in Paris to discuss the run-up to the Evian G8 Summit and to encourage him to make time for a discussion on development aid and debt in the low- and middle-income countries. I followed that with a visit with Chancellor Gordon Brown in the UK and then met with Prime Minister Silvio Berlusconi and the mayor of Rome, Walter Veltroni, in Italy. I was delighted by Veltroni's work, which involved linking up with a group of NGOs to bring programs to Africa. The idea was to demonstrate that a city like Rome could, on its own, make an important contribution to development. The mayor was especially concerned that his citizens understand that while they lived with the glories of their past, they had responsibilities in the present. Mayor Veltroni ran against Berlusconi in Italy's 2008 general election, but was defeated. He was one of the more enlightened leaders whom I met during my period at the Bank, and I hope that he has a considerable political life ahead of him.

After a quick trip to Paris for an informal dinner of G7 finance ministers and a productive discussion with French Finance Minister Francis Mer, I returned to Rome for a forum on the harmonization of development. This meeting was a precursor to a larger forum held in Paris two years later, at which a declaration was agreed establishing international targets to improve the effectiveness of aid delivery. It was vital that developed nations streamline the procedures that guide the delivery of aid. Far too much of every dollar allocated to development was spent in overhead, a cost that was repeated in each organization. Some estimates indicated that for every dollar, only thirty cents went to projects, with the remainder spent on operational costs, write-offs of debt, other accounting devices, and, sadly, corruption.

At Rome, I challenged the officials of twenty-six developing countries and dozens of representatives from donor institutions: "If, as a global donor community, we can get our act together, we will better serve those people in the poor countries who now want to lead their own development efforts." I pointed out that there were more than sixty-three thousand donor-funded development projects worldwide, each governed by countless demands, guidelines, and procedures designed to protect the project and ensure that aid gets to the poor. But these multiple demands were making the achievement of the projects even more difficult and were certainly wasting enormous resources in overhead because of an inability to rationalize our efforts and work together.

One of the great joys of the year was a visit in early May to the tiny mountainous Himalayan kingdom of Bhutan, which is nestled in the eastern Himalayas between its giant neighbors China and India, each with a population of over 1 billion, while Bhutan has less than 1 million. This was the first-ever visit by a president of the World Bank to that country. Emerging from self-imposed isolation in the 1960s, the kingdom had developed peaceful and cordial relations with its neighbors. Bhutan had established itself as a pragmatic and mutually beneficial partner with India through the development of its hydroelectric potential, which it exported to its neighbor. The hydroelectric projects contributed significantly to Bhutan's average 6 percent per annum GDP growth rate over the past eight or nine years and gave it one of the highest levels of GDP per capita in the South Asia region.

The kingdom was ruled by King Jigme Singye Wangchuck, who took the throne in 1972, when he was just seventeen. I was greatly impressed by this leader; he was calm and purposeful and had a view of an alternative path for development, reflecting the culture of his country and its quest for peaceful and equitable progress. The king was later succeeded by the crown prince, Dasho Jigme Khesar Namgyal Wangchuck, who now carries forward the vision of his father. The ethic of the country was embodied in the mantra of "Gross National Happiness." The priority was the overall development of people, measured in material, physical, cultural, and spiritual terms and embodied in the concept of national happiness, of human overall contentment and well-being. These values were tied to

Bhutan's Buddhist religion and unique Himalayan culture. I was awed by
the nation's ability to prioritize and preserve cultural and spiritual values.

Bhutan also had a staggering physical gift. We were mesmerized by
the magnificent rhododendron bushes native to the eastern Himalayas.
We saw these plants in full bloom as we drove across the mountains on
narrow, perilous roads to visit schools and meet people. Seventy percent of
Bhutan is covered in forest; indeed it is one of the most heavily forested
countries in the world. We left the country with an enduring sense of the
warmth of the people, its stunning environment, and its unique philosophy.

*   *   *

Over the previous few years, there had been a growing inclusiveness in the
international community. In 2003, for a portion of their June meetings in
France in which both the IMF and the World Bank were now regular attendees, the G8 decided to invite leaders of certain developing countries to
initiate a dialogue and to present their views. China and the other invited
developing nations, including India, Brazil, Mexico, South Africa, and
Nigeria, were rapidly gaining economic and political strength. Increasingly,
their voices were heard alongside those of the secretary-general of the UN
and the head of the European Union. And rich nations were beginning to
recognize that their elite club could no longer make decisions for a much
larger world without at least having some of its representatives present.

President Jacques Chirac, our host, began the meeting by inviting
the president of China, Hu Jintao, and the prime minister of India, Atal
Bihari Vajpayee, to address the group. Chirac then called on Luiz Inácio
Lula da Silva, president of Brazil. President Lula opened by discussing
his own family background in poverty and the labor movement and
then, in a warm and joking tone, he said something along the following
lines: "I am delighted to be here with my distinguished colleagues from
the developing nations. But I have a suggestion. Why not meet next
year in Rio so you members of the G8 can get used to the fact that in
the coming years, only the U.S. and Japan will be at G8 meetings and

the other members of this group will be replaced by your invited guests here today—starting with China, India, Brazil, and Russia? Maybe you can get used to the change by visiting us!" We all laughed as he said this, but how prescient he has proved to be. His prediction has been borne out even earlier than he anticipated, as we now have the G20 as the successor to the G8.

In July, I cochaired a meeting with my friend George Soros and Péter Medgyessy, the prime minister of Hungary, to discuss the issues of the Roma people, often referred to as gypsies, in an expanding Europe. They had been left behind in economic development for centuries, but with the collapse of the Soviet Union, their conditions had become even more acute. We heard remarkable opening statements from Roma youth and Roma women, who emotionally described the difficult state of their communities and detailed the enormous amount of work that needed to be done. The Bank's Dena Ringold had devoted herself for months to the preparation of this meeting, and I proudly stood on her shoulders to reflect our continued interest in the challenges faced by the Roma. Mark Malloch Brown, my former colleague and then the UNDP administrator, offered practical help and committed his own organization to the issue. Prime Minister Medgyessy and other leaders spoke movingly of the need to right the wrongs of the past.

We agreed first to establish and support a decade of Roma inclusion to run from 2005 to 2015, which was intended to bring to the public's attention the challenges faced by the Roma. Second, we would establish an education fund, designed in conjunction with the Roma people, which would address their difficult education and housing situations and the pervasive unemployment that prevailed in their community. In December 2009, Soros and I attended the fifth anniversary conference held in Brussels. I was moved to learn of the many Roma now attending university and of the two representatives elected to the European Parliament. While problems in Roma communities persist, a formidable start has been made, and I must pay tribute to George Soros for his continuing interest and financial support.

In July, we made another step toward the confrontation of corruption in Africa. Kenyan President Mwai Kibaki, who had announced that he had zero tolerance for corruption, held a National Anti-Corruption Workshop. My friend Peter Eigen, who had done admirable work as chairman of Transparency International, attended. It was a hopeful moment when it seemed we could work with the Kenyan government and its people to promote principles of democracy, transparency, accountability, and integrity. While progress has been made in some African nations, I am truly sad to say that today, corruption still holds back equitable development throughout too much of the developing world.

In Paris, early in the fall of 2003, I met with youth leaders who represented more than 120 million members worldwide. They included rural and street kids, children orphaned by AIDS and civil conflict, youth from the excluded Roma community, and young people with disabilities. They met in peace and with mutual respect. They asked why our generation could not do the same. They insisted that they did not want a future based only on economic considerations; there must be something more. They challenged me and my generation about our values and indicated that the standards that we had set were inadequate for them.

This exchange affected me greatly. By 2015, there would be 3 billion people under the age of twenty-five, and their expectations of us would be high. I told my young audience that I doubted our capacity to respond as speedily and effectively as they might want. But I believed that, at the least, we could address some of the more glaring imbalances—for example, the $300 billion spent on agricultural subsidies and $600 billion dollars spent on defense by rich nations each year, compared with the $56 billion that was then devoted to official development assistance. Even the poor countries themselves spent $200 billion on defense, dwarfing what they spent on education. I pointed to the Monterrey Conference, which saw developed countries promise to increase aid and open their markets for trade. But I also knew that it was far easier to identify the issues and draw up a menu for action than it was to implement the programs to make such ambitious goals a reality.

During my speech at the annual meetings held in September 2003 in Dubai, United Arab Emirates, I recalled the horror of the attack on the UN compound in Baghdad—an event that was seared in our memories. I confirmed the Bank's continuing commitment to help the people of Iraq just as we had worked to support the people of Afghanistan, Bosnia-Herzegovina, Kosovo, Timor-Leste, and the West Bank and Gaza. I knew that I was speaking for all my colleagues in our commitment to help.

Disturbingly, overall aid had reached its lowest level in recent decades, falling from 0.5 percent of GDP of the donor countries in the early 1960s to about 0.22 percent in 2002—and at a time when incomes in developed countries had never been higher. Chancellor Brown was, as usual, at the forefront in calling for more open trade and an additional $50 billion of aid, to be used immediately to assist the poorest developing countries. We had to move beyond projects that made us feel good to pursue initiatives that could be implemented in scale in 50 or 500 or 5,000 villages. This would require donors to come together with governments to move together to achieve more effective and more lasting solutions. I also spoke of the need to leverage technology and pushed for the development gateway to encourage partners to join us so that information and technology could help link the world in positive ways. "Delay is reckless," I said. This was a time for courage and action. I finished by saying: "I do not speak as a dreamer or a philosopher. Like all of you, I too have a family and worry about their future. We have the resources to make a difference. We know how to make a difference. We have the courage to make a difference. We must now act to make a difference. We all share one planet. It is time to restore balance to the way we use it. Let us move forward to fight poverty, to establish equity, and assure peace for the next generation."

In February 2004, the Second International Roundtable on Managing for Development Results was held in Morocco, attended by sixty representatives from developing countries and fifty representatives each from bilateral and multilateral development agencies. Our purpose was to discuss how the community could come together to ensure that the yardstick in measuring projects was the results they achieved and their sustainability.

I had been pushing this approach for over a year, and it was beginning to take hold as the international community recognized the need to eliminate rivalries between development agencies. We endorsed a joint memorandum that included a set of core principles for a harmonized approach to managing core development results—and a plan of action. I hoped that these principles and action plans would provide a foundation for broad consensus among development agencies and developing countries on how best to support countries in getting better results in the lives of the poor.

*   *   *

In February, I also took my first visit to Australia in three years. I was delighted to return to my native land and to speak to Prime Minister John Howard, Treasurer Peter Costello, Foreign Minister Alexander Downer, and many other leaders of the government and the community about the work that the World Bank had been doing. I encouraged the Australian government to take an even more active role in the development process. I also convened a roundtable in Melbourne with several key civil society groups to discuss priority issues on the development agenda. I met in Canberra with government officials to address the east Asia/Pacific region, including the assistance being provided to Papua New Guinea, the Solomon Islands, and Timor-Leste. I was impressed by the increased commitment of Australian leadership and civil society to development in the region, and I am delighted that successive Australian governments have remained committed to an active and generous involvement with development issues.

In Melbourne, I attended a Global Foundation meeting to speak in front of Sir Zelman Cowen, my dear friend and mentor and the former governor general, and Sir Gus Nossal, the chairman of the foundation's advisory committee and my friend from university days. I was moved at dinner to say: "I leave the country in the belief that it can punch beyond its weight, if it recognizes the generosity of spirit, if it recognizes that the values that it holds dear are not limited to behind the fence that surrounds our country. I believe that we can reach out and provide a light to this area and greater peace and security for our children. I think that it is not only a possibility, but I think it's a challenge that Australia must meet. If Australia does that, there won't be any question then of lengthy debates on migration or small issues that we address about immediate needs, because our kids will grow up with a sense of breadth, a sense of values, a sense of generosity and a sense of self-assurance which would make this country unique in the world." Immediately after the dinner, I flew to Singapore, but, as always, I left part of my heart in the country of my birth.

Later in the month, Gordon Brown and I met again for a conference titled "Making Globalization Work for All: The Challenge of Delivering on the Monterrey Consensus." Sometimes, I felt that Gordon and I were part of a regular Hollywood act, going around the world to present our program time and time again. Still, I was always impressed by Brown's remarks and by the integrity of his views. To me, he seemed a different man when dealing with development issues. He had a real sense of the problems and a big and generous heart. Somehow, he was more at ease in this role than as a politician in domestic issues. Had the 2010 British election included the poor and disadvantaged of the world in the electorate, he would certainly have retained his position as prime minister. At this gathering, we were joined by Development Minister Hilary Benn, Lords Carey and Griffiths, Live Aid leader and musician Bob Geldof, and—by video—President Lula and U2's lead singer Bono. The singer would become a leader in bringing development problems to the world's attention.

The following month, I made my first visit to Slovenia to mark its formal graduation from borrower status in the World Bank, an important transition for any country. I visited the Center of Excellence and Finance in Ljubljana, which had been established in 2001 by various regional ministers and the Bank. The main mission of this center was to build the capacity of finance management throughout Southeastern Europe at both the public and the private levels. It was clear that its work had already been successful, and in Ljubljana, we signed an agreement marking this small former Yugoslav state's status as donor member state. In the midst of the beautiful city, Finance Minister Dusan Mramor and I were confronted outside the building by an antiglobalization demonstrator who threw green paint all over us. I was somewhat shaken, but I cleaned up as best I could and continued with the formal proceedings in my Technicolor suit. Later, Prime Minister Anton Rop joked: "This is proof that we are in a democracy: we have antiglobalists as well."

The month continued at a busy pace with a visit to Jordan, where I gave a speech on the challenges facing the countries of the Arab Middle East and North Africa. Following a speech by King Abdullah II, Secretary Colin Powell made a moving address on the need for the alignment of the economies locally to allow for peaceful development. Sadly, the discussion we had at that time about economic development and unity for the Palestinian people has produced little progress, although finance minister Salam Fayyad is pushing ahead with courage and vigor.

I then flew to Shanghai for my last official visit to that country, where I attended the first real global conference on my favorite subject—scaling up poverty reduction interventions to make them more effective and more enduring. The conference had been organized by the Bank with the government of China, and it was attended on the Chinese side by Premier Wen Jiabao and Vice Premier Hui Liangyu, as well as by a number of heads of state, including President Lula of Brazil, President Yoweri Museveni of Uganda, President Benjamin Mkapa of Tanzania, and Prime Minister Begum Zia of Bangladesh. The conference, which drew nearly one thousand international participants and leaders of the major international aid agencies, reminded me of the enormous strength that China could bring to international development issues. China's hosting of the conference and the inclusion of such a broad range of participants demonstrated once more the important role that this nation would take in the international community. It was also clear that for a country of more than a billion people, scaling up and replication of successful project initiatives were essential to development.

During that meeting, I also met with Deng Pufang, the chairman of China's Disabled Peoples Federation and son of Deng Xiaoping. We discussed how the Bank might get more involved in the program for the disabled in China. Chairman Deng Pufang himself used a wheelchair, having been thrown out a window from a multistory building during the Cultural Revolution. Since that time, he has assumed a major position in leadership of disabled communities throughout the world.

During a televised speech I gave in Shanghai, I recalled an example of China's progress that had struck me particularly. Nine years earlier, at the beginning of my tenure at the Bank, I had visited the Loess Plateau, along the Yellow River. There I saw stark, barren valleys with no trees. The Yellow River was filling with sediment from water coming down the hills. It was a terrible situation. The people were living in unimaginable conditions, usually in caves on the tops of hills. I was told that there was a plan: The authorities would issue spades to people, and hundreds of thousands of workers would come through the valleys, picking up rocks and terracing the hills. There would be one bulldozer for each valley. On the top of each hill stood a small monument that read "World Bank Project No. 1" or "No. 20" and bore the signature of the team leader and the finance executive they had elected. As a result of the hard work of the citizens and the expert guidance of the Bank's Juergen Voegele, these parched areas now looked like Switzerland. They were covered with grass and trees, and the landscape was dotted with animals and houses. This project was an impeccable example of taking an idea to scale.

This was not magic; it was a simple idea carried forward by the diligence of the local people and one that would work year after year. The success was not the success of the World Bank. The success belonged to the Chinese people; it came from their perseverance and their commitment to improving their way of life. I remain deeply impressed by the actions of the Chinese people in their organized plans to confront poverty.

I was interviewed for a TV show during that trip, and as a special surprise, a woman whom I had met on my first visit to China was brought to the studio. When I first met her, she had been living with her husband and son in a cave without water or electricity. This was her first visit to a major city. She told me—and the audience—that as a result of the World

Bank project, she now had much better accommodations, electricity, and water, and her son had a motorcycle. I was moved to tears as we embraced.

*   *   *

The annual meetings that took place on October 3, 2004, in Washington gave me the opportunity to address my colleagues in what I was sure would be my last speech as president. I would like to have matched Bob McNamara's tenure of thirteen years, but I already had received indications from the Bush administration that I would not get an extension of my second term. Although I had developed good relationships with Treasury Secretary Snow and a few of the White House staff, I knew that Bush and his political operatives would not miss an opportunity to place a Republican into an important international vacancy created by the term end of one of the last surviving Clinton appointees.

The Bank community had much to be proud of. With only $11 billion in equity capital contributed by shareholders during the life of the institution, and by the astute use of the debt markets and reliance on the strength of uncalled capital, the Bank had made almost $400 billion in loans during its sixty years. The International Finance Corporation had brought $67 billion to the emerging markets, and the Multilateral Investment Guarantee Agency had issued $13.5 billion in guarantees. On the strength of donor contributions and reflows from borrowers, the International Development Association (IDA) had committed $151 billion to the countries eligible for aid—countries that were home to 80 percent of the world's poorest people who live on less than $1 a day.

We might be sixty, I said, but we were young. We were diverse, with staff from more than 140 countries. More than two-thirds of our country directors were now hiring and working in the field. Our offices were linked through satellite, making videoconferencing and distance learning a part of our lives. We had broadened our approach to development to make it comprehensive rather than divided up into thousands of projects. We had confronted the issues of debt and attacked corruption by working with governments in more than 100 countries, and we were at the fore-front of the fight against AIDS. The health of our environment had be-come central to our work. We knew that true and lasting development was simply not possible without preserving our planet. I spoke of the fu-ture and of how we might better manage the big global issues such as trade, illegal drugs, migration, diseases, and, yes, terrorism.

In looking forward, I noted that there were three urgent priorities: The first was protecting the planet through better stewardship of our en-vironment, the second was scaling up our efforts on effective poverty re-duction, and the third was educating our youth differently for the twenty-first century—and giving them hope. I knew that my ten-year tenure at the Bank made me only a small part of an ongoing effort of making the planet a better place. I was proud of what my colleagues and I had achieved during our period, but it was equally important to set forth clearly the challenges that lay ahead.

Standing before the 2,500 people assembled in Constitution Hall, I wanted not only to sum up the lessons we had learned but also to deliver a stronger message of concern about the global environment. On our visit to Peru, Elaine and I had met a farmer living near Machu Picchu in the Peruvian highlands. He pointed above him and said, through an inter-preter, "My mountains are sad." The glaciers that had formed on them thousands of years ago had resembled a smile on the face of the moun-tains, and now they were shrinking every year. As they receded, there was no water to fill the lakes and rivers. The animals suffered. The income of his valley had dropped by half, and farmers were abandoning their home-lands. He had a simple question: "Can you help me get my glaciers back so that the mountains will smile again?"

For him, the climate crisis was not some abstract, long-term issue. Like poverty, it was of immediate concern, with local as well as global implica-tions. In my ten years at the Bank, that was the most important lesson I had learned. "The world has no walls," I said to the crowd. "We are one world. Damage to the environment somewhere is damage everywhere. Poverty somewhere is poverty everywhere. And terror somewhere is terror everywhere. If there is a bombing in Bali, or Madrid, or Moscow, we all get scared. We all feel insecure." I knew as I ended my speech that I would never again have a mandate of such importance, nor an annual opportunity to address representatives of the world on key global concerns.

*   *   *

However, my term was not quite yet finished. Later that fall, Elaine and I went to Madagascar upon the invitation of President Marc Ravalomanana. I had been keen to see for myself what enlightened leadership could do in an island country with such rich wildlife and biodiversity. The president and his colleagues diligently followed programs for the maintenance of their environment. They also managed to maintain a balance between the Christian and Muslim groups that lived in their society. I hope that Madagascar will be able to return to its once-promising path following the recent political turmoil.

Our next stop was Ethiopia for the fourth meeting of the African Development Forum, hosted by the Economic Commission for Africa. The theme of the forum was governance. We met with Prime Minister Meles Zenawi and key members of his cabinet; they presented a finely tuned development plan for the next five years. It was a unified vision of the prime minister and his colleagues, who conveyed notable competence. Prime Minister Meles had done a terrific job strengthening his government. He and most of his ministers had missed their tertiary education because they were serving as freedom fighters to liberate their country. But he insisted that they enroll in correspondence courses with London University, which allowed them to gain degrees and knowledge that would help them run the country. Though I am sympathetic to those critics who complain that he has not done enough to embrace democratic principles, I was enormously impressed by Meles Zenawi. I found him to be one of the most farsighted and important leaders in Africa.

*   *   *

On the morning of December 26, 2004, we awoke to another tragedy when Indonesia was struck by a massive earthquake, with its epicenter on the west coast of northern Sumatra. As the quake set off tsunamis, hundreds of thousands of people lost their lives, and millions lost their homes. At the time, Kofi and Nane Annan were visiting Elaine and me in Wyoming. As we learned the facts, Kofi and I were able to coordinate the way our organizations responded. In past crises, UN disaster-relief teams had always gone in immediately, with personnel from the IMF and World Bank following days or weeks after the initial crisis. This time, the UN, the Bank, and the IMF mounted a unified response.

By January 2005, I was addressing a special meeting of the Association of southeast Asian nations in Jakarta. There was an overwhelming and immediate need for water, food, sanitation, and medicine, but we also needed to be thinking about reconstruction. First, we had to ensure that communities were involved in assessing their needs and designing home-grown recovery programs. Second, emergency assistance had to be provided, kept simple, and focused on the most urgent priorities. Third, the longer-term development plans had to integrate risk reduction to avoid future losses from disasters. Finally, the international community needed to work in a coordinated way to help the relief efforts.

We mounted a Bank-wide response. My colleagues from the East Asia, Pacific, and South Asia teams came forward immediately with offers of assistance. We were able to adapt preexisting projects to assist immediately in the reconstruction of Aceh and Northern Sumatra. These plans included community development projects, special interventions in poor and disadvantaged areas, and the reconstruction of infrastructure that would be essential for the restoration of the normal life in the community. The international community galvanized to pour in money and aid, and as the UN provided food, shelter, and medical care, our teams immediately began planning for reconstruction. Kofi Annan and I visited the sites together in a helicopter—both to minimize the burden of our visits on local government and to demonstrate the combined resolve of the Bank and the UN. The coordinated global response to the tsunami was a true achievement.

*   *   *

As the end of my term approached in May, I clung to the faint hope of winning a brief extension of my presidency. I even went as far as to suggest to Treasury Secretary John Snow that the president must be so busy starting his second term that he might like to hold off for some months searching for my replacement. This would have allowed me to attend the G8 meeting scheduled for July in Gleneagles, Scotland, where I knew that the U.K. hosts Tony Blair and Gordon Brown would put debt relief, the Millennium Development Goals, and Africa at the top of the agenda—all matters dear to my heart.

However, sometime in March, the Bush administration confirmed my successor would be Deputy Secretary of Defense Paul Wolfowitz and that they wanted him in the presidential chair by June 1. Paul and I had known each other for years; I liked him personally, though I disagreed with almost every aspect of his politics. Still, I wanted to be sure to give him all the support I could—all the support that Lew Preston had wished to offer me, but had been unable to give me because of his illness. So in the weeks leading up to the changeover, I opened my entire schedule to him. But Paul had a full calendar at the Department of Defense, and I met with him only on a few occasions. I took those opportunities to explain my philosophy and give my assessment of the people he would work with. I expressed my deep wish that he preserve and protect the good things I had done and that he change and improve the things I had done less well.

Following the end of my term on May 30, I had little contact with Paul. He never sought my advice again, and although I kept an office at the Bank for infrequent visits and for correspondence for almost twelve months, I decided to close it. I took Paul to lunch twice in a restaurant outside the Bank, but he never asked then or at any other time for my opinion on any subject related to the Bank. By then I had moved into a new phase of my life. I knew I should not interfere, but I hoped that he would lead the Bank to greater heights. I trained myself not to look back, not to comment, and not to become involved in any way.

As the day of retirement approached, there was an outpouring of goodwill and warmth, which concluded with a crowd of two thousand or more filling the glass atrium at headquarters to say good-bye. It had been an emotionally rich decade, at times exhilarating and at times crushing, but the feeling of love and the kindness in that hour-long ceremony moved both Elaine and me to tears. The staff presented the two of us with a book of messages concerning our ten years at the Bank. They were generous and warm. I felt that we should have given each of our colleagues a book of appreciation also, for without our constructive partnership, I would have achieved little. At separate occasions, the Board of Directors and the ministers were also generous and thoughtful in their parting words that they offered to us.

Serving the Bank had been the biggest challenge I had ever faced, and it was the most rewarding and the most humbling experience of my career. I will always have regrets and frustrations over our failures, but I will also recall with intense satisfaction the programs and projects that succeeded. I am proud that the Bank I left was a changed institution. The concerns of staff and management at the beginning of my term that the Bank had reached its "sunset" had given way to a renewed sense of purpose. Under the leadership of our management team, the staff chose this motto for their mission: "To fight poverty with passion and professionalism for lasting results." Surveys in my last year showed that there had been a huge leap in morale: More than 90 percent of the staff were now proud that they worked at the Bank.

The World Bank remains an extraordinarily unique establishment that nurtures growth and development in the public and private spheres. It is, in my judgment, one of the jewels of the international scene.

I also am very proud of the way the International Finance Corporation developed as the bridge to private sector investment. In the last five years of my term, the institution built on its past and implemented new programs to take advantage of private sector skills and to supplement initiatives in developing countries. Finally, MIGA continued to grow and to develop a special niche in insuring risk.

Bob McNamara had once said to me, "Running the World Bank is the best job in the world if you are interested in bringing about change in the human condition." He was right. I was blessed to be chosen, and for Elaine and for me, it was the most important period of our lives. Indeed, I felt then, and still believe, that my decade at the Bank was the reason for my life. I will be grateful forever to the thousands of men and women at the institution who give so much to the betterment of our planet. They are often unseen, and frequently criticized, but they are the finest and most devoted group of people one could ever hope to know. They give so much of themselves to bring hope to those in poverty, to protect our environment, and to give a greater sense of equity and social justice to our planet.

17

⊶⊷

A NEW AND DIFFERENT CHALLENGE

A S MY TENURE AT THE WORLD BANK DREW TO A CLOSE, I BEGAN TO wonder what I would do next. By the end of March 2005, with two months to go, Elaine and I were planning to take a three-month vacation in Italy to learn Italian and spend some time thinking about our plans for the future. But when my phone rang on April 4, our dream of a quiet summer melted away.

Secretary of State Condoleezza Rice was on the line from Air Force One, flying to Rome for the funeral of Pope John Paul II. She explained that when she and President Bush returned in forty-eight hours, they wanted to discuss with me whether I might be interested in taking the position of special envoy of the Quartet to the Middle East, the peace-seeking unit involved in the Israeli-Palestinian dispute, consisting of the United States, Russia, the European Union, and the United Nations.

Over the years, the United States had sent a series of special envoys to the Middle East to help underpin peace efforts. Among the most famous envoys was Secretary of State Henry Kissinger, who, in the wake of the Yom Kippur War, helped to settle border delineation disputes between Israel and its neighbors, though some of these disputes continue. In the aftermath of the attacks of 9/11, the Arab-Israeli issue had been given less attention by the Bush administration. It had now been two years since the Quartet had presented "a road map for peace" to Israelis and Palestinians. The vision of the road map was two democratic states, Israel and Palestine, living side by side, an objective that was decades old and for which many plans existed.

Over the previous year and a half, the landscape across the Middle East had shifted dramatically. In early 2004, Israeli Prime Minister Ariel Sharon began to back away from the idea of a Greater Israel, a policy goal once at the heart of the right-wing Likud Party he had helped to found. Surprising many, he expressed his commitment to the withdrawal of Jewish settlers from the Gaza Strip. Sharon appeared to have come around to the view that if the Palestinians were given more freedom to run their own affairs, they might be more willing to end the terror attacks that so disturbed Israeli life. In addition, such a move would pave the way for establishing a Palestinian state linking the West Bank and Gaza. Political negotiations had been suspended, but Sharon believed that the withdrawal proposal would improve Israel's security and international standing. He also wanted to be rid of the political liability of the more than one million Gazans under the umbrella of a harsh occupation.

This willingness to give up part of the territory that Israel acquired in the 1967 war—and that the Palestinians viewed as integral to their future state—created a moment of real possibility. In addition, Yasser Arafat, the first president of the Palestinian National Authority (PNA, or PA), had become terminally ill, and that development had brought the region back to center stage. The news of his lapse into a coma broke just as the 2004 American election results were being counted. Arafat's death on November 11 bolstered Sharon's diplomatic position when the newly elected president of the PA, Mahmoud Abbas (also known as Abu Mazen), asked militants to put a stop to violence.

Hostilities had returned that spring, with the assassination of two Hamas leaders, Sheikh Ahmed Yassin and his successor, Abdel Aziz Rantisi. Still, there remained a core group of Israelis and Palestinians willing to work together. On the Palestinian Authority's side, Ahmed Qurei (also known as Abu Ala), the deputy prime minister, and Nabil Shaath, the first foreign minister, made attempts to keep communications open. On the Israeli side, Shimon Peres continued his constructive approach to the Palestinians and remained willing to discuss building a basis for a two-state solution.

Whereas previous negotiations had been conducted mainly between Israel, the Palestinians, and the United States, now it was clear that it was time to install an envoy supported by all the Quartet members, someone who could be permanently represented on the ground and who could participate on a continuous basis within certain parameters. Once the United States agreed to this, the question was, who would be an acceptable candidate to all the parties? The United States wanted an American, but it had to be an American whom the other members could tolerate.

Condoleezza Rice had replaced Colin Powell as secretary of state in January 2005, and by the spring, she was beginning to shift her focus to the Israeli-Palestinian conflict. Relations across the region had been painfully strained by the Iraq War. The appointment of an envoy would enable the United States to bring in other international partners to work directly on the issues and gain greater international support in the search for an enduring peaceful settlement.

*   *   *

When Rice suggested I take the position of envoy, I felt I had a rare opportunity to build on my experience and make a contribution to this process of peace. My business life had touched the Middle East at every stage in my career. And my work at the World Bank had made me a regular visitor to the region, giving me the opportunity to build personal relationships with the leaders of Israel and the Arab nations.

The Bank had been working in the West Bank and Gaza Strip since 1993, when it established the Trust Fund for Gaza and West Bank. The fund was created to overcome a legal problem: The area was not a sovereign state and thus could not be assisted directly by the World Bank. So we established a separate vehicle to help support the Oslo Accords through economic recovery and development. Initially, the Bank focused on creating policies, projects, and infrastructure, as well as administering a multi-donor budget support fund. Over time, the Bank's work grew to include assisting the Palestinians in building the institutions that would be needed if a Palestinian state were created.

On my first trip to the region as president of World Bank in March 1996, I had visited the Bank offices in Gaza and the West Bank. The offices were largely staffed by Palestinians. There was a distinctly pro-Palestinian mood, along with deep suspicion of me as the new, Jewish president. I recognized that this would be a problem if the Bank was to become a key player in underpinning the Oslo Accords. But over time, as my visits became frequent and the Bank made a series of loans and grants to the Palestinian Authority and managed the donor funds from the West, I started to win not only the confidence of the field officers but also the trust of the Palestinian leadership. I visited other countries in the Middle East and built warm and trusting relationships with many leaders. And at every annual meeting of the World Bank, I made a point of convening a meeting with finance ministers of the Arab nations to discuss all the issues affecting the region.

Yasser Arafat and I got along well. I visited him regularly when I was in the region, and whenever he was in Washington, he would come to see me at the Bank, dressed in his distinctive Palestinian fatigues. In January 2000, I gave a dinner for him at my home, a rare distinction for a Jewish host in the U.S. capital. It was a gesture he did not forget.

On one occasion in early 2000, when I was due in Israel to launch the idea of joint Israeli-Palestinian industrial parks, I took Sara and Adam along with me to meet Arafat. He invited all of us to stay in his Gaza guesthouse. My very adult offspring were a little surprised when they were shown to a bedroom with one double bed for them to share—I have no doubt a staff member thought they were a young married couple—and yet it was a touching act of friendship and recognition of the trust between us. At the crack of dawn, we left with Arafat in his Russian helicopter and flew around Israeli territory before landing in Bethlehem.

I had also built friendships with Israel's leaders. Over many years, Elaine, my children, and I had visited Israel for vacations and had come to be friends with the late prime minister, Yitzhak Rabin, and his wife, Leah. We also developed a deep friendship with Shimon Peres, former foreign minister, prime minister, and later president. After our 2000 visit with Arafat, it was Peres who met us in Bethlehem and took us to visit the Church of the Nativity before we met with a large group of Palestinian and Israeli businessmen to discuss possible joint commercial activities in the region. The atmosphere in that meeting was constructive and the hopes were high, but sadly, political realities on the ground made progress nearly impossible in the years that followed.

When the second Intifada erupted in September 2000, the bulk of the Bank's work in the West Bank and Gaza came to a halt. I felt pressure from the United States to curtail my trips to see Arafat, who was increasingly isolated in his Ramallah compound. Although we could no longer move around the territory easily or make much progress with capital development projects, the Bank, with resident local representation, led donor efforts to cope with the emergency caused by the stringent restrictions on movement that Israel's security policies entailed.

The years 2001–2004 saw a rash of suicide bombers in Israel's main cities, followed by harsh retaliation by the Israel Defense Forces (IDF). The Bank had a staff of nearly thirty people working in the region under the strong leadership of Country Director Nigel Roberts, who reported to a succession of vice presidents for the Middle East and North Africa region, Kemal Dervis, then Jean-Louis Sarbib, and then finally Christiaan Poortman. In the summer of 2004, we produced our first plan for the Palestinian economy in the event of Israel's withdrawal from Gaza and the West Bank.

Throughout the summer, I was greatly impressed by the commitment of my colleagues, who were operating under the most difficult—and at times dangerous—conditions. They kept hope alive for our Palestinian friends. And we tried earnestly to convince our Israeli colleagues that it was essential to give hope to the Palestinians if there was to be a chance of enduring peace. My commitment through this unspeakable period earned me the trust of the Palestinian leadership and possibly the support of at least a few of the Israel leaders. My friendship with Shimon Peres deepened and grew during this period.

Around this time, I was also pursuing a private dialogue with Secretary of State Colin Powell. Both Elaine and I admired Powell and his wife, Alma. For two years, from 2002 to 2004, Powell and I traded information on the ups and downs in the region. We often conducted our exchanges through our private e-mail addresses, out of sight of the Bank and the State Department. I offered my observations as an outsider to the diplomatic process; I had contacts on the ground with real insight into what was happening. He had enormous experience and fine judgment.

I also worked with U.S. Treasury Secretary John Snow in 2004 to develop better relations with Arab finance ministers in support of a broader Middle East peace process. Ultimately, he supported a proposal that would engage the Arab leadership and the finance ministers of the G8 in economic development in the region.

In November 2004, our man on the ground, Nigel Roberts, produced a searing report on the Palestinian situation. It concluded that four years after the outbreak of the second Intifada, Gaza and the West Bank were mired in an unprecedented recession, with the unemployment rate surging to 25 percent and a staggering 37 percent among young people. The report warned that there were 600,000 Palestinians who could not afford the food, clothing, and shelter to survive. It was a strong indictment of the cost of the Intifada, underlining the critical importance of reducing obstacles to Palestinian movement and economic activity. It urged reopening the crossings that linked Gaza to Israel, the West Bank, and the outside world. The study showed that the imposed closures, justified by Israel on security grounds, had fragmented the Palestinian economic space, raised the cost of doing business, and eliminated the predictability needed to conduct business.

*   *   *

Now Israel had announced a plan to withdraw from the Gaza Strip by the end of 2005, and these problems had taken on a new urgency. Bush wanted to move forward and appoint an envoy to monitor and assist the withdrawal. When Rice called me from Air Force One, she told me that she wanted to see me immediately upon her return. President Clinton, who was also on that flight, would later tell me that he had supported the idea of my assuming the position. He added that he was not sure that he had done me a favor by mentioning our friendship, but it did not seem to do me any harm!

When I told my family about the position that was about to be offered, Elaine and the children were initially skeptical. After ten grueling years at the Bank, I needed to be with my family. Sara had married Neil Mayle, a gifted MIT-trained engineer, about a year earlier, and they were about to have their first child. Taking the appointment would mean canceling the trip to Italy that Elaine and I had planned for the summer. My family was also scared. The assignment was potentially dangerous, and I would require round-the-clock security surveillance.

As soon as Secretary Rice returned to Washington, we met at the State Department, and she handed me a single piece of paper outlining my assignment. It charged me with "leading, overseeing and coordinating the international community's efforts in support of the disengagement initiative." This was an enormous undertaking, one that many people would have dismissed as impossible to complete, even if it was worthy of effort. But I was full of optimism. I felt a deep, personal investment in this assignment.

As I met Rice in her office, I took a moment to read through the description of my position. I suggested that military aspects that had been

included in the assignment should be excluded; they were decidedly beyond my competence. We agreed that I would focus my efforts on two
areas: coordination between Israel and the Palestinians on the nonmilitary
aspects of the pullout, including the disposition of assets left behind by
the Israeli settlers, and the revival of the Palestinian economy. She made it
clear to me that the assignment would be on behalf of the Quartet and
that if I agreed, she would clear my nomination with her partners that
day. To help me, I would have a team of people, which I could choose according to conditions and a budget offered by the Quartet. We also
agreed to limit the assignment to seven months, through December 2005,
with three-month extensions thereafter. If the mission was not working,
this allowed either of us to call it off without the appearance of a problem.

There were more hoops to jump through. I knew that the UN secretary-
general and Russian President Vladimir Putin would support me, but I
was concerned about French President Jacques Chirac's response, as
Washington's relations with France had soured over Iraq. But by
lunchtime the following day, the principals of the Quartet had given their
approval, and all that remained was for me to meet with President Bush
the next day and for Secretary Rice to announce the decision in a short
State Department ceremony.

The following morning, I was ushered into the Oval Office to meet
with President Bush and Secretary Rice. The president thanked me for
my work at the Bank and for my assistance in smoothing the way for
Paul Wolfowitz to assume the presidency. He went on to say that I would
have his total support at all times and might well need it to bring the Israelis along.

"If they do not agree with you, tell them they will lose the support of
George Bush," he said.

"Mr. President, if I'm going to tell them that, I will tell you first," I
replied.

"If you have time," he shot back.

I was then whisked off to the State Department for a brief swearing-in
ceremony in which the secretary expressed her support for my mission. I

was not completely starry-eyed. I had some notion of the difficulties that my team and I would face, not just from the Israelis and Palestinians but also from Quartet members. I knew that the job would be stressful, and the chances of failure were very high. I had survived the political infighting of investment banking and the World Bank, but I did not yet know whether there were tensions between the American government and the other Quartet members and, if so, how they would affect me.

A much more cynical view of my appointment was given to me by Martin Indyk, a friend from my youth in Australia, who later became a senior U.S. government official and U.S. ambassador to Israel. In his view, Bush never took the Israeli-Palestinian peace process seriously. I was being used by the United States and Israel, and behind my back, Bush and Elliott Abrams made fun of me. The access I was given to the White House and the encouragement and the apparently serious discussions I had with the president, the vice president, and their cabinet colleagues were all a show. I was never a serious player. This cynical view extended to my relations with Sharon. It was said that he had zero interest in a deal with the Palestinians and was open with discussions with me simply to show "progress," feeling that events on the ground—and the efforts of his Defense Minister Mofaz—would ensure that none of my ideas would be implemented.

Perhaps this view of my role is correct, and because it was given to me by a friend with an inside view, I recount it for the record. But at the time, I was convinced that I was making a real contribution to the process of peace. I never doubted that I was being treated seriously. I was encouraged by my colleagues in the UN, the European Union, and in Russia. The fact was that I was their only hope to be participants in the process that historically had been run almost entirely by the United States. I worked directly with Secretary-General Kofi Annan, EU Foreign Policy Chief Javier Solana, Russian Foreign Minister Sergey Lavrov and, of course, Condoleezza Rice. Certainly, my team and I worked very hard to build understanding and to make progress that would be constructive for the future peace discussions. I also felt that I was receiving the full support of the president and the U.S. team.

*   *   *

The official start date for my Gaza assignment coincided with the day I left the Bank, June 1, 2005, but the Quartet wanted me on-site earlier. The Bank board had little choice but to accede to a request that I visit the region in May. My plan was to take the temperature, make the necessary new contacts, and find a base where I could set up shop. I arrived in the region three months before the planned Israeli withdrawal from Gaza. I decided that my team of representatives from the four Quartet powers should work out of the American Colony Hotel in Arab East Jerusalem. Established in a former pasha palace by Christian immigrants to the Holy Land, the American Colony Hotel was replete with elegant arches and lavishly decorated tiled floors. It had always been regarded as an oasis of calm in a divided city. Arabs and Jews used it as a place to meet discreetly, and journalists and diplomats saw it as somewhere they could go about their business in quiet comfort. It seemed like the ideal spot from which to conduct a peace mission. The gardens were beautiful, and many important negotiations had taken place in the open air under moonlit skies.

When I was shown up to my rooms, my heart almost stopped. The corridor outside was hung with World War I images that were deeply familiar to me from my youth. I was convinced I could see my late father in one of the photographs of General Allenby and his British army troops in Jerusalem almost ninety years earlier. As I lay on my hotel bed, I was overcome by the feeling that my father was with me.

In a hotel annex, across a narrow driveway, we found space for the Quartet offices. Our group set about learning as much as we could about the current political dynamic. Our task during this first visit was to start building personal trust with both sides. I needed to listen and show that the Quartet would have an even-handed approach. I also had to show that I was not arrogant, that I recognized the difficulties in seeking peace, and that I was not the first person to be sent to this region to help. I had to find a way to differentiate my efforts from those that preceded me.

In addition to Ariel Sharon, who provided decisive leadership, the key players on the Israeli side were Sharon's chief of staff and close confidante, the able lawyer Dov Weissglass; the hard-line defense minister, Shaul Mofaz, often an immovable force; and Shimon Peres, who had quit the Labour Party to serve in Sharon's newly founded Kadima Party. Sharon himself was an unlikely negotiator of peace. Yet he was pragmatic. He was not fond of Palestinians, but he knew that there was no future in the idea of an Israel full of Palestinians.

The key Palestinian figures were Arafat's successor as president, Mahmoud Abbas, a moderate who preferred well-tailored suits to fatigues; Prime Minister Ahmed Qurei, restored to power after falling out with Arafat; the highly competent finance minister, Salam Fayyad, who went on to become prime minister; and the dynamic security chief of Gaza and coordinator of the disengagement as minister of civil affairs, Mohammed Dahlan. They had all been involved in the Palestinian Authority for a long time and, with the possible exception of Dahlan, were all well known and respected by the international community.

I was very impressed by the advisers brought to the table by these Palestinian veterans of the region's conflicts. These bright young technocrats held an array of degrees from the best international universities. I particularly responded to the young negotiation team of Minister Dahlan, which included Diana Buttu, Nisreen Haj Ahmed, Lamia Matta, and Leila Hilal, all of whom were to become my trusted friends. They gave me background and color on the position of the Palestinian leadership, and though they were tough and unyielding in defending Palestinian positions, they were an enormous help in educating me and in preparing me for negotiations.

After my first round of meetings, I quickly came to realize that each side had a stereotype of the other, which they felt obliged to rehearse to any diplomatic newcomer to the region. The Palestinians saw the Israelis as oppressors, militarily strong and insensitive to the terrible human conditions of the Palestinians. As far as they were concerned, the Israelis delighted in humiliating them at crossing points, ignored international law and signed agreements, and were blatantly provocative. To illustrate this, the Palestinians would point to the indefatigable expansion of Israeli settlements on occupied land and the path of the security barrier and describe the terrible humanitarian consequences for the Palestinians in the West Bank.

Just as damaging was the Israeli view of the Palestinians. Despite many personal friendships, they regarded some Palestinians as terrorists not to be trusted. Palestinians, I was told time and time again, were an uncivilized people who callously used women and children as cover in the war against the Jewish state. They were devious and unable to govern themselves with any degree of integrity. Finally, the late Arafat himself was corrupt, unreliable, and willing to do anything to keep himself in power—and so were those around him, dating back to the days of exile in Tunis. The common refrain on both sides was, "With such people, how could you make a deal?"

I confronted this pessimistic dynamic head-on by demanding from each side that in their dealings with me going forward, they must at least attempt to discard these stereotypes and look to the future rather than the past. Withdrawal from Gaza could be a step toward an equitable peace and the two-state solution. President Bush believed that as part of the global effort to combat terror, it was time to drive the agenda forward, and that is why I had been appointed.

The vivid stereotypes on both sides could not, of course, be torn down in any series of meetings, and they remained as a sharp remainder to me of the huge gulf between neighbors living cheek by jowl on a tiny strip of land. At the same time, there were informal but strong relations between realistic peacemakers on both sides, which I had not anticipated. Many Israelis and Palestinians had concluded that a true peace was the only solution. These people continue to this day to work behind the scenes— and sometimes onstage—for cooperation and peaceful coexistence, freed from prejudice on either side. While I was in the region, it was as easy for me to have a meal with a Palestinian family as it was to dine with a Jewish family, and given the culture of hospitality, I had many occasions to do so.

Experiencing firsthand the similarities between these two peoples made me painfully aware—as never before—of the tragedy of our failure to establish a peace that is so deserved and so vital.

*   *   *

On returning to Washington after my first week-long trip to the region as special envoy, I recognized that we needed a strategy to jolt all the parties into action. Up until this point, my involvement in discussions had been largely procedural. It felt as if we were negotiating the positioning of the tables at the start of the 1973 Vietnam peace talks in Paris. I was eager for things to start happening. We needed a top-down approach that engaged the world leaders who were backing this peace mission as well as a more practical process to effect real changes on the ground. We had to create hope for both sides. For the Israelis, this meant an assured peace and security, and for the Palestinians, it meant their own state and a better life after the promised withdrawal of Israeli settlers and soldiers from Gaza.

I figured the best place to target world leaders would be at the G8 Gleneagles summit, scheduled for early July 2005. Months earlier, I had planned to attend Gleneagles to address the importance of the World Bank's work on Africa. Now I wanted to go wearing a different hat. Agendas and draft communiqués for such meetings are prepared months in advance to allow for prior negotiation and extensive preparations. So I went directly to President Bush and asked him to get the Middle East on the G8 agenda. He was immediately receptive. He said he felt that the issue was at least as urgent as Africa and global warming, the dominant agenda items that had been set in advance. However, the host, the British government—although sympathetic to the need for a Middle East deal—had other priorities. The United Kingdom was preparing for a massive push for poverty relief in Africa, including a Live Aid concert in Hyde Park, London, organized by Irish singer-songwriter and political activist Bob Geldof and featuring some of the world's top recording artists. Authorities at Gleneagles were gearing up for as many as 100,000 demonstrators from around the world. Prime Minister Tony Blair and Gordon Brown, chancellor of the Exchequer, wanted no diversions and no last-minute changes in the agenda.

I enlisted the help of Canadian Prime Minister Paul Martin, a friend for nearly five decades, and Lord Michael Levy, a prominent member of the Anglo-Jewish community. Levy was close to Blair, acting as his chief political fund-raiser and his envoy to the Middle East. I told them that the time was right for world leaders to dig deep on the Israel-Palestine issue. Then I went to Gordon Brown, with whom I had the pleasure of working closely during my years at the Bank. At first he was reluctant to get involved, because of his strong personal commitment to the African agenda. But persistence paid off. With Brown's help, I got a last-minute invitation to attend the G8 finance ministers' presummit meeting held in London in early June.

When I arrived at the meeting, the experience of passing the begging bowl at the World Bank served me well. Sitting around the table with all the ministers and their assistants, I pointed out that with the world spending $1,000 billion a year on defense and the war on terror, it was absurd that less than $1 billion went toward resolving the Israel-Palestine dispute—especially since it was seen by many people around the world as one of the causes of terrorism. Could we not spend $3 billion a year for several years in a real, coordinated effort to resolve the Israeli-Palestinian conflict? The Israeli withdrawal, I said, could be the start of the road map to a two-state solution. This seemed to be the moment. Not everyone was convinced, but with the invaluable help of Gordon, Palestine was now on the Gleneagles agenda for July.

On July 7, a series of bomb blasts struck the London subway system during morning rush hour, killing fifty-two commuters and injuring seven hundred. It was the second day of the summit at Gleneagles, and all of the energy surrounding Africa and global warming was immediately overwhelmed by the bombings. At noon, I waited in the background while Blair told the gathered press that it was "reasonably clear" that these were terrorist attacks and that he would be leaving the G8 immediately to go to London for meetings with the police and emergency services. It was one of the most moving and sad statements that I had ever witnessed, and it brought back to me the memory of being at the Bank when the World Trade Center tragedy occurred.

Foreign Secretary Jack Straw flew in to replace Blair at the summit that afternoon. In many ways, the London bombings made the discussion of the Palestinian issue all the more relevant and poignant. Before the meeting, President Bush surprised me by taking me aside to rehearse what I would say, offering me suggestions and encouragement. I could not have had a more remarkable launch into an assignment on behalf of global leadership than I was given by George Bush that day. When the meeting began, the president presented me to the leaders of the G8 world, all of whom I knew from my work at the Bank. Around one large table sat President Silvio Berlusconi, President George W. Bush, President Jacques Chirac, Prime Minister Junichiro Koizumi, Prime Minister Paul Martin, President Vladimir Putin, Chancellor Gerhard Schröder, and José Manuel Barroso, president of the European Commission (EC). President Bush said that I was his man. He allowed me to take center stage, and only after I had spoken and several others had intervened did he express his full and undivided support. He had empowered me and given me a unique start to my assignment.

The meeting had been scheduled to last one hour, and it took exactly that. I asked the G8 leaders to set a target of $3 billion a year for three years—a total of $9 billion—to support the peace deal, rather than the smaller amounts currently being raised. This would allow me to go to the richer Arab countries and raise $1 billion a year from them as part of this goal, in contrast to the dribble of $100–$200 million currently on offer. My personal links with each of the G8 leaders proved invaluable. Everyone was supportive. Perhaps galvanized by the tragic events a few hundred miles south in London, they unanimously agreed that this was the moment to act in the Middle East.

As my Royal Air Force helicopter soared above Gleneagles to return me to London, I left the summit that I had never expected to attend with

a feeling of disbelief that so much had happened in just two months. I felt
a surge of excitement that I had left the World Bank to work on something that could have lasting consequences, not only in the Middle East
but also globally.

*   *   *

Now that I had received political backing, it was time to knuckle down to
some hard negotiating. At the core of my team were the representatives of
the four Quartet powers: U.S. ambassador Bill Taylor, Christian Berger
from the European Commission, Lynn Hastings from the UN, and Niko-
lai Makarov from the Russian Armed Forces (later replaced by his colleague Leonid Barkovsky). We also had Nicholas Krafft from the World
Bank and a first-rate team of international assistants both in Washington and in Jerusalem: Alexei Monsarrat from the U.S. State Department,
Stefano Mocci from the World Bank, and Katiana Orluc from the EC.
The World Bank's country director, Nigel Roberts, also lent his indispensable wisdom.

I was lucky to have an Israeli, Didi Remez, as well as a Palestinian,
Khader Abusway, onboard as press officers. The rest of the team, including Catherine Downard from the U.S. Treasury Department, Pauline
Hayes from the British Department for International Development,
Katharina Lack from the German Foreign Ministry, and aid worker Ram-
sey Jamil, was equally competent. All of my new staff had worked for
years on the Israeli-Palestinian conflict, so their knowledge and expertise
were a great support to my work. The office was determined not to be just
a talking shop, but to achieve something meaningful.

On June 20, after my second visit to the region and before this G8
summit, I wrote to Sharon and Palestinian Prime Minister Ahmed Qurei
in an effort to cut through the rhetoric and confront the main issues surrounding the Israeli disengagement. I outlined a program that we had developed out of the Bank's proposals in two disengagement reports

published in November and December 2004. It came to be known as our "six-points-plus-three" strategy.

The first and most important challenge was to make sure there were sufficient arrangements for crossings from Gaza for people and goods to reach Israel, the overseas market, and the West Bank. Without such access, Gaza was in danger of becoming a large, overcrowded prison cut off from the rest of the world. This was going to be hugely complicated. The fundamental question was this: How, without the Israel Defense Forces present in Gaza, could Israel's security and customs regulations be guaranteed? Would Israel trust the Palestinians—or a combination of the Palestinians and the Egyptians—to maintain order?

We had to find a way to link centers of Palestinian population in Gaza and the West Bank. Gaza, with a population of 1.4 million people, was the smaller and the less prosperous of the Palestinian territories. It could only survive economically and socially with free movement of goods and people to the West Bank, home of 2.4 million Palestinians with a higher per-capita income. The issue had been addressed in the Oslo Accords as "safe passage" and was seen as a moral as well as practical issue by the Palestinian leadership.

The second issue of key significance was the movement of goods and people inside the West Bank itself. The area was crisscrossed by Israeli roads and highways linking settlements and providing free passage to Israeli citizens. But the original system of roads, mainly for use by the Palestinians, was controlled by five hundred separate checkpoints—cement-block and earth-mound constructions carved out by the Israel Defense Forces during the Intifada to intercept potential terrorist attacks. Clearly, the checkpoints were an enormous restraint on commerce, a nasty symbol of occupation, and a social affront to the population of the region. There would be no economic progress until these barriers were reformed and reduced.

The third and fourth closely related issues demonstrated the need for the Palestinian people to have their own links to the outside world—

without Israeli constraints. They badly needed to complete their own port, whose donor-funded construction had barely begun at the start of the Intifada. The airstrip and technology at the Gaza airport had been destroyed in 2001 by the Israel Defense Forces. Israel was deeply suspicious of Gaza's having these facilities. Having spent years searching and blowing up alleged and real tunnels between Egypt and Gaza, the IDF was not inclined to allow Gaza transport links to the rest of the world through which terrorist armaments could be moved.

Housing, the fifth issue, had also become a flash point between Israel and Palestine. Some of the best housing stock in the region had been put in place by the Israeli settlers. In Israeli settlements, some eight thousand people were occupying up to 20 percent of Gazan territory. This was not an efficient use of an overcrowded slip of land, and the Palestinians wanted to use the land for more intensive housing units.

But the last thing Israel wanted on leaving Gaza was an explosion of images of the Israel Defense Forces and settlers torching and bulldozing housing and community centers. Israel also feared that the settlements might be grabbed by militias and used by their leadership, while most of the population continued to live in grossly overcrowded quarters. As events transpired, after quiet negotiations, the Israelis and the Palestinians resolved that the properties be destroyed. The issue then became what to do about the rubble that would be left. The Israelis said they had enough debris of their own and did not want it moved to their sovereign territory. The Palestinians did not want it in Gaza. Eventually, the Israelis agreed to a cash transfer to cover the removal of the wreckage.

The sixth and final issue—and one in which I would play a personal role—was what to do about the greenhouses that had provided the economic foundation for the Israeli settlers in Gaza. These settlers had developed a system of a hundred acres of greenhouses, packing sheds, and storage facilities through which the Israelis sent high-quality produce, including soft fruits such as strawberries and vegetables, to Western grocery chains. The high-tech greenhouses were producing an astonishing $100 million in produce a year. Taking them over would be an economic opportunity for Gaza, creating four thousand to six thousand jobs, and it would foster Israeli-Palestinian economic cooperation. We needed a private-sector solution.

Beyond the issues of withdrawal, the Palestinians needed to get their financial house in order. Despite aid flows, the Palestinian Authority was running a persistent budget deficit. The finance minister, Salam Fayyad, had fought against the odds to put the embryonic nation's finances in order and had shown a great deal of skill and integrity. But he frequently found himself overruled by the political leadership and the Palestinian Parliament. Fayyad needed immediately to raise $400 million to cover the deficit by the end of 2005.

Once past debts had been cleared, the Palestinian Authority needed to budget for the future. I wanted to see a three-year plan for the period 2006–2008. If possible, I wanted such a plan to be built through the cooperation of all political parties, the private sector, and civil society groups. It was also critical for the PA to establish credibility for future donor conferences. My experience from other postconflict situations—including Bosnia-Herzegovina and Rwanda—had taught me that people become impatient when the fighting stops. They want to see tangible signs of progress very quickly. Israel's withdrawal was scheduled for August 15, 2005. There was already a huge amount of governmental and nongovernmental donor activity, including a large and very successful operation by the United Nations Relief and Works Agency (UNRWA), established in 1950 to support the Palestinian refugees who lost their homes during the 1948 Arab-Israeli conflict. But there was precious little coordination between the various other donors.

In the weeks leading up to the disengagement, my team and I focused on finding a way for the Palestinians to take control of the Israeli settler greenhouses. This would be a vital economic boost to an emergent Palestinian-run administration in Gaza. If the greenhouses could be kept functioning, it would be all the more important to put border crossings rapidly into place to ensure that produce could reach Western markets in a timely fashion.

The major obstacle was the Palestinians' refusal to allow international donor money to fund the withdrawal of Israeli settlers and leave the greenhouses functioning. They believed that the settlers who had occupied their land had done so in violation of international law and that this illegal activity would be legitimized if international funds were used to compensate them. Providing public funds for what would have been regarded as "settler compensation" was also a dubious policy for most donor countries.

I hoped to break this deadlock by raising the funds from private sources. I called my friend, the distinguished publisher, property developer, and Jewish community leader Mort Zuckerman, in New York. After several discussions, he suggested that I speak to Lester Crown of General Dynamics, renowned as a businessman and philanthropist in Chicago, and to Leonard Stern, the highly regarded investor in New York. Both men had been supporters of peaceful development in Israel, and they could respond quickly. I added my own modest donation, and with their generosity, we raised $4.5 million. Then I approached a large private foundation, one of America's finest charities, and after only days of discussions, it donated $10 million. The foundation insisted on anonymity, which we kept completely, though a year later, *Forbes* magazine identified the source of this extraordinary gift as the Bill and Melinda Gates Foundation. I can never express adequately the extent of my gratitude to these donors.

In just a few days, we had raised $14.5 million, the majority of which came from a non-Jewish source—even as there was misinformed criticism about "Jewish money" being at the center of this effort. These donors showed enormous generosity and courage; without their timely assistance, the greenhouse infrastructure would have been destroyed, along with any economic hope for the Gaza residents. Bill Gates later told me that he knew that this would be a big risk, but that it was worth the effort and the investment to advance the cause of peace. He remains deeply committed to justice in this area and to creating a better future for both peoples.

With the financing in place, we could now help to smooth the Israeli withdrawal and promise the Palestinians the chance to inherit a mature export market of flowers, plant cuttings, cherry tomatoes, and soft fruits. If this was to work, however, it was critical that the borders to Israel remain open so that the produce could reach Ben Gurion Airport, outside Tel Aviv, for the daily flights to European markets.

During the summer of the withdrawal, I saw how difficult my mission would become. On August 28, a suicide bombing killed or injured fifty-two Israelis outside the Beersheba Central Bus Station. The Palestinians claimed that the Israeli side had its share of responsibility, flowing from its frequent incursions into "their" territory and the resultant deaths of many Palestinians. According to an annual report of the Israeli human rights organization B'Tselem, during the time of my mandate—from June 2005 to April 2006—Israeli security forces killed 197 Palestinians in their campaign against terrorists, predominantly in Gaza. The vicious circle of violence on both sides continually undermined the effort to create a constructive environment for lasting agreements between the parties.

We completed the greenhouse deal in the early days of August. Within a few days, the Gaza pullout plan, or Tokhnit HaHitnatkut, was under way. On August 15, Jewish civilians were evacuated, many forcibly and in tears, and bulldozers moved in to start demolishing the settlements. Places of worship were left intact, but this exemption was too provocative for Palestinian extremists. They moved in and set some of the settlers' synagogues on fire, creating dramatic pictures that flashed around the world. All twenty-one Israeli settlements were demolished, as well as four small settlements in the northern West Bank. As part of the withdrawal, the Israel Defense Forces destroyed numerous military installations in the Gaza Strip, some of which had been in place for almost four decades. The last IDF soldier departed on September 12, 2005.

After a day or two of Palestinian looting, Gaza was briefly stabilized. During this period, some damage was done to the greenhouses, but they came through essentially intact. Peace was restored not because of an Israeli military presence but because Palestinians recognized that if they wanted to have any hope, they needed to create a peaceful environment and the opportunity for economic development. I toured the Gaza Strip with Palestinian Authority Finance Minister Salam Fayyad immediately after the PA took control of the territory, and we visited greenhouses, which now were protected by security forces. Everywhere around us, people were excited about building hotels, fostering tourism, and creating a thriving economy. There was a rare possibility of normality, and the atmosphere was joyous. Salam was later to become prime minister, a role he has occupied with distinction.

But we had to act fast to prepare and gain agreement on an overall plan to assist the Palestinians and to preserve peace—or all this optimism would disappear as Gaza remained shut off from the world. We had to turn the detailed proposals my team had crafted into a deal acceptable to Israel and the Palestinians, which in turn had to be signed formally by the Quartet powers. I spent most of the autumn of 2005 in a Kissinger-style shuttle, moving from Washington to Jerusalem, Ramallah, and Gaza, checking in with my other "shareholders"—the European Union, the United Nations, and Russia—whenever possible. I also visited several Arab nations to explain the plan and to gain support.

My frantic schedule proved to be too much for someone at the start of his eighth decade, and not surprisingly, it took a heavy toll on my health. In late September, my heart started to pump erratically. I had to have two pacemaker operations, the second one to correct a malfunctioning device. I arrived back at my headquarters at the American Colony Hotel in October physically exhausted and somewhat damaged by the experience. Yet I was determined to begin the final push toward an agreement. The clock was ticking loudly, and my first mandate would expire at the end of the year.

*   *   *

During the fall, President Bush was faithful to his offer to be of help at any time. I had two meetings in the Oval Office at the White House with the president, the vice president, the secretary of state, and the national security advisers. Each time, I was given an hour for freewheeling discussion. President Bush dominated the discussions and posed incisive questions. He was concerned about the balance of complaints from each side and constantly looked for ways to move forward and uncover issues on which he could use his special leverage. These meetings brimmed with good intentions, but they did not result in specific action plans. I was proud to be consulted, and I believe my judgments were valued. But I was not involved in crafting action plans that the United States would pursue. I would often wonder—after these and other encounters—what was really going on behind the scenes and whether, after I left, the president and his colleagues decided on a separate course of action.

Although my team and I were working furiously, commentators could already sense the precariousness of our mission. In late October 2005, bitterlemons.org, an Internet newsletter that presents Palestinian and Israeli viewpoints on prominent issues, gave voice to this concern. "The Wolfensohn mission is the product of a careful American policy calculation. But if it doesn't receive stronger administration backing, it will fail, thereby denying us all one of the more attainable fruits of the Gaza disengagement," wrote Yossi Alpher, an Israeli political analyst. Ghassan Khatib, a Palestinian analyst and minister of planning in the Palestinian Authority, echoed these sentiments: "There is a real sense that this mission is in danger of floundering."

We all felt that unless we came up with an agreement and a plan for future development, the withdrawal alone would leave the Palestinians in Gaza worse off than before. It would virtually guarantee a descent into complete chaos.

By early November, I felt we had done sufficient groundwork to complete a feasible framework for agreement between the Palestinian Authority and the government of Israel. I met regularly with Defense Minister Mofaz of Israel and Mohammed Dahlan of the Palestinian Authority and his team. We had a real negotiation going on, and I believe we all were working genuinely for a positive solution.

If my years of negotiations on Wall Street and at the World Bank had taught me anything, it was that there is nothing like a deadline to galvanize people into action. I gathered my team, and as each of my colleagues briefed me on the state of play, I became even more convinced that the time for leisurely talking was over. We needed to close a deal, and soon. Palestinian elections were scheduled for January 25, 2006. The Arafat-founded party, Fatah, led by Abu Mazen, Abu Ala, and Mohammed Dahlan, was in charge, and any change could disrupt our plans. At the time, we had no real idea what it would mean if the strongly anti-Israel rival party, Hamas, were to gain power.

The Israeli political landscape was equally disturbing. The Gaza withdrawal had torn Sharon's governing Likud Party apart, and following changes in the Labour Party leadership, elections for a new coalition government loomed. This distracted attention from an agreement with the Palestinians. If the prime minister was to press ahead with his rumored disengagement plans in the West Bank, he would need broader political support, which would mean an election in April or May. I felt confident that Sharon would be able to hold it together. There was even talk in Israel of a new breakaway "disengagement" party, though the reality was some way off.

Several people warned me that once an Israeli election campaign gets under way, the elected political leaders lose authority and the security services and the generals take command. With the hard-liners running the show, there would be little prospect of forging any kind of deal over Gaza. Security-minded officials would never agree to opening the border crossings and more tightly linking Gaza to the West Bank.

This meant that we had a small window of opportunity to forge a deal—weeks at best, but probably days—and I did not want to see the chance slip away. The Gaza Strip was open for imports and exports on some days for some hours, but the security provisions for loading and unloading made the passage of trucks painfully slow. Incidents of violence by the Palestinians and vigorous reprisals by the Israelis had made our dream of an open border a distant hope. Gaza had been effectively sealed off from the outside world since the Israeli disengagement, and the humanitarian and economic consequences for the Palestinian population were profound. There were already food shortages. Palestinian workers and traders to Israel were unable to cross the border.[1] Unemployment had sky-rocketed to 35 percent, and 65 percent of the population was living below the poverty line. Although a sound Palestinian economy alone did not guarantee security, it was hard to imagine how peace and stability in the Middle East could be achieved without it. We had to unlock the borders to Palestinian workers and move produce out of the greenhouses so they could reach the shelves of the supermarkets in Europe.

It was no use trying to resolve every minor detail; we did not have the time. We had to extract the main points, present them clearly and con-cisely, and, if necessary, bang heads together to get an accord. We had to keep all the border crossings open, not just at Rafah, but the crossing to Egypt as well. We had to address the free movement of goods and people in Gaza to and from the West Bank. We also had to press for a more normal social and economic life. I wanted something firm that I could present to both sides immediately. If we didn't present a coherent plan, we would lose momentum, and the opportunity before us would vanish. Five months of work would be wasted. I wanted to see something drawn up on a single sheet of paper, which could be shown to the Pales-tinian Authority minister of planning, Ghassan Khatib, and Israeli de-fense minister, Shaul Mofaz. I told my team members to lock themselves up in a room and not come out until they had a plan.

In the first week of November, while the drafters retreated to their of-fices, I repaired to a bench in the hotel courtyard under a cloudless sky with my cell phone. I took a deep breath and began a series of calls to the key players—Mohammed Dahlan and Ghassan Khatib on the Palestinian side, Shaul Mofaz on the Israeli side, and U.S. ambassador Richard Jones. If there was to be a deal on Gaza, I told each of them, it had to be very soon. When the Israelis left Gaza, I explained, we had hoped that there would be constructive conditions for Palestinian workers to move through Israel each day. However, the violence had led to total or at least partial closure of the crossings, with even more dramatic consequences for the Gazan population than we had anticipated. This was quickly turning into a humanitarian crisis. We all needed to act soon.

*   *   *

Secretary Rice and her entourage were due in Jerusalem in mid-November for events commemorating the tenth anniversary of the assassination of Yitzhak Rabin. Although my team had cleared the way for an agreement with the Israelis on many issues, the Israelis were unwilling to show flexibility on the border openings. It would take a more powerful force than me to get any kind of resolution. Secretary Rice's impending visit offered a major opportunity for agreements to be brokered before the Israeli election season would take its toll. The big question for me was whether Mofaz and the Israeli cabinet would compromise before we met Secretary Rice and lay out conditions that we could refer to her to negotiate.

After trying unsuccessfully to get the framework of an agreement that was clear and unequivocal, I needed even more urgently to meet with the secretary of state on her visit. I had a strong grasp of the issues I was addressing, but I always had the feeling that there was a great deal more that I did not know about the discussions between the Israelis and the U.S. representatives. And I did not know how much Rice was prepared to push.

Rice arrived in Jerusalem for a dinner on November 13, accompanied by Elliott Abrams, deputy national security adviser in charge of disseminating democracy in the Middle East, and C. David Welch, assistant secretary of state for Near Eastern affairs, among others. Arrangements had been made for negotiations on the main points of the Gaza agreement to take place the following day. I was eager to sit down with Rice immediately after her arrival so that I could update her on what I knew and to learn how it all fit into the larger picture.

The dinner was a stately occasion at the King David Citadel Hotel in the presence of Ariel Sharon and most of the Israeli cabinet. Sharon and I had become much closer by that stage. Initially, he had been hugely suspicious of me, as he was of the Quartet, but in the end, I believe that he accepted me and concluded that the Gaza withdrawal and the assistance we gave were positive contributions. Nonetheless, I was surprised when, as I was about to sit, Sharon came over from the table next to mine where he was sitting with Rice, gave me a huge hug, and thanked me for all that I was doing. It was an unexpectedly generous gesture in front of such distinguished company, and it could not have gone unnoticed by the assembled group of Israeli and American leaders. If, as some others have suggested, he was just stringing me along, then he was a consummate actor. I took it as a real expression of support.

After Rice had delivered her speech, I asked if I could have a word with her before the next day's talks. She agreed, and I followed her and her associates to a secure exterior staircase leading to her car. As we stood at the top of the stairs, I explained to the secretary that there was a great deal of information that I needed to pass on to her and that although she already had the written overview of the six-plus-three agenda that we had developed, I wanted to give her color and insight that I could not put into the report. She said she thought that was a good idea, but after five minutes, she and her colleagues left in their car for the hotel, explaining that they were very tired after a day of travel. No arrangements were made to meet the following morning.

Although I knew that talks had been fixed by the U.S. delegation for the next day before the afternoon Rabin memorial ceremony, I had no idea where they were being held or whom the Americans had invited. My distinguished and very able friend Javier Solana, the European Union's high representative, and I both expected to be part of the talks as we were part of the Quartet structure. But neither he nor I had heard anything about arrangements from the Israeli side or from the Americans. Finally, I heard from my Palestinian friends that a negotiation between Palestinian and Israeli teams and Secretary Rice was under way at the King David Citadel Hotel.

I was dumbstruck. I had spent seven months working tirelessly to put a deal together, and neither I nor the Europeans were being included in

the meeting to negotiate this deal. I called Javier and told him what was
going on. We were both furious, but what could we do? I decided to
stick to my schedule and go to the Mount Herzl Cemetery, high above
Jerusalem, for Rabin's memorial service that afternoon. As I entered the
cemetery, I was approached by one of Rice's military aides, who said
the secretary wanted to see me. Rice was in the front row, and as I greeted
her, she suggested that I ride back in the car with her after the ceremony.

The gathering took place under bright skies, with Sharon, never a political ally of Rabin's, delivering a dignified and moving eulogy. When it
was over, I headed straight to the secretary's car. I waited inside the vehicle
with Sharon's adviser, Dov Weissglass, for fifteen minutes. Although we
had been in constant touch in prior weeks, I felt so angry at my exclusion
from that day's negotiation that I could barely speak.

At long last, Secretary Rice climbed into the car with one of her aides
and explained that she was on her way to Jordan to keep an appointment
with the king. There she would express American condemnation and con-
dolences for the casualties resulting from the terrorist bombings of hotels
in Amman that had occurred a few days earlier. After that, she was going
directly to Pakistan.

For a moment, I was speechless. I had been blindsided. I had no idea
what had gone on in the negotiations. I gathered my thoughts and said,
"But you must come back." After a few minutes of discussion, it became
clear that they had not agreed upon a way forward. I told Rice that if she
had not pinned down a deal yet, she had no option but to return. "This
cannot be left in the air to be resolved later," I said. I explained that she
was the only person who could nail it down. "That's why I wanted you to
come over. This is not something for me to do; it's something for the secretary of state to do."

Rice turned to her staff aide, who was in the car with us, and asked if
it was possible to arrange the trip to Jordan, then return to Israel, and still
arrive in Pakistan on time. He reassured her that he would handle the logistics, and she promised to come back after a three-hour visit to Jordan.

We agreed that she would negotiate through the night, then hold a press conference in the morning, and then leave for Pakistan.

From 5:00 PM to 9:00 PM, while Rice was in Jordan, neither Javier nor I heard anything further about the negotiations. Eventually, I could restrain myself no longer. I went over to the King David Citadel Hotel and paced the floor outside the guarded meeting room like a substitute player waiting to get into a football game. Then, through an open door, I saw my Palestinian friends in a smoke-filled room. They were on their own. The Israelis and Americans were negotiating in another meeting room. The Palestinian team immediately invited me into the room. I saw that Dahlan was ready to leave and the whole team was exhausted and angry after a daylong experience resulting in almost no progress toward an agreement. I told them that the secretary of state would be returning, and there was no way they could leave.

When I saw Elliott Abrams come out of the suite where the Israelis and the U.S. team were talking, I approached him and suggested we have a coffee together. He readily agreed.

"Look, Elliott," I said, when we sat down, "I think you are a son of a bitch. I have made ten trips over here and negotiated this deal for seven months. My team has been working on the agreement day and night. I suggested that Secretary Rice come visit, and she came for the Rabin event. You have been negotiating all day. No one has had the courtesy to tell me one word about what is going on in there." I went on to tell him that I felt that my team and I had made real progress toward an agreement between the parties. Now we were being ignored. I could barely contain my rage. "So I just want you to know before I resign why I'm resigning and what I think about your behavior," I finished.

Abrams was plainly rattled. He said he would discuss this with the secretary of state when she returned around 10:00 PM. A few minutes after she arrived, I was invited to call on her. The secretary was at her most imperious. Why, she wanted to know, did I think I could talk to Elliott that way? It was outrageous, she said, that I was taking such a stand when she had been working with me the whole time. She then tried to reassure me that I remained a trusted adviser.

I stopped her. "I'm seventy-two years old. I have been negotiating at a reasonably high level for forty years. I know when I am in, and I know when I am out, so please don't tell me that I am in. Don't tell me that I'm a trusted adviser."

The secretary looked at me, took a moment to think, decided not to argue, and coolly declared, "Well, why don't we get on with it?"

The two of us then worked through the night with the Israelis and the Palestinians, talking through the framework of the deal. In the hours after midnight, Rice held a round of discussions alone with the Israeli team, telling me, quite appropriately, that she needed to use her personal authority to convince them on certain points. While she was talking with them, I sat with the Palestinians.

Weeks later, I would understand that Rice and Abrams were trying to make it clear that intervention in peace negotiations was not part of my job description. I was working on behalf of the Quartet for economic development, not as part of an American peace initiative, and the Quartet was not seen as a player—it was only the United States that counted. On top of that, I was told that Israel was suspicious of including me in the shuttle diplomacy that was going on between the rooms of the Israelis and the Palestinians.

At the time, though, I was baffled. I still assumed that the Quartet had a role. By 5:00 AM the next morning, we had worked through the night to settle most of the issues. I suggested to the secretary that Javier Solana be fully informed and included in the press conference. Secretary Rice and I then adjourned to grab a couple of hours' sleep.

At about 9:00 AM, the American team presented the documents it had drawn up at the end of the discussions. The core deal, dubbed by the media the "Rice Agreements," followed the pattern that my team had worked up over so many months. It set several deadlines to be met within the coming months, concerning the opening hours of the crossings, the number of trucks to pass through them, and the creation of bus and truck convoys between the West Bank and Gaza, as well as the reduction of obstacles to movement in the West Bank. There was also agreement to open the airport in Gaza and to build a port that could be used for import and export.

At the morning press conference, the secretary, flanked by Solana and me, paid handsome credit to the work of our team. She gave no hint of the bitterness of some of the exchanges the previous evening, telling the gathered journalists that the important thing was to achieve a balance between security on the one hand and allowing the Palestinian people freedom of movement on the other hand. Everybody recognized that if the Palestinians could move freely and export their agriculture, Gaza would be a much better place, a place where the institutions of democracy could begin to take root.

Now it looked to both Javier Solana and to me as though the Quartet might be involved after all. The all-night mediation by the secretary had delivered the deal we had been working on so intensely. We were very pleased.

In reality, the Israelis and the Americans subsequently took apart our agreement piece by piece. The Rice Agreements differed from the original agreement hammered out by the Quartet team on the crucial point that responsibility for implementation now rested with the Americans and not the Quartet. All that was now left for the Quartet team to do was to publish, every two weeks, a report taking stock of the implementation of the agreements. The consequences of this change, which essentially disenfranchised my team, were soon to be felt.

Some of the most prophetic words that morning may have been spoken by Ghassan Khatib, the Palestinian Authority's planning minister, who had been deeply involved in the talks. "The situation in Gaza," he observed, "is becoming a little bit dangerous because of the lack of economic progress. This is playing into the hands of [Hamas], the only alternative to the Palestinian Authority."[2]

*   *   *

The satisfaction I felt after the deal faded quickly as events overtook us at a pace no one could have anticipated. On December 18, just a month after the Rice Agreements were signed, Ariel Sharon suffered his first mild stroke. Sharon's illness and the almost exclusive focus placed by the international community on the upcoming Palestinian elections meant that there was a vacuum in leadership on both sides at a crucial time. In January 2006, after there had been little or no effort to enforce the agreements, almost none of the deadlines set by the Rice Agreements had been met. The only crossing that was fully functioning since its opening on November 26 was the Rafah crossing to Egypt, where the EU and several of its member states had quickly established an efficient Border Assistance Mission to support Palestinian border police and ensure security.

The crossings to and from Gaza and Israel were more problematic. The main crossing for agricultural goods at Karni initially operated continuously, but because of Israeli security concerns, the number of daily export truckloads was still way below the number needed to export all the products. The closures at Karni effectively blocked access to markets outside Gaza. This was particularly hard for the hitherto resilient textile and furniture industries. Erez, the main crossing for Palestinian workers and businesspeople, was also closed frequently, due to alleged security threats. Neither bus nor truck convoys began to operate by their respective deadlines of December 15, 2005, and January 15, 2006. And the rubble from the destruction of the Israeli settlements had still not been removed, even though the funding had been provided.

The greenhouse initiative was also suffering. In early December, the much-awaited first harvest of quality cash crops—strawberries, cherry tomatoes, cucumbers, sweet peppers, and flowers—began. These crops were intended for export via Israel to Europe. But their success relied upon the Karni crossing, which, beginning in mid-January 2006, was closed more often than not.[3]

The Palestine Economic Development Corporation, which was managing the greenhouses taken over from the settlers, said that it was experiencing losses in excess of $120,000 per day. Economic consultants estimated that the closures cost the whole agricultural sector in Gaza $450,000 a day in lost revenue.

I visited the crossing several times. The procedures at Karni—spreading out perishable cargoes of goods on sun-exposed blacktop for lengthy inspections—meant that routinely 10 percent or more of a shipment was spoiled before it even left Gaza. Fruit was rotting on trucks or in the fields because it could not be exported, and there were no local markets in Gaza capable of absorbing the product, even at severely discounted prices. It was excruciating. This lost harvest was the most recognizable sign of Gaza's declining fortunes and the biggest personal disappointment during my mandate. Almost as depressing were the bribes obviously being paid to allow a small number of trucks across the border in both directions. It pained me to admit that the arrangements for these bribes were the best example of Israeli-Palestinian cooperation at the official level. I also visited the crossings at dawn to see the civilian workers from Gaza who had already been there for hours, waiting to enter Israel to work. With each passing week, the delays grew longer and longer and those admitted to Israel fewer and fewer. That, too, was tragic.

Violence erupted in Gaza at the end of 2005. Within a month—between December 5 and January 19—two suicide bombings in the Israeli cities of Netanya and Tel Aviv and one other suicide attack against Israeli soldiers near Tulkarem killed five people and injured seventy. These events were devastating for the peace process and for the people on both sides who were fighting for an end to violence and for more normal commercial relations. These eruptions of violence also meant that the Israelis would be even less willing to ease their security measures at the crossings. Discussions on a permanent territorial link, internal movement in the West Bank, the airport, and the seaport ground to a halt.

On January 5, 2006, while recuperating on his ranch south of Jerusalem, Sharon suffered a second massive stroke, from which he never recovered. The leader who had come to dominate Israeli politics, shown the courage to pull out of Gaza, and supported future unilateral easing of conditions and reorganization of the West Bank was no longer a player.

Sharon's successor, Ehud Olmert, had the unenviable task of earning the trust of the Israeli people while carrying forward a policy that was based on Sharon. Most important, it was not Olmert but the generals and security services who would decide—in the end—if it was safe to follow through on the agreements and prevent Gaza from becoming a prison camp, where rival militias warred with each other and with the Israeli forces. The total change in Olmert's position from when he was mayor of Jerusalem began with his period as prime minister and would lead him to become an advocate of a two-state solution.

On January 25, 2006, the Palestinian people demonstrated that they were fed up with the performance of the Fatah-led Palestinian Authority. Ten years after the last elections for the Palestinian Legislative Council had been held, Palestinians voted overwhelmingly for a parliament in which the Hamas candidates were the dominant force. Of course, the January 2006 Hamas election victory did not arise solely from the collapse of the border-crossings agreement. It grew out of a long history of a corrupt Fatah leadership as well as the perception among Palestinians that the Oslo peace process, which was widely regarded as Fatah's strategy toward Palestinian statehood, was going nowhere.

We had reached a political deadlock as control passed to an organization condemned by the international community for its support of terrorism. My fear was no longer about whether the agreements to open borders could be carried through. Now I worried that the Palestinians might be facing an even more serious humanitarian crisis with the suspension of international assistance.

*　　*　　*

I was on my way to the annual meeting of global business and political leaders in Davos, Switzerland, on the day of the Palestinian elections. From there, I issued the first of several grave warnings about how the Hamas election sweep would affect the life of people in the West Bank and Gaza. "The Palestinians are basically bankrupt," I told the meeting in

Davos. "If you do not have the money to pay 135,000 Palestinians, you are going to have chaos." Almost half of Palestinian government employees belonged to the security forces; armed and unpaid, they constituted a formidable potential for anger and unrest.

I reiterated my concerns at the Quartet meeting in London on January 30, 2006. I explained to Secretary Rice, Kofi Annan, Javier Solana, and Sergey Lavrov that the Palestinian Authority lacked the resources to pay monthly salaries. If funding were to be provided for salaries to be paid in full, with only minimum operating costs covered, the PA would still face a monthly deficit of $60–$70 million, despite the inclusion of the agreed-upon contributions already announced by some donors. At the very least, the PA needed $500 million in funding to stay afloat through September.

On January 30, the Quartet, shocked by Hamas's victory, "congratulated the Palestinian people on an electoral process that was free, fair and secure." It expressed the view that "all members of a future Palestinian government must be committed to non-violence, recognition of Israel, and acceptance of previous agreements and obligations," and concluded that "it was inevitable that future assistance to any new government would be reviewed by donors against that government's commitment" to these agreements. It quickly became clear that raising funds in the absence of a change of heart by the new Palestinian government would be very difficult. But as an EU position paper rightly pointed out, the main problem was less the money needed from donors than the withholding of the Palestinian Authority's own tax revenues, which were being collected and retained by the Israeli government. In the words of the International Crisis Group, Israel was able to "virtually turn the Palestinian economy on and off."[4]

On the ground, the improvements for which we had worked so hard were vanishing before our eyes. The first six common issues of the border-crossings agreement had essentially collapsed. The Karni crossing had finally been closed for exports from Gaza. After January 15, it had been restricted to the import of basic humanitarian goods. The Israelis claimed that Palestinians were digging a tunnel under the crossing with explosives in it, but despite a massive earthmoving effort, the tunnel was never found. The second part of the agreement, concerning future financing for the Palestinian Authority, simply disintegrated. It had been part of my intention at this stage to work with the Palestinian leadership to create jobs for Palestinians, in particular for Palestinian youth. Now my aim was to prevent draconian measures from being taken against the newly Hamas-led Palestinian Authority.

As long as Mahmoud Abbas was still the Palestinian president and until a new cabinet was installed, the West could pretend that the power had not shifted and could continue with funding. Abbas agreed to hold off on cabinet selection until after the Israeli elections on March 28. This, I calculated, would give us two months to engage with the Hamas leaders over their stated position, which sought the destruction of the state of Israel. Polls taken immediately after the elections indicated that the overwhelming majority of Palestinian voters were in favor of negotiations toward a peace settlement, even as they elected a more confrontational alternative to the previously Fatah-led Palestinian Authority.

I knew that we had little time for a negotiation in which Hamas might be persuaded to change its public position on negotiations with Israel. I tried to explain to my Palestinian friends that my attempts to persuade Hamas to modify its views about Israel were not anti-Arab. I asserted that the G8 was not inherently anti-Palestinian, but that Hamas must change or modify its position on Israel before there could be a constructive engagement.

Soon after the elections, Hamas indicated that it wanted to start talking to the Quartet. But despite my urging, this never received even momentary consideration. The Americans jumped the gun. On January 29, Secretary Rice suggested that the United States would end financial aid to the Palestinian government unless Hamas recognized Israel, honored the Palestinian commitments under Oslo, and rejected violence.[5] The Europeans followed suit. All insisted that Hamas must accept the existence of the state of Israel as a precondition to engagement.

My worst nightmare was that if the West cut off the Palestinians, radical Middle East leaderships with money but no real interest in a settlement could step into the vacuum. The situation in Iraq and the deterioration of relations with Iran could potentially transform the Israel-Palestine situation into a confrontation that would engage much larger forces than the 11 million people that constitute Palestine and Israel.

Yet I was cut off from the diplomatic information stream, and frankly, I had little or no leverage. I thought that my Quartet team had played a vital role and had much to offer, but sadly, we—and the Quartet itself—were suddenly not very important. Although I was privy to the secretary of state's movements and to the odd readout from the State Department, I was only nominally being kept informed by U.S. officials. In February 2008, a U.S. news magazine gave some insights into why my team and I were dropped. Apparently, the United States and Fatah were working on plans to throw out the Hamas leadership.

At the beginning of February, my colleagues in Jerusalem learned that the Americans had made a decision to close down our offices. I was furious. It was insane to close down the operation so soon after the Palestinian elections. We had no idea what would happen next, and it might be useful to have a Quartet team on the ground. This was not a question of lack of funding, and the State Department knew this. The Quartet had just received notice of a donation of a million dollars from Russia, which was still unspent. The office could have remained operational well into the latter half of the year. The truth was, the Quartet office no longer had a role if the United States, Israel, and Fatah had taken matters into their own hands. If there were plans to invade Gaza, our small initiative would be a liability, and my colleagues would be in danger.

I continued to stay in close touch with Tony Blair's office, with Kofi Annan, Sergey Lavrov, and Javier Solana and his special representative for the Middle East peace process, Ambassador Marc Otte, at the EU. But the Americans had effectively cut me off at the knees. Moreover, they were pretending that nothing had changed. The secretary of state continued to assure me that I could have anything I needed.

In March during a phone call, I pointed out to the secretary that since the November meeting, when we had hammered out the agreements, I had not been given any opportunity to brief the president, even though he had personally dispatched me to the region. Certainly, my clash with Abrams in Jerusalem had not improved my image as far as the White House was concerned. But the real issue was that the Quartet office was in the way.

In the end, the State Department's unwillingness to involve the Quartet office any further led to its slow shutdown. The U.S. representative to the Quartet mission, Ambassador Bill Taylor, had been prematurely withdrawn from Jerusalem at the end of January. Although the United States agreed that we could continue our work until just after the results of the Israeli election in March, part of my staff left before then. The office was finally closed at the end of April.

*   *   *

My term ended on April 30, 2006. The Russians, hosts to the G8 meeting in July 2006, had written me—on behalf of the Quartet—asking me to stay on until July. But I had no vote, no office, and no information, and I informed Minister Lavrov accordingly. It would be ridiculous to attend the G8 meetings. So I resigned, albeit allowing the short remaining time of my mandate to run its course.

The abrupt end to our mission was a huge personal blow, and I was sad for the members of my team, who had worked with such commitment and passion. We had won the confidence of the Palestinians. We had helped to raise money for the Palestinians across the Middle East—from Arab states, including Saudi Arabia, Dubai, Qatar, and Jordan. We also enjoyed a good relationship with many Israeli counterparts. But the policy had changed, and we no longer had a role. I was also very conscious of the failure of the greenhouse venture and the debt I owed to my friends who had supported this bold initiative. I still hope to give them the pleasure of seeing the project flourish someday when the enterprise could be started again. Although we had failed, my team did establish a remarkable network of diplomatic and financial contacts across the region that could still be useful one day, when and if a final settlement to the Israel-Palestine confrontation is delivered.

Just before the end of my mission, on April 17, a suicide bomber killed eleven people and injured over sixty outside a fast-food restaurant in Tel Aviv. A few days earlier, the Israel Defense Forces moved into Gaza for the first time since the 2005 pullout. Gaza had also been suffering from air strikes. The Israelis were continuing to build the separation barrier in the West Bank. Again we saw how easily both societies can radicalize when they are not forced to negotiate.

I did not see President Bush until August 2006, when I belatedly called on him at the White House to bid farewell to my assignment. Three months after my resignation, I hoped that the meeting would bring closure. In preparation, I checked in with friends in Israel and in the Palestinian Authority for updates. I had decided I would say exactly what I thought.

I met for no more than twenty minutes with the president, who, to my surprise, was joined only by Elliott Abrams. Not a great omen, I thought, for an open exchange of views. The president put me immediately at ease, and we sat down in two adjacent chairs in the Oval Office. I told him that there would be no peace between Israel and the Palestinians unless we went back to the November plan, agreed on by Secretary Rice, the Israelis, and the Palestinians, in my presence. This agreement was key to giving hope to the Palestinians, and without hope of economic development and improvement of human conditions, there would be no prospect of peace. Hamas would become stronger and more radical, and a frustrated and angry youth would give their lives against a dominant Israel.

I left with the president's thanks ringing in my ears. He had been courteous, but I do not think that either he or Abrams gave any weight to my views. This was simply a courtesy meeting. About two months later, in

October, Kofi Annan called to tell me that the Quartet had met and agreed to reappoint me as the envoy to the region. I was astounded. I told Kofi that I would call Secretary Rice, who had been present at the Quartet meeting, to see if she was in full support. When I got Rice on the phone, she said yes, she had supported the appointment and that I should go to the region and assess the situation on the ground.

I asked Rice two questions. First, would I have U.S. personal security backing from the team that had kept me safe for my year of negotiations? No, she said. I should ask the Europeans for security. Second, I asked if Abrams and David Welch would give me periodic briefings on the state of the negotiations. That would be difficult, Rice said. With these two answers, I called Kofi, thanked him for the offer, and said that I would not accept an appointment I could not carry out.

The Middle East turned out to be my mission impossible. President Bush sought my help, and he seemed to treat me as a peace envoy, but that was not, in the end, the real appointment that I had received. I had been authorized to create and implement an economic program. The moment I extended this mission, my head was cut off. I don't think President Bush was trying to undermine my efforts. But whatever he had in mind, Rice and Abrams did not view me as their partner. Rice and Abrams were the ones implementing Bush's policy. I was not useful, and I was going beyond my mandate. In the end, the Quartet was a necessary camouflage for U.S. initiatives.

If the cynics are right, then President Bush never really intended me to be successful. I was to follow the line of other unsuccessful envoys and had never been given a political mandate to deal with negotiating an agreement. Sharon wanted out of Gaza, but wished to keep the West Bank. Rice saw my appointment as a double-edged sword. On the one hand, my standing in the international community demonstrated her seriousness. On the other hand, my independent relations with world leaders threatened her and her colleagues. Accordingly, Abrams and Welch—not always together—had license to neutralize me and to keep me out of the loop.

In this view, the Palestinians were also part of the failure. Their inability to control their territory after Israel withdrew, and the corruption that was so widely evident, meant that there was no credible single entity with which a deal could be done. I recount this view not because I believe it in every respect, but because it is credible and consistent with events. I was not a total innocent abroad, although for twelve months I acted as one, believing fully in my mandate and the bona fides of all who gave it to me.

In June 2007, Tony Blair, who had stepped down from his position as Britain's prime minister, was appointed the next Quartet representative for the Middle East. I spoke to him on the phone shortly after the announcement and warned him to read the fine print. I hoped that Blair would have a broader mandate than I had been given, but despite the fact that he went to his friend President Bush to discuss the limits to his authority, that mandate never came. I fear that Blair found himself in the same position I did and was unable to use his considerable experience and skills to the benefit of the region.

I remain convinced that the Palestinians, and even more crucially the Israelis, must not waste time. In the end, both sides have to recognize that they are 11 million people in a sea of 350 million Arabs. Over the last four years, the conflict in Israel and Palestine has cost the international community—including military expenditures—somewhere between $10 and $20 billion. Estimates say that the Iraq War has cost $1,000 billion. The war in Afghanistan has cost between $50 billion and $100 billion. There is a nuclear threat in Iran. Meanwhile, the Arab population will grow by 50 percent in the next twenty-five years, reaching 530 million by 2035. Israel's population could grow from 7.3 million to 8.7 million.[6]

There has to be a moment when Israelis and Palestinians understand that they are not the most important regional issue. The real global politics involve the politics of Iran, Iraq, Afghanistan, the Sunni-Shia divide, oil wealth, economics, education, war, nuclear weaponry, and the weight of population. In the Western press, the Israeli-Palestinian conflict receives coverage, but in developing countries, it is a peripheral issue. Israel and the Palestinians cannot afford to wait any longer. In my view, they must resolve their differences speedily and arrive at a two-state solution that will be recognized in the region and by the world community. I believe that a one-state solution will lead ultimately to the end of Israel as a Jewish state, if only due to the impact of demographics.

*   *   *

When my Middle East assignment ended, I felt that I had come to the end of my public life, after eleven years at the center of work in the international field. It was an empty feeling. More troubling was that in April, back in New York, I was getting calls from former colleagues and friends about the developments at the World Bank. Most of their comments were negative. In May 2007, my successor at the Bank, Paul Wolfowitz, resigned after weeks of painful investigation into alleged violations of the Bank's ethical rules. Paul and I had never grown close, but I was greatly saddened for the Bank and for him.

Both before and after Paul's resignation, I was endlessly being asked to comment by media outlets all over the world. I never said a word. I decided then that I would not get involved, that I would not engage with the critics or with the board. I did not think it would help. It was a period of great frustration, and I felt a crippling incapacity to do anything to help the institution that meant so much to me. The Bank showed the institutional fortitude to remain a unique and necessary institution. With Robert Zoellick as president, and with a great team to support him, the Bank is in good hands.

EPILOGUE

With the conclusion of my work in the Middle East in 2006, I had to decide what to do. Although I was approaching the age of seventy-three, I still felt passionate about the needs of the developing world and wondered how I could remain involved without the extraordinary support of the World Bank while still having time to pursue personal interests as well as leisure time to read and fish, to play sports, and to make music.

I somehow convinced Naomi and Adam to create a small enterprise with me, and in 2007, we raised a fund of $250 million to invest in banking, retailing, and clean energy principally outside the United States in the BRIC countries—Brazil, Russia, India, and China. We started slowly and deliberately, but were interrupted by the economic crisis of September 2008. We have been fortunate with our investments so far and are now seeking to expand our interests in our energy portfolio. We also have engaged in consulting for several firms, and since 2006, I have held the position of chairman of the International Advisory Board of Citi, the global U.S.-based banking group.

Over the last ten years, my family has expanded the activities of our foundation, in which Sara plays a central role. Key among our interests for the last five years has been the Wolfensohn Center for Development at the Brookings Institution in Washington, D.C., which has a small but talented staff. We have focused on four principal areas of interest. First has been the effectiveness of the international aid system. With the proliferation of aid donors and projects, but little in the way of coordination between them, the aid system is struggling to convert well-meaning efforts into development results. The potential for efficiency gains is vast. Second, we have been involved in the challenges facing the hundred million young Arabs between the ages of fifteen and twenty-nine. At the rate of four to five million a year, these young people come of age to face inadequate job prospects and become increasingly frustrated as they realize that they can neither marry nor get on with their lives without gainful employment. The lack of opportunities for them has resulted in a challenge to the stability of their communities. In addition, with Elaine's guidance, we are seeking to close the gap between what we know and what is actually done in early childhood development in the developing world. Such issues exist even in the richest countries where, despite resources, early education programs are not implemented. In the developing world there is the added problem of inadequate schools and inadequate funds. This five-year period of critical development in our young people affects the whole of their lives and has been given much less attention than is required. Happily, President Obama raised the subject of early childhood education at the outset of his presidency. Finally, as a separate project, we are working with Jacob Rothschild on the issue of bringing young Arab and Israeli experts together to study the coming challenges in water supply and agriculture in the Middle East.

In 2007, I retired after twenty-three years as chair of the board of the Institute for Advanced Study at Princeton, and I am doing my best to take a less active role in other cultural and academic activities. Yet somehow I cannot resist engaging in an ongoing series of challenges by participating in several groups addressing issues ranging from peace in the Middle East to development in Africa, Asia, and Latin America. I know that at my age, I should take it easier and spend more time in Jackson Hole playing the cello, engaging in active exercise, improving my golf game, and going fishing. There are so many books I want to read, and I still crave time to travel and enjoy life both in the United States and abroad. But as much as I hope to relax with family and friends, it is difficult to change the habits of a lifetime.

I hope that this book might encourage younger readers to follow to their fullest ability at least some part of the path I have taken. I was given the chance not only to establish a financial base, but more importantly, as part of my "global life," to contribute to the enormous challenge of making our world a better and more equitable place for the next generations—for the generations of my children and their children, Benjamin, Micah, Samuel, and Isabella.

ACKNOWLEDGMENTS

THERE ARE MANY PEOPLE WHO HAVE helped me to write this book, and I must thank initially Jill Margo, who recorded my first twenty-three years in Australia and conducted extensive interviews with friends and family. I also wish to acknowledge all the work that was done by Alex Brummer, who researched much of my business career from the time I graduated from Harvard Business School in 1959 and pieced together my efforts in the international banking community. Without the assistance of these two fine researchers and journalists, this work would have been less interesting and surely less accurate.

For the segment on the Middle East, I am grateful to Katiana Orluc for her work on checking facts and providing me with the correct sequence of events in a most hectic period. Also my thanks go to Ambassador Martin Indyk for his comments, and I must also say a special thank you to Caroline Anstey for all of her help over the years.

I am extremely grateful to Strobe Talbott, Brooke Shearer, and Michael Beschloss for reading an early version of the text and making many suggestions for editing and improvement in the story. I can never thank them adequately for their acts of friendship.

I must also express my gratitude to Peter Osnos, founder of PublicAffairs; to my publisher, Susan Weinberg; and to Lindsay Jones, who took a key role in editing this text and in making helpful suggestions for the improvement of the story. I also wish to thank Laurence Chandy and Geoffrey Gertz for their work in checking facts to make this account as accurate as possible.

I am very thankful to my wife, Elaine, for the countless hours she spent on reviewing the various versions of the manuscript. Somehow, she has a far better memory than I for events in our lives. Her contribution has been invaluable, both in my career and in this account of my life.

But most of all I must thank the hundreds of people who showed me friendship over the years and who have given me opportunities and invaluable advice and help. No achievements in life are possible without friends and colleagues. I have been truly blessed by those beside whom I have lived and worked. I thank them all for their friendship and support. I hope that in this story they will find some recognition, satisfaction, and reward.

Finally, I wish to take full responsibility for any errors and omissions in the text. I have done my best to give an accurate account of my life but I have no doubt that there will be blemishes on the story. I hope that I can be forgiven for any errors and that nonetheless the story will remain interesting and reasonably accurate.

NOTES

CHAPTER 7: BECOMING A BANKER

1. American commercial banks established holding companies in an effort to circumvent the tough laws on interstate banking and new activities, such as mergers and acquisitions, imposed by the Depression-era 1930s legislation, the Glass-Steagall Act. The 1970 act was an attempt to reimpose stringent regulation. It would take a further three decades before restrictive laws were swept away.

2. Egyptian and Arab forces launched a surprise attack on Israel on the holiest day in the Jewish calendar. The Egyptians crossed the Suez Canal and scored military successes before Israel, with the assistance of arms shipments from the United States, restored its military dominance.

CHAPTER 8: THE OUTSIDER

1. A Conservative government headed by Edward Heath, which was engaged in a bitter battle with the unions.

2. Commercial Union merged with Norwich Union to become part of the Aviva group.

3. Jim Callaghan, former chancellor of the Exchequer and foreign secretary, replaced Harold Wilson as Labour prime minister in April 1976.

4. Guarneri was the name of an Italian family of violin and cello makers.

5. The Davydov Strad dates from Stradivarius's golden period in the late 1680s. It was purchased for Jackie for $90,000 by her benefactor and godmother, Ismena Holland, in 1965.

6. I am indebted to Harold Brown for this clear account of what happened in the board. Richard Roberts skips speedily through these events in his official account of the succession to Verey, in *Schroders: Merchants and Bankers* (New York: Macmillan, 1992).

CHAPTER 9: SALOMON BROTHERS AND A NEW YORK-BASED CAREER

1. The Kennedy Family Trust was then valued at about $600 million, and most of it was tied up in the Chicago Furniture Mart.

CHAPTER 10: ON MY OWN

1. Stuart Ray became managing director and partner in BT Alex Brown. Brian M. Powers became chief executive officer of Hellman & Friedman, a private equity firm

based in San Francisco. Elliot Slade eventually moved on to BT Alex Brown and Deutsche Bank and then to his own firm. Donald Zilkha formed his own firm.

2. Lord Sandberg of Passfield retired as chairman of HSBC in 1986 and was succeeded by Sir William Purves.

3. Marine Midland and Midland Bank were two entirely separate institutions that, by coincidence, have similar names.

4. *Forbes*, December 26, 1988.

5. Fannie Mae, the "Federal National Mortgage Association," was established in 1938 by the federal government to provide a secondary market in mortgages on residential homes. Its shares are traded on the New York Stock Exchange.

6. James McClure, a Republican senator from Idaho, was first elected in 1972; George Mitchell served as a Democratic senator from Maine from 1980 to 1995.

CHAPTER 12: A DIFFICULT ENTRY

1. The other CEOs on this advisory board were Franco Bernabe of ENI in Italy, Lorenzo Zambrano of Cemex, Louis Gerstner of IBM, Pieter Korteweg of Robeco Group in the Netherlands, Dr. Stephan Schmidheiny of Switzerland, Juergen Schrempp of Daimler-Benz in Germany, Morris Tabaksblat of Unilever N.V. in the Netherlands, Lynton Red Wilson of BCE Inc. in Canada, and Ratan Tata from the Tata Group in India. Subsequently, the group was joined by Sir John Browne of BP Amoco in the United Kingdom, Orit Gadiesh of Bain and Company in New York, Daniel Vasella of Novartis International AG in Switzerland, and Jorma Ollila of Nokia Corp. in Finland.

CHAPTER 13: CREATIVITY AND CHANGE DURING THE CLINTON YEARS

1. James D. Wolfensohn, Chronology, July 7, 2000, World Bank Group Archives, March 2003.

2. Free Tibet Campaign, "Tibet Movement Claims Victory," press release, July 7, 2000.

CHAPTER 14: A FRESH LOOK AT DEVELOPMENT

1. Remarks I made at the Kampala conference on January 27, 1998. See James D. Wolfensohn, Chronology, World Bank Group Archives, March 2003.

CHAPTER 17: A NEW AND DIFFERENT CHALLENGE

1. In the late 1990s, a significant share of the Gazan workforce had worked in Israel, but by 2005 this share had dropped to virtually zero.

2. Robin Wright and Scott Wilson, "Rice Negotiates Deal to Open Gaza Crossings," *Washington Post*, November 16, 2005.

3. According to the United Nations Office for the Coordination of Humanitarian Affairs, *Gaza Strip Situation Report, March 29, 2006*, the Karni crossing had been closed forty-six days in 2006, or 53 percent of the current year.

4. International Crisis Group, "Palestinians, Israel and the Quartet: Pulling Back from the Brink," International Crisis Group Middle East Report no. 54, June 13, 2006, p. 24. See also "EC Assistance to the Palestinians," European Commission draft position paper, April 27, 2006: "The looming crisis is not the result of suspension of [donor] aid—nor will the crisis be averted by a resumption of direct aid. The key underlying factor is the continued freeze in Israeli transfers of PA fiscal revenue and the strict Israeli policy on closures and other restrictions. . . . The latest tightening of this policy has had a dramatic effect on the banking sector with a shortage of hard currency in the Palestinian Territories and difficulties to transfer money into Palestinian banks."

5. Condoleezza Rice, "Remarks En Route to London," January 29, 2006, available at www.state.gov/secretary/rm/2006/60016.htm

6. UN Population Prospects 2008 Revision, available at http://esa.un.org/unpp/

INDEX

JAMES D. WOLFENSOHN was born in Australia on December 1, 1933, and is a naturalized United States citizen. He holds a BA and LLB from the University of Sydney and an MBA from the Harvard Graduate School of Business. He served as an officer in the Royal Australian Air Force, and was a member of the 1956 Australian Olympic Fencing Team. Wolfensohn was president of the World Bank from 1995 to 2005. Prior to joining the Bank, Wolfensohn established his career as an international investment banker with a parallel involvement in development issues and the global environment. Mr. Wolfensohn is a Fellow of the American Academy of Arts and Sciences and a Fellow of the American Philosophical Society. He has been the recipient of many awards for his volunteer work, including the first David Rockefeller Prize of the Museum of Modern Art in New York for his work for culture and the arts. He and his wife, Elaine, have three children—Sara, Naomi, and Adam.

PublicAffairs is a publishing house founded in 1997. It is a tribute to the standards, values, and flair of three persons who have served as mentors to countless reporters, writers, editors, and book people of all kinds, including me.

I. F. STONE, proprietor of *I. F. Stone's Weekly*, combined a commitment to the First Amendment with entrepreneurial zeal and reporting skill and became one of the great independent journalists in American history. At the age of eighty, Izzy published *The Trial of Socrates*, which was a national bestseller. He wrote the book after he taught himself ancient Greek.

BENJAMIN C. BRADLEE was for nearly thirty years the charismatic editorial leader of *The Washington Post*. It was Ben who gave the *Post* the range and courage to pursue such historic issues as Watergate. He supported his reporters with a tenacity that made them fearless and it is no accident that so many became authors of influential, best-selling books.

ROBERT L. BERNSTEIN, the chief executive of Random House for more than a quarter century, guided one of the nation's premier publishing houses. Bob was personally responsible for many books of political dissent and argument that challenged tyranny around the globe. He is also the founder and longtime chair of Human Rights Watch, one of the most respected human rights organizations in the world.

•　　•　　•

For fifty years, the banner of Public Affairs Press was carried by its owner Morris B. Schnapper, who published Gandhi, Nasser, Toynbee, Truman, and about 1,500 other authors. In 1983, Schnapper was described by *The Washington Post* as "a redoubtable gadfly." His legacy will endure in the books to come.

Peter Osnos, *Founder and Editor-at-Large*